M000222246

Portraits

SUNY series in Contemporary Jewish Thought

Richard A. Cohen, editor

Portraits

The Hasidic Legacy of Elie Wiesel

David Patterson

SUNY
PRESS

Published by State University of New York Press, Albany

© 2021 State University of New York

All rights reserved

Printed in the United States of America

No part of this book may be used or reproduced in any manner whatsoever
without written permission. No part of this book may be stored in a retrieval
system or transmitted in any form or by any means including electronic,
electrostatic, magnetic tape, mechanical, photocopying, recording, or otherwise
without the prior permission in writing of the publisher.

For information, contact State University of New York Press, Albany, NY
www.sunypress.edu

Library of Congress Cataloging-in-Publication Data

Names: Patterson, David, [date] author.
Title: Portraits : the Hasidic legacy of Elie Wiesel / David Patterson.
Description: Albany : State University of New York Press, [2021] | Series:
    SUNY series in contemporary Jewish thought | Includes bibliographical
    references and index.
Identifiers: LCCN 2020056927 (print) | LCCN 2020056928 (ebook) | ISBN
    9781438483979 (hardcover : alk. paper) | ISBN 9781438483993 (ebook)
Subjects: LCSH: Wiesel, Elie, 1928–2016—Criticism and interpretation. |
    Hasidism.
Classification: LCC PQ2683.I32 Z84 2021 (print) | LCC PQ2683.I32 (ebook) |
    DDC 813/.54—dc23
LC record available at https://lccn.loc.gov/2020056927
LC ebook record available at https://lccn.loc.gov/2020056928

10 9 8 7 6 5 4 3 2 1

Contents

Preface

Although I never had the honor of sitting in one of Professor Elie Wiesel's seminars at Boston University, I have counted him among my teachers ever since one of my own students placed in my hands a copy of *Night* in 1978. Reading his first book not only set me upon a path of reading everything he published, but it also launched me on a never-ending journey through an ocean of Jewish texts and teachings, as well as Jewish thought and testimony. I began corresponding with Professor Wiesel in 1982, whereupon he graciously invited me to meet with him should I ever be in Boston or New York. In 1984 I had my first meeting with him in New York; as a result of that meeting I wrote a now-obscure book, *In Dialogue and Dilemma with Elie Wiesel*, which consists of transcripts of our conversation followed by my reflections on his words and works. With his characteristic generosity, he told me that he regarded that book as an expression of friendship; those who knew him know that friendship meant a great deal to him, and his words meant even more to me. Over the subsequent years I was blessed to sit with him and to learn from him on many other occasions.

Although I could never attain the merit of calling myself a Hasid, I count myself among the heirs to Wiesel's Hasidic legacy, and my own embrace of Jewish tradition has been shaped by that legacy. Therefore this book is, in a deep sense, the work of one of Professor Wiesel's students and not the work of one who comes to this subject matter with the cold distance of scholarly objectivity. The Baal Shem's call, Wiesel insisted, was a call to subjectivity, to passionate involvement. This study of Elie Wiesel's teachings, as they unfold through his personal engagement with the portraits of Judaism's sages and dreamers, is an attempt at just such an involvement. Years ago a critic once said that to read Wiesel is to burn with him. And so, at least for me, it is true: my attempt to convey the Hasidic legacy of this soul on fire is an attempt to transmit the fire he has transmitted to me.

I should also note that when, for example, I refer to "Jewish teaching," I am aware that my understanding of Jewish teaching is not the only legitimate one; it is my best understanding, informed by my own study of Judaism, as well as by what I have learned from the Hasid Wiesel. Indeed, Wiesel's portraits of biblical figures and Talmudic sages are rooted in his Hasidism; so all of these portraits, not just the portraits of the Hasidic masters, belong to his Hasidic legacy.

One other thing: the Holocaust. If there can be a post-Holocaust legacy, it must include a Hasidic legacy, a legacy that stems from that segment of world Jewry so profoundly and so brutally ravaged in the Shoah. And if it can be expressed as a Hasidic legacy, who better than Elie Wiesel to give voice to that expression, to that summons? A legacy is above all an inheritance, and an inheritance is a summons. It is a call, even a commandment, to *zakhor v'shamor*, to remember and to observe; it is a commandment that, says the Talmud, is woven into in a single utterance from Mount Sinai (*Shevuot* 20b). Turning to Mount Sinai—turning to those who turned to Mount Sinai—Professor Wiesel bequeaths to us an inheritance couched in the commandment to remember and observe voiced in a single utterance. His Hasidic legacy is a summons to remember what happened and why it matters. It is a summons to remember the testimony reduced to ashes and the voices that cry out from those ashes. It is a summons to remember and observe—to remember and *watch over*—the teaching and tradition consigned to obliteration as the Jews made their way to the gas chambers under the towers that watched over them in Auschwitz. Just as the teaching is embodied in the teachers, so too is the tradition embodied in their portraits.

Dallas, Texas
2020

Acknowledgments

I would like to express my deepest thanks to SUNY Press and to Rafael Chaiken, James Peltz, and Richard Cohen for their support, encouragement, and insightful suggestions in the preparation of this book. I am also grateful to the readers who took the time to review the manuscript and offer valuable recommendations to make this a better book. Most importantly, many thanks to Alan Rosen, who had the great blessing of being one of Professor Elie Wiesel's students and who has become one of my teachers. A great scholar, a true Hasid, and a dear friend, Alan has been a profound inspiration for this endeavor.

A Post-Holocaust Hasidic Legacy

Where are we going? Tell me. Do you know?

I don't know, my little girl.

I am afraid. Is it wrong, tell me, is it wrong to be afraid?

I don't know. I don't think so.

In all my life I have never been so afraid.

Never. . . .

Say, do you know? Where are we going?

To the end of the world, little girl. We are going to the end of the world.

Is that far?

No, not really.

You see, I am really tired. Is it wrong, tell me, is it wrong to be so tired?

Everybody is tired, my little girl.

Even God?

I don't know. You will ask Him yourself.

—Elie Wiesel, *A Jew Today*[1]

A legacy is not only something that we preserve in the mind. It is something that we receive into the heart and the soul. We embrace it in our words and in our deeds. We hold it in our arms and in our hands, like a weary child who asks whether God is weary, too. Elie Wiesel's friend Nikos Kazantzakis once commented that perhaps God is not so almighty after all but is as helpless as a child—and if we do not save Him, He will die: "He cannot be saved unless we save him with our own struggle; nor can we be saved unless He is saved."[2] So we see what is at stake in receivng Wiesel's Hasidic legacy, for it is just such a struggle. And it is just as fragile as the imperiled God, who is as weary as a child.

To acquire a sense of the post-Holocaust context of Weisel's Hasidic legacy, we turn to the Hasidic master, Rabbi Kalonymos Kalmish Shapira, Rebbe of the Warsaw Ghetto, who was murdered in the camp at Trawnicki on November 3, 1943. On February 14, 1942, he wrote, "A Jew, tortured in his suffering, may think he is the only one in pain, as though his personal pain and the pain of all other Jews has no effect above, God forbid. But . . . we learn in the Talmud (*Chagigah* 15b; *Sanhedrin* 46a) . . . God, as it were, suffers with a Jew much more than that person himself feels it."[3] Whereas Rabbi Yose "heard a Divine Voice like the cooing of a dove" over the ruins of the Temple, the Rebbe goes on to say, we know from Jeremiah 25:30 that "God roars, howling over His city."[4] And yet the Midrash tells us that God sits in silence over His city (*Eykhah Rabbah* 1:1:1). Why in silence? Because, as the Hasidic master Menahem-Mendl of Kotzk once said, the scream we hold back is more powerful.[5] If "God is silence," as Wiesel declares,[6] in a post-Holocaust world His is the silence of a silent scream. For there are times when, like the five-year-old Joel the Redhead in Wiesel's *A Jew Today*,[7] like the child Hanna in his drama *The Trial of God*,[8] God, too, screams without a sound. How, then, does God roar? He roars not only through the screams of "Mama!" that reverberate throughout the camps and ghettos, screams that threaten to undermine the very fabric of creation, but also through the whisper of a child who, like a Hasid shouting out a silent prayer, wants to know if God is weary, too.

Elie Wiesel begins his testimony in *Night* with a reference to a "Hasidic house of prayer."[9] His Hasidic legacy is one of prayer, without which we are left utterly homeless. These words, indeed, embody the primary targets in the Nazis' project to annihilate the teaching and tradition of the Jewish people and with them the Hasidim of Eastern Europe. "Most of the victims who ascended the burning altar were Hasidim: the killers and they could not coexist under the same sky," Wiesel has attested.[10] And so the killers transformed the sky into a cemetery. "For Hasidism," as David Biale and others have said, "the Holocaust meant decimation."[11] It meant the decimation of everything that the word *Hasidic* signifies.

As for the house, one recalls that before they annihilated the Jews of Europe the Nazis rendered them homeless, with every Jew under Nazi occupation sooner or later consigned to a camp, a ghetto, or a hiding place. Indeed, the house or the *bayit* is at the origin of Torah and creation, for the Torah begins with a *beit*, a *bayit*, which is a dwelling place. Thus, the meaning of creation is given in the first letter of creation: it is to transform this realm into a dwelling place for the Holy One. How? Through Torah, prayer, and acts of loving kindness, as it is written (*Pirke Avot* 1:2). Thus the Nazis forbade the study of Torah,[12] deemed prayer an act of sabotage,[13] and punished anyone who extended even a kind word to a Jew.[14]

And it is a house of *prayer*, of *tefillah*. In Judaism *tefillah* is not merely supplication or petition. It is also reckoning, confrontation, and wrestling, as the cognate *naftolin* suggests. The Hasidic house of prayer is a house of confrontation, as when the beadle in one of Wiesel's tales used to run to the synagogue and declare, "Master of the Universe! I am here . . . but where are You?"[15] Assuming the mode of prayer, as he himself has said,[16] Wiesel's writings frame just such a moment of reckoning and confrontation. Without this house of confrontation, there is no dwelling in a post-Holocaust world. Why? Because without this prayer, this *tefillah*, there is no reckoning—and therein lies the true horror, the horror to which Wiesel responds: where the post-Holocaust world is emptied of prayer, it is also emptied of reckoning, for both God and humanity. The problem that plagues us in our time, Wiesel once said to me, is that we no longer know how to pray. "My life?" asks Wiesel. And he answers: "I go on breathing from minute to minute, from prayer to prayer."[17] Just so, those of us who are heirs to this Hasidic storyteller's legacy are summoned to the task to which the Hasidic master Nahman of Bratzlav summoned his heirs: "Make my tales into prayers."[18] Thus we must go on breathing, from tale to tale, from prayer to prayer, from reckoning to reckoning.

Certain groups of especially pious Jews have been known as Hasidim for centuries. A text as old as the 149th Psalm, for example, opens with a call to the "assembly of Hasidim" to "sing unto HaShem a new song and His praise" (Psalms 149:1). The Talmud, moreover, invokes the *Hasidim ha-Rishonim* (*Nedarim* 10a; see also *Mishnah Berakhot* 5:1), the "first of the pious ones," who went far beyond the requirements of the commandments to show their love of God and neighbor; indeed, Rabbi Meir regarded Adam, the first human being, as the first of the ancient Hasidim (*Eruvin* 18b). Among the most famous texts of the thirteenth century is the *Sefer Hasidim* attributed to Judah ben Samuel of Regensburg, known as Yehuda HeHasid; it is a collection of tales and teachings from the *Hasidei Ashkenaz*, or the "Pious Ones of Germany."[19] In the seventeenth century, following the advent of Lurianic Kabbalah, one finds other examples of the use of the term *Hasid*; in his comments on the *Shulchan Arukh Ha-Ari*, a Kabbalistic rendering of the Code of Jewish Law, for example, Jacob ben Hayyim Zemah maintains that only one who acts in the manner of the Pious, of the *Hasidim*, can ever have access to the hidden wisdom.[20] By the time Hasidism came to Eastern Europe, then, the notion had its precedents.

Still, it must be asked: what does *Hasidic* mean? How are Hasidic Jews different from other Jews? What do they espouse? On one level, simply stated, Hasidic Jews thoroughly embrace the traditional observances of Judaism but with a dose of Jewish mysticism to inform the mind and enflame the soul. In fact, as Moshe Idel points out, both Martin Buber and Gershom Scholem viewed Jewish mysticism as a "bridge between Jewish tradition and the Judaism of the present,"[21] a bridge that obtains when other bridges have been burned. Elie Wiesel's Hasidic legacy—a legacy that has its mystical dimension—might also help to construct a bridge between a recent catastrophic past and an imminent Jewish future. Says Idel, "Only the coexistence in Judaism of a variety of mystical paradigms can explain how Hasidism was able to put back in circulation a whole range of key mystical concepts that were either marginal or absent from both Lurianism and Sabbateanism,"[22] which were among the mystical and messianic movements of the sixteenth and seventeenth centuries. One category inherited from Lurianic Kabbalah that the Hasidim, including the Baal Shem Tov, embraced was *gilgul*, or reincarnation; indeed, the Baal Shem declared himself to be a reincarnation of the great sage of the tenth century, Saadia Gaon.[23] Two key concepts in Hasidism, however, that are absent from Lurianism are *devekut*, or "clinging" closely to God in all things, and *hitbodedut*, which is a retreat into "solitude," not for the sake of removal from human relation but in order to return to that relation with even greater intensity and devotion for the sake of a higher relation.[24] For Hasidism, as for Judaism, there is no higher relation without human relation, no *ben adam leMakom* without the *ben adam lehevero*.

Modern Hasidism arose in Transylvania with the coming of Israel ben Eliezer of Medzhibozh (1700–1760), better known as the Baal Shem Tov (the "Master of the Good Name"). Born in the town of Okopy, he appeared in the aftermath of the Chmielnicki Massacres of 1648–1649, which took place in the Ukraine during an uprising between Roman Catholic and Orthodox Christians that left up to one hundred thousand Jews dead—about 90 percent of the Ukrainian Jews. That slaughter was followed by the trauma of the false Messiah debacle of Shabbatai Tzvi (1626–1676), who had duped several thousand Jews into following him to the Holy Land, only to convert to Islam when they were detained by the Turks. Martin Buber and Gershom Scholem believe that these catastrophes played a significant role in paving the way for the rise of Hasidism.[25] Idel, however, believes that Scholem and Buber may have overestimated the influence of the Shabbatean debacle,[26] since such disasters could just as well have stood as an obstacle to any new promises. Because no one was sure of what to make of him, the Baal Shem provoked such suspicions.

Rachel Elior expands on the source of these suspicions in the Jewish world, as the Baal Shem came on the scene just a generation before Jacob Frank (1726–1791), who was deeply incluenced by Shabbatai Tzvi. The scandal of Frankism came to a head in 1759, when he and his followers converted to Christianity. The Hasidim, Elior explains, were persecuted and excommunicated for their presumed association with Frankist Shabbateanism, "even though their outlook and way of life were very different from those of the Shabateans. The error is easily explained by the proximity of time, place, and sources of inspiration. The traditional communal leadership feared any divergent organization, and any attempt to replace the established ritual practices of Ashkenaz with kabbalistic liturgies and rites."[27] As it turned out, their fears were unfounded.

Elior notes an early Hasidic tradition concerning the relationship between Shabbateanism and Hasidism:

> The Baal Shem Tov . . . related that Shabetai Tsevi came to him and sought rectification [tikun] and he said . . . that tikun is to become bound up together soul and spirit. So he [the Baal Shem Tov] began to connect himself to him—carefully, for he was afraid, for he [Shabetai Tsevi] was a great evildoer. Once the Baal Shem Tov was asleep and Shabetai Tsevi, may his name be obliterated, came to the Baal Shem Tov in his sleep and tempted him to apostatize, God forbid, and he threw him down with a mighty throw until he fell into the deepest Sheol.[28]

Unlike Frank, Elior adds,

> the Baal Shem Tov did not cut his followers off from the traditional world. He did not demand secrecy, blind obedience, or submissiveness, and he did not offer his followers a future

beyond the limits of human comprehension. Instead he sought to illuminate existence in this world in the light of the divine spirit, which is apparent to all who want to see it and dispels the enigma of being. In the reality he posited, the state of human being is enlightened by the all-embracing divine being, which he conceptualized as the abundant effusion of hesed, divine joy, and sanctity.[29]

The Baal Shem was so distressed over the presumed association between the Hasidim and the Shabbateans, says Nahman of Bratzlav, that "they say in the name of the Baal Shem Tov that he suffered two perforations in his heart because of the Shabetai Tsevi affair and that is why he passed away" (*Likutei Moharan*, 1:207).

Most of what is known about the Baal Shem Tov belongs to Hasidic lore. It is said, for example, that he received the "Hidden Wisdom" from the great mystic Rabbi Adam Baal Shem of Ropczyce, who discovered a manuscript containing the secrets of Torah hidden in a cave; it was revealed to him in a dream that he should pass the secrets on to Israel ben Eliezer.[30] Early on the Baal Shem underscored the immanence of God's presence in the world and taught the ways of *devekut*.[31] Before long he became known for his wisdom, erudition, and righteousness. Immanuel Etkes observes that "the Besht's abilities to combat supernatural entities was evident also in his efforts to heal the sick. In one story, the Besht cures a child on his deathbed by confronting the soul of the child and commanding it to return to its body."[32] As Biale has noted,[33] contrary to some legendary accounts, when the Baal Shem arrived in Medzhibozh—a town destroyed in the Chmielnicki Massacres and rebuilt in 1660[34]—in the 1740s he was already known as a great healer and mystic. Moshe Rosman reinforces this view.[35]

The potency of the Baal Shem's presence, prior to the advent of any -*ism*, set into motion a transformation of everyone who encountered him. Etkes reminds us that "the Besht did not regard himself as the leader of a movement, not only because in his day the Hasidic movement did not yet exist, or because it had never even occurred to him to found such a movement, but mainly because he perceived himself as bearing responsibility for the welfare of the Jewish people as a whole."[36] There we have one category that defines the Hasidic movement and Wiesel's Hasidic legacy: the responsibility that devolves upon each for the sake of all. The Baal Shem's popularity drew reproach from Jews known as the Mitnagdim, or the "Opponents," chief among whom was the renowned Elijah ben Solomon Zalman, the Vilna Gaon; he believed that the Hasidim were spreading too many of the esoteric teachings among too many people too quickly. Biale maintains, however, that the conflict between the Mitnagdim and the Hasidim was relatively insignificant.[37] Still, he concedes, when the Hasidim celebrated the death of the Vilna Gaon in 1797, the spilt took on an unprecedented intensity.[38] In 1798, for example, the Mitnagdim went to the Russians and accused Rabbi Schneur Zalman of Liadi, the founder of the Chabad Lubavitch Hasidic dynasty, of espionage.

The Baal Shem attracted numerous followers, both from the elitist segments of East European Jewry and from the not-so-elitist segments of that world. Key figures in the transmission of his legacy were Yaakov Yosef of Polnoe and Dov Ber, the Maggid of Mezeritch. Through these leaders there emerged the person of the *tzaddik*, a "righteous one," who is able to elevate his entire following and to serve as a bridge between this realm and the upper realms. This particular understanding of the *tzaddik*, as it evolved over the generations immediately following the advent of the Baal Shem Tov, is another distinctive feature of Hasidism.

The *tzaddik*, Biale and others explain, "must bridge the chasm between himself and his followers by 'descending to the people.' He must periodically interrupt his state of communion with God and go down to the level of his followers in order to raise them up by joining himself to them. . . . What, more precisely, is the relationship between tsaddik and Hasid? The tsaddik is obliged to take care of both the spiritual and material needs of his followers, while the Hasidim are obliged to believe in the powers of the tsaddik and consequently to 'adhere' to him."[39] It is important to note, he adds, that "the tsaddik is not a passive conduit between the upper and lower worlds. Instead, he is the quintessential expression of the movement in and out of the state of devekut."[40] Note well: the *tzaddik* draws his Hasidim into the upper realms not only spiritually but also physically. This view of "the whole person of the *Zaddiq* as a channel, and not only his soul," Moshe Idel observes, may be traced to the time of the great Lurianic mystic Moshe Cordovero (1522–1570), if not before.[41] He goes on to note that "there can be no doubt" that the Hasidic masters were familiar with Cordovero's most famous kabbalistic text, the *Pardes Rimmonim*, the writings of Isaiah Horowitz (1555–1630), and other Kabbalists, which expound on this notion of the *tzaddik* as a channel.[42] In the nineteenth century, Hasidic dynasties stemming from the *tzaddikim* would come to the fore, based on the places where their followers lived, such as Belz, Bobova, Lubavitch, Bratzlav, Ger, Satmar (Szatmárnémeti), and Vizhnitz, the Yiddish name for Vizhnytsia, a town in present-day Ukraine. It is the dynasty to which Elie Wiesel was heir: he always identified himself as a Vizhnitzer Hasid.

For Hasidic Jews and for Wiesel's Hasidic legacy, gratitude and joy resting upon *relationship* are paramount. That is one way in which Hasidism epitomizes Judaism: in its accent on *relationship*. "What is Hasidism," writes Wiesel, "if not the belief that man must have faith in God *and* in people? You suffer? Pray to God but speak to your friend."[43] Few of us can fathom how extraordinary these words are, coming from a Hasid who emerged from the gullet of the antiworld. Faith in God? Faith in people? What can these words mean in the aftermath of Auschwitz? And yet Wiesel's Jewish teachings and testimonies are an effort to restore meaning to these words in the aftermath of a radical assault on the bond between word and meaning. Indeed, his is an effort to restore meaning to the very word *after*. "After?" he has written. "Did you say: after? Meaning what?"[44] Only a legacy can restore an *after*.

And so we come to the *after* in the Hasidic legacy. Here Arthur Green, with his notion of Neo-Hasidism, is of particular help. The Shoah is such a radical, unprecedented rupture of Jewish life, teaching, tradition, testimony—including the life and teaching of the Hasidim—that we should think of Wiesel's Hasidic legacy in terms of a Neo-Hasidic legacy. What does *Neo-Hasidic* mean? Green explains that it is "the notion that Hasidism has a message wider than the borders of the traditional Hasidic community, that Jews and others who do not live the lives of Hasidim and who have no intention of doing so might still be spiritually nourished by the stories, teachings, music of Hasidism—indeed by the telling of the narrative of Hasidic history itself."[45] Here Green has captured the meaning of *legacy*, as well as the innovation that Wiesel brings both to Hasidism and to Judaism. Wiesel's Hasidic legacy—his Hasidic *demand*—is for all humanity, and not just for the Jewish people, the traditional audience of the Hasidic sages. The Nazis obliterated the Hasidic world that was confined to Eastern Europe; Wiesel is chief among those witnesses who extend that world throughout the wider world. In *A Beggar in Jerusalem* he gives voice to the teaching couched in this universality: "There comes a time when one cannot be a man without assuming the Jewish condition."[46] If, as Green says, "Wiesel offers the first significant retelling of the story of Hasidism after the Holocaust,"[47] it is because Wiesel's legacy is Hasidic through and through. For Wiesel, *Jewish* and *Hasidic* (not to mention *human* and *Hasidic*) have virtually become the same thing.

I once repeated to Elie Wiesel a story about the Hasidic master Rabbi Uri of Strelisk, from his book *Somewhere a Master*. According to the tale, Rabbi Uri would make his final farewells to his family each morning before he set out to the synagogue for the morning prayers. Rabbi Uri was convinced that if he should attain the ascent to the upper realms that the prayers required, his soul might not return to this world.[48] Realizing that Wiesel's soul would not ascend but would descend into dangerous realms when he took up the task of writing his novels, I asked him: "How do you survive writing one of your novels? Do you not approach the edge of an abyss when you sound those depths?" He answered: "Yes. I descend . . . somewhere. But I have my . . . safety measures. My lifelines. I never write a novel without also studying or writing about something else: the Bible, the Talmud, Midrash, Hasidism. Without that lifeline, I could not find my way back to life." That lifeline was fundamentally Hasidic. Many of Wiesel's first lectures at the 92nd Street Y in the 1960s were on the Hasidic masters. His first collection of portraits were portraits of Hasidic masters. And he always prayed according to the custom of the Vizhnitzer Hasidim, just as he prayed in Auschwitz.

The Talmudic sage Shimon ben Azzai maintains that the most foundational of all Jewish teachings—and therefore of all Hasidic teachings—is that all human beings have their beginning in a single human being (*Talmud Yerushalmi, Nedarim* 9:4; *Bereshit Rabbah* 24:7). This teaching contains what Wiesel refers to when he says that "at Auschwitz, not only man died, but also the idea of man."[49] This most fundamental of Jewish teachings would become the teaching most fundamentally opposed to the Nazi view on what imparts meaning and value to the other human being. Why did God begin with just one human being and not two? The sages say it was so that no one may declare to another, "My side of the family is better than your side of the family" (*Tosefta Sanhedrin* 8:4). There is only one side of the family, which means that all of humanity is interrelated, physically through Adam, metaphysically through the Creator, with all the ethical demands that come with being part of a family. Indeed, the Hebrew term for "human being" is *ben adam*, a "child of Adam." There is no teaching more inimical to National Socialism's pivotal claim that there is no connection between the Aryan and the non-Aryan and no ethical obligation of one human being toward another. And this ethical demand lies at the core of Wiesel's Hasidic legacy.

The Baal Shem did not call for a resurgence of the study confined to the narrow circles of scholars, nor did he turn to the asceticism that had been associated with earlier Hasidim. To be sure, the Baal Shem drew one of his closest disciples, Yaakov Yosef of Polnoe, into his circle by turning him away from asceticism.[50] Rather, he opened up the gates to God to anyone capable of gratitude and joy, precisely in a time when all were blind to anything for which they might be grateful or that they could rejoice in. The Baal Shem Tov, says Wiesel, "taught them to fight sadness with joy. 'The man who looks only at himself cannot but sink into despair, yet as soon as he opens his eyes to the creation around him, he will know joy.' And this joy leads to the absolute, to redemption, to God; that was the new truth as defined by the Baal Shem."[51] Given their post-Holocaust context, these words are as extraordinary as Wiesel's post-Holocaust legacy.

Equally extraordinary is the Hasidic emphasis on gratitude, which is also a key to redemption. Says Wiesel in his commentary on the Passover Haggadah, "A Jew defines himself by his capacity for gratitude. A Jewish philosopher was once asked, 'What is the opposite of nihilism?' And he said, '*Dayenu*,' the ability to be thankful for what we have received, for what we are."[52] Wiesel's Hasidic legacy tells us that the path to redemption, both for God and for humanity, lies in joy even in the midst of despair, in gratitude even when we are hungry, and in struggling with God.

When in Wiesel's *Ani Maamin* Abraham, Isaac, and Jacob confront the Holy One with the murder of the children, we read, "Abraham, Isaac, and Jacob go away, heartened by another hope: their children. They leave heaven and do not, cannot, see that they are no longer alone: God accompanies them, weeping, smiling, whispering: *Nitzhuni banai*, my children have defeated me, they deserve my gratitude. Thus he spoke. He is speaking still. The word of God continues to be heard. So does the silence of his dead children."[53] So you see, just as the redemption of humanity rests upon human gratitude, so too does the redemption of the Shekhinah rest upon divine gratitude, even amidst the silence of her dead children: gratitude not for their immense suffering but for the truth that their suffering *matters*, despite the impossibility of deriving any meaning from it. As the character Gregor declared to the Rebbe in *The Gates of the Forest*, "I tell you this: if their death has no meaning, then it's an insult, and if it does have a meaning, it's even more so."[54] The redemption opened up by joy, gratitude, and struggling with God, even as God struggles with Himself, does not come through suffering but rather in spite of suffering.

If Auschwitz is central to Wiesel's post-Holocaust legacy, Jerusalem is central to his Hasidic legacy. The Hasidic master "Rabbi Nahman of Bratzlav," Wiesel relates, "the storyteller of Hasidism, liked to say that no matter where he walked, his steps turned toward Jerusalem."[55] As the site where the Temple stood, Jerusalem signifies the emanation of Torah into the world, and Torah signifies the sanctity of life in the world. The Midrash teaches that the windows of the Temple were designed not to let light in but to allow the light of Torah to radiate out from the Temple and into the world (*Tanhuma Tetzaveh* 6). Thus the third-century sage Rabbi Yehoshua ben Levi taught that the Temple was a greater blessing to the nations than it was to Israel (*Bamidbar Rabbah* 1:3). The nations, and not just the Jews, can no more live without Jerusalem than they can live without God. Like a *tzaddik*, Jerusalem is for everyone a bridge between this realm and the upper realms. "That's where the town of my childhood seems to be now," says Wiesel, "up there, in a Jerusalem of fire, hanging onto eternal memories of night."[56] That is why the young Eliezer would weep at night over the destruction of the Temple,[57] even though he may not have known it at the time: the town of his childhood would be the heavenly Jerusalem of fire, hanging on the eternal memories of fire, of flames such as there have never been.

"How was I to reconcile Auschwitz and Jerusalem?" asks Yedidyah, the main character in Wiesel's *The Sonderberg Case*. "Would the former merely be the antithesis, the anti-event of the latter? If Auschwitz is forever the question, is Jerusalem forever the answer? On the one hand the darkness of the abyss, on the other the dazzling light of daybreak? At Birkenau and Treblinka, the burning bush was consumed, but here the flame continues to warm the hearts of messianic dreamers."[58] Amidst the flames of the Hasidic house of prayer consumed in the Holocaust there is another flame, one that warms the hearts of the messianic dreamers. It is the flame of the Hasidic legacy that Elie Wiesel has bequeathed to us through his portraits of the patriarchs and prophets, as well as the sages and masters. It is a legacy that we receive from a Hasid who loves Jews and Judaism and celebrates both. His first two volumes of portraits, in fact, were celebrations: *Célébration hassidique: portraits et légendes* [Souls on fire: Portraits and legends of Hasidic masters] (1972) and *Célébration biblique: portraits et légendes* (Messengers of God: Biblical portraits and legends (1975).

Finally, with regard to Elie Wiesel's Hasidic legacy, we should note one more thing about his innovative approach to Judaism. Wiesel understood that after the Holocaust nothing remained the same. "In the beginning there was the Holocaust," he asserts. "We must therefore start all over again."[59] Wiesel's Hasidism enables him to start all over again. It opens up for him the *and yet*, which he describes as his "two favorite words"[60]

and are so crucial to his approach to Judaism in the aftermath of the
Shoah. It is a Judaism that leads us to put God on trial but to pause for
Minhah, the afternoon prayers. It is a Judaism that leads us to cry out
Ayekah!?—Where are You!?—to God in the midst of the *Hineni!*—Here
I am for You!—that we offer up to Him. It is a Judaism that makes it
possible to love Jews, love God, and celebrate both in the aftermath of
the unthinkable.

His Hasidism leads him to the reintroduction of another category
in Jewish texts: the portrait. The Jewish tradition of portraiture is, from
one perspective, ancient. Examples can be found in the writings of Flavius
Josephus (CE 37–100),[61] *Tzena Ureina* of the 1590s (sometimes called the
Women's Bible),[62] and the *MeAm Lo'ez* of Yaakov Culi (d. 1732), as well as
in the hagiographic literature, such as portions of the *Sefer HaKabbalah*
of Abraham ibn Daud (1110–1180),[63] the martyrologies from the time
of the Crusades, and portions of the Zohar. Others include the *Sefer
HaHezyonot*,[64] which contains portraits of Isaac Luria sketched by his student Chayyim Vital (1542–1620), as well as the *Shivhei HaBesht* compiled
by the disciple of the Baal Shem, Dov Ber of Mezeritch.[65] Although there
are later precedents for portraiture, such as Hillel Zeitlin's (1871–1942)
volume on Nahman of Bratzlav,[66] the post-Holocaust context imparts to
Wiesel's portraits an unprecedeneted dimension. And, unlike the earlier
examples of portraits of the sages, Wiesel uses the word *portrait* in the
titles of his essays on the sages.

Through his portraiture Wiesel brings out the flesh and blood, the
heart and soul, and the very humanity of these men and women who
otherwise get lost in the teachings and traditions they bequeath to us.
For the *meser* or the "message" transmitted through the *mesorah* or the
"tradition" is not merely the teachings that belong to a doctrine; if that
were all Judaism amounted to, it would indeed have been lost in the Shoah.
No, the message transmitted through the tradition lies in the *humanity* of
our teachers and not just in their teachings. It lies in the very meaning
of humanity that came under a radical assault in the time of the Shoah.
Let us consider, then, this innovation that Wiesel brings to Judaism and
that constitutes his Hasidic legacy: the portrait.

The Portrait of the *Who*

"Who is like You!"
Exodus 15:11

When Elie Wiesel won the Nobel Peace Prize in 1986, the Nobel Committee hailed him as a "messenger to mankind." And a messenger he was, a *malakh*, with a message and a summons to humanity, not only from the Kingdom of Night but also from the millennial testimony of the Jewish people. From within his teaching and testimony there emanates a trace of the light that was born upon the first utterance of Creation, the light that went forth from Mount Sinai, the light of the black fire on white fire that is the Written and Oral Torah (see *Tanhuma Bereshit* 1; *Devarim Rabbah* 3:12; *Shir HaShirim Rabbah* 5:11:6; *Zohar* II, 226b). Without the remnants of the Jewish tradition that came under a most radical assault in the time of the Shoah, Wiesel would never have emerged from that nefarious Kingdom. Indeed, he once said that what kept him alive after surviving Auschwitz and Buchenwald was not his unflinching faith in God, for that had been profoundly shaken. No, it was his unyielding love for learning and for studying the *sifrei kodesh*, the holy texts and teachings of the Jewish tradition that the Nazis had consigned to the flames. "I have never ceased studying the Bible, the Talmud, and the commentaries," he declares. "It is my passion."[1] It was also his salvation.

Wiesel was a world-renowned novelist, a revered teacher, and an outspoken advocate for humanity everywhere. The son of Sarah Feig and Shlomo Wiesel, he was born in the town of Sighet in the Romanian Carpathians on 16 Tishrei 5689 (September 30, 1928). He came from a highly distinguished line: a descendant of the great Kabbalist Rabbi Isaiah Horowitz, known as the Holy Shelah from the massive work *Shnei Luhot*

13

HaBrit (The two tablets of the Covenant, 1648), Wiesel could trace his lineage all the way back to great explicator of the Torah and Talmud, Rabbi Shlomo ben Yitzhak (1040–1105), better known as Rashi. On 26 Sivan 5776 (July 2, 2016), a Sabbath, Elie Wiesel's soul returned to the upper realms, where he perhaps now studies with his illustrious ancestors.

A tale told of this sage: When he was eight years old his mother took him to receive a blessing from the local Rebbe. Mother and son entered the Rebbe's study. The Rebbe looked up, caught sight of the boy, and gave a start. The Rebbe's reaction frightened Sarah. She ushered little Eliezer out of the room, told him to wait there for a moment, and asked the Rebbe, "What did you see?"

The Rebbe took a deep breath and answered, head in hands, "Your son will become a voice for the people of Israel, but only after he has endured unspeakable suffering."[2]

And so it came to pass.

Wiesel and his family were taken up in the whirlwind that swept across Hungary when the Germans entered the land of their Hungarian allies in March 1944. Between May 15 and July 9, 1944, nearly half a million Hungarian Jews—almost as many as during the previous two years combined—were gassed and burned in Birkenau. Almost a year later, after losing both parents and his sister Tzipora (his older sisters Beatrice and Hilda survived), Wiesel lay on a plank thinly strewn with straw in an abandoned block of Buchenwald. Then an African American unit of the US Third Army suddenly stumbled across the camp.

Wiesel once told me a story about the black American GI who walked into the block where dozens of inmates were lying in their wooden bunks waiting to die. The soldier paused for a moment and looked around, his eyes adjusting to the dimly lit space.

"He was a giant," Wiesel said of the man decked out in battle gear. "Like some mythical hero." Most of these Jews had never seen a black man.

This soldier, this warrior, had witnessed all the horrors of war. And yet, as the giant began to make out the skeletal shades surrounding him, tears started to run down his cheeks. The ghostlike creatures crawled down from their planks and shuffled over to comfort him, their bony hands patting him on the shoulders.

"The harder we tried to console him," said Wiesel, "the harder he sobbed. Like a child."

Wiesel spent the postwar years in France, where he studied at the Sorbonne and worked as a journalist for French and Israeli periodicals.

He once related to me a story from those years. It seems that a rabbi with whom he wanted to study asked him what he did for a living. Wiesel answered, "I am a writer." The rabbi was shocked, scandalized. "A *writer*!?" he retorted. "Don't you know that words create and destroy worlds? And you have the temerity to take yourself to be a *writer*!?"

Wiesel, of course, knew very well what the rabbi was saying. He knew very well the episode in the Talmud, where upon their meeting, Rabbi Meir's teacher, Rabbi Ishmael, asked about the disciple's profession. "I am a scribe," Rabbi Meir replied. "Be careful, my son," said Rabbi Ishmael, "be very careful. By omitting or adding a single letter, you may destroy the entire world" (*Eruvin*, 13a). Perhaps that is why for ten years Wiesel would make no public comment on his passage through the antiworld from which he had emerged as one who, like Moishe the Beadle in *Night*, had crawled out of a mass grave to relate to us the story of his own death. "He lived our destiny before any of us," writes Wiesel. "Messenger of the dead, he shouted his testimony from the rooftops and delivered it in silence, but either way no one would listen. People turned their backs so as not to see his eyes, as though fearing to glimpse a truth that held his past and our future in its steely grasp."[3] Just so, Wiesel exercised great care over his words. And over the silent space between the words, a space haunted by the cries of the children and the muteness of the Muselmänner.

As a young Jewish journalist, Wiesel visited François Mauriac, the Nobel Laureate in Literature, to interview the French Catholic author in 1954. According to the story, Wiesel sat and listened to the devout Christian compare the horrific sufferings of the Jews to the sufferings of Jesus. Finally, the young Jew could not take any more. He rose up and declared to Mauriac that a million and a half Jewish children suffered far more than the Nazarene could ever have imagined. He spoke of the sealed trains, of the babies thrown alive into the flaming pits, of the beatings and burnings, the starvation and deprivation, all of which he had seen with his own child's eyes. Suddenly he fell silent: here he was, a nobody, telling off the great François Mauriac. The embarrassed Jewish upstart bolted from the Catholic thinker's apartment, with the elderly Mauriac running after him. He caught the young man and led him back into his home. Dragging Wiesel's story out of him, word by word, phrase by phrase, Mauriac was soon in tears, pleading with the young man to tell his tale. He was subsequently instrumental in seeing to the 1958 publication of *La Nuit*.

In 1955 Wiesel moved to New York. In 1969 he married Austrian Holocaust survivor Marion Erster Rose, who would become the translator of many of his books from French into English. Their son, Shlomo Elisha, was born in 1972. In 1976 Wiesel was appointed Andrew Mellon Professor of the Humanities at Boston University, a position that he held for the remainder of his life. He used the money from the 1986 Nobel Peace Prize to establish the Elie Wiesel Foundation for Humanity, through which he came to the aid of suffering humanity throughout the world. Many people know these things. What many do not know is that Wiesel always identified himself as a Vizhnitzer Hasid. His maternal grandfather Dodye Feig was well known among the Vizhnitzer Hasidim for his wisdom and his righteousness. After the Shoah his grandson would recognize him in a photograph from the antiworld; the Nazis were cutting off his beard, humiliating him as they had tens of thousands of other devout Jews.[4]

"From the wandering Maggidim [Hasidic teachers and storytellers] of my childhood," Wiesel tells us, "I learned how to read and interpret a biblical text. Spellbound, I would listen as they juggled parables and quotations, verses and explanations, trying to extract a hidden meaning, a moral precept: a lesson. Then, after the war, in Paris, my strange teacher and master, Harav Shushani, guided me along the same path."[5] Thus Elie Wiesel transmits not just the teaching of the Jewish tradition but also the flesh and blood, the heart and soul of that tradition revealed in the Hasidic tradition, the *Who* and not just the *What* of a tradition that lives and breathes. The Hasid in him understood that a living tradition is a *Who*, just as he understood that the Shoah was above all an assault on the *Who* that is HaShem, as well as the *Who* that is the human being: it was, in other words, a radical assault on the Holy One and the human soul created in His image and likeness. How else to transmit the image and the likeness but through the portrait of the *Who*?

So we glimpse the meaning of Wiesel's enigmatic statement that "the ultimate mystery of the Holocaust is that whatever happened took place in the soul."[6] And because each human soul is tied to every other, the Holocaust had a profound impact on the soul of every human being.

The Hasidic Legacy of the *Who*

Neither the First Principle nor the God Idea of the philosophers is a *Who*. Indeed, no one ever cried out "Father!" to the First Principle, and no one ever prayed to an idea. Nor is the God who is the object of theological speculation a *Who*. On the contrary, God is all subject, as Abraham Joshua

Heschel, whom Wiesel knew very well, implies: "We approach Him, not by making Him the object of our thinking, but by discovering ourselves as the objects of His thinking."[7] The God whom the pagan would equate with nature is not a *Who*. The pagan God is a force or a power with which there can be no covenantal relation. Only the God of the Covenant, the suffering God, the God with whom one may argue, as Abraham and Moses argued, not just for the sake of "our people" but for the sake of all people, is a *Who*. Wiesel's Hasidic transmission, through his portraits, of the life made of the *Who* comes in response to the Nazi assault on the God that is a *Who*: Wiesel's portraits represent everything that the Nazis set out to obliterate in their assault on the bond between word and meaning and between the name and the soul within which the Holocaust transpired.

According to a teaching from the Hasidic master Levi-Yitzhak of Berditchev (1740–1809), "One of the names of God is: *Who*, as we know when Pharaoh challenged Moses by saying: '*Who* is HaShem' [Exodus 5:2]" (*Kedushat Levi, Vayera* 29). If God is a *Who*, then Israel is a *Who*, and if Israel is a *Who*, then the Torah is a *Who*. "The Torah is presented to us as a person," says Wiesel. "The Jew has a personal attitude toward the Torah, an intimate love for it. In the Talmud this bond is so extreme that God, we are told, consulted the Torah before creating Adam, and sometimes He talks to the Torah, which answers Him. The Torah is therefore like a living person, and in that sense we love it as much as we love God."[8] And so we see that Judaism is a *Who*, to be handed down not just through the elucidation of texts but also through the rendition of living *portraits*, as Elie Wiesel realized. He presents us not merely with commentaries on the sages, nor even merely with their teachings, but with their living and breathing *portraits*. In Wiesel's Hasidic understanding of Judaism, the teaching and the teacher, the *What* and the *Who*, are inseparable.

Through his portraits of these souls on fire Wiesel transmits the flame of his own soul and ignites the souls of those who encounter them. In the aftermath of an unprecedented assault on the soul, Wiesel declares, "*Hineni*—Here I am!" as a Hasid and as a witness who transmits the life of the *Who*, the life of the soul, contained not only in the teachings but also in the personas of the teachers: in Judaism, the portrait, the soul, the persona *is* the teaching. Through the portrait we come *face to face* with the teacher and the teaching. Through the portrait we gaze into the eyes that look into our souls. Through the portrait we step before the countenance.

To love the *Who* that is God is to love the *Who* in the human being; to be sure, there is no loving one without loving the other, as Wiesel's friend Emmanuel Levinas, the great Jewish thinker who also studied with Harav Shushani, affirms: " 'Going towards God' is meaningless unless seen in terms of my primary going towards the other person. I can only go towards God by being ethically concerned by and for the other person."[9] Why? Precisely because God is a *Who*, as taught in the Zohar:

> When the most Mysterious wished to reveal Himself, He first produced a single point which was transmuted into a thought, and in this He executed innumerable designs and engraved innumerable engravings. He further engraved with the sacred and mystic lamp a mystic and most holy design, which was a wondrous edifice issuing from the midst of thought. This is called *Mi*, or "Who," and was the beginning of the edifice, existent and non-existent, deep buried, unknowable by name. It was only called *Mi*. It desired to become manifest and to be called by name. It therefore clothed itself in a refulgent and precious garment and created *eleh*, or "These," and . . . the letters of the two words intermingled, forming the complete name *E-l-o-h-i-m* [God]. (*Zohar* I, 2a)

The *Who*, says the Zohar, created heaven and earth through a movement into a covenantal relationship, as the great sage Nahmanides (1194–1270) has explained, noting that the Hebrew word for "created," *bara*, is a cognate of the word for "covenant," *brit*.[10] No one ever entered into a covenant with a *What*, with an object, a concept, or a principle, first or otherwise.

That is, in part, why the great Hasidic Master Moshe-Leib of Sassov taught that "the beginning of all knowledge is to know that God created everything."[11] For to know that God created everything is to realize that the soul lives only in the midst of a relationship with a *Who*. Left only with a *What*—left only with the material neutrality of all there is—we are left without meaning, without a *Why*. We are left ultimately with Auschwitz, the realm in which there is *kein Warum*, no *Why*, as Primo Levi attests.[12] Where there is no *Why*, there is no *Who*, and where there is no *Who* there is no *Why*. Without this bond between the *Who* and the *Why*, there is nothing to hear except the infinite and terrifying silence, the silence that haunts the sound and the fury signifying nothing. These portraits are set over against *that*.

"Auschwitz," writes André Neher, "is, above all, silence."[13] In Auschwitz, he says, "Silence—the 'inert' silence, great and solemn—comes forward not as a temporary suspension of the Word but as a spokesman for the invincible Nothingness. Thus Silence replaces the Word because Nothingness takes the place of Being."[14] Yehiel De-Nur, the Holocaust survivor and author known as Ka-tzetnik 135633, calls it "the Site of Silence": "No screams here, no speech. The Site of Silence. Soundlessness was all around, engulfing the outflow of humanity from the cattle trucks. . . . Night muffled, stealing inaudibly on tip toes to envelop you, inaudibly, so as to keep from trespassing upon the terrifying silence reigning supreme."[15] And so Wiesel's words return to us: "Never shall I forget that night, the first night in the camp, that turned my life into one long night seven times sealed. . . . Never shall I forget the small faces of the children whose bodies I saw transformed into smoke under a *silent* sky. . . . Never shall I forget the nocturnal *silence* that deprived me for all eternity of the desire to live."[16] Thus the deafening silence of the What, of the indifferent It, crushes the soul. Thus Wiesel undertook a mending of the Who through an engagement with silence by way of language, by way of the word that issues from the face, by way of the face that emerges from the portrait. Indeed, "what is language," he writes, "if not a metamorphosis of silence?"[17] It is a metamorphosis of the *What* into the *Who*. That is what we have in his portraits: a metamorphosis of the *What* into the *Who*.

Wherever only the *What* obtains, all we have is the anonymous rumbling of the "there is," as Levinas says: " 'There is' is the phenomenon of impersonal being: 'it.' . . . [It is a] 'rumbling,' . . . as if the emptiness were full, as if the silence were a noise."[18] If the *Who* of the Revelation at Mount Sinai created the heavens and the earth, then all of creation harbors an elusive, ineffable, yet ineluctable *Why* that penetrates the silence of the ontological "there is." The assault on the *Why* is an assault on the Holy One. It is the assault to which Elie Wiesel responds through his portraits, indeed, precisely by means of *portraiture*: the portrait of the Patriarch, the Prophet, the sage, and the Hasidic master is precisely a portrait of the Why pursued in the aftermath of the radical assault on the *Why*. It is a restoration of the *face*, which is always the subject of the portrait.

Because it is the dimension of meaning, the *Why* is the dimension of the future, which, Levinas realized, is a *Who*: "The other is the future."[19] Wiesel's portraits are not only of the sages of the past but also of the possibilities for a future. For the *Who* is the future, the one to whom and for whom we have *yet* to fulfill an infinite responsibility, as commanded by the Infinite *Who*. Where there is a sense of meaning, there is an answering to the call of *someone* who summons us to a horizon that we have *yet* to reach, a horizon that, indeed, recedes as we approach it. That *someone* lurks in these portraits. With the demolition of meaning in the antiworld of Auschwitz, therefore, comes the demolition of time itself, the demolition of the *after*, as Wiesel has noted.[20] And yet this *after*, the future, the *Why* and the *Who*—all of it—form the matrix of the portraits that go into Elie Wiesel's Hasidic legacy. These portraits are not the ghosts of a fading past but the living voices who summon us to a living future and a living testimony. In his portraits Wiesel cries out, "*Hineni*—Here I am!" not just to the teachings but to the teachers of the tradition to bring about a kind of resurrection of the soul in the *after*math of the desolation of the soul. For the soul is made of meaning. Which is to say: the soul is made of relationship. These are portraits of the *relationship* that is soul.

The Recovery of Human Relationship

In his response to the Nazi assault on human relationship, Elie Wiesel transmits the portraits and the souls that embody a Jewish legacy through storytelling, without which there is neither a *Why* nor a relationship. Transmitting the portraits, he engages his listeners and his readers in a dialogue, in a speaking that is a relating. Note well: the *Why* that sustains the life of the soul emerges not from any philosophical or theological treatise but from storytelling. The stake in Wiesel's transmission of these portraits and tales can be found in a Hasidic tale, one that Wiesel relates as an epigraph to his novel *The Gates of the Forest*.

As the story goes, whenever a calamity threatened the Jewish community, the Baal Shem Tov would go to a special place in the forest, light a fire in a particular manner, and say a special prayer. And the community was saved. A generation later, the task fell to the Baal Shem's disciple Dov Ber, the Maggid of Mezeritch. He, too, would go to the place in the forest. However, he did not know how to light the fire. But he knew the prayer, and that was sufficient. After the Maggid came Rabbi Moshe Leib of Sassov. When catastrophe threatened the Jews, he would seek out the place in the forest, but he knew neither the ritual of fire nor the proper prayer. And yet, that was sufficient. Finally, the responsibility fell to Rabbi Yisrael of Rizhin, who stood paralyzed in his study, whispering, "Oh, Lord, King of the Universe! The secret of the Baal Shem's ritual of fire and his prayer for salvation are long forgotten. Here I stand, unable even to find the place in the forest. All I can do is tell the story. And this must be sufficient!" And so it was.

Gershom Scholem takes this to be a tale about the decline of the Hasidic masters from one generation to the next.[21] Not so Elie Wiesel; for him, as Nehemia Polen points out, "The master remains central."[22] Will transmitting the tale now be sufficient? Will entrusting to us the portraits of the sages and the patriarchs—so that we may tell the tales—be sufficient? There lies the desperate faith against faith, the hope against hope, of Elie Wiesel and his Hasidic legacy. Faith in what and hope in what? In human relationship, without which there can be neither faith nor hope. Faith is not about believing in God but about embracing the other human being. Hope is not about waiting for something to come but about declaring, "Here I am," in a movement toward the other human being. The Who targeted for annihilation in the Nazis' assault on the soul lay not in the inner recesses of the psyche but in the between space of human-to-human relationship, which is essential to human-to-divine relationship. Hence the two tablets of the Covenant signify the relation *ben adam leMakom* (between human and God) and *ben adam lehevero* (between human and fellow human). Both relationships, which are actually one, come under a definitive, radical assault in the antiworld. In Wiesel's *Night* we have one of the most chilling lines in all of the testimonies to emerge from the Kingdom of Night: "Here there is no such thing as father, brother, friend. Each of us lives and dies alone."[23] Primo Levi provides a brief but profoundly powerful elaboration on this *alone*: "Everyone is desperately and ferociously alone."[24] Yes, *ferociously* alone in a universe void of charity and compassion. As ferociously alone as God is.

Suddenly we understand on a deeper level the truth of the divine assertion that "it is not good for the human being to be alone" (Genesis 2:18). You cannot be charitable or compassionate in isolation; in isolation there can be no peace, no *shalom*, because there can be no wholeness, no *shalem*, apart from human relationship. For the soul lives not *within* us but *between* us, in the between space of human relation, where the soul draws its breath.

"Just as man can attain his ultimate truth only through other human beings," writes Wiesel, "God can be united to His creation only through man. Man needs the other to be human—just as God needs man to be God."[25] How, then, does a Hasid transmit the millennial legacy of Jewish teaching and testimony? Through storytelling. And the Hasid Elie Wiesel is above all a storyteller. He is a teller of tales who has a sense of the life-and-death stake in telling these tales that transform us into witnesses and messengers. He is like the old man in his novel *The Oath* who saves a young man bent on suicide by relating to him a tale and thus turning him into a messenger. Listen: "I'll transmit my experience to him and he, in turn, will be compelled to do the same. He in turn will become a messenger. Once a messenger, he has no alternative. He must stay alive until he has transmitted his message."[26] That is why knowing the story must be sufficient: Wiesel returns us to life by transforming us into messengers through these portraits that are made of the tales of the Patriarchs and Prophets, the tales of the sages and the Hasidim, the very tales that the Nazis sought to silence in their assault on the meaning and sanctity of humanity.

As in the case of the old man relating the tale to the young man, Wiesel relates his tales of the sages to us, transforming us into messengers and thereby extending to us a lifeline. Having heard this storyteller's cry of "Here I am," we must in turn declare, "Here I am for *you*." Understanding Elie Wiesel's portraits to be a restoration of human relationship in the aftermath of a radical assault on that relationship, we understand them, if one may say so, as a restoration of the divine presence. This he accomplishes through storytelling, through what in Jewish tradition is known as Aggadah.

Recall the *Sifre* on Deuteronomy 11:22: "You wish to recognize the One who spoke and brought the world into being? Learn Aggadah for in Aggadah you will find God." Where do we encounter Aggadah? In the face that gazes upon us from the depths of Wiesel's portraits. Says Levinas, "The face speaks. It speaks, it is in this that it renders possible and begins all discourse."[27] This returns us to the dictum: because the face speaks, "the face is what forbids us to kill."[28] Wiesel's portraits forbid us to kill. They forbid us to kill *because* they speak: to speak is to forbid murder. To speak is to relate; to relate is to tell a tale; and to tell a tale is to forbid murder, beginning with self-murder. Once again, note well: the power of the prohibition against murder comes to bear not in the treatise but in the tale, for the tale—the portrait—confronts us with the face from which the prohibition originates. You wish to recognize the Holy One, who was singled out for a unique annihilation in the extermination of His witnesses? Learn the aggadic tales that go into Wiesel's portraits. In those faces you will encounter—or collide with—the faces of the dead who are not dead, the faces of those who, Wiesel once told me, look over his shoulder and examine every line he writes. If they look over his shoulder, they look into our eyes. Sketching his portraits, Wiesel brings us face to face not only with the teaching but also with the teacher, whose lips move as we repeat the teaching that came from those lips.

Portraiture: Elie Wiesel's Hasidic Response to Auschwitz

When considering the matter of portraiture, what usually comes to mind is a visual image, often of the famous portraits, both in painting and in photography, such as Leonardo's *Mona Lisa*, Courbet's *The Desperate Man*, or Ansel Adams's photograph of "The Migrant Mother." Very often the eyes are the portrait's most striking feature: they follow us, question us, and plead with us. Gazing into those silent eyes, we search the face that gazes upon us, and we encounter the truth that is searching for us. The portrait *speaks*. More than that, the portrait *questions*: as we peer into those eyes, they peer into our souls. That is what makes Wiesel's portraits as unsettling as they are edifying.

Wiesel's portraits convey a trace of the spoken word, as they are based upon talks and lectures that he presented over the years: there is something strikingly *aural* about these textual renditions. To be sure, those of us who were blessed to hear him deliver a talk can hear his voice rising up from these pages charged with memory, testimony, and the flames of souls on fire. Through the voice of Professor Wiesel, through the voice of his portraiture, there emerges a kind of Oral Torah, transmitting the teachings and the Torah of the sages in a distinctively midrashic manner. One of Wiesel's students, the noted Holocaust scholar Alan Rosen, described to me Wiesel's portraits as encounters between Professor Wiesel and the subject of his portraiture, a saying of "*Hineni*—Here I am" to the prophet, the sage, or the Hasidic master: whether it is Jeremiah or the Kotzker Rebbe, Wiesel engages a living voice in a living dialogue. What we encounter in these portraits cannot be an object of analysis. Rather, there is a between space that opens up as Wiesel addresses his audience. In that between space the soul in the portrait draws a breath. And from within that breath a story unfolds.

Wiesel's portraits are haunted by what Emil Fackenheim calls "midrashic madness." He explains: "If sanity is not of the spirit only, but rather contact with the world (and with God *in* and *through* the world), then such sanity, when the world is Auschwitz, is destroyed by madness. And if sanity consists of flight from the world (and to gods who have themselves fled from the world), then such flight, when the world is the Nazi holocaust, is necessary if even a shred of sanity is to remain."[29] Fackenheim relates a tale he heard from Elie Wiesel. It is about a group of Jews who had gathered to pray in a city in Nazi Europe. Suddenly a pious Jew, stealing his way from shadow to shadow in the city's streets, bursts through the door, and, in a loud whisper says, "Shhhh, Jews! Do not pray so loud! God will hear you! Then He will know that there are still some Jews left alive in Europe!"[30] You see the madness in this midrashic tale. After Auschwitz, the only way to remain sane is to go mad. But that is just where Midrash comes in. Not only did the madman belong to Wiesel's world, but the specter of the madman, as he once told me, haunted all of his writings. In these portraits one senses in Wiesel a mad desire to dance, which, among the Hasidim, is a mad desire to pray. There lies a key to Wiesel's portraiture: it is a form of prayer—and of dance. Reb Leib, the son of the Great Maggid, once declared to his Hasidim, "Your dancing counts for more than my prayers."[31] Not only does Wiesel voice these portraits—he *dances* them.

One begins to see why Wiesel turns to portraiture not only as a response to the Nazis' assault on the soul but also as a means of transmitting a distinctively Hasidic legacy. To be sure, Wiesel's earliest portraits from his presentations at the 92nd Street Y in the 1960s and 1970s were of Hasidic masters, and the method of transmission through those portraits is what makes his legacy at once Hasidic and thoroughly Jewish. Says Wiesel, the Vizhnitzer Hasid: "In our tradition a human being is defined above all by his ties with other human beings. Only the face to face with the other is of importance; the life of the other alone is the measure of a life, and not the death that awaits us or has preceded us."[32] Wiesel's portraits draw us into this *face to face*. The great sage of the Talmud, Rabbi Akiba, maintains that the humanity and the dignity of the human being are revealed in the face; in the face, he held, lies the image of the Holy One,[33] and in the image of the Holy One lies the exigency of the holy.

Through Wiesel's portraits we encounter not only the faces of the unique individuals of the Jewish tradition but also the meaning of the face *as such*—and therefore the meaning of his portraiture *as such*. Because the face *as such* signifies holiness, says Levinas, "the face is signification, and signification *without context*. I mean that the Other, in the rectitude of his face, is not a character within a context. Ordinarily, . . . the meaning of something is in its relation to another thing. Here, to the contrary, the face *is meaning all by itself.*"[34] Indeed, without this meaning beyond context, without this absolute, that enters this world through the soul embodied in the flesh and blood of the face, this world has no meaning; it is simply there, mute and indifferent. Only the face of the other human being can penetrate this mute indifference. Because the face has meaning without context, it imparts meaning to every context, to every instance, of human relation. In Wiesel's portraits we encounter meaning beyond context. We encounter what imparts meaning to any context. We encounter—or collide with—the *Who* beyond the *What*.

As we receive the portraits that Wiesel lays before us, we are summoned to an infinite ethical responsibility that no other can meet, summoned not only by memory but also by the immemorial, which is the substance of memory, for it summons and sanctifies all that can be remembered. If, as both Elie Wiesel and Primo Levi have said, the Holocaust was a war against memory,[35] it was a war against God and the Good revealed in the face, God and the Good that choose us prior to every choice we make and that therefore make our choices matter. This *prior to*, this *always already*, is the immemorial transmitted through Wiesel's opposition to the war against memory and his restoration of the transcendent ethical demand. His weapon? Portraiture.

Wiesel's portraits profoundly implicate us, not only with regard to the living and the yet unborn but also with regard to the dead, those relegated either to remembrance or to oblivion. If we have no ethical responsibility to the dead, then we have no ethical responsibility to the living. That is why the Nazis robbed the Jews of their dead, just as they robbed the Jews of their deaths, as Wiesel has said: "My generation has been robbed of everything, even of our cemeteries."[36] The sky was transformed into a cemetery, the sky in which the might of the Infinite One lies, as it is written (Psalms 68:34). Deprived of their cemeteries, where do they lie? Wiesel once said, "We are their cemeteries."[37] Elsewhere he cries out, "I am nobody's grave!"[38] Where, then, do these souls lie? Where do they abide? In Wiesel's portraits.

In his portraits of these souls on fire we encounter the soul of the other and our own soul, the other that *is* our own soul, as Levinas has said: "The soul is the other in me."[39] The soul is the Torah in me. The soul is the outcry of the other who invades me and disturbs my sleep. Yes, that is it: calling us to an encounter with these portraits, Wiesel's outcry of "*Hineni*—Here I am" brings us a hope of redemption by disturbing our sleep. From within his declaration of "Here I am" a question—or a plea—singles us out, as it singled out the first human being: "*Ayekah?*— Where are you?" (Genesis 3:9). Through his portraits of the sages of the Jewish tradition Elie Wiesel, the master and the sage, ignites the soul in us by shaking us from our insidious sleep. Wiesel's portraits summon from us the response of "Here I am." And "the subject who says 'Here I am,'" Levinas asserts, "*testifies* to the Infinite,"[40] testifies, that is, to an infinite responsibility to and for the one who is infinitely dear. In Wiesel's portraits of our sages and teachers, the infinite and the finite merge into a commanding voice. Therefore there is no innocent reading of Wiesel's portraits and no encountering them without being implicated.

Levinas once said that "the attributes of God are given not in the indicative, but in the imperative. The knowledge of God comes to us like a commandment, like a *Mitzvah*. To know God is to know what must be done."[41] Just so, to know God's witness and messenger Elie Wiesel is to know what we are commanded to do and therefore what must be done. As Wiesel sketches his portraits, we hear the prophets and sages speak: originating in voice and not in ink, what he sketches is not so much a visual image as it is a voice, through which there resounds a *commanding* voice, arising not only from the millennial Jewish tradition but also from the ashes of the antiworld that now engulf our own world. Because here we come before the faces of our teachers, we come before the faces of our mothers and fathers, as Wiesel points out in his portrait of Rashi.[42] The love with which Wiesel portrays them is a love not only for these teachers whose voices come to us from over the centuries; it is also a love for his listeners and his readers, who are his students, whom Wiesel loved as a father loves his children. And so we arrive at the secret of Wiesel's portraiture: exploring his portraits of the Patriarchs and the Prophets, of the Talmudic sages and the Hasidic masters, we discover a profound, living portrait of Elie Wiesel himself as it unfolds in his love for the other human being. That is what, I hope, will emerge from the pages that follow.

Portraits from the Torah

For those who, like Elie Wiesel, take the Torah to be revealed at Mount Sinai, these portraits from the Torah fall into a category of their own. Beginning with these portraits from the Torah, we begin from an immemorial origin, from a "time" and "space" outside of space and time, from the depths of the revelation of the Infinite One. For these portraits, coming to us as they do from Torah, are rooted in that revelation. Elie Wiesel puts it this way: "As I reread the story of Noah and his children, I see myself as a child in a Heder, leaning over a tattered Bible. . . . I see myself and the world before . . . before the other deluge. . . . That is the profound beauty of Scripture: its characters are not mythical; their adventures are not imaginary; they vibrate with life and truth, and thus compel those of us who approach them to enter their lives and search for their meaning."[1] Searching these portraits for their meaning, we search for the meaning of our own lives.

"*The Jew*," says Wiesel, "*is haunted more by the beginning than by the end.*"[2] Haunted by the beginning, by the *Bereshit*, the Jew is haunted by the Commanding Voice of Creation, which is echoed in the Commanding Voice of Revelation. To be sure, the Ten Utterances of Creation parallel the Ten Utterances of Revelation, as it is written (*Bahir* 118; *Mishnah Avot* 5:1; see also the *Or HaChayim* on Exodus 20:1). Unlike other portraits that we shall consider—based on historical, cultural, and legendary accounts—these portraits, according to the Jewish religious tradition, were initially sketched by the Holy One Himself. Therefore what we engage here transcends the event horizon of ontological thought. As we shall see in what follows, these portraits harbor a trace of transcendence, of a "thinking" that precedes thought, of the primal, an anarchic movement of the creation and revelation of the *You*.

Looking to the tradition, we find that the creation of the *You* in the beginning makes portraiture possible: a portrait is not a "still life" but the emanation of a living soul, of one whom we address as a *You*, the one who eludes the eye. Elie Wiesel's Hasidic mastery of portraiture is precisely about rendering *present* the invisible *You* and the *Who* of the subject—a *subject* of relation, who is a person, and not an *object* of contemplation. As the subject of a relation, these portraits unfold through the relation of tales. It is precisely because HaShem was the first to tell the tales of these persons that we inherit a capacity for saying *You* to one another. Wiesel's Hasidic legacy, a legacy of telling tales, strengthens and continues that capacity, which was in the beginning. So let us begin from the beginning, with the first one to be addressed as *you*.

Portrait of Adam the First

If the portraits from the Torah are unique among Wiesel's portraits, unique among these portraits is the portrait of *Adam HaRishon*, "Adam the First," as he is known in the tradition (e.g., *Bereshit Rabbah* 8:1). For one thing, he had no parents. And yet we are all his children. In a profound sense, Wiesel's portrait of Adam is a portrait of each of us, as he indicates when he invokes a teaching from the Talmud (*Eruvin* 18a): "*Panim in Hebrew is used in the plural form: man has more than one face. His own and Adam's.*"[3] To gaze upon this image is to peer into our own souls. The face of Adam reveals the face of the other human being, the *ben adam*, the child of Adam placed in our care. Gazing upon this portrait of Adam, we collide with the question put to Adam: "Where are you?" Without Adam, there is no question. "Perhaps God intended to begin His work with a question," says Wiesel. "Perhaps He sought, through Adam, to continuously interrogate His creation."[4] And to interrogate Himself: to be created in His image and likeness is to be eternally turned over to questioning. Thus we have the questioning that belongs to the creation of the first human being.

The questioning penetrates the horrific solitude of our being to create an opening for a relationship with another. That is why, Joel Rosenberg observes, "if there is a single characteristic most commonly shared among biblical heroes, in Wiesel's handling, it is their solitude."[5] It is also why, as Wiesel says, "the secret of creation may be dwelled upon only when one is alone—as Adam was alone."[6] It is because the secret of creation lies in the human and divine longing for relation. Inasmuch as creation transpires through a divine word, it is a movement into a relationship: the word is spoken by *someone* and implies someone to whom it is addressed, someone who is summoned to respond. The most fundamental thing, the first thing, is that the Holy One *created* and thereby entered into a *covenant*. Where there is covenant there is responsibility, which is an overcoming of the solitude of the Creator and of Adam, which brings us back to the centrality of the *You*: prior to his appearance Adam is *already* singled out for a relationship with another, to whom he may say, "You." "In the beginning," writes Wiesel, "man is alone. Alone as God is alone. As he opens his eyes he does not ask: Who am I? He asks: Who are you?"[7]

And yet in his novel *The Oath* we read, "When he opened his eyes, Adam did not ask God: Who are *you*? He asked: Who am *I*?"[8] A contradiction? No. For the soul that comes to life in the midst of a relation, there is no *I* without the *You*: to ask, "Who are you?" is to ask, "Who am I?" In the words of Martin Buber, "When one says You, the I of the word pair I-You is said, too."[9] Looking further at the opening line of Torah, we find an important teaching from the Zohar, a teaching essential to Wiesel's portrait of Adam. Instead of reading *Bereshit bara Elokim et ha-* . . . as "In the beginning God created the—" the Zohar reads it as "In the beginning God created the *alef, tav, hey* of *atah*: You." Says the Zohar, "The word *et* consists of the letters *alef* and *tav*, which include between them all the letters, as being the first and last of the alphabet. Afterward, *hey* was added so that all the letters should be attached to *hey*, and this gave the name *atah* (You)" (*Zohar* I, 15b). What is most essential to the life of the soul is to answer, "*Hineni*—Here I am for *you*!" when summoned by another soul, as God Himself summoned the first human being with a cry of "*Ayekah?*—Where are you?" (Genesis 3:9). Wiesel points out that God puts to each of us this question put to Adam.[10] It is a cry of anguish and pain, for the word *ayekah* is the same as the first word in the Book of Lamentations, *Eykhah*, which is a howl of "How?" or "Why?" as though He were crying, "How could you?" God knows precisely where we are. Shall we answer, "*Hineni*—Here I am for you," or shall we hide, as the first Adam hid?

The Zohar relates that when God was about to create the first human being, the Torah, from which all of creation is made, warned him that the human being would surely break the commandments of the Holy One and thereby provoke Him to anger. Indeed, the Torah warned the Creator that He might become so angry that He would destroy His creation.

God then decided to make the Torah His assistant in the creation of the human being, since the chief attribute of the Torah is Mercy: whenever God might grow angry at humanity, the Torah would restrain him with mercy, patience, and a measure of loving kindness (*Zohar* II, 35; see also *Bereshit Rabbah* 12:1–2).

One can understand God's anger. But why the pain? Why does God suffer so much over Adam's fall from the relationship, when he succumbed to the temptation to eat the fruit and become as God? The Midrash tells us that the ministering angels tried to talk Him out of it (*Bereshit Rabbah* 8:5). Why? I think because they knew it would hurt Him. Indeed, when the Spirit of the Holy One "hovered" over the face of the deep, the word is *merahefet*, which may also mean "hesitated": He hesitated because He knew it would hurt. It is, indeed, striking that, according to the Talmud, when God created the heavens and the earth He prepared a place for Himself in the uppermost realms, a place called *Mistarim*, knowing that He would need a place to go, a place where He could weep in hiding (*Hagigah* 5b; see also *Sefer HaIkkarim* 4:23), lest His suffering undo His creation. According to the Midrash, this hiding place is the realm of darkness, the realm of *hoshekh*, from which God drew the plague of darkness, the darkness in which "a man could not see his brother" (Exodus 10:23), so that the very darkness in which God hides makes God weep (*Midrash Tehillim* 1:18:16). As a movement into a relationship, the act of creation is an act of love, and there is no loving without suffering. So we have an inkling of the pain in the "*Ayekah!?*" Wiesel provides us with more. After calling out the names of the animals, he notes, Adam called God by His Name. "He understood intuitively that God Himself receives His name from man—illustrating the basic Jewish concept that while God is God, and man is only His instrument, still God needs man to make Himself known."[11] God needs man if He is to be God.

Exploring the tradition further, we discover more reasons for God's anguish over Adam's falling prey to the primal temptation to be as God. We discover, for example, that one cannot eclipse God without erasing the prohibition against murder; "whoever sheds human blood renounces the Likeness," as it is written in the Tosefta (*Tosefta Yevamot* 8:4), the "Likeness" not only within one's own soul but also within the soul of the other. "Whoever kills, kills Adam," Wiesel states it. "Whoever kills, kills Adam's vision, kills in Adam's name. Every man should be Adam to all others."[12] Why God's anguish? Because in the loss of the higher relation, Adam did horrific damage to his own soul and to the souls of those of us who are bound to him. This is not to suggest any notion of inherited sin, which is alien to Jewish teaching. As Wiesel has said, "We are linked to Adam only by his memory, which becomes our own, and by his death, which foreshadows our own. Not by his sin."[13] And, linked to Adam, we are linked to each other.

That each is connected to all, both physically and metaphysically, can also be found in the Talmudic teaching of Rabbi Meir: "The dust of the first man was gathered from all parts of the earth" (*Sanhedrin*, 38a). And God "breathed the soul of life into the dust" (Genesis 2:7), breathed the "Word," says the Targum, to create a speaking being, a *medaber*, with the implication that a speaking being is also a listening being. Thus the very possibility of portraiture and the tales that characterize it come into being upon the creation of the first human being. This is the meaning of other Talmudic teachings. Rabbi Eleazar, for example, said: "The first man [extended] from the earth to the firmament." And Rabbi Yehuda taught, "In the name of Rab: 'The first man [extended] from one end of the world to the other'" (*Hagigah*, 12a), indicating that the First Adam is gathered into all of humanity. Therefore, as Wiesel says, "more than the Messiah, Adam is present. . . . Embodying every man's quest for meaning, justice and truth, Adam remains the contemporary."[14] Adam remains the contemporary precisely because with the creation of Adam comes the creation of the messianic mission. "Some go so far as seeing in him the future Messiah," says Wiesel.[15] Thus, we have the Jewish teaching that in addition to a trace of the soul of Adam, every soul harbors a spark of the soul of the Messiah, the Anointed One of the House of David.[16]

But we have almost forgotten the relationship most crucial to making Adam Adam, to making him a human being possessed of a divine spark and a human soul: it is the relationship with Eve. Indeed, God gave the name *Adam* to the man and woman together: "Male and female created He them" (Genesis 1:27). Created as an *ezer k'negdo*, a "helper against him" (Genesis 2:18), Wiesel explains, Eve was "to help him by opposing him, by defying him. . . . Eve: a remedy against solitude, the unfathomed side of man. Without Eve, Adam would have been a man but not human."[17] Here Emmanuel Levinas may be of some help:

> Woman does not simply come to someone deprived of companionship to keep him company. She answers to a solitude inside this privation and—which is stranger—to a solitude that subsists in spite of the presence of God; to a solitude in the

universal, to the inhuman which continues to well up even when the human has mastered nature and raised it to thought. For the inevitable uprooting of thought, which dominates the world, to return to the peace and ease of being at home, the strange flow of gentleness must enter into the geometry of infinite and cold space. Its name is woman.[18]

That is why it is not good for the man to be alone. That is why, according to the Talmudic sage Rabbi Shimon ben Menassia, "the Holy One, blessed be He, plaited Eve's hair and then brought her to Adam" to perform the marriage ceremony (*Eruvin*, 18a). That is why, without Eve, Adam would have been a man but not human.

And without Adam and Eve we would not have Cain and Abel.

Portrait of Cain and Abel

Cain and Abel: no two brothers, no two men, are so intimately bound to one another, each in need of the other to be who he is. No two men are so intimately bound to all humanity, indeed, to God Himself, as Wiesel suggests: the tale of Cain and Abel "describes a threefold confrontation: between man and God, at once present and hidden, between man and his brother, at once rivals and associates, and ultimately between man and himself."[19] Why between man and himself? Because these were the first men to be born of a man and a woman: "For the first time there was human collaboration in the creation of a man; for the first time a human being was entirely human, that is to say, man's work and entirely man's responsibility."[20] And with that responsibility comes the prospect of murder.

As for God, Wiesel has this to say: "God is judge. God is participant. Accomplice."[21] Accomplice? So it was not *entirely* man's responsibility: yes, God is a participant, as well as an accomplice, from the beginning. Born of a man and a woman, Cain and Abel came into the world thanks to God's participation, as the sages of the Talmud have taught: "There are three partners in the creation of a human being: the Holy One, blessed be He, the father, and the mother. Therefore when a man honors his father and his mother, the Holy One, blessed be He, says 'I ascribe [merit] to them as though I had dwelt among them and they had honored Me'" (*Kiddushin*, 30b). That is why the Fifth Commandment, the commandment to honor our mother and father (Exodus 20:11), falls in the category of the relationship *ben adam leMakom*, between the human being and God, rather than *ben adam lehevero*, between human and fellow human. But brothers who honor their mother and father do not quarrel; one certainly does not murder the other. Indeed, the act of murder is a repudiation and usurpation of God.

Cain is no exception. Says Wiesel: "Like God, he thought to offer himself a human sacrifice in holocaust. He wanted to be cruel like Him, a stranger like Him, an avenger like Him. And like Him, present and absent at the same time, absent by his presence, present *in* his absence. Cain killed to become God. To kill God."[22] Thus Cain succumbed to the primal temptation to be like God. You cannot become God without murdering, and you cannot murder without becoming God, without thereby killing God. For it is written that we are to read the commandments not from top to bottom but from right to left (in Hebrew): "I am God" means "Thou shalt not murder" (see, e.g, *Mekilta Bahodesh* 8; *Pesikta Rabbati* 21:19; *Zohar* I, 90a).

Wiesel understood this better than most. In his novel *Twilight* the sanitarium patient Cain declares to the main character Raphael, "When I killed my brother, it was really Him I wanted to kill. And He knows it. Any fool knows that whoever kills, kills God.' "[23] But the God that Cain would kill so that he might become God is not the Creator who, in a movement into a loving, covenantal relationship, spoke and brought heaven and earth into being, the God of the Thirteen Attributes of Mercy, who is "compassionate and gracious, slow to anger, abundant in loving kindness and truth," and so on (Exodus 34:6–7). No, it is the false, idolatrous god, for whom power is the only reality and weakness is the only sin, the self-styled ego-god who is free of all limitations, in complete control, and completely self-justified, not only knowing but devising good and evil. If the *yetzer hara*, the "evil inclination," is an inclination to get rid of God, it is an inclination to commit murder. Thus the Hasidic master Rabbi Simha Bunim of Pshishke taught that "the evil inclination should be imagined as if it were a murderer,"[24] a murderer of God and humanity.

According to one tradition, the two brothers quarreled so that Abel shares at least a portion of the blame. For one thing—even if it is the only thing, it is problematic—Abel did nothing to reach out to his brother at a time when his brother's "face had fallen," *vayiplu panayiv* (Genesis 4:5). Abel was unable to behold his brother's fallen face, a face inscribed with suffering, whatever the source of the suffering might have been. "To watch over a man who grieves," says Wiesel, "is a more urgent duty than to think of God. Though too weak to oppose God, man is strong enough to defend his fellow-man or at least to dress his wounds. Abel did nothing—such was the nature of his fault."[25] Still, Cain was the murderer, and, as Wiesel observes, his transgression toward Abel was much more egregious than Abel's fault: "By envying Abel, by refusing to understand him, to love him *in spite* of everything, by judging him and thus repudiating him, Cain became guilty. He was guilty even *before* he killed."[26] Here the sin runs deeper than Abel's failure, because Cain's judgment and repudiation of his brother was steeped in hatred, and, as it is written in the Talmud, "Whoever hates another is as though he were his murderer" (*Kallah Rabbati* 54b [1]).

Whom do we hate when we hate another? The one who "resembles us," Wiesel wisely observes. "The first murder was a fratricide."[27] Because all of humanity stems from a single human being, as well as from God, every murder is at once a fratricide and a deicide. Hence, the Talmud tells us, a brother's hatred of his brother was the reason for the destruction of the Second Temple (*Yoma* 9b), and the destruction of the Temple is the obliteration of God's Presence in the world—that is why it is so devastating, why it is a *Hurban*, a total destruction. In this first act of murder, Wiesel points out, we have the paradigm for other acts of murder, particularly for acts of mass murder. For in this first act of murder we have the three roles necessary for mass murder to happen: perpetrator, victim, and bystander. "Cain and Abel: *they* were mankind," writes Wiesel. "The choice was limited and absolute: assassin or victim, nothing else."[28] And the bystanders? They were none other than Adam and Eve: "Adam was conspicuously absent. . . . But then, where was Eve?"[29] Do not we, the offspring of the parents of all humanity, resemble these parents? Do not we, the descendants not only of Adam and Eve but also of Cain and Abel, hear "the bloods" of our brothers and sisters cry out, as God heard the outcry of the bloods of Abel and all of his descendants, hence the plural *bloods* (Genesis 4:10)? If, as it is written in the Mishnah, saving a single life is like saving an entire world (*Sanhedrin* 4:5), then how many worlds are destroyed in the act of murder that arises from a brother's hatred of his brother?

Yes, *a brother's hatred of his brother*, a hatred that washes over humanity. Hence Wiesel's focus on the Scripture's repetition of the word *brother*: "Whoever kills, kills his brother; and when one has killed, one no longer is anyone's brother."[30] Where does the murder of the one who resembles us lead? To suicide. "Cain killed Abel, and it was only a first step," says Wiesel. "Every murder is a suicide: Cain killed Cain in Abel."[31] Killing the one who resembles us is the manifestation of a desire to kill ourselves, a manifestation of a hatred of ourselves, and, in killing ourselves, a rebellion against God. "Self-hate," Wiesel has written, "is more harmful than hate toward others. The latter questions man's relationship to man; the first implicates man's relationship to God."[32] Self-hate, a hatred that can lead a person to commit every manner of atrocity as an act of vengeance against the Divine Nothingness, is hatred of God. Taking out our vengeance on creation, we take out our vengeance on the Creator in an expression of hatred for ourselves. And so those who would kill others by deeming them deicides end by killing themselves. Cain's design? To annihilate God in the annihilation of himself—which is the project of every murderer. Indeed, we often hear about a gunman who kills others and in the end kills himself.

And so the brothers quarreled, as brothers do east of Eden. What did they quarrel about? According to the Midrash, it was over the three things that prove to be the most common motives for murder. The first is wealth: they fought over which of them would own which portions of the earth and how much each would possess. The second is jealousy: they fought over which of them would have which of their sisters for a wife; some say that both of them wanted to lie with their mother. The third is religion: they fought over which of them would have the Temple built on his tract of land (*Bereshit Rabbah* 22:7). This third motive is the most insidious, since it involves a repetition of succumbing to the temptation that was the ruin of Adam and Eve: the temptation to be as God. For to suppose that one may be in possession of the Temple is to usurp the Divine Throne, a move that, again, is already manifest in the act of murder. Therefore, according to Jewish understanding, Jerusalem is not *our* city—in our prayers it is *irkha*, "*Your* city," God's city: He is the *Boneh Yerushalayim*, the Builder of Jerusalem. Therefore Jews do not lay claim to Jerusalem—Jerusalem lays claim to the Jews.

Cain's name, *Kayin*, means to "acquire," "possess," "appropriate." And in his name we have a key to this ancient tale. In his effort to become as God through the act of murder, Cain had to appropriate God. "His purpose?" Wiesel raises the question. "To destroy, to uproot creation. His reasoning? If this is man, I refuse to share his fate; if this is life, then I don't want it."[33] Cain, he writes, "no longer knew what to do with a life that now seemed shallow and useless. How could he fill its void and give it meaning? He set out to find a deed that would not be lost but would be inscribed in time, in a memory other than his own. He was the outsider, who kills to feel alive, to arrive more quickly at the inevitable and inevitably tragic end. Conditioned for this kind of spectacular, definitive gesture, Cain could not help but kill: he did not choose the crime; instead, the crime chose him."[34] Like so many others, he wanted the headline. Did he rush headlong into the crime precisely in order to relieve himself of all responsibility, professing to be ignorant of being his brother's keeper (Genesis 4:9)?

Ah, yes. We come to yet another insight into what this tale is about: in our effort to be as God, not only do we usurp God, but in doing so, like Cain, we judge God and thus lay the responsibility at the feet of God. The effort to be as God, which leads to murder, is an effort to detach ourselves from our humanity and thereby detach ourselves from all responsibility—all in the name of justice! The usurpation of God always takes place in the name of justice. "Cain is Cain," as Wiesel declares, "because he believes in justice!"[35] And so Wiesel teaches that, according to one tradition, when God says, "The bloods of your brother cry out to Me" (Genesis 4:10), "it should not be read as *to* Me but as *at* Me, *against* Me. What you have done, Cain, you have done also in My name; you have shared with Me your projects and daydreams; you have made Me responsible for your acts as I make you responsible for My creation."[36] Yet laying the responsibility for human action at God's feet is precisely what turns humanity over to a condition of exile and wandering.

Thus the first murderer was marked, so that no man may touch him (Genesis 4:15), so that he may have no human contact with any human—not even any human who might take revenge against him. Cain is a murderer on parole, only to be murdered by his very offspring (see Genesis 4:23–24). His is the so-called freedom that comes when "one no longer is anyone's brother."[37] Without the commandment, we are turned over to wandering, as the murderer Cain who was turned over to *Nod*, to "wandering." Can any term more accurately define the problem of a homeless humanity? If we are homeless, it is because we are either murderers or the accomplices to murder. If, as Wiesel says, "Cain's true punishment" was that "he unlearned the meaning of Shabbat,"[38] it is because Cain had lost all understanding of what it means to dwell the world. For the purpose of creation and therefore of Shabbat is given in the first letter of the Torah, in the *beit*, which means "home": the purpose of creation is to transform creation into a dwelling place for the Creator. Where does the Creator dwell? In the Shabbat.

Just one more point—a very important one. We have seen that the first question put to the first human being—Where are you?—is put to each of us. We now realize that so are the two questions put to the first man born of a human being: Where is your brother? And what have you done? (Genesis 4:9–10). And it is the Holy One who asks.

Portrait of Noah

Wiesel draws us into this tale with a single word: *corruption*, a term that also permeates the Talmudic discussion of the generation of Noah (see *Sanhedrin* 108a). "Corruption," says Wiesel, "is the key word in the story—or rather, in the preparation of the story: corruption of the flesh, of the senses, of the population, corruption of the land, of the values. Corruption begets *hamas*: theft, violence, hatred—total disdain for one's fellow man."[39] The corruption of the flesh lies in sensuality, where we rush from one intoxication to another. Corruption of the senses lies in hedonism, where the Good is reduced to whatever feels good. Corruption of the population lies in the retreat into the current fashion and fad, which in turn allows us to slip into the cave of an indifferent, solipsistic isolation, free of all responsibility. Corruption of the land lies in our disregard for the creatures whose lives are sustained by the land, a disregard for the land itself. And corruption of values lies in the collapse of all distinction between good and evil.

Hence the violence, the chaos, that is *hamas*. "Creation had become chaos," writes Wiesel. "As a result of Adam's sin, animals and beasts had begun to rebel. Man was no longer their sovereign,"[40] no longer their caretaker: cruelty to animals was part of the corruption of that generation. This chaos is characterized by a mass confusion, a *bilbul*, between above and below, between light and darkness, between good and evil, so that this ultimate confusion brought on the ultimate punishment: a radical "confusion," the *Mabul*, the Great Flood. Indeed, it is no coincidence that the Torah portion named for Noah ends with the story of the Tower of Babel and the Confusion of Tongues. For the chaos and confusion of *Babel*, a cognate of *Mabul*, lay in the tearing of word from meaning—that is what begets violence and murder. But more about the Tower later.

In this question concerning the bond between word and meaning lies a key to the Baal Shem Tov's commentary on Genesis 6:16, where God instructs Noah: "You shall make a window (*tzohar*) in the ark (*tevah*)." According to the Baal Shem, this means that one should bring light (*tzohar*) to each word (*tevah*) we speak.[41] The light we bring to each word is the light of meaning and sanctity in life. It is the light that God summons into being in the first utterance of the Creation (Genesis 1:3). It is, moreover, the silence of the Divine Presence that abides within the word, the silence of all tongues, signified by the silent letter *alef*, which, according to the Baal Shem, abides in every word (*Keter Shem Tov* 45). Made of a *yud* above, a *vav* between, and a *yud* below, the letter *alef* has a numerical value of twenty-six, the same value as the *yud-hey-vav-hey* of the Divine Name, so that the *alef* in every word is the divine spark in every word, as the Talmud states (*Shabbat* 88b).

Recall the insight from Levinas: "Language is the fact that always one sole word is proffered: God."[42] When the word is torn from its meaning—when no light can enter the *tevah*—the anonymous rumbling of *tohu vavohu*, of "chaos and void," erupts in a darkening of creation. Because creation includes this world and the upper worlds, the sages of the Talmud teach that all worlds, this world and the upper worlds, were destroyed during the Flood (*Sanhedrin* 108a). Indeed, the Flood, the *Mabul*, that descended upon creation was an undoing of creation: whereas at the time of the Creation the waters were separated above and below (Genesis 1:7), with the Flood came a reversion to the chaos and void, as the waters rained down from above and rose up from below (Genesis 7:11–12). In his commentary on Genesis 8:22, Rashi declares that in the time of the Flood the distinction between day and night, between light and darkness, collapsed. In a word, meaning collapsed. That was the massive confusion of the Flood in the time of Noah.

And Noah? He "found favor in God's eyes" (Genesis 6:8), says the Torah, enough favor for God to establish a covenant with him and his descendants. But the Talmud is a little harder on Noah: " 'Noah was a just man, and perfect in his generation' (Genesis 6:9). Rabbi Yohanan said: 'In his generation, but not in other generations.' Rabbi Oshaia said: 'As an illustration of Resh Lakish's view, to what may this be compared? To a phial of spikenard oil lying amidst refuse' " (*Sanhedrin* 108a). Wiesel adds his own reminder of the Talmudic tradition: "The Talmud tells us: Noah went on living as before, even after the rains came; he waited for the waters to reach his ankles before he tore himself away from his home and boarded the ark. Rabbi Hanina son of Pappa may be exaggerating, but this is his version. Noah, he said flatly, did not deserve to be saved; but without him, there would have been no Moses—and God wanted Moses."[43] Wiesel, however, reminds us of a Midrash that is more sympathetic toward Noah: "Noah and his children attended the wild beasts and the other animals, bringing them food and calming their anxiety."[44] Thus, when Abraham asked Shem, son of Noah, why God preserved their lives as the ark was tossed over the deep, Shem explained that it was because they stayed up all night every night feeding the animals (*Midrash Tehillim* 2:37:1). Still, the matter is not so simple, as Wiesel points out, for we have yet another Midrash, which says that Noah delayed feeding a lion, "who leaves him a reminder of his error: Noah is bitten on the leg and will limp till the end of his life [*Tanhuma Noah* 9]."[45] Even with regard to the care for the animals, then, Noah was perhaps not so completely righteous.

However, if Noah, the most righteous in his not-so-righteous generation, was not so worthy, it was not because he was too slow to feed a lion. No, it was because when God told him to build an ark, warning him that He was about to destroy the world, all Noah did was obey: he did not raise an uproar to challenge God. According to tradition, Abraham demonstrated that he was righteous enough to enter into the Covenant of Circumcision because he argued with God over the fate of the innocent in Sodom and Gomorrah; Moses received the Covenant of Torah because, unlike Abraham, he argued with God on behalf of both the innocent and the guilty on the occasion of the Golden Calf (see *Zohar* I, 67b). Wiesel calls our attention to yet another Midrash along these lines (see *Zohar Hadash* 42a): "When Noah came out of the ark and saw the devastation, he questioned God, asking, 'Where is Thy mercy, Thy charity, Thy compassion? And God put him right back in his place: You are nothing but a mindless shepherd, said the Almighty. *Now* you are asking these questions—when it is over? Why didn't you speak up before? . . . I told you . . . that I considered you a Tzaddik. . . . I said it for one reason only: to move you to become aware of your mission, to force you to intercede on behalf of mankind.'"[46] The portrait of Noah is the portrait of one who was too late, just as each of us is too late for the appointment, for the saying of "Here I am for you," when called. Anyone who has heard a child cry out in the night knows that there can be no getting there fast enough.

I once heard Wiesel say that if, when the Shoah came to an end, he had started to weep, he would never have stopped. He says the same of Noah: "Had he [Noah] wept once—only once—he could not have stopped. Ever."[47] Instead of weeping, Noah prayed (Genesis 8:20). Just so, Wiesel recalls, when the Jews emerged from another *Mabul*, they prayed: "Jewish inmates welcome their sudden freedom in a strange manner: they do not grab the food offered by their American liberators. Instead, they gather in circles and *daven*: their first act as free human beings was to say Kaddish, thus glorifying and sanctifying God's name."[48] In the concentrationary universe that haunts Wiesel's portraits there was no *depth*, no *height*, as in the time of the *Mabul*, when above and below collapsed into a sameness but with a difference: in the time of the Holocaust, the earth below and the heavens above were flooded with the silent ashes of the Jews. As when the waters rained down from above and rose up from below, there was a great confusion of above and below, for the sky was transformed into a cemetery. Thus in Wiesel's novel *Twilight* we have the mad patient Zelig, whose gaze is constantly turned toward the sky, declaring, "They are all here," in the sky.[49] Zelig saw no rainbow in the sky above—only the dead.

As for the tale of the tower, it is not intended to explain how the multitude of languages came to be. In his thirteenth-century commentary Jacob ben Asher, the Baal HaTurim, says that the confusion lay in the fact that they "had one language with unique words" (Genesis 11:1), where any word could mean anything, so that words were "empty and void" (Baal HaTurim on Genesis 11:1; cf. *Zohar* I, 75a). According to the four-teenth-century sage Ovadiah Sforno, the confusion lay in the supposition that the people could "make a name" for themselves and therefore gener-ate identity and meaning from their own autonomous selfhood (Genesis 11:4): they had no knowledge of the Name of the Holy One, from whom all names and all meaning issue, as it is written in the Zohar (*Zohar* II, 124a). It also lay in the fact that through building a tower to the heavens they thought they could define their own dimension of height (see Sforno's commentary on Genesis 11:4). Making one's own name and forging one's own height go hand in hand. The height is in the name and the name signifies a height; however, as in the case of anyone who makes his own name, the dimension of height is here a counterfeit.

The Midrash reveals the consequence of this confusion exemplified in the Tower of Confusion: when a man fell to his death during the construction of the tower, no one even noticed; but when a brick was dropped and broken, a great lamentation went up, and the people cried out, "When will another come in its stead?" (*Pirke de Rabbi Eliezer* 24). Hence we have the reading of Genesis 11:7 from the eighteenth-century sage Rabbi Yaakov Culi, who notes that in the phrase *navlah sham sfatam*, "Let us confuse their tongues," the word *navlah* (a cognate of *bilbul*, or "confusion") may also be read as *nevelah*, which means "corpse." The word *nevelah* is from the verb *naval*, which means to "wither," to "perish," or to "be destroyed." The noun *naval* refers to one who is base and vile; it can also refer to one who is godless—an "unbeliever." Read in this way, says Rabbi Culi, the verse means "let us make their speech produce corpses."[50] And so it has come to pass: the confusion of tongues was a confusion of life and death. With the tearing of the meaning from the word—the tearing of the *tzohar* from the *tevah*—there comes a corresponding tearing of sanctity from the human being. And so during the Holocaust the confusion of speech produced corpses.

Hate is a defining feature of the tearing of word from meaning; it cannot happen without hate. Hatred *is* the tearing of word from meaning and therefore of human from human, of human from God. The confusion of tongues is manifest in the collapse of human relation and of the understanding of what makes the other human being *matter*. This confusion that characterizes the time of the Shoah carries over to the time after the event, into the matter of remembrance. As the Talmudic sage Rav taught, "the atmosphere of the Tower causes forgetfulness" (*Sanhedrin* 109a). Thus we stand before the Carbide Tower in Buna, what Primo Levi called the *Babelturm*,[51] in the aftermath of Auschwtiz. What, then, are we to do? Do we look back upon the destruction? Do we dare?

Portrait of Lot's Wife

The transition from the Tower of Babel to the generation of Sodom is all too smooth. In the Mishnah, for example, Rabbi Nehemiah compares the generations of the Flood and the Tower of Babel to the generation of Sodom and Gomorrah (*Sanhedrin* 10:3; see also *Bava Metzia* 4:2). Why the comparison? The explanation may lie in a passage from the Gemara: "R. Jeremiah b. Eleazar said: They [the people of Babel] split up into three parties. One said, 'Let us ascend and dwell there'; the second, 'Let us ascend and serve idols'; and the third said, 'Let us ascend and wage war [with God].' The party which proposed, 'Let us ascend, and dwell there'—the Lord scattered them: the ones that said, 'Let us ascend and wage war' were turned to apes, spirits, devils, and night-demons; whilst as for the party which said, 'Let us ascend and serve idols'—'there the Lord did confound the language of all the earth'" (*Sanhedrin* 109a). When the language of the earth is confounded, the human image itself is confounded. For the human image is clothed in the word: the human being is a speaking being only when his or her words are bound to meaning.

When the word is torn from meaning, violence ensues. Thus God Himself added his anguished outcry to the outcry of humanity, saying, "Verily, the cry of Sodom and Gomorrah is great, and, verily, their sin is exceedingly grievous" (Genesis 18:20).

What was their sin? Without going into the graphic details, it was, according to the twelfth-century sage Rabbi David Kimchi, the Radak, a wanton violence and violation of human beings, in which all limiting principles were erased (*Mikraot Gedolot*, Radak commentary on Genesis 18:20). To enter Sodom is to enter a realm not of the unimaginable but of everything imaginable. "All trips to Sodom," says Wiesel, "were one-way. It was possible to enter the city but not to leave it."[52] There were four judges in Sodom, the Talmud tells us: Liar, Lying Liar, Forger, and Perverter of Justice (*Sanhedrin* 109b); the Midrash names at least one of them: Hidod (*Sefer HaYashar, Vayera* 1). Liar? Very well, we understand that. But Lying Liar? That is one who lies about telling the lie, the one who swears to the truth of his lie. Forger? A Forger is a falsifier of reality, one who would make you believe not only an untruth but an unreality, such as all evil is Jewish or the Holocaust did not happen.

As for the Perverters of Justice, Wiesel explains, they were the "worst of all: they pretended to act in accordance with the law of the land. . . . In other words, there *was* a system in Sodom."[53] Which means: Lying was institutionalized, legalized, socially acceptable. The Perverters of Justice were the judges, like the Nazi judges who stood with the other war criminals in the Judges' Trial on March 5, 1947. As in the time of the Holocaust, human beings were officially no longer human beings. God was officially no longer God, since the status of God and the status of the human being are interwoven. Indeed, the animals were no longer animals. "Cruel to human beings?" Wiesel asks. "The Sodomites were equally cruel toward animals and birds, in other words, toward any living creature whose life and movement escaped their authority."[54] In other words, they were not like Noah, the lion's bite notwithstanding.

In order to illustrate the evil of the generation of Sodom, Wiesel relates a Midrash on Lot's daughter Paltit: one day "she noticed a hungry beggar and couldn't help but feel sorry for him. Unfortunately, that was forbidden in Sodom."[55] She was seen to have brought the beggar food, but that was forbidden, as it must be in a place where lying had become institutionalized. Paltit was arrested and sentenced to be burned at the stake. But God heard her cry and intervened (Ginzberg, *Legends of the Jews* 1:5:155; *Sefer HaYashar, Vayera* 6). Another midrashic account relates that when she cried out, as she was being burned alive for feeding the poor, that was the outcry that God heard (*Pirke de Rabbi Eliezer* 25), whereupon He declared, "I will go down to see whether they have acted together according to the outcry that has reached Me" (Genesis 18:21). According to this version, however, it was not on her behalf but on behalf of humanity: it was *too late for Paltit*. But why did God have to go down to see whether the outcry was justified? Did He not know? Is this the God who "searches the hearts of men" (Jeremiah 17:10) and" knows the secrets of the heart" (Psalms 44:21)? Or is it that when we are indifferent to the suffering of our neighbor, God too grows indifferent? The Baal Shem Tov commented on Psalms 121:5, "HaShem is the shadow on your right hand," saying that as we act, so does God act (*Kedushat Levi, Beshalah* 21).

A singular passage in the Torah illustrates the singularity of the moment that drew God and Abraham into a covenantal confrontation: for the first time, the only time, we are privy to what God is thinking to Himself: "Shall I hide from Abraham what I am about to do?" (Genesis 18:17). God provokes an argument with the one with whom He has entered into a covenant precisely to determine whether Abraham understands what it means to be in a covenantal relation with Holy One, what it means to be an *ezer k'negdo*, a "helper against Him." In short, God wanted to see if Abraham would argue with Him. Wiesel asks, "Why did He allow Abraham to go on arguing, when He knew there were no righteous men in Sodom?"[56] The answer: God *wanted* Abraham to argue, to object, to be His helper against Himself. Whereas Noah did nothing but obey when God announced the destruction of humanity, God wanted someone who would speak out on behalf of humanity. As Wiesel points out, He wanted Abraham to ask, "Will the Judge of the world be unjust?" (Genesis 18:25).[57]

Abraham argues God down from fifty righteous people to ten, getting God to agree to save at least ten, and He would spare the cities. Of course, there were not even ten. Nevertheless, God agreed to spare four: Lot, Lot's wife, and two of his four daughters, the two who were not married. Lot tried to tell his sons-in-law to take his married daughters away to avoid the impending destruction, but they thought he "jested" (Genesis 19:14); just as Noah's neighbors did not believe the waters would rise up, so they did not believe the fire would rain down.

And Lot's wife in all of this, the mother of Paltit? Who was she? What sort of person was she? What sort of mother? The Bible does not mention Lot's wife by name, but the Midrash refers to her as "Idit" or "Edah" or "Edith" (*Tanhuma, Vayera* 8). One tradition tries to justify her punishment, which would suggest that God tried to save at least one from among the unrighteous. Commenting on "Lot's wife looked back and became a pillar of salt" (Genesis 19:26), Rashi says, "By salt she sinned, by salt she was punished." How did she sin by salt? The Midrash explains: "Lot asked her to provide the strangers with some salt, and she refused" (*Bereshit Rabbah* 50:4). So she deserved it.

Other sources treat Idit more sympathetically. The Midrash says that when Lot and his wife were fleeing from the destruction, she took pity on her married daughters, who had remained in Sodom, and looked behind her, hoping that she would see them following after her (Baal HaTurim on Genesis 19:26; *Sefer HaYashar, Vayera* 7). Not surprisingly, Wiesel is drawn to these sympathetic sources in his portrait of Lot's wife, noting their accent on Idit's maternal instinct and why that led her to look back, despite the warning: "Suddenly, the mother appears as a positive figure. Disobeying the angels' order, she looked back, and what she saw filled her with . . . with what? With fear, says one source: she saw the magnitude of the catastrophe and died. She was filled with light, claims another source: she saw the Shekhina with impunity."[58] Perhaps only a mother can look upon the *Shekhinah*, the Supernal Mother, with impunity. And yet it was not exactly with impunity that Lot's wife looked back. For yet another source teaches that as soon as she saw the back of the *Shekhinah*, she was transformed into a pillar of salt (*Pirke de-Rabbi Eliezer* 25).

Wiesel once spoke to me about Lot's wife, saying that the transgression that transformed her into a pillar of salt was to rob the victims of the privacy of their suffering, thus adding to their and humiliation. If the Nazis set out to murder souls before they destroyed bodies—if they systematically tortured and humiliated the Jews before murdering them—then we must not add to the crime by gazing upon the victims. And so one is led to wonder: Is looking upon, say, the photographic images of the Nazis' victims akin to Lot's wife gazing upon the devastation of Sodom and Gomorrah? Does our voyeuristic fixation upon those photographs embody what Isabel Wollaston calls "a Nazi gaze," one that "objectifies, humiliates and violates those photographed?"[59] Perhaps so. Wiesel seemed to think so.

The portrait of Lot's wife is a portrait of a pillar of salt. But what does that mean? In the Torah one of the more mysterious of the expressions of a covenant with God is the "covenant of salt," which is associated with the offerings brought to God; the heave offerings, for example, affirm "a covenant of salt forever before HaShem unto thee and to thy seed with thee" (Numbers 18:19). The meaning of this covenant that affirms a higher relation is manifest in the ancient custom of dipping bread three times in salt prior to eating it after the blessing on bread. In Hebrew "salt" is *melah*, which (with a numerical value of seventy-eight) is three times the value of the Divine Name (twenty-six), the Name of the One with whom we enter into the Covenant. The letters that form *melah*, moreover, also form the word *lehem*, which is "bread," the symbol of all that sustains life. The Nazis transformed it into what Primo Levi calls "the holy grey slab,"[60] the antithesis of bread, the stuff that destroyed both body and soul, as it was transformed in currency to be hoarded, and not sustenance to be shared. Is that transformation of bread into antibread forbidden to look upon? After all, where bread is not bread, Levi has demonstrated, the human being is not a human being; it may indeed be questionable to gaze upon such a transformation.

Wiesel's portrait of Lot's wife provides a lens through which to consider the risk we run in a post-Holocaust context, a risk that places in jeopardy any Hasidic legacy. "Escape for thy life; look not behind thee, neither stay thou in all the plain," it is written in the Torah, "lest thou be consumed" (Genesis 19:17). There are, however, important differences. Lot's wife looked upon the destruction of the guilty; turning toward Auschwitz, we turn our gaze toward the humiliation and murder of the innocent. She saw the fire of retribution raining down; the Jews endured the flames of destruction rising up. In a word, the people of Sodom and Gomorrah were punished, while the Jews of Europe were simply annihilated, body and soul: "For us," says Levi, "the Lager is not a punishment."[61] If Lot's wife paid a price for gazing upon the destruction of the guilty as she fled to Zoar, how much greater is the price exacted from us for looking back at the murder, torture, and humiliation of the innocent? Does it ultimately render us as numb, mute, and lifeless as a pillar of salt?

Portrait of Abraham and Isaac

We now go from the annihilation of the guilty to the slaughter of the innocent, in a "going forth" into our own souls, a *lekh-lekha*, as when Abram was commanded to "go forth" from the land of his father to a land that God would show him (Genesis 12:1). Indeed, the Torah portion that begins with Genesis 12 is called *Lekh-Lekha*. Reflecting on the words *lekh-lekha*, literally "go forth, into yourself," we are reminded of Wiesel's statement that what took place in the Shoah "took place in the soul."[62] To "go forth, into yourself" is to sound the depths of the soul. This movement into the soul that marks the emergence of the first Jew also characterizes the struggle to respond to the attempted extermination of every Jew, down to the last Jew. Here God is telling Abraham, as He tells every Jew at every hour, to depart from the egocentric will of the self and to enter into the higher Will that makes us who we are. A movement into the *you*, the *lekh-lekha* is a movement into the capacity to say *you* to another, the capacity to say, "*Hineni*—Here I am for you," a phrase that appears three times in the story of the *Akeda*, the Binding of Isaac.

To be sure, the only other time that the phrase *lekh-lekha* appears in the Torah is when God commands Abraham to offer up "Isaac, [his] only son, the son [he] loves," and "go forth" to the land of Moriah (Genesis 22:2). As he moves into the depths of his portrait of Abraham and Isaac, Wiesel goes forth into the depths of his own soul, perhaps more than in any other portrait. To be sure, the story of the *Akeda* is so fundamental to Jewish teaching and tradition that we repeat the tale every morning in our preliminary prayers. As Joel Rosenberg has noted, for Wiesel the *Akeda* is, next to the revelation at Mount Sinai, "the most important event in the Bible."[63] In the Midrash, Wiesel points out, "The theme of the *Akeda* occupies as important a place as the creation of the world or the revelation at Sinai."[64] One thing that characterizes the creation of the world and the revelation at Sinai is silence, but each has its own silence, as Katriel in Wiesel's *A Beggar in Jerusalem* says: "There is the silence which preceded creation; and the one which accompanied the revelation on Mount Sinai. The first contains chaos and solitude, the second suggests presence, fervor, plenitude."[65] We shall come back to the silence of the *Akeda*, the silence of Abraham—or rather it will come back to haunt us. When Isaac lay upon the altar, says Wiesel, "all the worlds in all the spheres were in tumult: Isaac had become the center of the universe."[66] Why? What was at stake?

In a reference to a Midrash, Wiesel provides us with a hint:

> Stretched out on the altar, his wrists and ankles bound, Isaac saw the Temple in Jerusalem first destroyed and then rebuilt, and at that moment of the supreme test, Isaac understood that what was happening to him would happen to others, that this was to be a tale without an end, an experience to be endured by his children and theirs. Never would they be spared the

torture. The father's anguish, on the other hand, was not linked to the future; by sacrificing his son to obey God's will, Abraham knew that he was, in fact, sacrificing his knowledge *of* God and His faith *in* Him.[67] [see *Bereshit Rabbah* 56:5, 56:9]

There are several important points to note here. First, the issue of human sacrifice would haunt not only the Jewish people but all of humanity over the centuries. This goes to the core commandment concerning the sanctity of human-to-human relation revealed at Mount Sinai: "Do not murder" (Exodus 20:12). At stake in the tale of the *Akeda*, therefore, is our most fundamental understanding of the value of the other human being and therefore of any meaning that human life may have. Wiesel's insight here also reminds us of a connection already noted, namely the parallel between "Do not murder" and "I am God" (Exodus 20:2). Thus, upon laying his son on the altar, Abraham was sacrificing his knowledge *of* God, as well as his faith *in* God. He was turned over to what Martin Buber calls "that decisive hour," when he "had to forget everything [he] imagined [he] knew of God, when [he] dared to keep nothing handed down or learned or self-contrived, no shred of knowledge, and [was] plunged into the night."[68] In this portrait of Abraham, then, we see a man to whom the Creator of heaven and earth is revealed as the One who eludes all knowing, all faith, the One who demands not so much our faith as our deeds. But what sort of deed is this?

It was, first of all, an event that drew father and son into an intimacy unlike any other. "The sacrifice," writes Wiesel, underscoring the togetherness of the two, "was to be their joint offering; father and son had never been so close."[69] The portrait, therefore, is of Abraham *and* Isaac—and of God as well, "the God of Abraham and the Fear of Isaac," as it is written (Genesis 31:42). Yes, fear, not *yirah*, which also means "awe," but *pahad*, "fear": fear is a prominent feature of this portrait. Wiesel recalls, for example, the Midrash that says Isaac—a man of thirty-seven, and not a child—cried out to Abraham, "Father, I am afraid, afraid of being afraid. You must bind me securely, lest I flinch and the knife will miss its precise mark, thus rendering me unfit for a sacrificial offering" (see *Bereshit Rabbah* 56:8; *Tanhuma Vayera* 23; *Sefer HaYashar, Vayera* 21).[70] Another Midrash says that Isaac asked to be bound tightly, lest he curse his father and violate the commandment to honor his mother and father (*Pirke de Rabbi Eliezer* 31). Isaac's greatest fear, it seems, was not that his father would offer him up in sacrifice but that he would not be a pure and proper sacrifice and that he might, God forbid, compromise his relation with the Holy One—*even as his father raised the knife over him!*

Turning to Abraham, we come face to face with a silence in a category of its own, an unnerving silence that is the most uncanny aspect of his portrait: he who, according to one tradition, was known as *HaIvri*, the Hebrew, because he conversed with God in Hebrew,[71] suddenly loses his tongue. Abraham "could have spoken up just as he had done when trying to save Sodom and Gomorrah," Wiesel reminds us. "Why didn't he? According to the Midrash[*Pirke de Rabbi Eliezer* 31; see also *Talmud Bavli, Yoma* 28b], he knew and observed the laws and commandments of Torah; didn't he know that by killing, he would mutilate the very image of God? Didn't he know, he who knew everything, didn't he know that in Jewish tradition God is bound to obey His own Law, including the most urgent of all: Thou shalt not kill!"[72] *Mutilate* the very image of God? Was God Himself, then, laid upon the altar in the Binding of Isaac? Is that where God was in this terrible moment that shook heaven and earth—laid bound upon the altar? Is that why He sent angels to stop Abraham rather than do it Himself? Is *that* the Fear of Isaac, a fear not only *of* God but also a fear *for* God?

Not only did the Patriarch fail to raise an outcry *against* God—worse, he lied *for* God, as Wiesel points out in his portrait: "To his wife he said: we are going to pray. To his son he said: We shall study and meditate. The secret was his alone; he alone knew there was a secret."[73] What a secret! And let us not forget that, unable to "get it over with," Abraham not only journeyed silently for three days to Mount Moriah but lay silently at the side of his son *for three nights!* "Silently he arranged the firewood, bound Isaac; silently he drew the knife," as Kierkegaard has observed,[74] only to collide with the most terrifying silence of all, as "Isaac lay on the altar, silently gazing at his father."[75] Abraham, however, was not entirely silent. Three times he cried out, "*Hineni*—Here I am!": once to God (Genesis 22:1), once to Isaac (Genesis 22:7), and once to the angel (Genesis 22:11). If, as Levinas asserts, one "who says 'Here I am' *testifies* to the Infinite,"[76] in this instance it is a testimony to the infinite silence of the Infinite One: after God commanded Abraham to offer up his son in sacrifice, the two of them—Abraham and God, the two who conversed in Hebrew—*spoke no more to one another.*

Madness lurks in this silence. Madness always foments in silence. And so, as Wiesel so profoundly understood—he for whom madness was a category of thought—madness became the most tempting of the temptations that Satan could place before Abraham, as the Patriarch and his son made their way to Moriah. On the way, Wiesel relates a Midrash: Satan appeared to Abraham and said, "Tell me, old man, have you lost your mind, have you emptied your heart of all human feeling? Will you really sacrifice your son?" Abraham said, "Yes." And if God should send harsher trials, said Abraham, he will try to live up to them. And even if God should later accuse him of murder, Abraham declared that he would still go through with it. Even when Satan finally told Abraham the truth—that a lamb would be provided in Isaac's place—Abraham refused to believe him (*Bereshit Rabbah* 56:4; see also *Tanhuma Vayera* 23). "Satan personifies the doubt Abraham *had* to have," says Wiesel, "in order to remain human. The same is true for Isaac's fear."[77] Fear, doubt, and the temptation of madness: madness offers the one who doubts and the one who fears a place to hide, as Adam hid. But Abraham did not hide. Abraham declared, *Hineni!* and moved into a most radical vulnerability, which is precisely the movement into the Covenant: the meaning of Covenant lies not in assurances or guarantees but in a radical vulnerability.

Why did Abraham not take this way out, thinking, "Perhaps I am insane. God would never ask this of me"? "One begins to wonder," as Wiesel says, "since God and he loved one another so much and collaborated so closely, why these tests? Because God tests only the strong. The weak do not resist or resist poorly; they are of no consequence. But then, what good is it to resist, since God knows the outcome in advance? Answer: God knows, man does not."[78] Still, this Midrash, where Abraham insists that, no matter what—even if a lamb should be provided to take the place of Isaac—he will go through with it, is striking to say the least. There is a certain defiance here, as Wiesel insightfully understands, and a certain temptation of God. "A double-edged test," writes Wiesel. "God subjected Abraham to it, yet at the same time Abraham forced it on God. As though Abraham had said: I defy you, Lord. I shall submit to Your will, but let us see whether you will go to the end, whether You shall remain passive and remain silent when the life of my son—who is also Your son—is at stake!"[79] Even more powerfully, the Midrash says Abraham would not listen to the angel who tried to stop him but insisted that God Himself should face him (*Tanhuma Vayera* 23), as if to say to God, "*You* commanded this—I want *You*, and not Your messenger, to rescind the commandment!" It sounds very Hasidic, doesn't it?

If the defiance of Abraham has a Hasidic ring about it, then the reaction of Isaac has it even more so. Isaac, Wiesel attests, "will be entitled to say anything he likes to God, ask anything of Him. Because he suffered? No. Suffering, in Jewish tradition, confers no privileges. It all depends on what one makes of that suffering. Isaac knew how to transform it into prayer [after all, he is the author of the Minhah service (Talmud Bavli, Berakhot 26b)] and love rather than into rancor and malediction. This is what gives him rights and powers no other man possesses. His reward? The Temple was built on Moriah, not on Sinai."[80] On Mount Moriah the silence of Creation converged with the silence of Revelation, the silence of chaos, and the void with the silence of plenitude and mystery. Without Mount Moriah there would be no Messiah; for without Mount Moriah, as suggested in the Talmud, the yirat HaShem, the "awe" or the "fear of God" would not emanate into the world (Taanit 16a).

According to tradition, Mount Moriah has at least two other distinctions. It is the site from which the dust of Adam was gathered to form the first human being (Zohar I, 34b). And it was the site where Jacob had his dream of the angels ascending and descending the ladder, the point of contact between this world and the upper worlds (Pirke de Rabbi Eliezer 35), and the site where he awoke and declared, "God was here all along, and I did not know it" (Genesis 28:16). Indeed, this realization fundamental to Jacob is fundamental to us all: God has been here all along, and I did not know it. It is a realization that comes with fear and trembling: all this time I have stood before the Judgment, only to be judged for not knowing.

Portrait of Jacob and the Angel

Wiesel notes that two moments marked Jacob's life: having a dream and receiving a name.[81] The two decisive moments transpired in two distinctive places that themselves received new names: Beth-El and Peniel, the House of God, and the Face of God. Both are required for the covenantal relation that makes dwelling in the world possible. The dream at Beth-El was a prelude to the confrontation at Peniel, and the confrontation at Peniel was a consummation of the dream at Beth-El. "The future victor of Peniel," says Wiesel, "trembled with fear at Beth-El [Genesis 28:17]."[82] Why? Because this site where he dreamed was the site where his father was bound to the altar. This was the place where a father raised his knife over his son and where God was too embarrassed to face the father He had commanded to raise the knife over his son. It was now *the dwelling place of the Holy One*, destined to become the site of the Temple from which the Divine Light would emanate into the world—the "Word of God going forth from Jerusalem" (Isaiah 2:3) from the *Har HaBayit*, the Mount of the Dwelling Place! No wonder Jacob trembled with fear!

On this site where heaven and earth are just a hair's breadth apart, Jacob had a vision of a ladder connecting the upper worlds to this one, with angels—*malakhim* or "messengers"—ascending and descending (Genesis 28:12), passing in and out of the "gate of heaven" (Genesis 28:17). The sages of the Talmud understand well enough who the angels descending the ladder are: they are the emissaries of the Holy One. But who, they ask, are these angels ascending the ladder? And they answer: they are the angels we create with our thoughts, words, and deeds—the angels who then go out into this world to do their work for good or for ill and ascend into the upper realms to do the same (see *Avot* 4:11; *Hagigah* 41a). When we create angels of evil, the souls of the murdered dead accompany them into the upper realms to confront the Celestial Tribunal. Perhaps one of them caught up with Jacob at Peniel. Perhaps that is why he trembled with fear at Beth-El. Perhaps that is why much of Wiesel's portrait of Jacob dwells upon the encounter at Peniel.

But there is even more reason not only for Jacob to tremble with fear at his dream but for all of us to be frozen with fear as we look upon this Hasid's portrait of Jacob. "*In his dream*," Wiesel writes, "*Jacob saw a ladder whose top reached into heaven. It still exists. There are those who have seen it, somewhere in Poland, at the side of an out-of-the-way railroad station. And an entire people was climbing, climbing toward the clouds on fire. Such was the nature of the dread our ancestor Jacob must have felt.*"[83] Yes, the dread: a dread that spans the history and the eternity of the Jewish people. The survivor and author Ka-tzetnik 135633 was one of those who saw a ladder somewhere in Poland. Among the nightmarish visions he relates in *Shivitti* is the vision of a ladder ascending into a watchtower at Birkenau. This time, however, the "angels" ascending and descending the ladder were not the souls of the dead but the guards who murdered them.[84] Those ladders, too, still exist.

So what do these angels have to do with Peniel? Wiesel points out that even though the Torah refers to the stranger of Peniel as *ish*, or "man" (Genesis 32:25), tradition takes him to be an angel.[85] The prophet Hosea, for example, refers to Jacob's adversary as an angel (Hosea 12:4). Rashi identifies him as the guardian angel of Esau, the evil angel Samael, whom tradition also identifies as the Angel of Death (see, e.g., Bahya ben

Asher on Exodus 21:23). If at Peniel Jacob saw God face to face, does it mean that he saw death face to face? Is God death? Can it be that, contra Nietzsche,[86] God is not dead but rather that God is death? It may well be so, if we are to understand Jacob's defeat of God as a defeat of the Angel of Death, thereby, precisely through his wrestling with God, making God into the God of Life.

On the night before Jacob was to reconcile with his brother Esau and return to the land of his birth, the Angel of Death fell upon him, and the two of them wrestled until dawn. Jacob overcame the Angel and would not release him until he obtained a blessing from the unearthly being. The blessing began with a question: "What is your name?"

And the man answered, "Jacob."

To which the Angel of Death replied, " 'No longer will you be called Jacob. Henceforth you will be called Israel, for you have struggled against God and humanity, and you have prevailed. . . .' And Jacob called the name of the place Peniel: 'For I have seen God face to face, and my life is preserved'" (Genesis 32:25–31). Wiesel elaborates:

> This may be meant to imply that there is a connection between divine and human solitude: man must be alone to listen, to feel and even to fight God, for God engages only those who, para-doxically, are both threatened and protected by solitude. . . . But solitude contains its own share of danger precisely because it inevitably leads to God; whoever meets Him is irrevocably condemned to another kind of solitude. Thus to be chosen signifies not privilege but dignity and responsibility. *And none shall see My face and remain living* means: None shall see My face and live as he did before.[87]

Did Wiesel catch a glimpse of the face of God, to be left staggering, like Jacob, in the aftermath of the Shoah, unable ever again to live as he had lived before?

In his portrait of Jacob, Wiesel wrestles the name of Israel from the Angel of—dare one say it?—of the Shoah. Through his portrayal of the Patriarch that follows his passage through his own Peniel, Wiesel is left not so much with a new name as a reaffirmation of his own name as one of the *benei Yisrael*. The "aggressor," he relates, left Jacob with "a new name which in generations to come would symbolize eternal struggle and endurance, in more than one land, during more than one night."[88] Does this not describe Wiesel's journey? "Never shall I forget that night": his words return to haunt us. "Never shall I forget those things, even were I condemned to live as long as God Himself. Never."[89] Did Wiesel prevail?

"At night he [Jacob] was different," writes the author of *Night*. "Transfigured. . . . Thus the decisive event of his life took place at night. At Peniel he was attacked, at Peniel he responded."[90] One Hebrew word for "response" is *teshuvah*, which is also a movement of return; indeed, the encounter with the Angel took place as Jacob was undertaking a movement of return to his homeland. It was the land that would become known by his new name—the Land of Israel. And the essence of the Land of Israel is the essence of Torah, as it is written in the *Or Neerav* of Moshe Cordovero: "It is well known that the Land of Israel and the Torah have a closeness and a relationship similar to that of the life-force to the heart. For the Torah constitutes the life-force of the world, as [the liturgy] states, 'He planted eternal life in our midst.' The life-force and the soul dwell in the heart and its essential workings are there. Thence it spreads to the rest of the body. The same is true of the Torah. Its essence is in the Land of Israel, and many commandments are dependent upon [the land]" (3:5:38). Peniel, therefore, was a decisive step in the movement of return to the land of his birth, the land whose essence is Torah, to the land of Beth-El.

The decisive event of Wiesel's life also took place at night, and there would be many nights to follow the night of the decisive event— the night that was unlike any other—when his soul was "invaded—and devoured—by a black flame."[91] What were Elie Wiesel's nights like even after he emerged from the Night? What was it like for him to wrestle with the Angel of Night, night after night after night? We will never know. But Jacob, too, confronted a dark flame, as Wiesel suggests: "It was Jacob's own angel, . . . the other half of Jacob's split self. The side of him that harbored doubts."[92] What, then, was Jacob trying to wrest from the Angel in that decisive wrestling match? Was it not his own soul—his own name? Which brings us back to another question concerning the biblical account: if he received the name "Israel" because he wrestled with God and prevailed, what does it mean to "prevail"? The word translated as "prevailed" is *vatukhal*, a cognate of *takhlit*, meaning "aim" or "purpose," which in turn suggests that, upon wrestling a new name from the Angel, he received a renewed meaning and mission, a renewed soul and legacy, a renewed past and future.

What, then, is the difference between Jacob and Israel? The psalmist states it this way: "He has established a testimony in Jacob and placed a teaching [Torah] in Israel" (Psalms 78:5); thus, proclaims the prophet Isaiah, God shall draw Jacob into a movement of return (*leshuvev*), so that Israel may be gathered unto Him through Torah (see Isaiah 49:5). In the wrestling that Wiesel focuses upon, which is a reflection of his own wrestling, we have the testimony and the struggle to return; in the name that emerges from the wrestling we have the teaching and the Torah, which at times is not received from God but wrenched from God. And within the testimony and the teaching are both a summons and a blessing. Wrestling a blessing from the Angel of Death, Jacob attained meaning and purpose—attained a teaching, a Torah—for life by attaining a name: Yisrael. Receiving the name, Jacob received a summons. For the name *Yisrael*, Rashi points out, is a cognate of *serarah*, which denotes a blessing received through "noble and open conduct" (see Rashi's commentary on Genesis 32:29). Which means that in order to attain a name—in order to recover the name of Israel after the Shoah—the Jew must live according to the teachings of the Name. Thus the name and the Name, with the *N* writ large, are interconnected.

A Hasidic legacy is not simply taken from the past and bequeathed to subsequent generations—it is *wrested* from the past and entrusted to the care of those who receive it: the wrestling is what makes it at once Jewish and Hasidic. The name of the wrestler, Israel, is entrusted to us as a summons: receiving such a summons, we receive a name—in the aftermath of a radical assault on the Name. In the time of the Shoah, as well as before and after, the Jewish people have wrestled incessantly with the Angel of Death. The Shoah was an age of assault not only upon the body but also upon the soul of Israel, the soul attained as a blessing and a name. Therefore the Nazi affliction of the Jewish soul entailed an assault on the blessing and the name, both human and divine. Ka-tzetnik's Rabbi of Shilev understood this point even as he and his fellow Jews awaited their turn for the gas chambers of Birkenau. "Can't you feel," he addressed a man named Ferber, "that Jacob—in our bones—now wrestles with the Angel? We are the sinew of his thigh vein in this struggle!" And Ferber asked him, "Rabbi of Shilev, for whose sake does Jacob wrestle with the Angel, if his children did not cross the river, but stayed here in the blackness of the night?" And the Rabbi answered, "From the very blackness of this night Jacob will bring forth the name 'Israel!' "[93] From the blackness of that night Jacob wrestled a blessing and a name from the Angel, the name of the Angel himself, according to the Midrash: Israel (*Pirke de Rabbi Eliezer* 37).

The two events, the one at Peniel and the one in Birkenau, may be more closely connected than we realize. The Zohar tells us that the dust raised when Jacob wrestled with the Angel "was not ordinary dust, but ashes, the residue of fire" (*Zohar* I, 170a), ashes and fire that ascended, says the Talmud, all the way up to the Throne of Glory (*Hullin* 91a). As the Angel wrestled with Jacob, says the Midrash, "he put his finger to the earth, whereupon the earth began spurting fire. Said Jacob to him: 'Would you terrify me with that! Why, I am altogether of that stuff!' Thus it is written, *And the house of Jacob shall be a fire*" (Obadiah 1:18; *Bereshit Rabbah* 77:2). After Auschwitz that fire takes on a new dimension. Wiesel describes fire as "the dominant imagine in their tragedy,"[94] and now we see why. In the post-Holocaust wrestling with the Angel, the earth erupts in a strange fire. Just as Jacob wrestled a name from the Angel, we must now wrestle a name from the fire that would consume the Name. In this new wrestling match that devolves upon us we have the Hasidic legacy that comes with Wiesel's portrait of Jacob.

In *Night*, at the end of his wrestling with the Angel of Death, Wiesel looks into a mirror. And Death looks back at him. Gazing into the eyes of a corpse, he gazed into the eyes of the Angel with a Thousand Eyes, the Angel as yellow as the star that Nazis stamped on the Jews (see *Talmud Bavli, Avodah Zarah* 20b). Peering into this portrait, we look into those eyes too. Only this time the Angel comes not to take us but to leave us with new eyes, through which we gaze into the mirror of our soul where the Holocaust has transpired. And the Angel gazes back at us. From the depths of that gaze the Angel puts to us a question, in keeping with the ancient Jewish legend, going all the way back to Peniel.

According to the legend, when we die and lie in the grave the Angel of Death comes to us so that he might bring us into the presence of the Holy One. But in order to draw nigh unto the Divine Presence, we must correctly answer a certain question. The question is the same for all, but for each the answer is different. And so, his thousand eyes penetrating our soul, the Angel poses the fearsome question, the very question he put to Jacob: "What is your name?" (Genesis 32:28)[95] But what, indeed, do we know when we know our name? To know our name is to know the names of our mother and father. It means knowing a tradition borne by those who have borne our names before us; it means knowing a teaching that harbors our mission in life, as inscribed in our name; it means recognizing that we are called by name and must answer to our name. Hence Rabbi Chayim ben Attar teaches that one who knowingly violates God's commandment forfeits his original name (*Or HaChayim* on Genesis 3:30). Knowing our name, like knowing God, means knowing what must be done.[96]

The sages of the Talmud refer to the transmission of the legacy and the truth of the Holy One from one generation to another as a "handing down of names" (see *Kiddushin* 71a). As the names are handed down, so is the confrontation and the question: what is your name? It is a question that invites confrontation, a question that can be decided only through a confrontation that Jacob himself sought out, as Wiesel understood: "The adventure at Peniel? A conscious, deliberate act, a challenge by Jacob. The battle? Conceived and arranged by Jacob."[97] This is an indication, Wiesel observes, that "Jacob has just understood a fundamental truth: God is in man, even in suffering, even in misfortune, even in evil. God is everywhere. In every being, not only in the victim. God does not wait for man at the end of the road, the terminations of exile; He accompanies him there. More than that: He is the road, He is the exile."[98] He is the confrontation that is the Hasidic legacy of Elie Wiesel: if the Hasidim are known for anything, it is for their confrontations with God.

Portrait of Joseph the Righteous

Wiesel's portrait of Joseph is the portrait not just of Joseph but of *Yosef HaTzaddik*, Joseph the Righteous: "Joseph was and remains—in tradition and legend—a *Tzaddik*. Why?. . . . [T]he very existence of the question lends Joseph a new density. Suddenly we suspect a secret. If, despite all that is said about him, he is *the* Just Man in the Bible, it must mean that we have been misled by appearances. We have been looking at a mask, we have not seen the face."[99] The face of a *Tzaddik* is always hidden. But then that is precisely the aim of Wiesel's portraits—to reveal the hidden *as hidden*, as righteousness is always hidden. This portrait of a *Tzaddik* is the portrait of a secret.

Wiesel points out that Jewish tradition ascribes Joseph's righteousness to his ability to resist the wiles of Potiphar's wife.[100] Thus the Gemara says that "Joseph's eyes did not seek to feast on that which was not his, Potiphar's wife, the evil eye had no dominion over him" (*Berakhot* 20a), and that, says Rabbi Ovadiah Bartenura in his commentary on *Mishnah Makkot* 3:15, is why he is called *Yosef HaTzaddik* (see also Kaidanover, *Kav HaYashar* 2:5). Wiesel imagines the exchange: "Joseph: No, I cannot,

I will not.—She: But why not?—He: I am afraid.—She: Afraid? Afraid of what?—Joseph: Of your husband.—She: That's nothing to worry about. I'll simply kill him.—Joseph (in a cold sweat): No! What are you trying to do to me? Turn me not only into a rake but an assassin as well?"[101] Potiphar's wife had an answer for every objection Joseph could offer, except one: it is a sin against God (Genesis 39:9).

If Joseph could resist this irresistible sin against God, then what enabled him to do so? The Midrash tells us it was the memory of his father: "In all his wisdom a certain woman enticed (him), and when he wished to accustom himself to sin, he saw the image of his father, and repented concerning it" (*Pirke de Rabbi Eliezer* 39; see also *Kedushat Levi, Vayeshev* 7). Because he never forgot his father, Joseph forever honored his father. And the commandment to honor mother and father is in category of commandments pertaining to the relation between the human being and God. Hence Joseph the Righteous declared to Potiphar's wife that it would be a sin against God.

The *sefirah* most crucial to the flow of holiness into this realm is *Yesod*: that is where the holiness from on high flows into *Malkhut*, into this realm, as when a husband joins with his wife in holy matrimony. Thus *Yosef HaTzaddik* is situated in the *sefirah* of *Yesod*. Pivotal to this connection between above and below, Joseph, says Wiesel, also provided a pivotal connection between Israel and the nations, "the first Jew to bridge two nations, two histories; the first to link Israel to the world"[102] and "the first to know how to reconcile his love for Israel with his love of other nations."[103] He was the first, therefore, to link the world to the Holy One. When does that linkage occur? In a time of famine: the bond between Israel and humanity lies not in the proselytizing of Torah but in offering a fellow human being a bite of bread. To recognize the other human being *as* a human being is to recognize him or her as *hungry* and to offer him or her bread. Why does Joseph merit the title of *Tzaddik*? Because, in a time when people had no bread, he offered them bread.

Still, Joseph did not attain the status of *Tzaddik* overnight. His story, Wiesel understands, is about "man's capacity for transformation. The tale of Joseph is the tale of a metamorphosis—no, a series of metamorphoses."[104] His life, Wiesel elaborates, "is a perfect illustration of Kierkegaard's concept of man's existence as divided into four cycles: the first being that of beauty, the second that of morality, the third that of laughter, and the fourth devoted to things sacred. As an adolescent, Joseph was concerned only with external appearance and behavior. Later, in prison, he discovered the phenomena of good and evil. Still later, when he was king, he ridiculed his brothers, laughing at their expense. And finally, toward the end of his life, his demeanor approached that of a saint."[105] Before he became a saint, as Wiesel notes, Joseph assimilated into Egyptian society. "Jacob," says Wiesel, "did not forget what he had studied—Joseph did. Joseph, the assimilated Jew."[106]

But let's not be too hasty here. Let's turn to the Midrash:

> And he sent Judah before him (Genesis 46:28). Jacob sent Judah before him to establish an academy wherein he might teach the Torah. . . . When Joseph's brothers returned and told him: "Joseph is yet alive" . . . his heart fainted (Genesis 45:26). Jacob recalled the chapter of the Torah that Joseph was studying at the time of his departure. . . . Joseph had also remembered the chapter he was studying when he was separated from his father. What did Joseph do? He gave them wagons (Genesis 45:21). When Jacob saw the wagons (*agalot*), the spirit of their father revived forthwith. Word-play relating *agalot* ("wagons") to *kelayot* ("kidneys") stated in the next paragraph to be the organ through which Abraham learned and retained the law. This teaches us that wherever Joseph went, he devoted himself to the law . . . , even though the Torah itself had not yet been given. (*Midrash Tanhuma, Vayigash* 11)

Joseph learned not only Torah but also Kabbalah, as suggested by the teaching that says Jacob taught Joseph the mysteries of the twenty-two letters of the Hebrew alphabet (see, e.g., Bahya ben Asher on Genesis 37:3). Further, the Talmud says that on the day before Pharaoh was to appoint Joseph to rule over Egypt, he told Joseph that he would test him the following morning to see if he knew the seventy languages of the seventy nations, so that he might have the wisdom required to rule. That night the angel Gabriel came to teach Joseph the seventy languages, and so he demonstrated to Pharaoh that he knew all seventy, plus one: Hebrew. And Pharaoh asked him please not to reveal that he knew one more language than Pharaoh (*Sotah* 33a; see also Bahya ben Asher on Numbers 19:2).

And yet, despite Joseph's ability to speak the seventy languages of the seventy nations, there remains a secret, as we suspected from the outset: a silence that hangs over the portrait. "One recognizes the value of a text by the weight of its silence," writes Wiesel. "Here the silence exists and it weighs heavily."[107] We are reminded of Rabbi Kalonymos Kalmish Shapira's commentary on the sheaf of wheat, the *alumah*, in Joseph's dream (Genesis 37:7). Like the silence that pervaded the inhuman screaming and barking that defined the Shoah, a secret silence lurks in the background of Wiesel's portrait of *Yosef HaTzaddik*. The Hebrew word *ilem*, a cognate of *alumah*, Rabbi Shapira points out, means both "silent" and "mute." In his account of the Nazi assault on the body and soul of Israel, Rabbi Shapira reads *ilem* as a silence that overcomes a person "so broken and crushed that he has nothing to say; who does not appreciate or understand what is happening to him; who does not possess the faculties with which to assess or assimilate his experiences; who no longer has the mind or the heart with which to incorporate the experience. For him, silence is not a choice; his is the muteness of one incapable of speech."[108] Because this muteness is the muteness of a human being, within it lies hidden an outcry. Indeed, the muteness itself "stands erect," as Rabbi Shapira says, like Joseph's "sheaf." The muteness of *alumah* is more than deafening—it is haunting.

The image is especially haunting when Wiesel reminds us that Joseph was silent when his brothers plotted to kill him. As for Jacob, he was so broken and crushed that "for twenty years he did not speak. Not a word, not a complaint. He lived outside language, beyond hope. Bathed in silence and penetrated by it, he was distant and inaccessible. He seemed to have cut his ties with the world and its Creator. For, on another level, there was also the silence from above."[109] Jacob, who received the name of Israel when he came face to face with God at Peniel, no longer spoke to God. And yet Jacob had a dream, out of which God did, indeed, speak to him: "And God spoke unto Israel in the visions of the night, and said: 'Jacob, Jacob.' And he said: "Here I am'" (Genesis 46:2). Why would God call out, "Israel," and then address him as "Jacob?" Because, says Nahmanides, he was about to go into the exile of Egypt, and the name of Israel applies only to the one who dwells in the Land of the Covenant (Nahmanides on Genesis 46:2). One might think that retaining the name of Israel in exile would be even more crucial than being called Jacob. After all, Jacob was named Israel while in exile. He received the name, however, while undertaking a movement of return. And yet, it was not Jacob but Joseph who first truly experienced the meaning of exile, as Wiesel teaches: "Joseph, the first Jew to suffer at the hands of Jews, succeeded in mastering his grief and disappointment and linking his fate to theirs. Joseph—a *Tzaddik*? The title was, unquestionably, deserved."[110] At last we glimpse the secret of why Joseph was known as a *Tzaddik*, as Joseph the Righteous.

We have spoken of the first question God puts to the human being: where are you? (Genesis 3:9). The first question man asks of God, however, is: am I my brother's keeper? (Genesis 4:9). According to one of my teachers, Rabbi Sheldon Zimmerman, the rest of the Book of Genesis addresses this question, to culminate in the encounter between Joseph and Judah. This is an encounter that occurs upon the movement into exile: Judah puts his own life on the line in order to be the keeper of Benjamin, his half-brother, the son of Rachel (and not of Leah, Judah's own mother) (Genesis 43:9). Upon witnessing Judah's offering up of his own life for the sake of a brother, Joseph weeps for the first time (Genesis 43:30), as if he, of all the sages of the Book of Genesis, finally understands the question that Cain put to God. That is why he is *Yosef HaTzaddik*.

Portrait of Moses Our Teacher

Every artist who paints a portrait dips his or her brush into a palette of colors, textures, and themes. In the case of Joseph, Wiesel explored the transformations that Joseph went through in the stages along life's way. Here his palette for the portrait of Moses leans much more toward the death of Moses than toward the transformations he underwent during his life. Nevertheless, the portrait of his death is intertwined with the portrait of his life. If a portrait captures the identity of a person, then Wiesel's portrayal of the death of Moses, as well as his portrayal of Moses's life, goes to the core of the issue of identity, exile, and the movement of return, even unto death. Indeed, this is where the portrait of Joseph and the portrait of Moses intersect: in the realization that, unlike the death of an animal, the death of a human being is part of the testimony to which he or she summoned in life. For a human being *death is a task*.

According to one tradition (see Yaakov ben Rabbeinu Asher, *Tur HaArokh*, on Exodus 2:19), when God declared to Moses that he would not be allowed to enter the Land of the Promise but would be buried outside the land, Moses pleaded with God, saying, "If I may not enter the Land alive, then please allow my bones to be carried into the Land along with the bones of Joseph, whose remains I have brought out of Egypt."

To which God replied: "I am sorry, Moses, but I cannot do that. You see, Joseph never denied that he was a Hebrew. He was, indeed, known as Joseph the Hebrew. But you, Moses, when you fled from Egypt to Midian, you tried to pass yourself off as an Egyptian. Therefore your bones shall lie outside the Land."

Wiesel picks up on this teaching: "When [Moses] arrived in the land of Midian, he concealed his identity. They assumed he was Egyptian and he chose not to correct their mistake [Exodus 2:19]. He was a hidden Jew in search of assimilation, so much so that his second son was not circumcised. Moses, once more, was far removed from his people, though this time deliberately. Nothing is more painful than the sight of victims adopting the behavior and laws of their executioners. If the Jews behaved like the Egyptians, why should Moses be concerned with their fate?"[111] It will be recalled that Wiesel made a similar complaint about Joseph and his desire to assimilate and to imitate the ways of the murderers of the Jews.[112] To be sure, exile and assimilation are interwoven: assimilation *is* exile, the most insidious form of exile because it is the most comfortable. The Midrash teaches that those Israelites who were able to ascend from Egypt could do so for four reasons: (1) they did not change their language, (2) they did not change their names, (3) they did not intermarry, and (4) they did not inform on one another (*Mekilta de-Rabbi Ishmael, Pisha* 5). The vast majority of the Israelites in Egypt chose to remain in Egypt, even as a multitude of Egyptians chose to depart with the Israelites. Sounds familiar, doesn't it? How many Jews have forgotten their Hebrew? How many have shed their Hebrew names? How many have intermarried? How many have denounced Israel? And in the name of what? For the sake of what? To appease whom? In short, what have these Jews traded their Torah for?

Wiesel is all too sensitive to these issues in his portraiture. He knows that the self-hating soul is a soul in exile, and the Jewish paradigm of exile is the exile in Egypt, a realm ruled by a Pharaoh who thinks he is God and plagued by a darkness in which "a man cannot not see his brother" (Exodus 10:23). That is the exile out of which Moses led the Jews, and therein lies his greatness. The true horror of the Egyptian exile, as Rabbi Adin Steinsaltz expresses it, "was that the slaves gradually became more and more like their masters, thinking like them and even dreaming the same dreams. Their greatest sorrow, in fact, was that their masters would not let them fulfill the Egyptian dream."[113] And their greatest wretchedness was that they saw no harm in dreaming the Egyptian dream, one of power and possessions, of pleasure and prestige—a nightmare in which more is better but never enough. It is the nightmare of being lost in a strange surrounding, unable to find our way home. Thus we see in Moses the prototype of the dilemma that would confront the Jewish people throughout history: to convert, assimilate, or die. We see in him, too, traces of our own ominous dreams.

"Moses became a stranger in more ways than one," Wiesel observes, "a stranger to the Egyptian people, to the Jewish people and to himself. . . . Strange, for forty years Moses lived in his new adopted land without ever worrying about his family's fate. It seems unlikely somehow. What had taken place inside him?"[114] And yet it was Moses who was chosen to transmit the Torah to the people of Israel. Why? We have already discussed Joseph's identification with the *sefirah* of *Yesod*. Here we note that Moses is identified with the *sefirah* of *Netzah*, which stems from *Hesed*, which signifies the dimension of height, particularly in the Hasidic tradition (see *Kedushat Levi, Vaera* 6). Because the Israelites do not merely come out of Egypt but *ascend* from Egypt, they had to be led into a dimension of height, into the *sefirah* of *Netzah*, which is "eternity" or "infinity," and into the realm of *Hesed*—or loving kindness. Moses manifested this transcendent ascent in the most humble of ways, as Wiesel points out, noting a Midrash on the shepherd Moses: he went to great lengths to follow a lamb that had gone astray, whereupon God proclaimed, "Since you have such compassion toward the lamb, you'll have compassion for the Jews [*Shemot Rabbah* 2:2]."[115] In fact, as Wiesel portrays him, Moses had more compassion for the Jews—which is a compassion that extends to all humanity—than he did for God Himself.

Characteristically Hasidic in his profound love for the Jewish people and his confrontations with God, Wiesel notes, Moses complained of the Israelites, but:

> If others spoke ill of Israel, he was quick to come to its defense, passionately, fiercely; there are times when Jews—and Jews alone—may criticize other Jews. Moses defended them not only against their enemies but, at times, even against God. Says the Midrash: only by pleading for his people did Moses become an *Ish Elokim* [a Man of God]. . . . The moment the angels spoke out against Israel—and that happened frequently—Moses took its defense. When God decided to give His Law to Israel and the angels opposed His plan, Moses scolded them: Who then will observe it? You? Only man can assume the Law and live by its precepts. . . . [And he said to God (Exodus 32:32)], "If you wipe them out, erase my name from Your book."[116]

As often happens, what is characteristically Hasidic is characteristically Talmudic:

And Rabbi Yehoshua ben Levi said: When Moses ascended on High to receive the Torah, the ministering angels said before the Holy One, Blessed be He: Master of the Universe, what is one born of a woman doing here among us? The Holy One, Blessed be He, said to them: He came to receive the Torah. The angels said: The Torah is a hidden treasure . . . , and you seek to give it to flesh and blood? The Holy One, Blessed be He, said to Moses: Provide them with an answer as to why the Torah should be given to the people . . . Moses said to the angels: Did you descend to Egypt? Were you enslaved to Pharaoh? Why should the Torah be yours? Do you dwell among the nations who worship idols that you require this special warning? (*Shabbat* 88a)

From there Moses went through the Ten Commandments, noting there was no way they could pertain to the angels. And so the angels agreed that the Torah should be given to Moses and, through Moses, to the Israelites (*Shabbat* 89a).

Because Moses embodied the *sefirah* of *Netzah* and therefore the dimension of height, even as an infant in a basket floating down the river, says Wiesel, "his entire people was crying in him."[117] And because Batya, the daughter of Pharaoh, was so close to God, she could recognize that outcry. Indeed, so righteous was she that, according to the Talmud, she was among those who were able to ascend into the upper realms without undergoing the agony of death (see *Kallah Rabbati* 3:23; also *Derekh Eretz* 1:18).[118]

Wiesel relates the Midrash explaining how Moses happened to become "slow of tongue," that is, a stutterer (Exodus 4:10). He whom God chose to be His spokesman and teacher of Torah was a stutterer! Yet God needed a stutterer to encourage each of us to closely examine each word and to be sure that we have heard what we thought we have heard. As it happens, beautiful words are not truthful, and truthful words are not beautiful. Therefore God Himself made Moses into a stutterer, as per the Midrash that Wiesel relates.[119] According to the tale, the toddler Moses loved to play with the crown of Pharaoh. Pharaoh also took delight in pleasing his grandson, until one day his counselors warned him. This is a sign that the child will take your power away from you. Pharaoh ordered two cauldrons to be brought forth: one filled with gold, the other filled with burning coals. If little Moses should reach for the gold, his ambition would be exposed, and he would be executed; if he should reach for the burning coals, they would know that he had no ambition. Moses was about to reach for the gold, when an angel suddenly took his hand, leading him to the burning coals. He picked up a hot coal from the cauldron and put it to his lips, whereupon he became a stutterer (*Shemot Rabbah* 1:31).

When the Israelites emerged from the separated waters of the Sea of Reeds, Moses the Stutterer was able to burst forth in song. How? Says Wiesel, "The Hasidic explanation: *Vayaaminu baadoshem uv Moshe avdo*— And they had faith in God *and* in His servant Moses. For the first time an entire people rallied around Moses; for the first time he became its true spokesman. That is why he was able to sing; through him an entire people was singing."[120] Still, the Hasidic tradition would underscore a Talmudic teaching that pertains to this occasion: when the angels joined the Israelites in song, God silenced them, saying, "How can you sing when My children are drowning?" (*Megillah* 10b). When the price of deliverance is so high, there must be no celebration on high. Let humanity rejoice, but let not the angels rejoice.

The reason for humanity's rejoicing is the giving of the Torah. The Torah alone, as Wiesel makes clear in his portrait of Moses, is an occasion for joy and thanksgiving. If, as he says, "Moses was gratitude personified,"[121] it is because Moses realized that without the Divine Revelation of the infinite sanctity of the other human being and the infinite responsibility of each for the other—without an infinite gratitude for that infinite responsibility—nothing can have any meaning. Thus Wiesel turns our attention to the Scripture, saying that the "Israelites were gathered at the foot of the mountain," which was actually *betahtit hahar*, "beneath the mountain" (Exodus 19:17). The Talmud tells us that, with the mountain hanging over them, the Israelites had a decision to make (*Avodah Zarah* 2b). "It was either the Torah or death," Wiesel relates. "They had no choice, and so they accepted the Law against their will."[122] Once again, however, we mustn't be too hasty. God is not threatening the Jews. No, He is saying that without Torah humanity will be crushed by the emptiness of a strictly material and therefore meaningless world, where power is the only reality and weakness the only sin.

Like the cloud of smoke and pillar of fire, however, the mountain that now threatens to bury us is a mountain of ashes. Not only does the mountain hang over us—it abides within us, as literally and as graphically as the mountain of ashes under the concrete dome at Majdanek. For the winds have spread a mountain of ashes—the ashes of six million Jews—

over the face of the earth. They inhabit the ground that yields our bread. They curl up in the crumbs we place in our mouths. If, as the Talmudic sage Rabbi Ammi once taught, he who eats from the earth of Babylon is as though he ate the flesh of his ancestors (*Zevahim* 113b), what shall we say of this bread that we now harvest from the ashen earth? As we are made of that bread, so are we made of those ashes: we are the grave to those denied a grave. Survivor and author Arnošt Lustig states it more eloquently: "These ashes will be contained in the breath and expression of every one of us, and the next time anybody asks what the air he breathes is made of, he will have to think about these ashes; they will be contained in books which haven't been written and will be found in the remotest regions of the earth where no human foot has ever trod; no one will be able to get rid of them, for they will be the fond, nagging ashes of the dead who died in innocence."[123] No one will be able to engage Mount Sinai without engaging this mountain. And Elie Wiesel knew it.

This vision of humanity's need for redemption is expressive of the Jewish understanding of redemption exemplified by Moses. As Wiesel correctly states it, in Judaism, from Moses forward, there is no concept of personal salvation: when Moses declared, "If You will not redeem all of Israel, then Erase my name from Your Book" (Exodus 32:32), he declared that either all of us will be redeemed or none of us will.[124] Says Wiesel, "Though chosen by God, he refused to give up on man. Just as God brought Moses closer to man, Moses brought Him closer to man."[125] And that is why Moses was the beloved of God, the one unto whose care the Torah was entrusted. That is why at the moment of his death, despite—or because of—the questioning between Moses and God, we have this moment at the end of Wiesel's portrait: "Then, silently, God kissed his lips. And the soul of Moses found shelter in God's breath and was swept away into eternity"[126] (see Rashi on Deuteronomy 34:5), just as He had taken Miriam and Aaron by a Divine Kiss (see Rashi on Numbers 20:1). Remarkable siblings, indeed.

Portrait of Miriam

Part of the Hasidic legacy are the Hasidic prayers. And in Hasidic prayers, such as the prayers of the *Tehillat HaShem* of Chabad Lubavitch, the remembrance of when Miriam was stricken with leprosy is among the Six Remembrances that come at the end of the morning service.[127] In the

Torah she appears on the scene before Aaron: as Wiesel points out, the first time Aaron is mentioned in the Scripture is when God is sending Moses on a mission (Exodus 4:14),[128] but the sister of Moses is invoked at the moment when Pharaoh's daughter Batya saved his life (Exodus 2:4–5). It was his sister who stood watch over Moshe Rabbeinu when he was turned over to the waters of the river that had been used to murder the male infants of Israel (Exodus 1:22). Even before Moses was born, according to the Midrash, Miriam and her mother were saving the male Israelite infants, a point not lost on Wiesel in his portrait. "Of all the women who dwell in the turbulent universe of the Bible," he writes, "she seems the most elusive."[129] But the Midrash specializes in the elusive; to be sure, the whole point of Midrash is to make things less elusive (or is it more elusive?). She is not referred to by name until Exodus 15:20, when, we are told, "Miriam the prophetess" led the Israelite women in song upon their crossing of the Sea of Reeds. Or rather, if she is mentioned by name, it is a different name: Puah (Exodus 1:15). Between the Aggadah of the Talmud and the tales of the Midrash, we have an explanation.

It is written in the Talmud that when Pharaoh decreed that the Israelite male infants should be murdered, Amram, the head of the Jewish community, ordered that there be no more marital relations among the husbands and wives of Israel, so that there would be no newborns to be murdered. His daughter Miriam, who even as a child had prophetic powers, says Wiesel,[130] convinced her father to revoke his ruling and to encourage the Israelite husbands and wives to have babies, despite the Pharaoh's decree. This is because from him and her mother, Yoheved, would arise the man who would deliver the Israelites from their bondage (*Sotah* 12a–12b; *Pesikta Rabbati* 43).

The Midrash takes it further still. After urging her father to encourage the birth of Israelite babies, Miriam and her mother Yoheved saw to it that as many as possible would live: they were the midwives Puah and Shifrah, who saved Israelite babies (Exodus 1:17). The Talmud says that she was called Puah, from *poah* or "cry out," because she cried out her prophesy that her mother would give birth to Israel's savior (*Sotah* 11b). And so, the Talmud relates, when Moses was born, Miriam stood guard over her infant brother to assure that her prophecy would come to pass (*Megillah* 14a; see also *Mekilta de-Rabbi Ishmael, Beshalah* 10). For her vigilance over her brother, says the Mishnah, Miriam received healing for her affliction of leprosy when Moses and all of the Israelites pleaded with God for her healing (*Sotah* 1:9). Indeed, has this not been the response of Jews in the post-Shoah period—to have Jewish babies and to bring them up as Jews, despite the fact that a large portion of the world would still like to see their destruction? Is this not the legacy that devolves upon all Jews?

Essential to a Hasidic legacy is song, and whose song is more central to the Torah's account of the Jewish people than Miriam's Song at the Sea? Says Wiesel, "Interestingly, the [sixteenth-century] commentator 'Kli Yakar' says that she did not burst into song because she was a prophetess, but rather she became a prophetess *because* she burst into song" (Shlomo Ephraim ben Aaron Luntschitz, *Kli Yakar* on Exodus 15:20).[131] And because she rose up and danced, reminding us of the Hasidic view of dancing as a form of prayer—indeed, even higher than prayer. In the dance the spiritual descends and the physical ascends to arrive at new levels of insight, joy, and gratitude. In the dance, thought becomes praise, so that the psalmist enjoins us to praise God through the dance or *mahol* (see, e.g., Psalms 150:4). Thus becoming a "dancer," a *meholelet*, Miriam concretely affirmed the holiness of God.

Why, then, is the memory of her affliction with leprosy, rather than her dancing, among the Six Remembrances in the *Tehillat HaShem*? On the simplest level, it is because the Torah commands us to remember that she was stricken with leprosy (Deuteronomy 24:9). On a deeper level it lies in the reason for her affliction, which is even more powerful than the dance: according to Rashi's commentary on Deuteronomy 24:9, Miriam was stricken because she spoke slander against Moses; that is, she was guilty of a most grievous sin, of *lashon hara*. "More than evil speech," Wiesel explains, "it means the tongue of evil. To insult someone, to discredit him, to defame him behind his back, is to serve the powers of evil."[132] Evil thrives on the evil angels created by words of evil. Therefore the psalmist cautions us: "Who is the man who desires life and loves his days, so that he might behold goodness? Guard your tongue from evil and your lips from speaking slander" (Psalms 34:13–14). When Miriam spoke against Moses it threatened to undermine all of creation and therefore the Torah itself.

"How remarkable, says the Midrash [*Vayikra Rabbah* 15:8]: it was God who punished her, God who determined her illness, and God who cured her."[133] When God cured Miriam and then took her, as Wiesel notes, the Israelites were suddenly in desperate need of water.[134] Why? Because, as Rashi explains, as long as she was alive, they enjoyed the waters of Miriam's well (commentary on Numbers 20:2). They were sustained, in other words, by the nourishment of Torah. For the Torah is associated with water (see, e.g., *Talmud Bavli, Avodah Zarah* 5b), and water is associated with Miriam and the mothers and daughters of Israel. So we recall Rashi's commentary on Exodus 19:3, where it is written, "Thus shall you say unto the House of Jacob and the Children of Israel." "The House of Jacob," says Rashi, refers to the women, and "the Children of Israel" refers to the men. The women are mentioned first because they are closer to God: without the women, the men would have no hope of receiving the Torah. If the Torah is the foundation of creation, the mother, through her tie to the *beit* (the first letter of the Torah), is the foundation of the Torah itself: the *beit* is the womb from which creation is born (*Zohar* I, 22b). Indeed, the Talmud says that Miriam's well was among the ten miraculous phenomena created on the sixth day of Creation, on the eve of the first Sabbath (*Pesahim* 54a),[135] miraculous because it moved about the desert with the Israelites (*Shabbat* 35a).

Realizing the profound association between Torah and water, between Torah and Miriam, we now understand why Wiesel would say, "What do I love about Miriam? First of all her name. Perhaps it bears her secret and her destiny. *Mar-yam*: the bitterness of the sea. Or perhaps *meri-yam*, the revolt of the sea, the rebellion at the seashore, against the sea. Remove the *resh* and you have *mayim*—water. Her whole life was lived under the sign of water. We meet her on the banks of the Nile, we find her on the far shore of the Red Sea. We leave her, or she leaves us, as her people are clamoring for water."[136] Which is a clamoring for Torah. Yes, Wiesel finds her to be elusive. And his favorite feature about her is her name, with all of its elusiveness.

Portrait of Aaron

Professor Wiesel gives Aaron his own well-deserved portrait. But for the task at hand, and for the transmission of Elie Wiesel's Hasidic legacy (which is about loving relationship), I attach the portrait of Aaron to that of his sons Nadab and Abihu, for reasons that, I think, will soon become clear. Wiesel calls his portrait of Nadab and Abihu, the priestly sons of the High Priest Aaron, a "story of fire and silence."[137] The sons are central to the fire, and Aaron is central to the silence. But we shall come to that.

"Moses personifies the rigor of the Law and its inflexibility," says Wiesel. "Aaron incarnates warmth, goodness, kindness, indulgence. One could almost state, not without some reticence, that Moses wants to be closer to God, and Aaron to people."[138] Almost, but not quite. Recall that when God declares to Moses, "Now therefore let Me alone, that My wrath may wax hot against them, and that I may consume them; and I will make of thee a great nation" (Exodus 32:10), Moses replies, "Turn from Thy fierce wrath, and repent of this evil against Thy people" (Exodus 32:12), *calling God Himself to repentance* for the sake of Israel. Aaron, who did not stutter and was known for his eloquence, did no such thing. "Unlike Moses," Wiesel points out, "Aaron did not argue."[139] Wherein lay his power, his strength, his priestly righteousness? In his silence. Yes, there are times when silence becomes the most deafening outcry.

Silence, however, takes many forms and harbors many meanings. Aaron, God's first High Priest, stood by silently when the Israelites were crying out for the golden calf. "Aaron's conduct," says Wiesel, "is indeed incomprehensible. But Moses' and God's are more so."[140] He adds that tradition tries to whitewash Aaron. For example, he postponed a feast for the false god to the next day, in the hope that Moses would return and put a stop to it (Rashi commentary on Exodus 32:5; see also *Midrash Tanhuma, Ki Tisa* 19). And the Midrash says that if God elevated Aaron and his sons to the priesthood, it is because He did not blame Aaron for the incident of the golden calf (*Midrash Tanhuma, Tetzaveh* 10). Whom, then, did God blame? According to the Baal HaTurim, the people were to blame for ganging up on Aaron and forcing him to make the golden calf (*Tur HaArokh* on Exodus 32:35).

Wiesel suggests another reason. He points out that the women among the Israelites refused to participate in the worship of the golden calf. When Aaron asked the women to give their jewels, Wiesel reminds us, he was sure that, "unlike their husbands, they knew the meaning of gratitude: having witnessed the miracles accomplished by God, they would not repudiate Him just like that."[141] The lesson? Gratitude is the best defense against slipping into idolatry. For idolatry is always about me, about the ego, whereas gratitude is about you, about the Eternal You. Could Aaron's silence be rooted in gratitude? Why not? Aaron himself is associated with gratitude.

Among the Ten *Sefirot* Aaron is associated with *Hod*, which means "praise" or "thanksgiving." Indeed, it is the word that begins the morning prayers: *Hodu*—"We thank You and praise You." And yet it comes from the side of *Gevurah* or *Din*, of power and judgment. It comes from the side of Aaron, the High Priest of Israel, who was chosen not only for thanksgiving and service to God but also to witness the consumption of his sons by fire in the midst of serving God. So here, too, we have Aaron—who did not argue! Who said nothing when *his sons were consumed* for offering God a "strange fire," consumed, indeed, by a "strange fire." What can this "strange fire" mean? And how can Aaron, the one who remains silent, possibly grasp it? No, he cannot grasp it: that is why he remains silent. But wait! No! He *does* grasp it, in all his prophetic vision, a vision as acute as his sister's vision. And yet the vision of the prophet is precisely the vision of the incomprehensible. His is the silence of incomprehension, foreshadowing other silences. Perhaps he does not remain silent; perhaps he screams—silently. Those untransmittable silences are the silences that bind us most profoundly to one another, to Aaron, and to the God whose "appearance is announced by a deep silence" (*Berakhot* 58a). But when? And where?

Nadab and Abihu

The tale of these sons of Aaron, says Wiesel, "comprising a few short verses is among the saddest and most mysterious in the Bible. It grips us; it takes us by the throat."[142] *By the throat*: taking us by the throat, it strangles the word and the outcry that struggle to escape the throat. It is stark in its devastating simplicity. So Wiesel begins with simplicity, with the all-too-brief tale from the Torah. Nadab and Abihu, the beloved sons of Aaron and priests charged with the service of the Holy One, "each brought his censer before God, and put fire therein, and laid incense thereon, and offered strange fire before HaShem, which He had not commanded them. And there came forth fire from before HaShem, and devoured them. . . . Then Moses said unto Aaron: 'This is it that the HaShem spoke, saying: Through them that are nigh unto Me I will be sanctified, and before all the people I will be glorified.' *And Aaron held his peace*" (Leviticus 10:1–3; emphasis added). Wiesel cries out, as if in a whisper: "'*Va'yidom Aharon*,' and Aaron held his peace. He kept silent. He wrapped himself in silence; he *became* silence."[143] This is the untransmittable silence, the silence that announces the appearance of the God who is a consuming fire. And the fire is *silence*. Yes: *fire* . . . there are times when silence is made of fire.

"Need I say that the theme of this story has always fascinated and even obsessed me?" writes Wiesel. "Because of Aaron's silence? There is something else. This chapter gives a new dimension to the subject of brothers as they are presented in the Bible. . . . Nadab and Abihu are different. They are attached to each other, loyal to each other. . . . Together they fall, in the same moment that they breathe their last."[144] Because of Aaron's silence? Yes and no. Wiesel points out that in the Midrash (see, e.g., Horowitz, *Shnei Luhot HaBrit, Vayikra, Torah Or* 100) Aaron's wife, Elisheva, sobs and laments the news of their death, as any mother would. Nahmanides says Aaron did, too (see Nahmanides commentary on Leviticus 10:3).[145] But what is the "strange fire," the *esh zarah*, that the brothers brought as an offering to God? How is it that both brothers, without one questioning the other, could bring the same "strange fire" in lieu of the prescribed offering?

The simplest explanation, as Wiesel points out, is Rashi's explanation: they were drunk.[146] But why would they be drunk? Would the priests show up for work drunk? Or is it because drinking the wine of *Kiddush* is a *mitzvah*, and they got carried away with the *mitzvah*? Getting carried away by our own enthusiasm, even an enthusiasm for performing a *mitzvah*, can be dangerous. Other sources, Wiesel observes, take it deeper. The Talmud, for example, claims that it was due to lack of respect for their elders: Nadab and Abihu longed "for the death of Aaron and Moses, so that they could be the leaders—the strange fire was ambition [*Sanhedrin* 52a]."[147] In this account Nadab was the one who expressed a wish for Moses and Aaron to die; Abihu said nothing. So why was Abihu punished? Because he said nothing: "His silence made him an accomplice."[148] Elsewhere the Talmud explains: "The sons of Aaron died after daring to teach the Law in the presence of Moses" (*Eruvin* 63a): the strange fire, Wiesel observes, was arrogance.[149] According to still another Talmudic teaching, it was because they refused to get married and thereby observe the first of the commandments, namely to be fruitful and multiply (*Yevamot* 64a). Here, says Wiesel, the strange fire is pride and vanity.[150]

As a Hasid, however, Wiesel sees in this episode a challenge and a question for God, which makes the tale much *less* understandable. Like good Jews, "they wanted to abolish any space at all between the Creator and His creatures. '*Amdu le'hossif ahava al ahava,*' comments the Sifra [*Sifra, Aharei Mot* 1]: They believed they could, should, add to their love of God a greater love, more imposing, all-encompassing, in order to melt into his radiance and fulfill themselves in it."[151] In other words, in their love for God, they wanted to join in a mystical union with God, in the uppermost realms. "They have been compared to the four Talmudic masters who dared enter into the Pardes," says Wiesel, "the orchard of forbidden knowledge. Like Ben Azzai, they perished for gazing where one must not gaze."[152] The problem? The "strange fire" was the fire of their own personal, subjective passion, and not the fire ignited by the Holy One from on High. When it is about feeling good, it is never about God—it is about me, about the self, which, as Abraham Joshua Heschel rightly understood, is a "self-deception."[153] Worse, it is a form of idolatry.

In keeping with the brothers motif, Wiesel notes Moses's efforts to console his brother, despite the horror that rendered Aaron mute: " 'Aaron, my brother, I have known for a long time, because God told me, that God wishes to be sanctified by those closest to Him. I thought He was speaking of me, or of you, but I was wrong: your sons were closer to Him.' That is when and why Aaron held his peace, peace not of resignation but of acceptance."[154] They lost their lives by their love for God and *by God's love for them*, in a *Kiddush HaShem*. But Wiesel cannot accept Aaron's acceptance. No, he prefers the High Priest's outrage and outcry: "I like this explosion of grief on Aaron's part. Here the father is stronger than the High Priest,"[155] as he goes back to Nahmanides' commentary referenced above, namely that the silence of Aaron overcame him only after he had raised an outcry that shook the foundations of the earth and extended into the heavens, where the Father held *His* peace. "Why didn't the God of love spare so many descendants of Moses and Aaron? To bring them closer to Him, He tore them from our midst. Why? *Va'yidom Aharon*. And Aaron the father held his peace. Like God. For God. And all that we, his distant disciples, can do is to join our silence to his."[156] Here, too, more than ever, there is a danger. Here, too, we tread the razor's edge. Speaking of the survivors of the strange fire that consumed a generation, Wiesel writes, "Had all of them remained mute, their accumulated silences would have become unbearable: the impact would have deafened the world."[157] Yes, some silences can be deafening. Some silences transcend transmission.

Portraits from the Prophets

E lie Wiesel's portraits from the Torah fall into a singular category, a category forged by God Himself upon the Revelation of the Torah at Mount Sinai. Approaching his portraits of the prophets, we move into yet another singular category, as we encounter those upon whom the *Ruah HaKodesh*, the Holy Spirit, descended to transform them into messengers of the Holy One. Coming before the portraits of the prophets, we step before the person through whom the Word of God entered this realm. "In Scripture there is the problem of true and false prophets," Wiesel points out. "How can they be identified? The former are disturbing, the latter soothing. Also, the former reinforce and celebrate the Law, the latter bend it or oppose it. . . . The true power of the prophet derives from his moral conviction. . . . Should he fall silent, his silence itself bears witness."[1] If silence might be part of prophecy, then "what is the essence of prophecy?" Wiesel asks. "What is its function?" He answers: "Unlike the oracles of antiquity, the biblical prophet is not content merely to predict the future. For him, it is the ethical element that prevails."[2] The prophet is neither seer nor soothsayer. The future that concerns the prophet is the future that unfolds through the ethical demand that devolves upon us from on high, *here and now*, through the face-to-face encounter with the other human being, where we collide with the "Thou shalt" of the Holy One: the future is made of the "Thou shalt."

Therefore the prophet transmits not only a warning concerning the future but also an announcement concerning the present, which is the Holy One's demand for *presence*. "God is present, God is presence," writes Wiesel. "It is up to man to be present, too—present to God, to himself and to his fellow man."[3] There lie the prophetic message and the prophetic demand, without which there is no meaning. Prophecy addresses the *Why* of humanity and therefore the *Who* of humanity, both of which lie in the messianic *not yet* that imparts meaning to humanity. Because it is the dimension of meaning, the *Why* is the dimension of the future. Hence time "becomes biblical," as Wiesel says.[4] What does it mean for time to become biblical? It means that we now understand time in terms of the ethical demand that we encounter through the face of the other human being—the demand that constitutes redemptive time and defines prophetic time.

Wiesel asks further: "Who is a prophet?" And he answers: "Someone who is searching—someone who is being sought. Someone who listens—and who is listened to. Someone who sees people as they are, and as they ought to be. Someone who rejects his time, yet who lives outside time. A prophet is forever awake, forever alert; he is never indifferent, least of all to injustice, be it human or divine, whenever or wherever it may be found. God's messenger to man, he somehow becomes man's messenger to God."[5] The prophet is not only sought—he or she is laid claim to, seized, and sent on a search. Most crucial to searching is listening—as when we are commanded twice a day, *Shma Yisrael*—"Hear!" And most crucial to hearing is wakefulness. Wakefulness requires nonindifference toward the other human being. The prophet understands that our humanity lies in a capacity to transform difference into a nonindifference toward the other human being, a difference that, in the words of Emmanuel Levinas, "shudders as non-indifference."[6] Why the shudder? Because the prophet announces the demand of nonindifference as "a sign of this impossibility of slipping away and being replaced, of this identity, this uniqueness: here I am."[7] The future that the prophet proclaims is the future defined by answering to the other, "Here I am for you," which we have forever *yet* to utter. It is not merely what *will* come to pass; more than that, it is what we must *make* come to pass.

Wiesel's portrayal of the prophet is, indeed, distinctively Hasidic: even greater than being God's messenger to humanity, the prophet is humanity's messenger to God. As it is written in the Talmud and underscored by the Hasidic master Levi-Yitzhak of Berditchev, one who is a *tzaddik*, a righteous person, is devoted to God, but one who is a *tzaddik tov*, a "good *tzaddik*," is devoted to God and humanity (*Kiddushin* 40b; see also *Kedushat Levi, Noah* 1). How can there be a category that transcends that of the *tzaddik*? It lies in the *tzaddik tov*, where the devotion to humanity elevates the righteous person even higher than his devotion to God. A prophet is a *tzaddik tov*. Here we have a key to the solitude of the prophet, of the one who announces the profound importance of human and higher relation and yet who, for that reason, is profoundly alone. Wiesel underscores the solitude of the prophet as part of the condition that defines him: "Solitude: No solitude is greater than that of the messenger who is unable to transmit the message. No one is as alone as the prophet whom God chooses to isolate from those he is sent to warn and save. No one is as alone as the man who must speak and is not heard."[8] And how much greater is the devastating solitude of the prophet who, in his radical isolation, *cannot transmit his message to God*?

Here we realize that, if it is not good for the man to be alone, it is not good for God to be alone. We realize that there are times when God, too, might be ferociously alone. Dare we compare the situation of the prophet in the ancient world to one trapped in the antiworld? Absolutely not. And yet Wiesel, like Moishe the Beadle, emerges from the mass grave that was Europe to desperately transmit a message not only from God to humanity but from humanity to God. As humanity grows deaf, so does God, and both are ferociously alone. The difference is that God at least has a realm to retreat to, what in the Talmud is called *Mistarim*, the "Hidden Place," where God curls up so as not to allow His weeping to destroy all of Creation (*Hagigah* 5b). But to where shall a humanity devastated by an infinite evil retreat? And what, then, shall become of Creation? There can be no doubt that this desperation finds its way into Wiesel's portraits of the prophets. Indeed, that desperation lends to these portraits a certain prophetic dimension.

If, as Wiesel says, "One is not chosen by God without, at the same time, or at one time, becoming His victim,"[9] this victimization lies in the isolation of the messenger who cannot deliver his message. What can be more isolating, more maddening, than having been entrusted with a life-and-death warning that falls upon deaf ears, both on the part of humanity and on the part of God? In the Torah is it written: "Hear now My words: if there be a prophet among you, I HaShem do make Myself known unto him in a vision, I speak with him in a dream" (Numbers 12:6). Through these portraits of the prophets come visions akin to those of Madame Schächter in Wiesel's *Night*, who, in the mode of a prophet, repeatedly uttered cries of "Fire! I see fire!" that fell upon deaf ears.[10] Abraham Joshua Heschel proclaims that the prophet's words "must not shine, they must burn."[11] Like the words of Madame Schächter. Like the words of Elie Wiesel. For the fire that Madame Schächter beholds is not only the fire of the ovens of Auschwitz—it is the fire that surrounds us now, the fire that would consume humanity, beginning with the Jews, the fire that the enemies of the Jewish people promise to visit upon the Jewish state. Therefore Wiesel's portraits of the prophets have a bearing not only on how we understand the Scriptures but also on what humanity faces in this hour.

Portrait of Samuel

Samuel's name means "the Name of God." He was a Nazarite, that is, one who abstained from wine and who did not cut his hair (see 1 Samuel 1:11). Elie Wiesel adds:

> Born circumcised, he is among the eight princes and founders of humankind. He was twelve when he was endowed with prophetic powers. The Palestinian Talmud calls him "*rabban shel nevi'im*," a master of prophets [cf. *Midrash Tanhuma, Emor* 2]. Wealthy, he never profited financially from his position. Though thirsty, he never drank from a public well. When traveling to sit in judgment, he rode on his own donkey. His misfortune was his two sons: they aged him prematurely. It was because of their unworthy behavior that he died at fifty-two. His relations with Saul were not happy either. Did he ever have moments of happiness?[12]

Born circumcised: from birth Samuel bore the sign of the covenant. Circumcised by whom? Circumcised by God, as were others who were born circumcised. Among them, according to the Midrash, are Adam and his son Seth, Noah, Jacob, Joseph, Moses, and Job (*Midrash Tanhuma, Noah* 5). To be born circumcised is to be born already with a prophetic mission to affirm and uphold the Covenant of Circumcision, already, therefore, with a divine sanction. But isn't every soul that comes into this world born with a divine sanction—*already*? Yes, but not only does Samuel bear the sign of the Covenant from birth: born circumcised, he *is* a sign of the Covenant.

Wiesel's mention of the eight princes is an allusion to a passage in the Book of the Prophet Micah: "And this shall be peace: when the Assyrian shall come into our land, and when he shall tread in our palaces, then shall we raise against him seven shepherds, and eight princes among men" (5:4). The Talmud identifies the seven shepherds as Adam, Seth, Methuselah, Abraham, Jacob, Moses, and King David. The eight princes are Saul, Samuel, Elijah, Amos, Isaiah, Zephaniah, Zedekiah, and the Messiah. These eight princes, the Talmud explains, will rule over the world in the Messianic Age (*Sukkah* 52b). Their number is eight because, as one more than the seven days of Creation, the number eight signifies the Creator, the Infinite One, beyond Creation. In the ascent through the lower seven *sefirot*, which correspond to the realm established during the seven days of creation, where the seven shepherds watch over their flock, the eighth *sefirah*, *Binah*, represents the transition into the upper realm. It is the realm of the *Ruah HaKodesh* that descends upon the prophet.

But if Samuel is associated with such a transcendent realm, why is he counted as a "founder of humankind?" The answer: humankind is precisely where we encounter the transcendent as a foundation, for a foundation signifies the dimension of height—a teaching fundamental to Judaism in general and to Hasidism in particular. Living up to his name, the prophet Samuel lives up to this wisdom, even at the age of twelve. Wiesel takes care to relate the episode when God first called out to Samuel, and he answered, "*Hineni!* Here I am for you!"—but not to God: he thought it was the ailing priest Eli who was calling out to him.[13] It seems, then, that the prophet Samuel was a forerunner of a Hasidic outlook. The Baal Shem Tov, Wiesel relates, proclaimed that the path to God leads through this world, through your fellow human being: "Fervor? Yes—later. Study? Yes—later. Ecstasy? Yes—later. Not on a hungry stomach. Not with a sick child at home."[14] And not with an ailing priest in the next room. Not once but twice Samuel took the outcry to be the calling of his sick benefactor and teacher, until Eli finally convinced him that it was coming from God (see 1 Samuel 3:4–14). And if he thought the outcry came from an ailing man, then he understood that it came from an ailing God, a God afraid of no longer being God. Without God, the prophet is not a prophet, but without the prophet, God, in a sense, is not God. Without the prophet's response of "*Hineni!*—Here I am for you!" to a suffering humanity, God is not God.

God declares to Samuel that He will punish the house of Eli for its corruption. And what is its corruption? Wiesel notes that the corruption lay with Eli's sons Pinhas and Hofni, who "pretended that the heavens were empty."[15] If the heavens are empty, then there is no foundation. If the heavens are empty, the earth is empty, formless, and void—that is why God created the heavens *before* He created the earth, as it is written in the

Midrash: it was to introduce the dimension of height before proceeding with the creation because the foundation for *meaning* is above and not below (*Midrash Tanhuma, Bereshit* 1). With the prophet Samuel, prophecy is not prognostication: it is an affirmation of the dimension of height that forms the foundation of meaning. In the beginning God created the heavens and the earth—the heavens first and then the earth, as if to say, "Let there be height," before He declared, "Let there be light." Without this dimension of meaning—this dimension of transcendent height—the soul cannot endure. For this reason—because he twice answered to the human outcry before answering to God—Samuel is counted among the founders of humankind.

With the gift—and the curse?—of prophecy devolving upon him at the age of twelve, Samuel ran certain risks, as Wiesel points out. According to both Talmudic and Midrashic sources (*Berakhot* 31b; *Midrash Shmuel* 3:6), Hannah entrusted her son Samuel to the care of Eli the priest in Shilo in his "House of God," which was known to be corrupt. "She almost lost him," writes Wiesel. "He was too precocious. In spite of his tender age, he managed to solve a difficult Halakhic problem. And this he did in the presence of Eli the priest, who, visibly embarrassed, reprimanded him: didn't the little boy know that whoever teaches in the presence of his teacher is committing a transgression which theoretically deserves capital punishment? Luckily Hannah was still there. And of course she used her greatest weapon: her tears."[16] Recall the fate of Nadab and Abihu, who, according to one tradition, were consumed by the divine fire for teaching in front of their teacher Moses—precisely what Samuel had done in the presence of his own teacher (*Talmud Bavli, Eruvin* 63a). What protected this prophet, one of the founders of humankind, from such retribution? The tears of his mother, which moved not only the priest Eli but also the Creator of heaven and earth. For the tears of a mother reach into the heart and soul of *HaEl HaRahamim*, God the Compassionate One.

Why the tears of a *mother*?

The mystery of value and meaning in human life unfolds wherever we make room for another human being. A mother opens up space where there is no space: she is precisely the one who does not usurp the place of another. Instead, miraculously, she creates room for another life within herself, in the very depths of her physical being. Both physically and metaphysically a mother embodies the radical opposite of the ontological interest in occupying space. Associated with the "womb," or *rehem*, the mother personifies the "compassion," the *rahamim*, that lies at the core of our humanity. Levinas offers an insight: "*Rachamim* (Mercy) . . . goes back to the word *Rechem*, which means uterus. . . . *Rachamim* is maternity itself. God as merciful is God defined by maternity."[17] That is why the tears of a mother could assuage the Holy One, who is the Supernal Mother, as the Zohar describes the Creator (*Zohar* I, 22b). If he is "shielded by God," as Wiesel says, inspiring "admiration, respect, and awe,"[18] it is because he is shielded by the Supernal Mother, even by the tears of the Supernal Mother.

Why would the Supernal Mother shed tears? Perhaps for the same reason that Samuel himself shed tears: the Israelites pressed him to anoint a king so that they might be "like other nations" (1 Samuel 8:5). Indeed, in our own time we can sympathize with Samuel and his realization that presaged far more than even the prophet could have foreseen. In the time of modernity, Jews have been deceptively encouraged to be like other nations, to assimilate, and, in the end, to imitate the ways of their murderers. They have been encouraged, in other words, to disappear.

No one is more vulnerable to the primal temptation to be as God than the king; indeed, among the nations that the Israelites would resemble in their request for a king, many of the kings took themselves to be gods. That is why the Torah places so many restraints upon the king—a phenomenon unique in the ancient world. The Torah, for example, requires the king to write a Torah scroll (Deuteronomy 17:18). And where else in ancient cultures and societies is there a law limiting the number of horses that a king may own (see Deuteronomy 17:16)? This can be explained only by the proclamations of Samuel, beginning with his warnings concerning the appointment of a king. To be sure, few men have been as miserable as the first king whom Samuel anointed.

So what became of the king whom Samuel appointed so that the Israelites might be like all the other nations? According to one variation of the tale, as Wiesel relates it, the first king whom Samuel anointed, King Saul, was "a victim of his own compassion," who "had to endure Samuel's wrath and God's" for failing to slay Agag, the Amalekite king, forcing Samuel to kill Agag himself (1 Samuel 15). "Is he [Saul] commended for his gesture? The lack of unanimity in the Midrash is meaningful. One sage believes that Samuel tortured Agag before putting him to death. Another maintains that he castrated him [*Midrash Tanhuma, Ki Teitzei* 10]."[19] From this ambiguity there arises "a third theory: actually Saul was not as innocent as he appears. Nor was he as kind. If he refused to kill Agag it was because he wanted to humiliate him—and that is why he needed him alive. And that is why Agag preferred death [*Talmud Bavli, Megillah*

31a; see also *Pirke de Rabbi Eliezer* 49]."[20] So was King Saul compassionate or vicious? Did Samuel behead Agag to put an end to the suffering and humiliation that Saul had inflicted upon the Amalekite king? Or was it an act of extreme brutality? If Pinhas and Hofni corrupted the house of Eli by pretending that the heavens were empty, King Saul's transgression may well have been even greater: torturing the Amalekite king, Saul laid siege to the heavens in a usurpation of the Divine Seat of Judgment, which requires the radical appropriation of the soul of the other human being through torture.

As the "conversion of absolute pain into absolute power," in the words of Elaine Scarry,[21] torture is necessary to becoming god. Torture is about the totalitarian reign of terror over the body and soul of the other human being. Saul was not trying to extract information from Agag; no, if he tortured Agag, it was an act of an absolute possession of his soul. The torturer is as god, knowing and determining good and evil, fusing good and evil into a single, nebulous nothingness, where the horror is not an impending death but an unending death, not the imminence of death but the impossibility of death. Instead of the suffering God, we have the god who inflicts suffering, in an assault on what Levinas calls the "exigency of the holy."[22] The opposite of the arbitrary, the exigency of the holy is an ethical imperative that issues from a face naked and exposed to blows.[23] As an assault on the ethical exigency itself, torture is an assault on the Holy One. That is why, according to one midrashic tradition, Samuel put a stop to it and delivered Agag from his agony.

Wiesel's portrait of Samuel is titled "Samuel and the Quest for Mercy." Perhaps the prophet's longing for mercy ran so deep that he found a way to show mercy even to the Amalekite king, one of humanity's truly evil specimens.

Portrait of Elijah

Elijah is among the most enigmatic of the prophets. Certainly he is the one most intimately tied to the Messiah. Other prophets proclaim the signs of the coming of Messianic Age. Elijah measures humanity to see whether we are worthy of the advent of the Messiah. Ultimately, in a time of great goodness or in a time of great evil, he will go to the Messiah and draw him into this realm, either riding on an ass (Zechariah 9:9) or soaring on wings of eagles (Isaiah 40:31). Indeed, Wiesel notes that "for the Messiah to come, he must be preceded—and announced—by Elijah."[24] Why? Because if we are unworthy, Elijah's announcement of the Messiah's coming will lead us to a last-minute *teshuvah,* to a return to a relationship with Holy One. Many of the scenarios of the coming of the Messiah are not pretty. So Elijah precedes the Messiah as much out of his love for humanity as for his love of God—both of which were unbounded.

If Samuel put Agag to death in an act of mercy, the Talmud tells us that Elijah's last act as the herald of the Messiah will be to put an end to death itself (*Ketuvot* 77b). The one who is destined to defeat death—who was spared the tribulation of death—wanted only "to be alone as death is alone," says Wiesel, "as God is alone."[25] Because he did not endure the throes of death, he never knew what it meant to be alone as death is alone. But he knew what it meant to be alone as God is alone, alone and wrapped in the tentacles of silence. As Wiesel suggests, God is alone as death is alone: the mystery and ubiquity of God lie in the mystery and ubiquity of death. So much did Elijah long for the solitude of God and death, he wished "not to be seen by anyone."[26] He wished to be as invisible as God and the Angel of Death—Elijah, who turns up everywhere, in the midst of so many, both in this world and in the upper worlds. Says Wiesel, "When he is alone, he is the loneliest creature on earth; when surrounded by crowds, he is even lonelier."[27] Like God and the Angel of Death. And yet, the agony of Elijah's loneliness lay in his longing for relation, in his longing for presence, in his longing to be in the presence of the Holy One through his bond to the human one.

The thread running through Elijah's longing for the solitude of God and death is silence: God and death are most profoundly revealed in the solitude of silence—that is where they converge. Wiesel once invoked the thirteenth-century Hebrew poet Eleazar Rokeah, saying, "Some people complain that God is silent; they are wrong—God is not silent; God is Silence. It is to this silence that I would like to direct my words."[28] In his novel *The Gates of the Forest* Wiesel reiterates this insight: says the character Gavriel, "Men talk because they're afraid, they're trying to convince themselves that they're still alive. It's in the silence after the storm that God reveals himself to man. God is silence."[29] If God has something in common with death, the link lies in silence, as Wiesel's friend André Neher has suggested, saying, "Death is silence."[30] To be sure, the angel who rules over the dead is called Dumah, which is "Silence" (see *Talmud Bavli, Sanhedrin* 94a). Longing to be alone, as God and death are alone, Elijah is the prophet of silence: yes, silence itself can be part of prophecy.

Thus in God and in the Angel of Death—the Angel of Silence—we have the key to the prophet Elijah. True to Wiesel's Hasidic legacy, his confrontations with God lay in his love for God; his desire to be as alone as the Angel of Death lay in his love for the people. "He took God to task," writes Wiesel, "and God thanked him for his courage—God, but not the people. The people he defended actually made fun of him."[31] And yet he loved them: Elijah "does not talk; he commands. But when he listens to one person, he listens to no one else."[32] Even when he is performing the most miraculous of miracles—the raising of the dead—he prefers to do so in isolation, as Wiesel observes: it happened on the occasion when Elijah raised a widow's son from the dead (1 Kings 17:17–22). Like Moses, he performs miracles, but this one "takes place in quasi-secrecy. Whereas most miracles are meant to impress as many witnesses as possible, this one was witnessed by only three persons, Elijah included. He did the same again later, centuries later, when he comforted, consoled, and saved despair-stricken victims in exile by appearing to them alone."[33] Despite his longing for solitude and silence, Elijah never remained silent for long: over the generations he has appeared to those who were most alone because they had been most profoundly silenced. He who longed for the silence of solitude could never remain silent in the face of human suffering and idolatry. Thus he never attained the solitude he longed for. Instead, he encountered—or collided—with a silence that infinitely transcended any silence he could have imagined, a silence as transcendent as the Infinite One Himself: the silence of an indifferent humanity.

"Ahab loves Jezebel," Wiesel tells us, "who loves Elijah, who is in love with God alone. And God? Whom does He love? This is the question Elijah faces in the desert,"[34] where, like Moses on Mount Sinai, he spent forty days. What does it mean to be in love with God? The question is not *what* do you love but *whom* do you love when you are in love with God. To love God is to love the *Who*: the opposition of Elijah to Jezebel is the opposition of the love for the living *Who* to the love of the idolatrous *What*. As for the desert, it signifies silence—that is why the prophets, almost without exception, dwell in the "desert," in the *midbar*, where in the silence unlike any other they come before the *davar*, the "word," without which there is no silence, as without silence there is no word. In this tension we see the task laid out by the prophet Elijah and articulated in Wiesel's novel *A Beggar in Jerusalem*: "Happy is he who unites his words and his silence with the words and silence of the Shekhinah."[35] Is that not what the prophet Elijah sought and continues to seek—the silence of the Divine Presence, the Divine Presence *as* silence?

Wiesel enables us to see that at least two forms of silence provide the key to the portrait of the prophet Elijah. The first is the silence of a darkening, and the second is the silence of an unfolding. These two forms of silence appear on Mount Carmel: the first when Elijah confronted the priests of Baal (1 Kings 18:19–40), the second when he retreated to the solitude of the cave (1 Kings 19:9–12). Elijah challenged the priests of Baal to see which sacrificial offering would be consumed in fire—the one offered to Baal or the one offered to the God of Abraham. When the priests of Baal implored their false god to send fire to consume their offering, they met with nothing but silence (see Ginzberg, *Legends of the Jews*, 4:7:10). "Only silence," Wiesel comments, "like the silence that reigned when God gave the Law: the birds did not sing, the oxen did not bellow, the angels did not fly, the sea was calm, no creature made a sound. God caused creation to be silent, and void, and empty, as if no living thing existed"[36]—as if, eclipsed by the false gods of the idolaters (then and now), God did not exist. There is no silence more terrifying.

If, during an eclipse the moon blots out the light of the sun, during a time of idolatry, the idolaters blot out the word of God: as one leaves us in darkness, so the other leaves us in silence—not the pregnant silence of Sinai but the horrific silence that was before the beginning, the silence that continues to haunt us. The Kingdom of Night is the Kingdom of Silence. Ka-tzetnik expresses the cosmic nature of this silence in *Star of Ashes*, where he writes, "Silent are the heavens, silent the yellowed fields; silent the readied rifles, silent the ghetto hovels."[37] At the Site of Silence that was Auschwitz the word was sucked forth from the soul and into the silence of the chaos and void of the anticreation.

In the cave, however, Elijah met with a silence more akin to the silence of Mount Sinai. Plunged into despair, he longed for some sign of the Holy One. God told him to stand on the mount, where the prophet beheld a wind so strong that it broke the rocks of the mountain, followed by an earthquake and fire. But after the fire came the *kol demamah dakah*, "the voice of a thin silence" (1 Kings 19:12), and that is where Elijah encountered the Holy One. "Does that mean that God is in silence?" Wiesel asks. "The text does not say so explicitly."[38] But it might mean that God is in the "voice" of silence, a voice revealed as a "deep silence." Indeed, the voice of silence is what imparts depth to the deep silence.

The Talmudic sage Rabbi Isaac asks, "What should be a man's pursuit in this world?" And he answers, "He should be silent" (*Hullin* 89a). Why? So that he may attend more carefully to the voice of a thin silence. For listening more carefully to the voice in the silence may enable us to hear more clearly the human outcry all around us.

The motif of silence follows Elijah all the way to his last moment on earth, when he was taken into the heavens in a chariot of fire as he was walking with his disciple Elisha (2 Kings 2:11). When Elisha saw his teacher ascend in "a whirlwind of flames," writes Wiesel, "a cry, profound as painful, left his lips, a cry that was to shake the universe to its foundations: 'Father, father, chariots of Israel, and the horsemen thereof!' [2 Kings 2:12]. But no answer was to be heard. No echo. Nothing."[39] As we saw in the case of Pharaoh's daughter Batya, Elijah was not the only one to enter the upper realms without undergoing the ordeal of death. Wiesel reminds us, however, that unlike the others, Elijah returned "among his fellowmen throughout the centuries, so as to remind them of their rights to hope and memory—and to offer men not fascination with death but a taste of immortality,"[40] so great is his love for humanity.

Still, Wiesel suggests that the prophet's love for humanity was not always so great. He came to love humanity so much only when he was taken up to the heavens in a whirlwind of fire. Wiesel notes, for example, that Elijah brought a drought upon the land for the sins of the Israelite aristocracy (1 Kings 17:1). But what about the people? Wiesel asks. What about the children? God had to reign him in and demanded to know why the prophet was so harsh with His children. "God was angry at Elijah," says Wiesel, "for having obeyed Him too well. And so it was time for him to leave and ascend to heaven. Only to return after having been cast into a totally different role. The post-biblical or post-ascension Elijah has undergone an astonishing metamorphosis. Talmudic legend now represents him as the friend and companion to all those who lack friendship, comfort, and hope."[41] True to his Hasidic legacy and the love that defines it, Wiesel leads us to realize that precisely Elijah's ascent into the uppermost realms in a chariot of fire led his soul to burn with a love for humanity, a love so great that he continuously returns to this realm—anonymously.

"Whenever a stranger appears," Wiesel explains, "he takes on the identity of Elijah. At first Elijah is unknown, then the unknown becomes Elijah. A stranger utters a true word, performs a true deed: it must be Elijah. The best proof is that he disappears as soon as his work is completed."[42] And, Wiesel adds, his disguises are many: he might be an Arab, a Persian, a Roman, a horseman, a soldier, even a prostitute, a disguise he assumed when he saved Rabbi Meir from being captured by the Romans (*Avodah Zarah* 18b).[43] An Arab? A soldier? Indeed, a prostitute? Why so many unlikely disguises? It is because the prophet is looking to see how we treat such individuals, those who are often subjected to our scorn and derision when we become blind to their humanity and therefore to our own. To be sure, Elijah specializes in the unlikely. The Talmud, for example, relates the story of Rabbi Beroka Hozaah, who one day was strolling through a market with the prophet. The sage paused and asked him if he saw anyone there who would have a share in the World to Come. Elijah looked around and said nothing, when suddenly he spotted a jailer, saying, "That one." Rabbi Beroka Hozaah was incredulous. "A jailer!? But how?" Whereupon Elijah explained that this jailer stays awake all night to be sure that the men and women in the jail remain separate. Elijah also identified two jesters who would have a share in the world to come. Again Rabbi Beroka Hozaah was surprised. Again Elijah explained: they promote gaiety, enable people to forget their grudges against one another, bring them beer, make them laugh, and in the end make peace (*Taanit* 22a).

The prophet Elijah, who heralds the Redemption of humanity, sometimes intervenes for the sake of humanity even before the time of the Redemption. Wiesel relates a tradition in this connection: when Haman plotted to exterminate the Jews of Persia, the angels, and the Torah, dressed like a widow, stood weeping before God and cried out, "If Israel is destroyed, of what use are we?" Says Wiesel: "When the sun and the moon heard the weeping, they withheld their light and Elijah hastened to alert Abraham and Isaac and Jacob and Moses: 'Your children are threatened and you are asleep?'" So Elijah roused the Patriarchs and the Prophet of Prophets to intervene, and the disaster was averted.[44] There are, however, other times when waking the three Patriarchs proved to be a little too risky. The Gemara relates that one day, when it was a New Moon, Elijah was late for his usual appointment in the academy of learning. Said Rabbi Yehuda HaNassi to Elijah: "What is the reason that the Master was delayed?" Elijah answered: "I had to wake up Abraham, wash his hands, and wait for him to pray, and then lay him down again. And similarly, I followed the same procedure for Isaac, and similarly for Jacob in turn." Rabbi Yehuda HaNassi replied: "Let the Master wake them all together." Elijah responded: "If I were to wake all three to pray at the same time, they would generate powerful prayers and bring the Messiah prematurely (*Bava Metzia* 85b). Yes, prematurely: no one knows better than Elijah the importance of the time and the season. Seeing to that synchronicity is his responsibility as the herald of the Messiah.

In the meantime, unable to turn away from human suffering, Elijah continues to turn up, both to resolve *halakhic* disputes and to alleviate human suffering, each of which is tied to the other: *halakhic* disputes are about human suffering. The Talmud presents a number of cases in which, after all the rabbinic debates, it is written that Elijah will have to resolve the question. For example: "Says Rabbi Yose," on the matter of inherited property, "let the whole amount be left with the depositary . . . until the conflict is ultimately resolved by Elijah" (*Bava Metzia*, 4b).

Whereas the *Halakhah* applies to every Jew, Elijah came to the aid of individual Jews. Wiesel notes that he saved Rabbi Nahum of Gamzu from execution at the hands of the Romans (*Taanit* 21a) and Rabbi Kahana when he tried to commit suicide by jumping off a roof (*Kiddushin* 40a).[45] Elijah also cured Rabbi Shimi bar Ashi of a snake bite (*Shabbat* 109b) and Rabbi Yehuda HaNassi of severe toothaches (Ginzberg, *Legends of the Jews*, 4:7:34).[46] The greatest sign of Elijah's love for humanity can be found in an interlude from the Talmud that Wiesel relates. There was a debate between Rabbi Eliezer and the other sages concerning the *kashrut* of an oven. In order to justify his position, Rabbi Eliezer invoked one miracle after another, all of which came to pass. Despite the miracles, despite a Voice from heaven declaring Rabbi Eliezer to be right, the sages nonetheless prevailed, declaring that the Torah is not in heaven. Later Rabbi Nathan asked Elijah what God was doing during the debate. "Elijah smiled and replied: 'God listened, and laughed and laughed, saying: *Nitzhuni banai*—"My children have defeated Me'" (*Bava Metzia* 59b). Wiesel adds: "As for myself, I would prefer to change the punctuation: *Nitzhuni, banai*. 'Please, children, defeat Me!'' "[47] This is as quintessentially Hasidic as it is quintessentially Jewish. Why would God beg the Jews to defeat Him? Because not only does the Redemption of humanity depend upon it, but so does the redemption of God Himself: unless humanity defeats God, God cannot be God!

Knowing this, says Wiesel, Elijah knows when the Redemption will come; more importantly, he knows the meaning of human suffering, the meaning that eludes all understanding. I would, however, add one more thing: our response to human suffering should rest not upon knowing but precisely upon *not* knowing the meaning of that suffering: I must help even if I know or understand nothing—even and *especially* if I do not know *why*. I think this question may underlie one more question that Elie Wiesel raises: "What does God do while we go on hoping or losing hope in Him, because of Him?"[48] Elijah knows but he does not tell. Nor should he tell: his not telling is the ground of our seeking, our testimony. So where does that leave us? It leaves us with attending to human suffering, no matter how long the Messiah may tarry, no matter what is hidden or revealed.

Therefore, as Wiesel points out, Elijah visits all Jewish homes at Passover, not only to sit at the table but also to see if we invite the hungry to come to our table.[49] He also attends all circumcisions (*Pirke de Rabbi Eliezer* 29), both to heal the infant and to cry out to the Holy One: "Behold! See how your children long for You and seek Your embrace, as they honor the Covenant of Torah!" They honor You by inviting the hungry to the table that takes the place of the altar, as it is written: since the destruction of the Temple, the table in our home where we invite a guest to share our bread takes the place of the altar, the most sacred space on earth, the place where heaven and earth meet (see *Hagigah* 27a). It is the site of the redemption that Elijah will herald.

Portrait of Isaiah

Commenting on his approach to the Book of the Isaiah, Wiesel relates that he took his approach from Rav Mordecai Shushani,[50] the mysterious teacher of various notable figures, including Emmanuel Levinas:

> The exegetical method applied to the Book of Isaiah I learned from a master who influenced my attitudes toward learning. His name was Harav Shushani, and his pedagogical powers cannot be exaggerated. He figures in many of my tales and memories. His legend was shrouded in a dense and fascinating mystery. No one knew where he came from or where he disappeared for days or weeks at a time. He was fluent in many languages and cultures. The Babylonian and Palestinian Talmud as well as Greek and Roman philosophers, Ugaritic and Akkadian texts, Homer and Shakespeare, Erasmus and Einstein: he spoke with passion about nuclear physics, Aztec history, and any other subject in the encyclopedia. It was with Shushani that I studied [the Book of Isaiah] in France after the war. The first chapter took us several months. The first verse . . . over a week.[51]

In keeping with this exegetical approach, Wiesel attends to the Book of Isaiah line by line, word by word. His care with words as a writer shows in his care for words as a reader. For Wiesel, it is not a question of how far we get in the text; what concerns us, rather, is how deep we go—or how high we ascend.

Addressing some of the distinguishing features of this prophet, Wiesel recalls the moment when an angel put a live coal on Isaiah's lips to purify them for the words they would pronounce. When God then asked, "Whom shall I send," Isaiah answered with his seared lips, "Here I am, send me!" (Isaiah 6:6–8). Says Wiesel, "Unlike his colleagues, Isaiah volunteered."[52] But there is more:

> Three terms are generally used to designate a prophetic mes-
> sage: *massa*, or verbal communication, *dvar* or divine word,
> and *hazon*. According to some Talmudic scholars, only Moses
> heard God while fully awake [see, for example, *Sefer HaIkkarim*
> 3:10]. The other prophets received His words in a dream or
> in a trance. In Isaiah's case the term *hazon* hints that he 'saw'
> the message. What did he see? The words? The reality they
> conjured? The deplorable state of the nation? Surely this injunc-
> tion implies a somewhat literal account of moral decadence in
> the culture of Judah. But later on the vision shifts, invoking
> celestial imagery not unlike Ezekiel's.[53]

Isaiah confronted four kings of Judah: Uzziah, Jotham, Ahaz, and Heze-kiah,[54] but his first vision did not come until 740 BCE, during the reign of Ahaz.[55] In that vision, according to the Talmudic sage Rava, "Every-thing Ezekiel saw, Isaiah saw" (*Hagigah* 13b). But what can it mean to see the words? Is it something akin to the moment when, according to the Midrash (*Shemot Rabbah* 5:9), the Israelites gathered at Mount Sinai saw the Voice? Of course, word and image are bound to one another: Isaiah not only beholds the images—he *reads* them and *hears* them crying out, "Holy! Holy! Holy! is the Lord of hosts, and all the earth is filled with His glory!" (Isaiah 6:3). The vision of the Most High opens his eyes to the glory, to the Presence, that fills all the earth. The glory inheres in this interweaving of *davar* and *hazon*, of divine word and the vision of the divine that eludes all portrayal and every theme.

The vision of the prophet is not a vision of the future. Rather, it is a vision of what makes a future possible, a vision of an immemorial past, of what is, always was, and always will be *already* present, like the Holy One who, Jacob realized upon waking from his dream, was there all along (Genesis 28:16). The portrait of the prophet is a portrait of what does not appear and what cannot be circumscribed by a theme: that is precisely why it summons us from our hiding place to put to us the question put to Adam: where are you? (Genesis 3:9). There lies the glory revealed from on high to fill the earth. That is why to come before the portrait is to step before the countenance, where the ego is shaken as the prophet announces our humanity.

Here we discover why the prophet is hated. The prophet is hated for the same reason that the Jew is hated, as it was expressed in Brian Percival's film *The Book Thief* (2013), based on the novel by Markus Zusak.[56] In the film, when a Jew is asked, "Why do they hate the Jews?" he answers, "Because we remind them of their humanity." Which is to say: like the prophet, the Jews remind them—remind all of us—of the absolute demand of meaning, which emanates from an immemorial origin, from an eternal beginning. Why would you want to kill someone for reminding you, be it prophet or Jew? Because the demand of meaning lies in an infinite responsibility, which requires an infinite vulnerability—that is the glory that fills the earth. "Moses first invokes the earth," Wiesel reminds us, "and then the heavens; with Isaiah it is the reverse. Why this disparity? The answer is simple. Moses was standing *above* his people when he spoke of their faults and duties; so he looked at the ground below first. But Isaiah stood *among* the people when he was conveying the divine word; so he looked up at the sky."[57] This upward glance announces the dimension of height that defines prophecy, which in turn enables the vision of His glory that fills all the earth. How does the glory of God fill all the earth? Through the love of one human being for another. Through one human being's saying of "Here I am" to another, just as Isaiah cried out, "Here I am," to the Holy One.

This is why "in the Talmud our sages are pleased with him," Wiesel observes. "He was born circumcised and lived a hundred and twenty years. Other prophets speak only of their own people, whereas Isaiah, in his vision, addresses the whole of humanity. . . . None of My children loved them so much as Isaiah, says God. Furthermore, according to the sages, none of the prophets understood what they were prophesying; they spoke the words in a kind of altered state, except for Moses and Isaiah."[58] We have seen how, each in his own way, Moses and Isaiah kept their feet firmly in contact with the earth, which is filled with the glory of the Holy

One, inasmuch as it is filled with loving kindness. Therefore Isaiah brings consolation with condemnation: "He who punishes through love ends by consoling through love," writes Wiesel. "He who predicts persecutions and oppression cannot fail to promise deliverance and redemption."[59] The Servant may be suffering (Isaiah 52:13–53:12), but the Servant remains a servant to God and therefore in a relationship with God. His suffering, moreover, is neither useless nor in vain: no, it is for the sake of the elevation of all of creation and for the sake of the promise of deliverance and redemption, not only for the Jews—who are the Suffering Servant (see *Pirke de Rabbi Eliezer* 10)—but for all humanity.

Says Wiesel, "Now we understand why, in Talmudic literature, it is the same Isaiah who accomplished a dazzling metamorphosis in the book bearing his name. There he is the eloquent consoler, unequaled as a bearer of promise."[60] The metamorphosis that Wiesel refers to is ascribed largely to the major shift in style from the so-called Isaiah One to Isaiah Two, where "biblical criticism," which renounces the categories of revelation and prophecy, argues for the existence of more than one Isaiah, if not multiple Isaiahs. However, writes Wiesel, "as Isaiah is only repeating God's words, why not admit that God was perfectly capable of changing style between chapter 1 and chapter 40?"[61] The problem, of course, is that one would have to acknowledge the reality of God and the prophet who reminds us of our humanity, which would mean having to come out of our hiding place and step before a reckoning. And that must be prevented at all costs—not for the sake of humanity but for the sake of the false god of the ego that would reign over humanity. It is because there are *not* "two Isaiahs" that there can be a transformation of condemnation into consolation, of rebuke into redemption. Wiesel says that "God commanded His messengers to criticize, to judge, to condemn; when they did, He lost His temper."[62] If He lost His temper, it was when the prophet lost sight of the consolation to be sought in redemption. What makes the exile from the land an *exile* is the promise of the return to the land: if the land were never the Land of the Promise, then the exile would not be the Exile—it would be merely a relocation.

Thus the prophet of consolation reveals the *galui*, the "revelation," in the *galut*, in the "exile." The exile of the Jewish people is the exile of the One in whose image and likeness the soul is created; it is the exile of Torah. And yet the Holy One is manifest in the Jewish people's infinite longing for holiness from the depths of the reeling unreality of exile. Which means: even in exile, even in *galut*, there is revelation, *galui*. Or better:

only in exile is there revelation. For only in exile is revelation needful for redemption—hence the teaching we have from Yaakov Yosef of Polnoe, a disciple of the Baal Shem Tov: the key to redemption (*geulah*) lies in exile (*galut*) (*Toledot Yaakov Yosef, Hukat* 15). Only a soul that has lost its way can make the movement of return, of *teshuvah*, to the Holy Land of the Covenant.

While the prophet brought consolation to the People of Israel, he was not so comforting to King Hezekiah when the monarch fell ill. The Midrash notes that God told Isaiah to go to Hezekiah and tell him to "put his house in order" (Isaiah 38:1). Said the King to the Prophet, "It is usual when a person visits an invalid to say to him, 'May mercy be shown you from Heaven. . . .' Even when he sees him near death he does not say to him, 'Set thy house in order. . . . I pay no attention to what you say, nor will I listen to your advice'" (*Kohelet Rabbah* 6:1). Wiesel reads this as a condemnation of Isaiah for going to King Hezekiah and telling him that he is condemned to die in this world and in the next.[63] Why so harsh toward the king? Because our leaders—kings, rabbis, and teachers—must be held to a far higher standard than the rest of us. And yet Isaiah's merciless confrontation with King Hezekiah might well extend to the rest of the Jews, who, after all, were chosen to be a nation of priests (Exodus 19:6).

Isaiah's determination to summon those who were in the highest stations of society to a reckoning might well be couched in his own sense of accountability. Indeed, Isaiah is known as the "Prince of Prophets" because he was the nephew of King Amaziah of Judah (*Megillah* 10b, 15a). So the prophet who accosted and accused the king for failing to live up to a higher standard is from the same bloodline. Here, in Isaiah's social and political "connections," we find the higher standard to which Isaiah himself was held. Once again, Wiesel brings the Talmud into play. "According to legend," he writes, "King Ezekias [Hezekiah] eventually married the prophet's daughter. One of their sons was Manasseh. The son, crowned king while still a boy (twelve years old), began to persecute the prophet [*Talmud Bavli, Berakhot* 10a]."[64] He goes on to invoke another Talmudic tradition: "Shimon ben Azzai found, in a genealogical scroll in Jerusalem, a passage saying Manasseh killed Isaiah. Rava commented that he accused him, judged him, and had him executed. In other words, everything unfolded according to the Law [*Yevamot* 49b]."[65] What a horrific end for the prophet: to be killed by his grandson! Did the young king fear the admonitions of the prophet? Or was it something simpler, something even more terrifying?

The explanation, Wiesel suggests, may lie in the king's name: "Manasseh's name itself derives from the verb *nasha*, which means 'he has forgotten.' "[66] If, in the words of the Baal Shem, "oblivion is at the root of exile the way memory is at the root of redemption,"[67] it is because the exile that stems from the loss of memory comes with the murder of the father—or, worse, with the murder of the grandfather. In any case, as we saw in the story of Cain, murder brings exile, and exile is the realm of murder.

Portrait of Jeremiah

Elie Wiesel's Hasidic legacy is one of storytelling, which provides us with an entry into his portrait of Jeremiah. In chapter 36 of the Book of Jeremiah we are told that God summoned the prophet to take the "scroll of a book, and write therein all the words that I have spoken unto thee" (36:2), whereupon Jeremiah dictated the book to Baruch, who then took the book and read it in the Temple (36:10–18). When King Jehoiakim heard the words of the book, he cut it into pieces and burned it (36:23), whereupon God commanded Jeremiah to write another book, the same book, but this time he must include the episode of the burning of the first book (36:28).

"Any other writer would have lost his mind," Wiesel asserts. "Not Jeremiah. He simply began writing the book all over again—adding the story of the destruction of the first version. And therein lies Jeremiah's ultimate lesson for all tellers of tales: to rewrite is more difficult and more important than to write; to transmit is more vital than to invent."[68] As we have seen, for the Jewish writer—for the Hasidic storyteller Elie Wiesel—what is needful is not to begin but to begin again. Not only is it given to us to begin again—it is commanded. And so Wiesel enjoins us: "We are beginning and beginning, again and again . . . ,"[69] with the ellipses, without a period. Beginning what? Beginning yet again the task of engaging in a testimony that defies death and sides with the living: for Elie Wiesel, as for Jeremiah, to write is to write as a witness. When Jeremiah began again, his soul hovered over the face of the deep. For the prophet, as for the storyteller, to write is to alter the face of creation itself. Just as words brought heaven and earth into being, so too can words alter the being of heaven and earth—for good or for evil. Could this be why Jeremiah cursed the day he was born (Jeremiah 20:14)? Because he understood what was at stake in the words he uttered and wrote?

"Jeremiah is reluctant," Wiesel points out. "God must use force. Without waiting for the boy's decision, 'the Lord put out His hand and touched my mouth, and the Lord said unto me: Herewith I put My words into thy mouth' [Jeremiah 1:9]. That is the end of Jeremiah's personal life, the beginning of, the initiation into, his prophetic mission."[70] Abraham Joshua Heschel once said that the prophet's ear can hear "the silent sigh."[71] Is that why he could hear the silent sigh? Because God's word was on his lips? And whose silent sigh does the prophet hear? Is it the sigh of God? Or the sigh of a child? Perhaps it is the sigh of truth.

As one writer—one storyteller—engaging another, Wiesel notices that the trepidation that Jeremiah experienced over his concern for the integrity of the word was tied to his concern for the integrity of truth: "Jeremiah's contradictions, his constant search for himself in a society which turned away not only from him but from itself, his determined quest for truth in times of falsehood (the very word 'falsehood' appears seventy-two times in biblical literature, half of them in the Book of Jeremiah), his doubts, his tears, his yearning for meaning and silence: few personalities possess his richness and even fewer his tragic depth."[72] This is extraordinary: half of the biblical references to falsehood appear in the Book of Jeremiah alone. Truth is not a datum. Truth is what draws one human being closer to another, which is how each is drawn closer to the Holy One. As the Talmud teaches, truth is what opens the door to the Shekhinah to dwell in the Land of Israel (*Sanhedrin* 7a). In the Talmud it is further written: "Rabban Simeon ben Gamaliel used to say: By three things the world endures: justice, truth and peace. Rabbi Muna said: The three are one, because if justice is done, truth has been effected and peace brought about" (*Derekh Eretz Rabbah*, 59a). Peace: *shalom*. *Shalom*: *shalem*: wholeness. Truth lies within the wholeness of human-to-human and human-to-divine relationship. There lies the agony of Jeremiah's outrage and outcry against falsehood: falsehood undermines the relationship without which nothing is true and everything is permitted, without which God is not divine and the human being is not human.

But the horror extends even further: "Of all the prophets," Wiesel relates, "he alone predicted the catastrophe, experienced it, and lived to tell the tale. He alone sounded the alarm before the fire, and after being singed by its flames went on to retell it to anyone who would listen."[73] Why go on telling it? Because, as history as shown, whatever befalls humanity befalls the Jewish first, as Wiesel has insightfully said: "Whoever kills Jews will end up killing himself and his own God."[74] That is why the Midrash relates that Jeremiah will be a prophet of the doom of other nations, with compassion for other nations (see Arama, *Akeidat Yitzchak* 82:1): Jeremiah realizes that "Israel's destiny affects everyone else's. What happens to Judah will eventually happen to Babylon, then Rome, and ultimately, to the entire world."[75] But, says Wiesel, God deceived him: there was no compassion for the other nations. When Jeremiah asks God about the deception, God answers, " 'Too late to turn the clock back; once you acquire prophetic powers, you cannot divest yourself of them.' Poor Jeremiah: opposed by the mighty, hated by the masses, even deceived by God."[76] Here we discover that, far more than a vision of the future, the prophet conveys a memory of the past: like Elie Wiesel.

The prophet's thankless task is to force the people "to remember: the covenant, the Law, the promise of the beginning, the moral thrust of Israel's adventure. To forget means to deny the relevance of the past. To forget the beginning means to justify the end—the end of Israel. Thus Jeremiah's magnificently rendered prophetic discourse is contrapuntal in structure and concept: set in the present, it reaches out simultaneously to the distant past and unattainable future and makes one dependent on the other."[77] If, as we have seen, "memory is at the root of redemption,"[78] what is at the root of memory? Storytelling, relating a tale, without which there is no human relation. Thus, says Wiesel of Jeremiah, "though alone he defines himself in relation to his fellowmen, who reject him. Though shattered, he does not try to escape the present and seek refuge in the future; he works with the present, on the present."[79] Could that be the destiny of the storyteller? When the present became a time of exile, Jeremiah worked with the exile; the first prophet to survive the catastrophe that he predicted, he was the first prophet to follow the Jews into exile.

Wiesel recalls the Midrash that relates a vision that Jeremiah had of a woman in mourning. "Who will console me?" the woman cried out. And Jeremiah answered her: "If you are a woman, talk to me; if you are a ghost, leave me." She replied, "I am your mother, your mother Zion [see *Pesikta Rabbati* 26:1]."[80] Thus Jeremiah came to the agonizing realization that the one in exile is also an orphan. Indeed, the Book of Lamentations describes the Holy City as a *nidah* or a "wanderer" (1:8): Jerusalem herself is in exile. Jerusalem herself is an orphan. And, tellingly, the vast majority of the survivors of the Shoah were orphans. Inasmuch as we have lost a sense of purpose and direction in our post-Holocaust morass—inasmuch as we are flooded with a sense of emptiness and aimlessness—we are all orphaned. Having lost a relation to our fathers, we have lost the ability to be fathers: we have lost the capacity for the fatherly care and the protection of other human beings. We have lost God. And so we understand why one of the names of God is *Avi Yetomim*, the "Father of the Fatherless" (Psalms 68:6).

In the Midrash it is written: "Rabbi Judah said: Come and see how beloved are the children by the Holy One, blessed be He. The Sanhedrin were exiled but the *Shekhinah* did not go into exile with them. When, however, the children were exiled, the *Shekhinah* went into exile with them" (*Eykhah Rabbah* 1:6:33). Without her children, the Holy City was no longer holy, laid waste and bereft, like Rachel, whom Jeremiah invokes, crying out, "A voice is heard in Ramah, lamentation, and bitter weeping, Rachel weeping for her children; she refuses to be comforted for her children, because they are no more" (Jeremiah 31:14). If, as Wiesel notes, "few prophets have spoken with such anguish and forcefulness against heavenly injustice—or heavenly justice, which is worse,"[81] it is because Jeremiah was especially drawn to the children. The Midrash, says Wiesel, describes him in exile "seeking out children, embracing and kissing them. When he finds a group of tormented young men, he joins them and wants to share their pain. When a number of Jews are about to be hanged, he tries to hang himself [see Ginzberg, *Legends of the Jews*, 4:10:35]."[82] He even has the temerity to declare to the exiled king Zedekiah—who lived to see his two sons murdered and then had his eyes torn out of their sockets (Jeremiah 52:10–11)—that he must do something to make exile meaningful. "Nothing is worse than suffering . . . except meaningless suffering. And meaning has to be found in the suffering itself."[83] Meaning found in suffering? I am not so sure that this sounds like Jeremiah. Nor am I so sure that it sounds like Elie Wiesel.

Is Jeremiah suggesting to the King that he should find meaning in the destruction of the Holy City, the exile of the children, and the murder of his own children? One can well imagine Zedekiah wanting to be blinded and wanting to see nothing more of this world after witnessing the murder of his sons. But how does he get to *meaningful* suffering? It is not suffering but *useless* suffering that drains life of its meaning: suffering without anything to suffer for and suffering that is nothing but suffering. It is simply there, and that is all. It is the suffering that the human being can make no sense of because it is the suffering born of the erasure of all sense from life. It has no cause, no purpose, no explanation. It cannot be situated in the world because it ensues upon the destruction of the world. Wiesel understands the problem all too well: "Obstinate, unyielding, merciless, He does what He wants. But what about pity, grace, compassion for innocent children? He weeps later? We can do without His tears."[84] Even if we can do without His tears, however, we cannot do without our own tears shed for the sake of others. And this is where Wiesel takes Jeremiah to task.

The Midrash, he notes, shows Jeremiah leaving Babylon, with the exiled pleading with him not to abandon them. But their plea falls on deaf ears: the prophet leaves behind the Jews whose exile he had foretold and cried out against (Ginzberg, *Legends of the Jews*, 4:10:41–42). "Jeremiah," Wiesel insists, "should go to Babylon and stay there; he should choose exile and suffer with those who, under hostile skies, along the shores of foreign rivers filled with Jewish blood, are marching with heavy hearts and bowed heads toward the unknown."[85] If the ones forced into exile—the ones whose children were sent into exile, who saw the Shekhinah sent into exile, who saw the Holy City bereft of its holiness, who wept for their children and would not be comforted because their children were no more—are to raise their heads, it can only be in outrage. And if Jeremiah should have stayed with them, it would be to voice their outrage to God, as he had voiced God's outrage to them: "The enemy Nebuchadnezzar, the invader, the destroyer of Jerusalem, is God's servant? Is this conceivable? If so, how can one resist anger or madness?"[86] Anger and madness haunt Jeremiah, just as they haunt Elie Wiesel's Hasidic legacy. He once told me that he still prays, but he prays, as a Hasid, with anger—with a certain anger called *barukh* or "blessed." This is where he feels a kinship to the prophet Jeremiah. This is where, in his portrait of the prophet, one may find traces of a self-portrait.

Jeremiah, Wiesel writes, "reminds us of the ghetto-survivor who returned from Ponar and Treblinka to warn his friends, but who was unable to make them pay attention. Solitude: No solitude is greater than that of the messenger who is unable to transmit the message. No one is as alone as the prophet whom God chooses to isolate from those he is sent to warn and save. No one is as alone as the man who must speak and is not heard."[87] This is not the man who is simply lonely, which is bad enough. This is the man who is in a relationship with the Holy One, who in turn has summoned him to move into a testimonial relation with the human one, and who is nonetheless refused. That is where the isolation of Auschwitz finds some point of contact with the isolation of prophecy and of exile that Wiesel sees in Jeremiah.

"Listen to Jeremiah," Wiesel summons us,

"I look at the skies and their light is gone. I look at the mountains and they are quaking. I look: no man is left and all the birds of the sky have left [Jeremiah 4:24–25]." Quaking mountains? What did Jeremiah mean to convey? I never understood the meaning of these words until I visited Babi Yar. Eyewitnesses had told me that, in September 1941, when the German invaders massacred some 80,000 Jews—between Rosh Hashanah and Yom Kippur—and buried them in the ravine, near the center of Kiev, the ground was shaking for weeks on end. The mountain of corpses made the earth quake. . . . And I understood Jeremiah. As for the birds of the sky that have fled, I understood the prophet's imagery only when I returned to Auschwitz and Birkenau in the summer of 1979. Then and only then did I remember that, during the tempest of fire and silence, there were no birds to be seen on the horizon: they had fled the skies above all the death-camps. I stood in Birkenau and remembered Jeremiah[88]

At his trial in Jerusalem Adolf Eichmann testified that he saw a "spurting geyser of blood" shooting into the heavens from a mass grave.[89] In those days of destruction, in that destruction of days, the earth moved not with the stirring of life but in the throes of death—indeed, the throes of the death of death. Donna Rubinstein recollects the mass graves at Krasnostav: "They covered up the graves but the soil heaved."[90] And, as though in a state of delirium, Judith Dribben writes, "They bury them half-alive . . . or half-dead . . . and the soil was moving . . . the soil was moving . . . they bury them half-alive . . . and the soil was moving."[91] What these witnesses beheld, Wiesel remembered in his portrait of the prophet Jeremiah. And he summons us to remember more than what happened. He summons us to remember this: while the prophets are those who can read the bird signs, when there are no birds, that, too, is a sign.

Portrait of Ezekiel

Like Jeremiah, Ezekiel was a prophet not only to the Jewish people but also to the nations. Like Jeremiah, he knew that what happens to humanity happens first to the Jews. Thus, Wiesel points out, Ezekiel "foretold the doom of Tyre and Egypt. That was his way of emphasizing again and again that suffering is contagious—as is evil itself."[92] Unlike Jeremiah, however, Ezekiel gave voice to his prophecy—to his visions—from outside the Land of the Covenant, alongside the River Kvar (Ezekiel 1:1; see also *Zohar* I, 6b). It is worth noting that *kvar* means "already." His prophecy unfolds in the midst of what is always already there, which is the responsibility that devolves upon the human being, the responsibility that is *already* at the core of our humanity, prior to any move or decisions we make—the *already* is what makes our every move, our every decision, *matter*. If Ezekiel's vision is a vision not only of the Creation but of the *meaning* of the Creation, it is a vision of the eternally *already*. Revelation is the revelation of the *already*. Without this *already*, there is no truth. This is the meaning of Ezekiel's vision along the River Kvar: beholding the secret of primordial creation, he beholds the secret of immemorial revelation. *Already* we are forbidden to murder; *already* we are commanded to have no other gods; *already* we are commanded to love the neighbor and the stranger. "Goodness," in the words of Levinas, "is always older than choice; the Good has always *already* chosen and required the unique one."[93] At the core of the prophecy beheld and pronounced on the banks of the River Kvar is the Good that has *already* chosen the prophet.

And so prophecy proceeds from exile to exile. In the case of Ezekiel, who speaks from the depths of exile, prophecy proceeds from danger to danger. To delve into the mysteries of the Creation (*Maaseh Bereshit*) and the mysteries of the Chariot (*Maaseh Merkavah*)—the two portions of Scripture (Genesis and Ezekiel) upon which the Kabbalah is based— is to risk death, insanity, or apostasy. Here Wiesel recalls the Talmudic teaching that says one is forbidden to discuss sexual relations with three students, the *Maaseh Bereshit* with two, and the *Maaseh Merkavah* with one (*Hagigah* 11b). "*Merkava* experiences are forbidden territory," he explains, "dangerous to outsiders. One cannot approach them with impunity."[94] Wiesel goes on to ask: why should the mystery of Creation be considered less perilous than that of the chariot? In reply he notes a comment from Maimonides: "The first is about Creation, the second about its Creator. Creation is immanent and therefore perceivable—the Creator is not."[95] In other words, the vision of the Chariot in chapter 1 of the Book of Ezekiel borders on a vision of the Holy One Himself. Maimonides knew very well the tale from the Talmud that Wiesel invokes. It is the tale of a child who opened the Book of Ezekiel and was reading the first chapter when "a fire came out of the fire and burnt the child down" (*Hagigah* 13a).[96] So the sages sought to suppress the Book. Of course, when he writes these words, Wiesel is mindful of other flames that consumed other children.

We recall the midrashic teaching that the Torah is made of black fire on white fire (*Tanhuma Bereshit* 1; *Devarim Rabbah* 3:12; *Shir HaShirim Rabbah* 5:11:6; *Zohar* II, 226b); we also recall that, according to Rabbi Chayim ben Attar, fire forms "the basis of the soul" (*Or HaChayim* on Genesis 23:2). But this fire that comes out of the fire runs even deeper than the fire of the soul or the fire of the Torah. According to the Talmud, Wiesel notes, whenever Rabbi Yohanan ben Zakkai and his disciples studied Ezekiel's vision of the Chariot, they were surrounded by fire (*Hagigah* 14b). "Was it there to shield them or to isolate them from reality? To protect them from the Fire of Sinai or to remind them of it? Perhaps it was there to bring them closer to the fire that consumed the sanctuary in their time—and other living sanctuaries in later generations—or perhaps to teach them the dangers inherent in language, or to teach them that some words have the ability to burn and burn."[97] The fire of Ezekiel's vision is the fire of the light summoned into being with the utterance of "let there be light." It is a light and a fire that precedes the creation of the luminaries of the heavens, the creation of any light or fire that can be seen or felt. It is the light and the fire of the silent Word, the light and the fire of the ineffable and the invisible, and the fire of the letter *alef* that precedes the letter *beit*. It is the light and the fire of the *hashmal* (Ezekiel 1:4).

"No other light," writes Wiesel, "was so forceful in tearing darkness apart. But then, no one had ever seen such darkness. . . . Ezekiel: Who has not heard of this intriguing and passionate speaker whose visions of horror and beauty have left an impact on innumerable generations? No messenger has hurt us more—none has offered us such balm."[98] Says Abraham Joshua Heschel, "The words of the prophet are stern, sour, stinging. But behind his austerity is love and compassion for mankind. Ezekiel sets forth what all other prophets imply: 'Have I any pleasure in the death of the wicked, says the Lord God, and not rather that he should turn from his way and live?'" (Ezekiel 18:23).[99] Wiesel underscores this teaching from Heschel, whom he counted among his teachers: "In the Jewish tradition, one may not rejoice over an enemy's downfall. The enemy's punishment offers no consolation to the victim."[100] What is critical in Wiesel's Hasidic portrait of Ezekiel is this: the profoundly dangerous details of the prophet's vision are rooted in the prophet's profoundly urgent call for compassion.

And the *hashmal*, this mysterious fire and light? It is often translated as the "electrum," that Ezekiel saw amidst clouds of flame. In modern Hebrew *hashmal* translates as "electricity"; some biblical scholars maintain that it is a brightly polished metal. On a deeper level, however, the sages of the Talmud teach that the word *hashmal* is made of the words *hash*—from *hashai*, meaning "silent"—and *mal*, which means to "speak" (*Hagigah* 13b). Where Elijah heard the "thin Voice of silence" (1 Kings 19:12), Ezekiel "saw" the silence of the Voice, the word that "speaks" silently in the fire and the light: he saw what surpasses, what is prior to, all utterance and therefore all meaning. He saw a "speaking silence" couched in the divine utterance, manifest in the shift from the silence of the *alef* to the eloquence of the *beit*.

The Torah does not begin with *alef*, the first letter of the alphabet; rather, it begins with *beit*, the second letter. But the *beit* is the first letter that has a sound: unless marked with vowel points, the *alef* is silent. It is the silence from which the first sound, the first divine utterance of "let there be light," emerges. Hence the *hashmal*, the "speaking silence," of Ezekiel's vision represents the move from the eloquent silence that preceded creation to the divine utterance that at every instant brings creation into being. Beholding the link between silence and utterance that lies at the heart of creation, Ezekiel beholds the word that brings the world into being and confers meaning upon it—silently. As the Hasidic master Levi-Yitzhak of Berditchev has taught, when God gave Moses the Torah, He gave not only the words but also the silence between and around the words.[101] In his vision of the Chariot, Ezekiel peers into the silence between the words, the silence that precedes the words, the silence that hovers over the face of the deep—there lies the danger of this fire and this light.

Wiesel points out that Ezekiel was the first of the prophets to speak of *Kiddush HaShem*, dying for the Sanctification of the Holy Name, for the sake of the teaching and testimony of Torah, without which Creation has no meaning—without which human life has no meaning. Wiesel relates the legend that says when Hananya, Mishael, and Azarya faced *Kiddush HaShem* in Babylon for refusing to worship idols, Daniel sent them to Ezekiel, who urged them to flee rather than be martyred. Ezekiel consulted God, who refused to save them. When Ezekiel burst into tears, God relented and saved them. During their time in the furnace of flames, says the legend, Ezekiel resurrected the dry bones (see Ginzberg, *Legends of the Jews* 4:10:88).[102] Thus, the voice of the prophet Ezekiel and the mystery of the Chariot have sustained the Jewish people throughout the centuries. "Through endless years of turbulent wanderings," says Wiesel, "it is his voice that we follow from agony to agony and then to rebirth."[103] What leads us from one agony to another? It is the trespass not against God but against our fellow human beings, as Wiesel suggests: "As long as people offended heaven, God, in spite of his anger, was willing to wait. But when they ceased to be human toward one another, He had to intervene—and punish them."[104] Note well: *when they ceased to be human*. We lose our humanity in the harm we do to another human being; we become as dead as the dry bones, as God suggests to the prophet: "Son of man, these bones are the whole house of Israel; behold, they say: Our bones are dried up, and our hope is lost; we are clean cut off" (Ezekiel 37:11). And only the God who punishes can, through His Torah, make those dry bones live again.

Between God and humanity stands the prophet Ezekiel. God declares that He will cause breath to be breathed into the bones to return them to life (Ezekiel 37:5), but it is the word of the prophet that summons the breath to breathe into the bones, "that they may live" (Ezekiel 37:9). Says Wiesel, "His fears and hopes, his joys and depressions, his moments of turmoil and his moments of ecstasy: they are not his alone. A prophet must have no ego, no individual memory. If he hears a voice, he must echo it. If he sees visions, he must share them—right? Yes and no. Yes as far as the voices are concerned. . . . But visions—that is something else. God rarely says, Tell them what you see, but rather, Tell them what you hear."[105] The tension between voice and vision is central to an understanding not only of prophecy but also of Jewish teaching and testimony. "The key phrase in the Talmud," Wiesel points out, "is *Ta shema*—Come and listen; in the Zohar, the key phrase is *Ta khazi*—come and see. See what words conceal, see what the mind fails to comprehend, see what man does to silence in whose sharply defined spheres God's presence is felt, glorified, liberated, *Ta shema*—for the oral tradition is language—*Ta khazi*—open your eyes and look, and say not what you see, for you will see it no longer."[106] There lies the challenge to the prophet Ezekiel: "It is the voice that matters: the word—the sound—complete sentences—precise thoughts—ideas—principles—ethical injunctions—memories and more memories." But Ezekiel revealed everything he had *seen*. "*That* was his mistake. . . . He did not understand the importance of silence—the occasional necessity for silence."[107] But I am not so sure.

Wiesel himself points out that when Ezekiel's wife died of plague, for a time he lost his power of speech.[108] In the Talmud Rabbi Yohanan says that a man who has witnessed the death of his wife is as one who witnessed the destruction of the Temple (*Sanhedrin* 22a), that is, as one who has witnessed the unspeakable. Perhaps that is why Wiesel lost his voice when he was writing *A Beggar in Jerusalem*: giving voice to the unspeakable had rendered him mute,[109] as it had happened to Ezekiel—not when he spoke of his visions but when he witnessed the death of his wife.

Portrait of Jonah

In his portrait of the prophet Jonah, who lived in the eighth century BCE, Wiesel underscores two themes. First there is *teshuvah*, the "movement of return," sometimes mistranslated as "repentance," which is *haratah*. Rather different from repentance, *teshuvah*, Wiesel explains, "means an act of consciousness, of awareness, of willingness to take sides and responsibility for the future." The word *teshuvah* means "response": it comes in a movement of answering and reckoning. *Haratah* is regret for the past; *teshuvah* is a return to the future. The second theme in the portrait of Joah is the universality of the Jewish message, which begins with the commandment, "You shall love the stranger as yourself" (Leviticus 19:34), which is the commandment repeated most frequently—thirty-six times—in the Torah. Says Wiesel, "Jonah is not the only prophet who, in the name of God, speaks to other nations; others did so before him. But Jonah is the only one whose mission is to serve other nations exclusively."[110] That is why we read the Book of Jonah as part of the Yom Kippur services. It is the same day, Wiesel observes, that the liturgy relates the story of Nadab and Abihu.[111] What is the connection between the story of Jonah and the tale of Nadab and Abihu? And what does it mean to serve other nations?

In Nadab and Abihu, we have the priests who are possessed of an intensely passionate longing to serve God for the sake of the Jewish people and the Jewish people alone. In Jonah, we have the prophet who tries to turn away from his prophecy to the nations because of his love for the Jewish people alone. Or does he turn from the call to become a light unto the nations precisely out of love for the nations, knowing the severe demand that his message would place upon them? To become a witness to the Holy One, the Creator of heaven and earth, who places upon us an infinite responsibility to and for the other human being, is not an easy path. In fact, it can be a very dangerous path. And yet, to call the nations to a movement of return—*not* to a conversion to Judaism—but to a return, a *teshuvah*, to a relationship of loving kindness toward their neighbors *and their strangers*, cannot but benefit the Jewish people, even God Himself. "Whoever hates Jews," Wiesel writes in his portrait of Jonah, "will end up hating all men."[112] Indeed, history has shown that the nations that fail to respond to the sanctity of the other human being as a *ben adam*, a child of Adam and therefore of God, begin by killing the Jews and go on to murder others. In the portrait of Jonah, therefore, we have a portrait of humanity that runs very deep, a portrait that provides a key to the millennial hatred that has plagued the Jewish people and has threatened the souls of all the nations.

Unlike the missionaries of creed-based religions, Jonah does not go to Nineveh to convert non-Jews to Judaism. No, he goes to draw them into the Jewish condition, a condition of testimony, reminding people of their humanity, which is a movement into a radical vulnerability that comes with an infinite responsibility to and for other human beings. It is a summons to be hated and even murdered for the sake of the truth of the absolute sanctity of other human beings.

Here we come a bit closer to understanding Jonah and his reluctance to undertake his mission to the nations. Again, his resistance may lie in a certain love for them: he does not want to be the one to summon them to this radical vulnerability. And yet, as Wiesel suggests, their very humanity lies in assuming this vulnerability for the sake of the other human being. No one can answer the question put to the first murderer, "Where is your brother?" (Genesis 4:9) without assuming this vulnerability. And no one can answer *innocently*. There lies the difficulty: Who does not want to be innocent, pure, free of responsibility? Could it be the reason for Wiesel's ambivalence? His portrait is, after all, both questioning and affirming. A good portrait leaves room for ambiguity, wondering, and wonder; a good portrait opens the gate to questioning. And no one is better at that than Elie Wiesel.

And so he asks about Jonah, as he is prone to ask: "A man who argues with God not to save men but to punish them—what kind of prophet is that anyway?"[113] Recall that when the people of Nineveh turned away from their evil, "it displeased Jonah exceedingly, and he was angry" (Jonah 4:1). Well, what kind of prophet *is* that? And consider this: "What kind of prophet would prevent people from returning to God's ways? By acting as he does, hasn't the prophet turned anti-prophet?"[114] An antiprophet, it seems, is a prophet who summons a people to a movement of returning to God but does not want them to heed that call. Other evidence that Jonah is the antiprophet: in Nineveh, Jonah "is more disturbed by his success than by his failure. Again he wishes to die. . . . No prophet has ever been gripped by so strong and so recurrent a death wish."[115] So what happened to the Torah's command to choose life (Deuteronomy 30:19)? Is the prophet not there to be a witness to Torah?

Here we have Wiesel's most scathing indictment of Jonah. Jonah's "self-image," he says, "stands between him and this knowledge; his concern is with that image and not with other people's lives and welfare. . . . Does he forget what Moses did—and would do—in similar circumstances? 'Let me die,' Moses said, 'but do not touch one child in Israel!' "[116] Not only is Jonah sick over his success—he is sick unto death, sick with the worst sickness of all, the sickness of egocentrism: "Therefore now, O Lord, take, I beseech Thee, my life from me; for it is better for me to die than to live" (Jonah 4:3). In other words, unlike Moses, who would die for the sake of a nation, Jonah appears to beg for death for the sake of his ego! The egocentric self-image is the sickness. A true prophet has no self-image because a true prophet has no self. Could Jonah be not only an antiprophet but a false prophet? Not according to the tradition.

Whereas the other prophets are singled out to deliver a singular message, Jonah's uniqueness lies, paradoxically, in his being a kind of Everyman, someone who reflects the internal tribulations of the first man. When God put to Adam the first question put to humanity—"Where are you?" (Genesis 3:9)—Adam fled and went into hiding (Genesis 3:10). Just so, Wiesel points out, "Elijah fled from Jezebel, Jeremiah from Jehoiakim, but only Jonah fled from God."[117] In his flight from God, Jonah was even more determined than the other prophets in his response to God: other prophets resist God, Wiesel points out, but "Jonah is different: he is the first—and the only one—to reject his mission not only in words but in deed."[118] Interestingly, with this insight, Wiesel turns from an interrogation and even a condemnation of Jonah to an admiration and affirmation of the prophet. But in order to show both sides of the human being, in his portrait, Wiesel, true to his Hasidism, shows both faces of God: "If He is cruel towards Jonah, it is for his own good; so as to teach him the importance of repentance, to show him the way to humanity rather than to abstract absolutes. He teaches Jonah not how to suffer but how to remain humble in the face of suffering. Justice must be human, truth must be human, compassion must be human. The way to God leads through man, however alien, however sinful he may be."[119] For Wiesel, the path to God is *through the fellow man*—not just through the fellow Jew.

The tradition teaches, Wiesel reminds us, that "we are even asked to believe he was equal to Elijah, who ordained him as a prophet. Midrashic legends describe him as a *Tzaddik gamour*—a true just Man, an absolute Just man, among the few chosen to enter Paradise alive [see Ginzberg, *Legends of the Jews* 4:8:34]."[120] The Zohar, Wiesel notes, says that the prophet Jonah died of fear but was brought back to life, so that he both endured the agony of death and then entered the Garden undergoing it again: thus Jonah lived through his own death—like Moishe the Beadle and Elie Wiesel himself—another unique feature of this prophet.[121] Those who entered Paradise alive merited the distinction through their devotion to the Jewish people. Does Jonah merit his entry into Paradise through his devotion to the non-Jews of Nineveh? At first glance, it would seem not, given his despair over their salvation.

Nevertheless, Wiesel observes, there is evidence of his devotion to others. The Midrash says the sailors were from each of the seventy nations, speaking the seventy languages. "After witnessing Jonah's successful intercession with his God, they throw their idols into the sea, sail back to the Jaffa harbor, go to Jerusalem," where they become learned men (*Midrash Tanhuma, Vayikra* 8; see also *Pirke de Rabbi Eliezer* 10). Indeed, Jonah even "entered the mouth of the whale as one enters a synagogue [Ginzberg, *Legends of the Jews*, 4:8:24],"[122] so devoted was he to the men with whom he pleaded to throw him overboard to quell the threatening storm (Jonah 1:12).

Thus in his Hasidic generosity, Wiesel allows:

> It is as if he told God: "I do not agree with Your way of running Your world. . . ." Jonah shuns Nineveh because of his enormous love for humanity. . . . He knows that when the life of a community is in peril, one may not indulge in philosophy or art. At that moment his anguish is even greater than it was while in the belly of the whale. His own death does not frighten him; the death of others does. Yes, Jonah acts as spokesman for mankind in general. A true prophet, he is faithful to tradition and wishes to serve not only as God's messenger to mankind and Israel, but also as man's and Israel's messenger to God.[123]

To add to Wiesel's Hasidic generosity toward Jonah, recall that, according to the Midrash, the King of Nineveh was none other than the Pharaoh of Egypt, who oppressed the Israelites, chased after them to kill them, and was the sole survivor of the waters that drowned his fellow Egyptians (*Yalkut Shimoni*, Exodus 176): Jonah ultimately went to Nineveh to restore the soul of an enemy of the Jewish people.

Coming to the end of his portrait of Jonah, Wiesel observes that "God makes sure He has the last word, always. But, uniquely, the book ends on a question."[124] What is the question? It is this: "And HaShem said: 'Thou hast had pity on the gourd, for which thou hast not labored, neither made it grow, which came up in a night, and perished in a night;

and should not I have pity on Nineveh, that great city, wherein are more than sixscore thousand persons that cannot discern between their right hand and their left hand, and also much cattle?' " (Jonah 4:10–11). Jonah had appeared to show more concern for the fate of a plant than for the fate of the people of Nineveh. Could it be that he knew what the Rebbe Nahman of Bratzlav would teach centuries later: that "when plants grow to completeness, love enters the world" (*Sefer HaMidot* Love 2:1)? Let us not make the mistake of supposing that God's question is merely rhetorical. If that were the case, it would not be a question at all. It would be an answer, part of a fixed formula and a ready answer, both of which all too often lead to mass murder: starting with the Jews, who precisely unsettle fixed formulas and ready answers.

Portraits from the Writings

We come to the third category of texts comprising the *Tanakh*, the *Khetuvim*, which are the "Writings." The Patriarchs are part of the Revelation of the Divine Word at Mount Sinai. The Prophets are those upon whom the *Ruah HaKodesh*, the "holy spirit," descended in words and visions so that they might declare, "Thus saith the Lord!" And the figures in the Writings? Some of them we have from the hands of the Prophets: according to the Talmud, for example, the Book of Job was written by Moses (*Bava Batra* 15a) and the Book of Ruth by Samuel (*Bava Batra* 14b), while the Men of the Great Assembly, the 120 sages of the Second Temple Period, wrote the Book of Daniel and the Book of Esther (*Bava Batra* 15a). In any case, the Writings were not revealed—they were authored, albeit with reverence and awe.

"To write," says Wiesel, "is to plumb the unfathomable depths of being. Writing lies within the domain of mystery. The space between any two words is vaster than the distance between heaven and earth. To bridge it you must close your eyes and leap. A Hasidic tradition tells us that in the Torah the white spaces, too, are God-given."[1] The domain of mystery is the domain of the transcendent, of the holy, of all that exceeds the categories of speculative thought. It is the domain of good and evil, of light and darkness. It is the domain of meaning, without which no soul can live. To write, therefore, is not only to plumb the unfathomable depths of being but also to ascend to the "otherwise than being" and alter the face of creation itself; if writing lies within the domain of mystery, it is because it lies within the domain of creation and the meaning of creation. Just as words brought heaven and earth into being, so too can words alter the being of heaven and earth, for good or for evil—something that the authors of the Writings understood very well, as did Elie Wiesel.

One more thing that Wiesel has in common with the authors of the Writings: like these ancients, Wiesel turned to the Written Torah, the model for creation itself (*Zohar* I, 134a), in order to come to an understanding of what writing is about. To write, to take up the word, is to return to the word of Torah, the word of truth, teaching, and testimony—that is how you "plumb the unfathomable depths of being." In his Torah-based approach to sounding the depths of being, Wiesel exemplifies a teaching from Emmanuel Levinas: "The meaning of being, the meaning of creation, is to realize the Torah."[2] And the realization of Torah begins and begins again with an extreme care for the word. In a very profound sense, then, both for Wiesel and for the authors of the Writings, the meaning of writing is to realize the Torah.

Portrait of Daniel

Wiesel's portrait of Daniel is a nice point of transition from the Prophets to the Writings. Why, indeed, is Daniel not counted among the prophets? We are told that he was very pious, careful not to "defile himself with the king's food" (Daniel 1:8) and that he "had understanding in all visions and dreams" (Daniel 1:17). So if Daniel "was so wise, so pious," Wiesel wonders, "if he saw more and better than the prophets, if he looked farther than they did, and deeper, why couldn't he be a prophet?"[3] He is known not as Daniel HaNavi (Daniel the Prophet) but as Daniel Ish-HaMudot (Daniel the Beloved) (Daniel 10:11). From what we know of the lives of the prophets, one can easily imagine that most of them would have preferred to have been counted among the beloved of God rather than among the prophets of God.

If the prophet's story is in some sense the story of a failure—the failure to get his people to listen to him—the story of Daniel is a success story, a repetition "of the story of Joseph in Egypt and of Mordecai in Persia," Wiesel writes. "Daniel passes the test and earns respect as a Jew. He is esteemed, congratulated, his advice is sought, as is his consent"[4]—clearly not the lot of the prophets. Thus Daniel the Beloved "prospered in the reign of Darius and in the reign of Cyrus the Persian" (Daniel 6:29), which leads Wiesel to ask: "Is this the reason that Daniel is not called a prophet? Because the king liked him too much? Because he was too happy? Must a prophet always be sad, pursued, and cursed? Would a happy Jeremiah not have been Jeremiah?"[5] Does prophecy, indeed, require misery?

It should be noted that neither Daniel nor his comrades Hananya (Shadrach), Mishael (Meshach), and Azarya (Abednego) were spared persecution. Daniel was cast into the lions' den (Daniel 6:17), and Hananya, Mishael, and Azarya were turned over to the flames of the furnace (Daniel 3:19). Like the prophets, Daniel had dreams and visions. To be sure, the entire Book of Daniel overflows with dreams and visions; when Daniel was not interpreting dreams in chapters 1 through 6, he was having them, from chapter 7 onward. And they were spectacular. "Mystical in essence," says Wiesel, "they refer to a grand denouement, and as we read them, and reread them, we feel hope, great hope: yes, all suffering has an end, all ordeals have a meaning. . . . Yes, God will be—God is—on the side of the victim."[6] Immediately we ask: if all ordeals have a meaning, does meaning require suffering through ordeals? The Rebbe in Wiesel's novel *The Gates of the Forest* says, "A man who is put to the trial . . . must give triple thanks to the Almighty: first for giving him strength to endure the trial, second for bringing the trial to an end, third for the trial itself."[7] Why for the trial itself? Because, writes Wiesel, "in a time of trial man is more than himself, he represents more than his own person."[8] Yes, a time of trial is a time of having to answer to our fellow human beings, "*Hineni!*—Here I am for you!" when answering is most difficult and most dangerous.

Hananya, Mishael, and Azarya are a good example. It was "the first time Jews were persecuted for their faith," Wiesel relates the incident. "The King said, 'If your God is God, let *Him* save you.' And they replied, 'Even if He does not come to our rescue, He remains our God' [Daniel 3:18–19]. How can one not see this as a prefiguration of countless ordeals to come?"[9] Jewish faith in God does not rest upon a barter system of "if you do this for me, then I'll do that for You." *Faith* means: "I'll do this for You, even if You never do anything for me": faith lies in the *even if*, as in "*even if* he may tarry, *no matter what*, I shall await his coming every day." Throughout Jewish history—indeed, human history—a defining feature of the ordeals endured has been the apparent hopelessness, meaninglessness, and uselessness of the ordeal. The meaning that might be derived from trial and tribulation does not lie in a happy outcome. That is why Hananya, Mishael, and Azarya were prepared to offer themselves up even if God did not come to their rescue. No, the meaning lies in God's being on the side of the victim throughout the ordeal.

God's being on the side of the victim, however, does not necessarily mean coming to the aid of the victim. Rather, it lies in the divine, absolute summons from on high, through the victim, for *us* to come to the aid of the victim *even if it means opposing God.* "Ah, yes, Daniel dares to rise against God when it's a question of defending tormented Jews. But didn't he say the suffering was the fault of the Jewish people? [Daniel 9:5] Between suffering and logic, he makes his choice; between victims and justice, he opts for victims: he conducts himself like so many of the great Masters of our people. . . . A Midrashic commentary: There were two defenders of Israel before the Lord: Moses and Daniel [*Shemot Rabbah* 43:1]."[10] Whereas Abraham pleaded with God on behalf of the few righteous people of Sodom and Gomorrah (Genesis 18:25), Moses pleaded with God for the sake of the righteous and the sinners alike (Exodus 32:31–32). And so did Daniel (Daniel 9:16–19), exemplifying a characteristic that, as we shall see, is reminiscent of the Hasidic masters.

The visions begin in chapter 7. Daniel beholds four animals coming out of the sea: a lion with eagle's wings, a bear, a leopard with four wings, and a terrible, hideous animal with teeth of iron. He sees the *Atik Yomin*, the Ancient of Days, seated on the throne of divine judgment, dressed in white, surrounded by a river of fire, with thousands of angels serving him. If, as Wiesel says, Daniel "faces the universe" and "confirms what is above, beyond man,"[11] his vision is a vision of the *already* that constitutes the eternity of God and the ground of meaning, similar to Ezekiel's visions at the River Kvar, the River of the "Already." The key lies in the *Atik Yomin*, the Ancient of Days. The Ancient of Days is the One whose antiquity signifies the eternity that is *already*, the *alef* that already precedes the *beit* of the beginning, of what we have referred to as "the immemorial." The Zohar associates the *Atik Yomin* with *Keter*, the highest of the *sefirot*. It is the bridge between what is beyond humanity and humanity's dwelling place in this realm. The Ancient of Days is the God who constitutes life time by imparting meaning to the days of our lives before the day begins, as Heschel has suggested. "Time," he says "is the presence of God in the world of space."[12] And the presence of God in the world of space is the presence of meaning in the realm of life.

The Book of Daniel deals largely with the matter of *teshuvah*, or the movement of return. Here, too, the *Atik Yomin* is significant, as Rabbi Adin Steinsaltz points out. Doing *teshuvah*, he explains, entails a movement to the "time" before creation; it is a return to the "home of the soul"[13] and to the singularity at the source. Thus, the One we have turned away from also longs to return: at every instant He cries out to us, "Return, and I shall return!" (Malachi 3:7). That is the whole aim of *teshuvah*: to bring an end to the exile not only of ourselves but also of the Holy One. That is why Daniel pleads with God, "O Lord, hear, O Lord, forgive, O Lord, attend and do, defer not; *for Thine own sake*" (Daniel 9:19). The mystery of God's *teshuvah* must remain a mystery. That is why the Angel Gabriel tells Daniel to keep the explanation of the visions a secret (Daniel 8:26).

When in chapter 10 of the Book of Daniel the Angel Michael proclaims the coming of wars in the future, he deems Daniel *Ish-HaMudot* (Daniel 10:11), the beloved one. Or is it, Wiesel asks, "someone who knows how to love well? Who loves others more than himself?"[14] Such love is essential for the *teshuvah* of both God and humanity. It is this love, and not, say, the faculty of reason that makes each of us a human being. "The Book of Daniel," he writes, "teaches us a solemn and essential lesson: Mystery must remain secret in order for it to affect man's destiny. To reveal the mystery at the wrong moment is to dissipate its substance. It is only when the secret is whole—sealed—that knowledge will increase. In other words, Daniel repeats for us what the angel told him: It is forbidden to trivialize certain subjects; it is dangerous to treat them lightly. All that Daniel is authorized to tell us is: 'Know that the secret exists.' "[15] Wiesel's portrait of Daniel, of the *Ish-HaMudot*, is the portrait of a secret—the secret of *Ish-HaMudot*. In the words of Moshe from Wiesel's *The Oath*, the secret harbored by this word is "a secret that dies and relives each time it is received, each time it is invoked. Only the Messiah can speak of it without betrayal."[16] And perhaps, too, only a child, one of the favorite disguises of the Messiah, as Wiesel once told me.

Perhaps that is why Wiesel opens his portrait of Daniel by saying, "This story, beautiful and disturbing, is about children, Jewish children."[17] It is the story of children taken out of the Holy City and into exile. The text tells us that King Nebuchadnezzar ordered Ashpenaz, the master of the King's eunuchs, to take the Jewish children and make them into eunuchs (Daniel 1:3–5). Daniel, Hananya, Mishael, and Azarya were among them. Wiesel notes that, worse than being made into eunuchs, they were taken to be converted to the religion of idolatry that ruled in Babylon and thus assimilated into Babylonian culture. But Daniel, Hananya, Mishael, and Azarya resisted.[18] Wiesel speculates: "Mutilated in the flesh, was Daniel no longer qualified to serve as God's prophet? Tortured by men, he clings to angels. Feeling diminished, he soars to the dizzying heights of the absolute."[19] And the Angels Gabriel and Michael cling to him, angels who had only limited contact with the prophets: Daniel, the mutilated child, not only had dreams and visions comparable to those of

Isaiah and Ezekiel, but he also enjoyed the intimate company of Gabriel and Michael as well as the angels of Gevurah and Hesed, through whom the forces of Creation—of the Absolute—channel into this realm. And yet he declares that he did not understand the visions (Daniel 8:27).

"Here is the end of the matter," says Daniel at the close of his first vision. "As for me, Daniel, my thoughts much affrighted me, and my countenance was changed in me; but I kept the matter in my heart" (Daniel 7:28). If Daniel kept watch over a secret, he himself became a secret, and that is the key to this portrait. "Poor Daniel," says Wiesel, "brave Daniel: wise and famous, he wasn't at all embarrassed to say, more than once, that he didn't understand. His role was only that of messenger. To listen and repeat; to listen and transmit; to listen and to be present."[20] Then he mysteriously disappears. We do not know where he came from or where he went. If he was not the Messiah in disguise, in Daniel the prophet Elijah may have been there in disguise. After all, recall Wiesel's observation concerning Elijah: "A stranger utters a true word, performs a true deed: it must be Elijah. The best proof is that he disappears as soon as his work is completed."[21] Was Daniel's work completed? Or are we the ones summoned to complete it? The answer to these questions, too, remains a secret to be kept within the heart, which, according to Hasidic teaching, is God's favorite dwelling place.[22]

Portrait of Ruth

With the portrait of Ruth we go back to an earlier time, to the time of the great-great grandmother of King David, from whose line the Messiah will emerge. "What do we owe Ruth?" Wiesel asks. And he answers: "King David and—our hope."[23] As in the case of Daniel, here we come up against the issue of prophecy, for the Midrash attributes to Ruth the capacity for prophecy: when she came before Boaz, "she prostrated herself with her face to the ground, and said to him, 'Why are you so kind as to single me out [le-hakireni, literally, to know me]?' (Ruth 2:10)—this teaches that she prophesied about herself, that he would know her intimately" (Ruth Rabbah 5:2). Elsewhere in the Midrash Boaz is the one who was endowed with prophetic powers, knowing as he did that Ruth was destined for greatness: "For he saw, unbeknownst to Ruth, with the spirit of Divine inspiration that the Messiah, the anointed king, will come from her, but he did not reveal this to her" (Ruth Rabbah 3:9). According to the Talmud, Boaz revealed to Ruth that six descendants are destined to emerge from her, each of whom would be blessed: David, Daniel, Hananya, Mishael, Azarya, and the Messiah (*Sanhedrin* 93b). Once again we see the connections and the transition from Wiesel's portrait of Daniel to his portrait of Ruth. In keeping with a motif found in all of Wiesel's portraits, what was revealed to Ruth and Boaz remained hidden from each of them.

Whereas Daniel was called Ish-HaMudot, Wiesel notes that Ruth was known as "Ruth ha-Moavia, Ruth the Moabite: her name conjures up a past filled with doubt and pain, and a future penetrated by an irresistible light that penetrates exile, the messianic light that will put an end to suffering and injustice."[24] This irresistible light that penetrates exile is what makes the portrait of Ruth ha-Moavia so extraordinary. In biblical lore there are few nations as ignoble as the Moabites, known as they were for their idolatrous worship of Chemosh, a god who thrived on human sacrifice. They were descendants of the unholy union between Lot and his older daughter (Genesis 19:37). Indeed, the Israelites were forbidden to consort with them. Which tells us, according to Wiesel, that "history is never finished. Good may emerge from bad. Evil's triumph must be temporary. Repentance is granted even to killers."[25] To say that history is never finished is to say that God is never finished drawing goodness from evil, light from darkness. On this view, history is, indeed, the history of transforming darkness into light. There lies its messianic dimension. There lies the meaning of Ruth: within the Messiah himself flows Moabite blood, so that the Messiah comes to redeem his very origin and with it all of humanity.

The Midrash relates that Ruth and her sister Orpah—whom the Talmud identifies as the great-great-grandmother of Goliath, the one who would be slain by Ruth's great-great-grandson David (*Sotah* 42b)—were the daughters of King Eglon of Moab, the son of the Moabite King Balak (*Ruth Rabbah* 2:9). It will be recalled that Balak was the king who had summoned the pagan prophet Balaam to curse the Israelites (Numbers 22:1–5). According to one tradition, "Ruth" was not her original Moabite name; rather her husband Hilion, the son of Naomi, gave her the Hebrew name Ruth (*Zohar Hadash* 79a), a name, says the Midrash, that underscores her loyalty to Naomi "because she saw [*ra'atah* or 'heeded'] the words of her mother-in-law" (*Ruth Rabbah* 2:9). In the Talmud Rabbi Yohanan says she was called Ruth "because she merited to have issue from her David, who saturated [*she-rivahu*] God with song and praises" (*Berakhot* 7b). Notice that, according to these two interpretations, Ruth's name derives from the sanctity of the human-to-human relation, *ben adam lehevero*, and from the sanctity of the human-to-higher relation, *ben adam leMakom*. Without the dimension of height signified by the latter, there is nothing holy about the relationship with the former.

When a person converts to Judaism he or she takes on a new name, a Hebrew name, and with a new name comes a new soul. Ruth is the most famous of all the converts, one of only two converts whose names appear in the title of the books of the Bible; the other is the prophet Ovadiah, who, according to the Talmud, was an Edomite convert (*Sanhedrin* 39b). Wiesel reminds us that the Scroll of Ruth is read on Shavuot, the day when the Torah was revealed at Mount Sinai. Why? Because "like Ruth, our ancestors became Jewish, that is, converted to the Jewish faith, when they received the law."[26] The Talmud teaches that all Jewish souls were gathered at Mount Sinai, living, dead, and yet to be born, including the souls of the converts (*Shavuot* 39a)—including Ruth. The story of Ruth is the story not only of a young widow's devotion to her widowed mother-in-law; it is also the story of a marriage. Ruth, then, is intimately associated with the two tablets given to Moses, which, according to the Midrash, symbolize a bride and groom (*Shemot Rabbah* 41:6; *Tanhuma Ki Tisa* 16)—a point to be kept in mind when considering Wiesel's portrayal of her betrothal to Boaz.

In his commentary on chapter 20 of Exodus Rashi tells us that at Mount Sinai the *Shekhinah* went "forth to meet them, as a bridegroom who goes forth to meet his bride"; in the words of the sixteenth-century mystic Rabbi Moshe Cordovero, "The people of Israel are the spouse of the Holy One."[27] The mystics also teach that "the day of His wedding" in the Song of Songs (3:11) refers to the day God gave the Torah to Israel at Mount Sinai.[28] In keeping with this tradition, we declare ourselves, in the words of the prophet, to be "betrothed" to God (Hosea 2:21–22) each weekday morning, as we wrap the tefillin, or phylacteries, around our finger. From the day Israel was gathered at Mount Sinai, says the Zohar, God began creating new worlds through the creation of marriages (*Zohar* I, 89a), and no marriage was more critical to creation than the marriage of Ruth and Boaz.

Commenting on this love story, Wiesel writes, "It contains sensuality, but no transcendent element. It is a story about human relations, not about God and His workings. Why then is it sacred?"[29] As a Hasid, indeed as a Jew, he knows very well why it is sacred: from a Hasidic standpoint, there is nothing more sacred than human relation and no human relation more sacred than marriage. Why? Because marriage is the human relation that connects us most intimately to God. From the depths of the flesh-and-blood between space of human marital relations, the Holy One enters the world so that there is no human relation holier than marriage. That is why it is called *kiddushin* or "holiness." The redemption of humanty comes not just from the union between God and humanity but also from the union between husband and wife, between Boaz and Ruth.

Wiesel's portrait of Ruth demonstrates the profound connection between how we understand marriage and how we understand the meaning and value of the other human being. Ruth is not just a woman who enters into a marriage with Boaz. More than that, she is a *stranger*, a *ger*. And—*this is crucial to the portrait of Ruth*—without a marriage with the stranger, the Messiah cannot find his way into this realm. Listen to Wiesel:

> It is because the "Other" is other, because he or she is not I, that I am to consider him or her both sovereign and instrument used by God to act upon history and justify His faith in His creation. When are we suspicious of the stranger? When he or she comes from our midst. There is a difference between *ger*, *nochri* and *zar*. All three words refer to the stranger. Scripture is kind to the *ger*, compassionate toward the *nochri*, and harsh toward the *zar*. For only the *zar* is Jewish. And a Jew who chooses to estrange himself from his people, a Jew who makes use of his Jewishness only to denigrate other Jews, a Jew of whom it may be said that "he removed himself from his community," who shares neither its sorrow nor its joy, that Jew is not our brother.[30]

The *ger* is closer to the Jews than a Jew who has severed himself from his people. Wiesel's portrait of Ruth is the portrait of a *ger*, of a stranger who longs to dwell among the Jews, without whom there can be no Messiah.

Another distinguishing feature of this portrait is *hunger*. Indeed, Wiesel's portrait of Ruth is a portrait of hunger: "The narrative, from beginning to end, is bathed in unfathomable suffering. From the very first sentence we are confronted by famine and misfortune. . . . We realize that hunger, too, is a character in the drama. . . . Hunger means humiliation. A hungry person experiences an overwhelming feeling of shame. The father who cannot feed his children. The son who witnesses his father's helplessness. All desires, aspirations, and dreams lose their lofty qualities and relate to food alone. Hence the feeling of degradation. Shame in Hebrew is linked to one disease alone: hunger. *Kherpat-raav*: the shame of hunger."[31] Yes, hunger, too, is a character in this tale: it is present as a radical emptiness that devours its host from within. It belongs to our humanity and to the loss of our humanity. Hunger also belongs to the Holy One, who hungers in the hunger of the afflicted, who in the cry of the beggar cries out to us, "I am hungry!" Like the Holy One, hunger is ubiquitous and definitive of the human-to-human relationship that defines who we are: who we are as human beings lies in our capacity to respond to the hunger of the other human being.

Among those deemed the closest to God are not only the strangers but also the widows. Ruth is both. Hence Wiesel's anguished cry: "Why so much sadness in one home? Why did death strike only the men? Why were the women spared?"[32] In the portrait of Ruth we encounter three widows: Naomi, who lost her husband Elimelekh; Orpah, who lost her husband Mahlon, son of Naomi; and Ruth, who lost her husband Hilion, son of Naomi. Widow after widow after widow. Of the three, Naomi is by far the most deeply bereaved: not only did she lose her husband, but she also lost her sons.[33] And so Naomi cries out, "God pained me, hurt me, punished me" (see Ruth 1:20). Yes, says Wiesel: "God, not people. Is she reproaching Him? Is she reproaching herself?"[34] Wait a minute. Reproaching herself? For what? Is she the survivor who, like so many, feels guilty for surviving?

Wiesel's questions bring to mind a teaching from the Hasidic master Levi-Yitzhak of Berditchev on the *Shema*'s summons to love God *bekol-meodekha*. The word appears in the phrase "You shall love HaShem your God with all your heart, all your soul, and all your 'might' [*bekol-meodekha*]" (Deuteronomy 6:5). As Wiesel once pointed out to me, *meod* actually means "more," so that God commands me to love "with all your 'more'": this is to love with an inexhaustible love. The *more* with which I love is a messianic more. Rabbi Levi-Yitzhak, however, reminds us of what this "more" might mean: "The word *meod* is understood as an alternative for the word *midah*, i.e. we are to accept with love every attribute of God with which He sees fit to relate to us" (*Kedushat Levi, Vayeshev* 3), that is, even when "God has pained me, hurt me, punished me." But . . . even when God has taken my children? Even when thousands go hungry? At times, to love Go with all the "more" means loving God with a kind of anger or outrage, with the *barukh* that is a "certain anger that is blessed from above and below," as Wiesel has said.[35] It means loving God against our will.

After all, God is known as the *Dayan Almanot*, the "judge" who watches over "widows" (as in Psalms 68:6). The phrase implies that inasmuch as a husband is a protector, God acts as a husband to the one bereft of a husband. How does He protect Naomi? By providing her with the companionship of her son's widow. Ruth the convert is Ruth the comforter, as if she, Ruth the widow, had taken on the role of *Dayan Almanot*. In fact, according to the aggadic tradition, Ruth was twice made a widow; for Boaz, it is said, died on his wedding day, whereas Ruth lived to behold the glory of Solomon (Ginzberg, *Legends of the Jews*, 4:2:34).[36] Continuing the theme of bereavement, the sages of the Talmud explain that the crowd of people who greeted Ruth and Naomi upon their return to Bethlehem were gathered for the funeral of Boaz's first wife: she had died that very day. As if that were not enough, the Talmud adds, Boaz had lived to see thirty sons and thirty daughters die, all except Oved, the one born of Ruth, the father of Jesse, the father of David (*Bava Batra* 91a). And Boaz died before he could see Oved, the son born of a miracle, since, according to the Midrash, Ruth was born without a womb; but "God shaped a womb for her" (*Ruth Rabbah* 7:14). The death of Boaz, however, drew Naomi and Ruth even closer: once again both are widows, but now they have a son to bring up together—a son whose seed would bring forth the redemption of humanity.

As for the men who made widows of their wives—Elimelekh, Mahlon, Hilion, and Boaz—the Talmud absolves them of their faults (*Bava Batra* 91a; *Ketuvot* 7b). Why? Because their deaths were necessary links in a chain that would ultimately bring the Messiah. "And so we discover," says Wiesel, "a new element—perhaps the most important of all—in this wondrous tale: that of coincidence. Or is it divine design?"[37] Wiesel's portrait of Ruth weaves together threads of faith, loyalty, and devotion with threads of bereavement, hunger, and suffering to lay before us what is required to bring the redemption of humanity that the Jewish people are chosen to bring. This realization imparts even greater depth to Ruth's affirmation to Naomi: "Wherever you go, I will go; and wherever you lodge, I will lodge; your people shall be my people, and your God my God. Where you die, will I die, and there will I be buried" (Ruth 1:16–17). *Where you die, will I die, and there will I be buried*. Thus Ruth attaches not only her life but also her death to the Jewish people. To die where the Jewish people die is to die for the sake of the Jewish people—and for the sake of all humanity, just as she gave birth to Oved for the sake of all humanity. The portrait of Ruth? It is the portrait of how a simple act of love and devotion can transform the destiny of humanity.

Portrait of Esther

The *Megillat Esther*, the Scroll of Esther, is literally "the revelation of the hidden," the revelation of the hidden precisely *as* hidden. This is the most significant feature of Wiesel's portrait of Esther: it is a portrait of hidden-ness, a portrait of the invisible or of the Invisible One. Levinas may be of some help. "The manifestation of the invisible," he has said, "cannot mean the passage of the invisible to the status of the visible,"[38] because here the invisible is not hidden from sight but rather transcends the categories of vision. It eludes the light because it is the source of light: it is the One who utters, "Let there be light." What is hidden in the portrait of Esther, then, is forever inviolable in its hiddenness. God Himself remains invisible here, for this is the one book of the Bible in which there is no mention of God. How, then, did it find its way into the Bible? According to one tradition, it is included as an eternal reminder of the mandate to "blot out the remembrance of Amalek from under heaven" (Exodus 17:14), for, according to the Talmud, Haman was a descendant of the King of the Amalekites (*Megillah* 30a).

The Talmud also points out a hidden allusion to Esther in the Torah, where it is written "I shall surely hide [*haster astir*] my Face" (Deuteronomy 16:18). The invisible God is invisible not because He cannot be "seen" but because He transcends the thematizing categories of the ontological realm to impart meaning to the ontological realm. "Invisibility," Levinas explains, "does not denote an absence of relation; it implies relations with what is not given, of which there is no idea. Vision is an adequation of the idea with the thing, a comprehension that encompasses."[39] The invisible God is the encompassing, not the encompassed. Only the One who invisibly transcends creation, can impart meaning to creation: the portrait of Esther is a portrait of the Most High, who exceeds our field of vision.

Looking more closely at Wiesel's brush strokes, it seems that Esther has to seek justice because somehow God will not: true to his Hasidic inclination to stubbornly seek out God, Wiesel sees God's hiddenness or invisibility as an *absence*. "What could be the reason for His withdrawal?"

he asks. "Nowhere in the entire Book are any of His sacred and ineffable names mentioned. Isn't the story about miracles? Could miracles occur without Him? Isn't He central to the tale? For Him to step out of history and become spectator, there must have been a reason."[40] If God is absent from the Book of Esther, He is not absent from the Midrash, as Wiesel points out.[41] Before she went to King Ahasuerus, Esther said a prayer:

> Lord, God of Israel, who has ruled from the days of yore and created the world, please help Your maidservant, as I was orphaned without father or mother and am comparable to a poor woman who goes to beg from house to house; so do I beg Your mercy, from window to window in the house of Ahasuerus. And now, Lord, please give success to Your maid-servant—this poor woman—and the flock of Your shepherding from these enemies that have risen against us, as You have no impediment from saving with the many or with the few. And, You, O Father of orphans, please stand to the right of this orphan, who trusted in Your kindness, and give me mercy in front of this man, as I feared him; and bring him low in front of me, as you bring the proud ones low. (*Esther Rabbah* 8:7)

Here we would do well to recall the words of a *tzaddik*: "Men believe they pray before God, but this is not so, for the prayer itself is divinity."[42] In response to her prayer, says the Talmud, the holy spirit of divine inspiration descended upon her so that she is counted among the seven women who were endowed with the gift of prophecy (*Megillah* 14a).[43] God has not withdrawn; nor is He a bystander. He is hidden in the hidden prayer of the one whose name means "hidden."

Of course, Esther is known by other names, most famously by the name Hadassah (Esther 2:7), which means "myrtle" (*hadas*), for the righteous are called "myrtles," as it is written in the Talmud (*Sanhedrin* 93a). "Ben Azzai said: 'Esther was neither too tall nor too short, but of medium size, like a myrtle.' Rabbi Joshua ben Korha said: 'Esther was sallow, but endowed with great charm'" (*Megillah* 13a). The Midrash elaborates further, saying that just as the myrtle has a sweet scent but a bitter taste, so was Esther sweet toward Ahasuerus but bitter toward Haman (*Esther Rabbah* 6:5). Indeed, Wiesel notes that when Esther accused Haman of trying to seduce her, so that the King would kill him, she lied.[44] The sweet scent of the myrtle is also compared to the *mitzvot* performed by the righteous.

The Midrash praises Esther for performing the commandment of taking the *hallah* from the dough when baking bread, for following the laws pertaining to a woman's menstrual cycle, and for lighting Sabbath candles, even when she was in the palace of Ahasuerus (*Midrash Tehillim* 1:22:16). Thus Esther illuminated Israel "like the light of the dawn" (*Midrash Tehillim* 1:22:5). If, as the Talmud says, she, along with Sarah, Rahab, and Abigail, is one of the four women possessed of unsurpassed beauty (*Megillah* 15a), it is because she emanated this transcendent light. In that light is hidden the One who summoned forth the light in the beginning.

While the sages of the Talmud extol Queen Esther for her devotion to the commandments of Torah, they also exalt her for her love of the people of Israel. When Esther asked Mordecai to proclaim a fast before her intercession with the king to avert Haman's evil plan, Wiesel points out, Mordecai said he could not do it because they were in the season of Passover. Whereupon she asked him, "But what would happen to Passover if there were no Jews left to observe it?" Mordecai agreed that she was right (*Megillah* 15a).[45] Here we discover that Esther's love for Torah and the people of Israel was a love steeped in *pikuah nefesh*, the rabbinic principle that saving a life takes precedence over the observance of the laws. It is based on a reading of the Torah's affirmation that the person who obeys the commandments of Torah will live by them (Leviticus 18:5) and not die by them: the highest priority of the laws of the Torah is to preserve human life (*Yoma* 85b). Could this deviation from the strict observance of the letter of the law be the reason for the Zohar's claim that it was not Esther who lived with King Ahasuerus but a demon who looked like her (*Zohar* III, 267a)? Or was it because, as the king's consort, she would certainly have lain with the pagan king? But then that, too, would have been for the sake of *pikuah nefesh*—to save the Jewish people from the exterminationist designs of Haman.

Haman was not a bigot or a racist. He neither succumbed to xenophobia nor did he suffer from any economic envy of the Jews. He is one of the original anti-Semites. He seeks to annihilate not only the Jewish people but also the teaching and testimony that the Jewish people represent by their very presence in the world. It is a teaching that undermines the anti-Semite's totalitarian project to become as God. Therefore, like the Nazis, as Wiesel indicates, "Haman had gone to the trouble of learning Jewish laws. . . . His opinion of the Jews was, in a way, quite flattering. He attributed to us an international power of infinite magnitude and was convinced that we were fully committed to helping one another and the

Jewish people, always. If only he were right."[46] The Talmud relates that Haman told the king about how the Jews were negligent of their own precepts. "Their laws," said Haman, "are diverse from those of every other people: they do not eat of our food, nor do they marry our women nor give us theirs in marriage; neither do they keep the king's laws" (*Megillah* 13b). If he were not thoroughly versed in the teachings and traditions of the Torah—like the Nazis—how would he know any of this?

Like Haman, the Nazis understood that because the God of Abraham is omnipresent, then the assault on the God of Abraham had to be omnipresent also. Jewish teaching and testimony were the designated targets of a project of total extermination, for Jewish tradition is itself a manifestation of the God of Abraham, Isaac, and Jacob. In the time of King Ahasuerus the Jews' devotion to Torah provoked the ire of Haman. Wiesel cites a Midrash in this connection:

> When Haman said to King Ahasuerus, "Look at His people which is faithful to its own traditions, its own tongue, its own laws, its own customs, its own memory," the angel Michael repeated the words after him and said to God, "See, Master of the Universe, see Your people and the way it observes Your laws, the way it affirms its faith in You." And, at the end, Michael added, "Admit it, Master of the Universe, your people is not accused of theft or rape or idolatry but only of wanting to remain Jewish. How can you not save it from massacre?" [Ginzberg, *Legends of the Jews* 4:12:133][47]

Where, Wiesel wonders, was the Angel Michael in the time of the Shoah? "Later," he says, "I resented the Book: everything in it seemed too artificial, *too* uplifting. . . . In my time the Jews of Shushan were not spared."[48] Nor was the retribution so severe: almost all of the more than 150,000 named Nazi war criminals avoided punishment, whereas in Shushan "the Jews smote all their enemies with the stroke of the sword, and with slaughter and destruction, and did what they would unto them that hated them" (Esther 9:5)—five hundred in all, plus the ten sons of Haman (Esther 9:12). "This must explain why God chose not to give His name to the Book of Esther," Wiesel suggests. "He refused to be associated with the denouement—with the bloodshed. It was His way of saying, Don't ascribe this to me."[49] Shall the same be said of the bloodshed of the Shoah?

Portrait of Job

If God is absent from the Book of Esther, He is all too present in the Book of Job, at times present *as an absence*. And that is the problem. Note an insight from Wiesel's portrait:

> Job would have preferred to think of himself as guilty. His innocence troubled him, left him in the dark; his guilt might give the experience *a meaning*. He would gladly have sacrificed his soul for knowledge. What he demanded was neither happiness nor reparations, but an answer, an answer that would show him unequivocally that man is not a toy, and that he is defined only in relation to himself. That was why Job turned against God: to find and comfort Him. He defied Him to come closer to Him. He wanted to hear His voice, even though he knew he would be condemned. He preferred a cruel and unjust God to an indifferent God.[50]

A meaning: that is what Job sought—not solace, peace, or happiness but a sense of *meaning*. Elsewhere Wiesel expresses it by saying, "The ultimate aim of humanity lies neither in happiness nor in suffering but in the search for the truth. The human being is born to seek out the truth and to live it."[51] The search for truth and for meaning amount to the same thing. That is what makes Job a kind of Everyman: the human soul hungers for meaning as the human body hungers for bread. In the portrait of Job we see that desperate hunger, that hungry desperation. In the case of Job, as in other cases, the undoing of meaning lies not in suffering but in *useless* suffering, suffering without anything to suffer *for*—suffering that is *merely* suffering. It is simply there, neutral and indifferent, in a realm where no one hears you scream and you hear the scream of no one.

What is worse, in the case of Job, there are moments when God, the very One who is necessary to meaning, seems to undermine meaning. Wiesel wisely cautions us on this point: "One must approach Job as a friend, and as such we have no right to develop any systematic theories: it is neither the time nor the place . . . : Job is a victim of God, *not* of Satan!"[52] Why as a friend? Because his problem, Wiesel asserts, is "about absurdity. His friends do not understand, and he has a pathetic need to be understood."[53] The difficulty—indeed, the *horror*—is not that there is so much evil in the world but that there is no evil. Nor is there any good:

there is no *Why*, no hidden aspect. There is nothing other than what is merely there, neutral and indifferent. Such is the situation in which Job finds himself. Wiesel elucidates: "It is not a question of seeing God but of being seen by Him. If Job complains that God hides His face from him, it is not because he cannot 'see God' but because he ceases to be seen by Him!"[54] Job is turned over to the horror of being neither seen nor heard.

Job is turned over to the "there is," to the indifferent neutrality of being that, as Levinas describes it, "has 'no exits.' "[55] There lies the anguish and the outcry of Job: *there is no exit*. Left only with the material emptiness of all there is, we are left without meaning—without a *Why*. Where there is no *Why*, there is no *Who*; where there is no *Who*, there is no *Why*. Simply stated, there is neither God nor humanity; God is reduced to a phantasm, and human beings are reduced to animals—or less. Without this bond between the *Who* and the *Why*, there is nothing to hear except the infinite and terrifying silence that haunts the sound and the fury, signifying nothing. Job seeks the *Why* in order to encounter the *Who*, the Holy One, the source of every *Why*. Even if he cannot fathom the *Why*.

For Job there is no "getting it over with." This explains the ubiquity of Job and the Everyman quality about him. Job, says Wiesel, is "a mirror a thousand times shattered reflecting the image of a solitude bursting with madness. In him come together legend and truth; in him come together silence and the word. . . . Whenever we attempt to tell our own story, we transmit his."[56] Why? Because the solitude bursting with madness does not belong to Job alone: "Job is alone with God, against God, and I would add: alone like God, because human solitude is a reflection of Divine solitude."[57] Who among us has not felt the outcry of Job stir within the depths of our own soul, in the cry of "Why!?"? Who among us has not awakened in the dead of night to feel bulwarks crack? According to one tradition, the Hebrew word for "face," *panim*, is plural because each of us has two faces: our own unique face and the face of Adam. Perhaps we have three: our own, Adam's, and Job's.

This is Job the Everyman. "Strange," says Wiesel, "he who knew no other land but his own—that of legend—seems to have lived in all of them; he who perhaps was never born, seems to have achieved immortality."[58] To be sure, the Talmudic sage Rabbi Shmuel ben Nahman says Job never lived (*Bava Batra* 15a). "There were those who claimed that Job did exist" Wiesel points out, "but that his sufferings are sheer literary invention. Then there were those who declared that while Job never existed, he undeniably did suffer."[59] What does it mean? What does it have to do with the portrait of Job? The portrait of Job is not precisely a portrait of useless suffering or of the meaninglessness attendant upon useless suffering. No, it is a portrait of the outcry that, at times, might restore meaning. There are times when we are powerless to mend the world, but *we are not powerless to cry out*, as Job cried out, whatever the outcome of the outcry. Like every word, every outcry transforms creation. That is what Wiesel teaches us in his portrait of Job.

On the other hand, Job is not exactly like everyone. Wiesel observes, for example, that "every day we invoke the God of Abraham, Isaac, Jacob, *and* of Job!"[60] He also notes a Midrash that counts Job among the wise counselors of Pharaoh at the time of the Exodus. According to the tale, when Satan, the "Accuser," saw the Israelites coming out of Egypt, he went to God and accused them of every transgression, insisting that they did not merit their liberation. That is when God said, "Have you considered my servant Job?" (Job 1:8). Thus, God diverted Satan's attention away from the Israelites and turned him on Job (*Shemot Rabbah* 12:2; 31:7; see also *Talmud Bavli, Sotah* 11a),[61] like a kind of sacrificial offering—but to whom? Wiesel also reminds us that, according to one tradition, Job "was reputed to have tried to save mankind through his suffering. Job: a different Messiah, working for the redemption of the Gentiles."[62] Still, Wiesel reminds us, "the difference between Job and Abraham is that Job speaks with anger, whereas Abraham speaks with compassion. Further, as explicated in the Hasidic tradition, Abraham speaks for the sake of others, whereas Job registers his complaint only for himself."[63] So in some ways, Job is not like everyone else.

Wiesel notes that "in the Midrash, Job is compared to the Jewish people. Israel too is alone; its best friends are ready to commiserate in its misfortunes but will do nothing to help. Israel too has been accused of acting against God, forcing Him to resort to punishment but of whom? Israel too is persecuted by men who, after inflicting pain, denounce the people of Israel for attempting to bear suffering in a proud and dignified way. If Job was not Jewish to begin with, he became Jewish."[64] Indeed, Wiesel tells us that the gematria of *Job* and of *my brother* (*achi*) is 19: "Job is our brother."[65] Is Job's condition of utter abandonment the Jewish condition? And is this utter abandonment characteristic of what it means to be a human being? "On a deeply human plane," Wiesel writes, "his [Job's] revolt was ultimately against his own solitude, which he knew to be irreducible, for it concealed God's face beneath that of man."[66] Only in the face-to-face of the human-to-human relationship does the exigency of the holy open up, without which we are turned over to the solipsistic isolation with the ego.

Wiesel has profound sympathy for Job's outcry, when he howls, "Oh that my vexation were but weighed, and my calamity laid in the balances altogether! For now it would be heavier than the sand of the seas; therefore are my words broken. For the arrows of the Almighty are within me, the poison whereof my spirit drinketh up; the terrors of God do set themselves in array against me" (Job 6:2–4). Here, says Wiesel, "I am with Job because I love him, and I am with him because he is against God."[67] But when he comes to the last verse, "Job died, being old and full of days" (Job 42:17), even Wiesel has run out of patience:

> This can be interpreted as: Saturated with life; he had had enough. In spite of his apparent happiness, in spite of his regained wealth, he no longer cared to live. . . . Yet, when taken literally, these words could indicate that Job, once his ordeals were behind him, lived in peace with his destiny, reconciled with God and mankind. And that is the point at which I register my protest. Much as I admired Job's passionate rebellion, I am deeply troubled by his hasty abdication. He appeared to me more human when he was cursed and grief-stricken, more dignified than after he rebuilt his lavish residences under the sign of his newly found faith in divine glory and mercy.[68]

This seemingly satisfied end comes to the man who cried out, "My days are swifter than a weaver's shuttle, and are spent without hope. O remember that my life is a breath; mine eye shall no more see good. The eye of him that seeth me shall behold me no more; while Thine eyes are upon me, I am gone" (Job 7:6–8). Surely there was truth in his outcry, just as there is truth in the silence, as Wiesel suggests when he says, "God is always listening within the silence,"[69] which would imply that God is not absent, even when He appears to be absent. No, He is listening—silently.

Even in a moment when it looks as if Job has capitulated, saying, "Though He slay me, yet will I trust in Him; but I will argue my ways before Him" (Job 13:15), Wiesel reads this outcry as a moment of rebellion and defiance:

> It is as if Job were saying to God, "Even if you do not want me to believe in You, yet shall I have faith in You. Even if You do

not want my prayers, yet shall I continue to pray." This remains my obsession. It goes to the depths of my people and our history. I have lived through too much with God to *not* question Him. I have loved Him too much to abandon Him. . . . Can one pray *against* God? Can one say to Him "You are great" and "You are harming us" at the same time?"[70]

Certainly from a Hasidic point of view the answer is yes—there lies the Hasidic legacy attached to the portrait of Job. In his conversation with Josy Eisenberg on the Book of Job, Wiesel recalls the time in the camp when somehow the inmates obtained a pair of tefillin. Wasting no time, they lined up to lay the tefillin and to say the blessing—but with a difference: "Every time, when the moment came to recite the prayer, it took the form of a protest, and we said to God: 'Is it You who merits our prayer? No, You do not merit our prayer!' And then we said our prayers."[71] Here too we find an expression of Wiesel's Hasidic legacy.

Did not God Himself declare to Eliphaz, Bildad, and Zophar, "For ye have not spoken of Me the thing that is right, as my servant Job hath" (Job 42:8)? Job's ultimate abdication—if, indeed, he abdicated—makes it look as if his three "comforters" had spoken rightly. Does God suggest that Job has spoken rightly in his moment of rebellion and defiance? Or is it in his moment of capitulation and abdication? Wiesel elaborates:

> I was preoccupied with Job, especially in the early years after the war. In those days he could be seen on every road of Europe. Wounded, robbed, mutilated. Certainly not happy. Nor resigned. I was offended by his surrender in the text. Job's resignation as a man was an insult to man. . . . He should have said to God: Very well, I forgive You, I forgive you to the extent of my sorrow, my anguish. But what about my dead children, do they forgive you? What right do I have to speak on their behalf? Therein lies God's true victory: He forced Job to welcome happiness. After the catastrophe Job lived happily in spite of himself.[72]

Elsewhere Wiesel cries out, "I am not Job! To raise Job up and then to bring him down is completely in keeping with the Jewish spirit. With us, the great men, our ancestors, our sages, our masters are altogether human—not super human!"[73] In a way, this ambiguity on the part of God and humanity has a value of its own. It belongs to working and waiting for the hour of redemption. "God is also in the wait," says Wiesel. "God *is* the wait. He waits, with man, for deliverance. Just like man, He awaits the Messiah."[74] Does God, too, then, defiantly declare with Job, "I know that my Redeemer lives" (Job 19:25)?

Although Wiesel speaks of God's victory, it seems to me that God's victory should have been in His defeat. If He enjoyed a moment of victory, was it not in Job's rebellion, rather than in his abdication? I have suggested that Wiesel's portrait of Job is a portrait of outcry, absence, and useless suffering. Is it, then, a portrait of God's victory or of God's defeat? Says Wiesel, "Job is for God and against God at the same time, but always *with* God."[75] There lies the sustaining tension that delivers us from any final solution. And the key to the tension, as Wiesel suggests, lies in what the tradition refers to as the "hidden light," which we have already seen in the Portrait of Esther.

The hidden light, Wiesel teaches, is "the most beautiful, the most pure, the most radiant. Thanks to it creation exists. Thanks to it we have the visible and the invisible. Thanks to this light, according to the Talmud, Adam was able to see all of creation [*Hagigah* 12a; *Sanhedrin* 38b]."[76] Therefore, Wiesel goes on to say, this is God's message to Job: "You cannot see the light. But you must believe Me when I affirm that it exists, that it is otherwise, more pure and more beautiful than anything you can know. For that which you take to be light is merely a reflection."[77] In the end, God restores the hiddenness of the light through the restoration of the relationship with which the story began. In the end, Wiesel reminds us, God refers to Job as "My servant" (Job 42:7–8), just as He had done in the beginning (Job 1:8; 2:3). "Nothing has changed!" Wiesel exclaims. "Job has suffered, howled, argued, but for God nothing has changed: Job remains His servant. . . . Here lies the infinite beauty of this text: God re-establishes friendship between Job and the three comforters and demands from us and others that we do something *together*,"[78] something that affirms the higher relation to the Holy One (Job 42:8). God demands that each of us become a servant to the other—*together*. Only in that way, as Levinas states it, can we hope to stop "murmur of silence" that is the "anonymous and senseless rumbling of being."[79]

In the end, then, the portrait of Job is a portrait of the togetherness without which we are turned over to the horror of meaninglessness.

Portraits from the Talmud

R euven Kimelman has correctly noted that for Elie Wiesel, "the Talmud
is the spine of Judaism, without which we would have gone limp long
ago. It is what kept Jews upright, walking tall throughout their lachry-
mose history. Without it, the spiritual reality would have succumbed to
the material one."[1] But what is this *it*, without which our spiritual reality
would be lost?

The word *Talmud* means "study" or "learning." We do not *read* the
Talmud—we *study* it. In addition to the Mishnah, which is the core text
of the Talmud, and the Gemara, which is the commentary surrounding
the Mishnah, there may be as many as a dozen other texts on any given
page of the Talmud. In Jewish tradition there are two Talmuds: the Talmud
Yerushalmi, produced by the sages of the Land of Israel, and the Talmud
Bavli, which is the creation of the sages of Babylon, the center of Jewish
learning from the time of the destruction of the First Temple in 586 BCE
to the end of the tenth century. When we speak of *the* Talmud we refer
to the Talmud Bavli, a massive work consisting of sixty-three tractates.
In the second half of the second century, when it was evident that the
Temple would not be rebuilt any time soon, Rabbi Yehudah HaNassi, the
leader of the Jewish community, began supervising the redaction of the
oral tradition into what would become the Mishnah. By the fifth century,
Rabbi Ashi (d. 427), Rosh Yeshivah in Sura for fifty-six years, assembled
the Mishnah and the Gemara to form the Talmud Bavli. As the great
Talmudist Rabbi Adin Steinsaltz points out, however, "No single scholar
is named as having officially completed the writing and editing of the
Talmud (as is the case with the Mishnah), hence the significant saying:
'The Talmud was never completed.' "[2] Over the centuries commentaries
have been added to each page of the Talmud, most notably that of the
great medieval sage Rashi.

The Talmud consists of a wide range of commentaries on the Tanakh, discussions of Jewish law, midrashic tales, and mystical ruminations. Rabbi Steinsaltz notes that while the Talmud is the source of *Halakhah* or Jewish law, it is not itself a "law book."[3] "Only in the Talmud," he writes, "can one read the following statement: 'On this subject there were differences of opinion between two Palestinian sages, and there are those who say that it was a debate between two angels from Heaven' [see *Bava Batra* 75a] without finding the juxtaposition strange. After all, mundane affairs, abstract discussions of *halakhah*, and questions pertaining to the heavenly sphere are all concentrated together within the concept of Torah, and each interacts with the others."[4] If the Talmud is not a legal text, it is even less a theological tract, for it is as much about the relation between human and human as it is about the relation between human and God. In fact, Rabbi Steinsaltz observes, in the Talmud "there is no clear division between offenses committed by one man against another and religious transgressions 'between man and God.'"[5] This means that the higher relation is of a piece with the human relation. "In learning," Wiesel asserts, "man can always go higher and higher. When it comes to learning, the more one gives, the more one receives. Hence the emphasis in the Talmud on study and good deeds. Theology matters less than human relations."[6] The point of studying Talmud is not to become theologically sophisticated but to become humanly engaged. That is how one ascends higher and higher.

The Talmud itself tells us how the Oral Torah was studied and transmitted from the time of its revelation: "Our Rabbis taught: What was the method of learning the Oral Law in the days of Moshe? Moshe would first be taught by the Divine Power. Aharon would then enter and Moshe would teach him the chapter. When Aharon had finished, he would leave the seat of study and take a seat at the left of Moshe. Aharon's sons would then enter and Moshe would teach them the chapter" (*Eruvin* 54b). Sounding the depths of the *yam Talmud*, the "sea of Talmud," in this way, Rabbi Steinsaltz explains, "the scholar is not only a man who has studied but also the personification of the Torah itself,"[7] so that "the sincere student becomes part of the essence of the Talmud."[8] That is why we have the teaching that "to repeat a saying in its author's name is to hasten redemption."[9] Indeed, in the Talmud it is written: "Rabbi Yohanan stated in the name of Rabbi Shimon bar Yohai: The lips of a [deceased] scholar, in whose name a traditional statement is reported in the world, move gently in the grave" (*Yevamot* 97a). The teacher is part of the teaching: these portraits of the teachers contain the wisdom of their teaching—the portrait *is* the teaching. Therefore, Wiesel teaches, "when sages protected one another, it was the Torah they sought to shield. In spite of the arguments and counterarguments in the academies of those days, there was finally a marvelous solidarity among the scholars. They were united by an irresistible passion for learning."[10] And their passion for learning found expression in their love for one another: in the love lies the teaching.

Elie Wiesel once said that God does not want to be studied—He wants to be lived.[11] And so it is with the Talmud. As it happens with the study of the Talmud, to study a portrait from the Talmud is to become part of the portrait. Wiesel's portraits *from* the Talmud, then, are portraits *of* the Talmud, as well as portraits of ourselves. Says Wiesel,

> Today I know that the study of a Talmudic text is an adventure not unrelated to a literary endeavor: a three-sentence legend often possesses the suggestive power of a lyrical poem. A discussion on a remote subject often contains more descriptive elements than a historical narrative. Today I also know that it would be wrong to look only for the past in the Talmud. The Talmud is eternally present. Nothing in it is ever lost. The sages continue their eternal debates and the children continue to be imbued with their fervor. The holiness of Shabbat is still celebrated and, right there, the Temple is burning. And we who read the corresponding passages burn with the Temple—and perhaps for the Temple.[12]

We now better understand Wiesel's anecdote about the poet who was asked what he would take from his house if it were on fire. He answered, "The fire, naturally." And Wiesel adds, "We steal the fire, but our fire does not destroy. Our fire burns and burns and burns—and we burn forever."[13] That is how a Hasid binds himself to the Talmud, how we bind ourselves to these portraits from the Talmud: by burning. Thus, the transmission of the teachings and traditions of Judaism is the igniting of one flame after another, passing one flame to the other.

"Jewish knowledge," writes Wiesel, "was passed from Moses to Joshua, from Joshua to the Elders, from the Elders to the Judges, to the

Prophets, to the Sages, to the Tannaim, to the Amoraim, to the Svoraim, to the Gaonim, to the Rishonim. There is creative beauty in the continuous movement of their ideas and stories—there is eternity in their words that refuse to die."[14] The fact that Judaism has such a chronology of sages tells us something about the uniqueness of its teaching and testimony and how central the sages are to the transmission of its millennial tradition of learning. "Sometimes," writes Wiesel, "a question that had been raised during the first generation of scholars was examined by the second and resolved by the third. Enchanted, you breathlessly read of its course, its progression: the adventure of words, ideas, principles is matched by none—for it transcends time itself. In some instances it took a century for the cycle to close. And yet the discussion among scholars of different ages is rendered as if they were contemporaries."[15] Wherever the eternal is eternally at stake, every Jew is contemporary with every other Jew and with all humanity.

The sages of the Talmud consist of the Tannaim and the Amoraim. Wiesel explains the difference between the two: "The Tannaic era began with Hillel and Shammai in the early period of Herod's reign. As authors of the Mishna, the Tannaim were innovators, creative thinkers, daring codifiers. . . . Then came the Amoraim. At first, they would translate into Aramaic what the Tannaim would say in public. Later they themselves were teachers. Still, protocol and seniority limited their authority: an Amora, for instance, would not dispute the views of a Tanna."[16] Here we shall explore only Wiesel's portraits of the Tannaim, portraits that almost invariably become portraits of two, not just one. Why two? In order to open up a between space for the question, without which the relationship essential to teaching, learning, and memory cannot happen.

Rabbi Steinsaltz offers this insight: "Voicing doubts is not only legitimate in the Talmud, it is essential to study,"[17] as it is written in the Talmud itself: "With scholars, the younger sharpen the minds of the older. . . . Rabbi Hanina said: I have learned much from my teachers, and from my colleagues more than from my teachers, but from my disciples more than from them all." Rabbi Hama bar Hanina said that just as iron sharpens iron, two students should always study together, each a teacher to the other (*Taanit* 7a). Thus we begin to glimpse the importance of the pairing of these sages from the Talmud: each portrait is a portrait of two, sometimes of two sages and sometimes of a sage and the one who encounters the portrait.

Portrait of the House of Shammai
and the House of Hillel

To look upon this portrait of the House of Shammai and the House of Hillel is to cast our gaze not only backward but also upward into the dimension of height. Hillel and Shammai, the most renowned sages of the first generation of the Tannaim, were disciples of Shemaya and Avtalyon, who were converts to Judaism. And so we have a pair born within the fold of the Jewish people fostered by a pair who, like Ruth, entered the fold from beyond. There is no portrait of one without the portrait of another. "Shammai," says Wiesel, "seems to have lived exclusively in relation to Hillel."[18] He notes that according to a tradition that goes back to Flavius Josephus (see *The Antiquities of the Jews*, 14:9:4), King Herod the Great massacred all the sages of the Sanhedrin except two: Shemaya and Avtalyon. Herod later confirmed Hillel's nomination to the presidency of the Sanhedrin (the Sanhedrin had two leaders: the president, or the *Nassi*, and the sage, or the *Hakham*). Shammai, Wiesel explains, joined the Sanhedrin when an Essene named Menachem vacated a seat (*Mishnah Hagigah* 2:2).[19]

Hillel and Shammai were defined not just by their *relationship* to one another but by their *opposition* to one another. Indeed, there are times when a relationship becomes most intimate when it assumes the form of opposition. For three years, Wiesel relates, the students of Hillel and those of Shammai argued over which of their masters was right on different issues. Finally a *bat kol*, a Voice from heaven, declared, "You are both right; both positions reflect God's word and God's truth—and yet—the law is according to the school of Hillel[*Eruvin* 13b]."[20] If both can reflect God's word and God's truth, then the word is not necessarily tied to its dictionary definition, and the truth is not reducible to a datum. Both belong to the realm of a covenantal affirmation, testimony, and relation, which, from the moment when God created for Adam an *ezer k'negdo*, a "helper against him" (Genesis 2:18), is at times oppositional: as in the beginning, the opposition between the Talmudic sages is for the sake of God and humanity.

In his portrait Wiesel brings out the most fundamental of their disputes, one that defines all others:

The school of Shammai said, It would have been better—or simpler—for man not to have been born. The school of Hillel

replied, Man is better off having been born. After thirty
months of discussion, the issue was to be voted on. And lo
and behold—this time, the school of Shammai emerged victorious. Yes, indeed, it would have been better for man not to
have been born—but, having been born, he must search his
conscience, his soul, he must scrutinize his actions, looking
for their meaning; in other words, his actions must confer a
meaning upon his existence [*Eruvin* 13b].[21]

Note that the debate is not about whether to choose life or death. It is
about whether it would be better if there were no life and therefore no
death. They were debating the meaning of the passage from Ecclesiastes:
"I praised the dead who are already dead more than the living who are
yet alive, but better than both is he who has not been born" (4:2–3). He
who has not been born does not have to endure death. So which is better?

Recall, too, the argument among the angels over whether the Holy
One, blessed be he, should create the human being (*Bereshit Rabbah* 8:5):
the House of Hillel and the House of Shammai are like the ministering
angels of God. And yet there is an important difference between the sages
and the angels: the matter of whether it would be better not to have been
created is not an issue for the angels, since they are *malakhim*, "messengers," who cannot but deliver their messages. Period. They do not suffer
for one another. They have no commandments that devolve upon them.
They are not asked, "Where is your brother and what have you done?"
In short, they bear no responsibility and are summoned to no reckoning.
Because the human being must toil to what seems to be no end, bear the
yoke of an infinite responsibility, and suffer the throes of death, surely it
would have been better not to have been born. Then there is the point
that had at least certain humans not been born, then certain evils would
not have transpired: in some cases, one may argue, it is better for what
has been not to have been.

But, like it or not, we have been born and have been given a name
not of our choosing, a name by which each of us is summoned to a task
not of our choosing, a task that no other can engage and for which we are
held accountable. One of Hillel's most famous teachings is his enjoinder:
"In a place where there are no men, you must strive to be a man" (*Pirke
Avot* 2:5), and to be a man is to bear this infinite responsibility. This is
why the House of Hillel invariably held sway over the House of Shammai:
Hillel proceeded from the realistic, concrete premise that, since we have

been born, like it or not, we must determine what must be done—we do not have the luxury of indulging in subjunctive-mood speculations on *what if we had not been born*. More importantly, *our neighbor has been born*, so that we must answer absolutely the questions: "Where is your brother and what have you done?" Because our neighbor has been born, we have been born to help. In my infatuation with myself and my narcissistic wallowing in my despair, it might have been better for *me* not to have been born, but it may well not have been better for my neighbor. Indeed, he could be the Messiah: would it be better for the Messiah not to have been born? Therefore we must not slip into a self-indulgent lament over the fact that we are here. *We are here.* So now what? That is Hillel's question.

The tension underlying the disputes between the two houses reverberates over the centuries, as Wiesel suggests. In Yavneh they said: " 'There will be a time when man will search for words of Torah and will not find them, search for words of scribes and will not find them—that is why we must begin with Hillel and Shammai.' They knew that with Hillel and Shammai you cannot go wrong: begin with them and their discussions and their eternal arguments, and you will be in touch with the living sources of Jewish learning."[22] Yes, the *living* sources, to be sought in the aftermath of the radical imposition of death and the death of death upon the Jewish people. Wiesel's portrait of the House of Hillel and the House of Shammai is a portrait of the eternal *afterward* that haunts humanity. It was said of Hillel, Wiesel writes, that "like Ezra the scribe, he came from Babylon so as to prevent the Torah from being forgotten."[23] We are reminded of the teaching from the Talmudic sage Resh Lakish: "When Torah was first forgotten in Israel, Ezra came up from Babylon and reestablished it. When it was once again forgotten, Hillel the Babylonian came up and reestablished it" (*Sukkot* 20a). Who now, in the aftermath of the Shoah, will come up and reestablish it? Perhaps Elie Wiesel.

It is said of Hillel that he "was wise, learned, and devoted; he mastered the sciences and understood all languages—those of the hills and those of the trees, those of birds and those of people, even those of demons."[24] In other words, he understood the language that the Creator used to bring about the Creation. There is a divine spark in everything, from quarks to quasars, and that divine spark is made of a divine utterance. Hence Adam did not make up the names of the animals—he "read the names" of the animals, *vayikra haAdam shemot* (Genesis 2:20): so great was his wisdom that he could discern the divine word of which each creature was made (see, for instance, Nahmanides, commentary on Genesis 2:20).

Perhaps Hillel possessed a measure of this adamic wisdom. Perhaps he, too, could read and understand the words of which all things are made. If Hillel understood all languages, it is because he understood what the Gerer Rebbe, Rabbi Yehudah Leib Alter, referred to as the *Sefat Emet*, the Language of Truth,[25] which is the language of *hesed* or loving kindness that lies at the heart of Torah and at the core of creation.

Of the 316 disputes between Hillel and Shammai, Wiesel points out, only fifty-five "stress the more indulgent position of the House of Shammai."[26] In all other instances the more tolerant view lay with Hillel. For example, says the Talmud, when Shammai's daughter-in-law gave birth to a son on Sukkot, he made a hole in the roof and put branches over it to make a Sukkah for his grandson (*Sukkot* 2:8). Wiesel relates that Shammai also made his young son fast on Yom Kippur. When the other sages objected, he relented but fed his son with only one hand.[27] That is why, when Wiesel was a child, he envisioned Hillel as a Hasid and Shammai as a Mitnagged.[28] However, he later adjusted his view.

Wiesel confesses that the anecdotes about Hillel's patience sometimes strained his own patience.[29] The Talmud, for example, relates the following: a gentile "came before Shammai and said to Shammai: Convert me on condition that you teach me the entire Torah while I am standing on one foot. Shammai pushed him away with the builder's cubit in his hand. This was a common measuring stick and Shammai was a builder by trade. The same gentile came before Hillel. He converted him and said to him: That which is hateful to you do not do to another; that is the entire Torah, and the rest is its interpretation. Go study." And so the converts declared, "Shammai's impatience sought to drive us from the world, but Hillel's gentleness brought us under the wings of the *Shekhinah*" (*Shabbat* 31a). In the popular reception of this incident, the admiration almost always goes to Hillel. Wiesel, however, declares, "Here again, my sympathy goes to Shammai. For he refuses to play games. He dislikes conditional converts and proclaims it aloud."[30] Conversion to a tradition that takes the truth to be a matter of life and death cannot be compromised. And Shammai understood this. So did Wiesel.

He suggests that it might be his own Hasidic legacy that drew him to Shammai: "Perhaps it is the influence on me of Menachem-Mendel, the solitary visionary of Kotzk, but I am fascinated by Shammai. I respect his extremism, his obsession with truth, no matter what the consequences."[31] It was Shammai's obsession with truth that led him to teach, "Make your Torah study a permanent fixture of your life. Say little and do much. And receive every man with a pleasant countenance" (*Pirke Avot* 1:15). Truth lies in the face of one who greets another with a kind word and a "pleasant countenance." What Wiesel describes as Shammai's "obsession with truth" comes to life through the *hesed*, the loving kindness, associated with Hillel.

"Shammai defends the absolute," says Wiesel, "and we are grateful to him for it; but Hillel defends human beings, and we are even more grateful to him. Both may be right, provided the two options remain open. . . . In the world to come, says the Talmud, Shammai's decisions will prevail. For here is an essential truth of Jewish thought: We need both, we admire Shammai and we love Hillel. I would like to follow Shammai, as far as *I* am concerned, and to emulate Hillel where others are involved—ideally, to be intransigent with myself and understanding with others."[32] Why does Shammai defend the absolute? What, exactly, is defended in the defense of the absolute? Levinas offers a helpful insight: "It is in the midst of the Absolute that the *beyond* takes on meaning."[33] Shammai defends the absolute because without the absolute, as revealed and commanded from On High, human life has no meaning. With a little more help from Levinas, we realize that Hillel, too, defended the absolute in his defense of the human being: "The absolute is a person."[34] The *person*, the *Who*, is the image and likeness of the Holy One in which the human being is created. Hence the refrain "*Who* is like You, O Lord" (Exodus 15:11) is taken to be an affirmation, and not a rhetorical question. The *Who* is the image and likeness of the Holy One. That is why the absolute is a person.

What happens when the concern for the absolute is divorced from the concern for person we discover in one last disagreement between the two houses. Wiesel relates that when the issue of whether to rebel against the Romans arose, Shammai encouraged rebellion, but Hillel opposed it (see *Tosefta Eduyot* 2:2). The people went with Shammai. The result was the destruction of the Temple and Jerusalem.[35] *Hesed* was divorced from *Gevurah*, which resulted in the loss of *Tiferet*: the loss, in other words, of the flow of Torah, light, and holiness from the upper reals into this realm. And so the second *Hurban*, the destruction of the Second Temple, ensued. From the ashes of a third *Hurban* we have this portrait of these two houses and of what is at stake in the relationship between them.

Portrait of Rabbi Hanina ben Dosa

Wiesel's portrait of Rabbi Hanina ben Dosa is a portrait of prayer. And wherever Wiesel is concerned with prayer, he is also concerned with silence. Indeed, it is a portrait of prayer and silence. A certain silence from the

"Third Prayer" in his novel *The Town beyond the Wall* comes to mind, where we read that the hero of the story "is neither fear nor hatred; it is silence. The silence of a five-year-old Jew."[36] As a portrait of silence and of prayer, this portrait of Hanina ben Dosa is, in some ways, a portrait of Elie Wiesel himself. "There are certain silences between word and word," Wiesel has written. "This is the silence that I have tried to put in my work, and I have tried to link it to that silence, the silence of Sinai."[37] If the human being is created in the image and likeness of the Holy One, it is in the image and likeness of silence. That is why Jews pray in silence, as in the Silent Amidah. That is where the "inner light," the *or pnimi*, burns.

If the absolute is a person, it is also a prayer, a face, and a plea shrouded in silence. "Prayer," says Wiesel, "draws the human being into an eternal dialogue with God. Thanks to prayer, God becomes present. Or better: God becomes presence. Everything becomes possible and meaningful: here is the Judge, here the Father, of humanity who has stepped down from His celestial throne to live and to move among His human creatures. And, in exchange, here is the soul who, transported by his prayer, has left behind his complacency and has ascended to the heavens. The substance of language and the language of silence—that is what prayer is."[38] Yes, the language of silence. It is an *unspoken* language, a language steeped in what Martin Buber calls "the silence of all tongues."[39] It is the silence couched in the silent *alef* that precedes the *beit* out of which the Torah is born, the Torah whose depths Rabbi Hanina ben Dosa penetrated.

How do we know that Rabbi Hanina ben Dosa indeed penetrated those depths? A story from the Talmud provides a hint. One Sabbath evening, as it came time to light the Sabbath lamps, the rabbi's daughter prepared the oil for the lamps and lit them, only to discover that she had filled them with vinegar instead of oil. She expressed her amazement to her father, who simply replied, "He who ordered that oil should burn, can order that vinegar should also burn" (*Taanit* 25a). Thus if Rabbi Hanina was known for his miracles, it was because he knew that a miracle is not a violation of the laws of nature but the manifestation of a divine utterance from the Creator. There, more than in scholarship, lay the wisdom of the man who taught, "If your fear of heaven precedes your wisdom, your wisdom will last; if it follows it, it will not. And also: If your deeds weigh more than your knowledge, then your knowledge will stay with you; if not, it will not [*Pirke Avot* 3:8–9]."[40] A master of prayer, Rabbi Hanina ben Dosa knew how to transform his prayers into deeds. There lay the miracles he performed.

"Known more for his miracles than for his erudition," says Wiesel, he was "a man of fervor and passion who, throughout his life, was intensely involved with his people, its heritage, and its aspirations—a man of inner strength and beauty. And yet. . . . This man somehow surrounded himself with silence."[41] Wiesel, too, was known for his fervor and passion. He was known for his ability to transform silence into a deafening outcry. What is behind his fervor and passion, his emphasis on prayer and silence, in this portrait of Rabbi Hanina ben Dosa? Perhaps this: "I remembered walking with the crowd toward the railroad station, where the sealed trains were already waiting for us, it had come into my mind that the silence would triumph, that it was stronger than we, stronger than they; it was beyond language, beyond lies, beyond time; it drew its strength from the very struggle which pitted life against its negation, brutality against silent prayer."[42] In Rabbi Hanina ben Dosa Wiesel sees the stirrings of that struggle. "His name has been linked to fables more often than to laws, to prayers and miracles more often than to ideas. He could be mistaken for a Hasidic rabbi. As a matter of fact, one wonders why Hasidism has not claimed him as it has Rabbi Akiba, Rabbi Shimon bar Yohai, and Rabbi Meir Baal-haNes."[43] Why, indeed?

In Wiesel's portrait of Rabbi Hanina ben Dosa, a sage famous for his capacity for prayer, we discover the dimension of a humanity whose history, Wiesel has said, is the history of prayer.[44] If the history of humanity is the history of prayer, it is the history of seeking out truth through prayer. This means prayer is about truth, not about supplication. There lies the heart of Wiesel's portrait of Rabbi Hanina ben Dosa. With or without the Hasidic claim to Rabbi Hanina, Wiesel draws the sage into his own Hasidic legacy. "All the stories and legends," he writes, "center on Rabbi Hanina—yet they do not shed much light on his personality. The biographical information is astonishingly sketchy. . . . He quite simply vanished, not *from* the Talmud but *inside* it."[45] What can it mean to vanish not *from* the Talmud but *inside* it? Where does that *inside* lie? To vanish *from* the Talmud is to fade into an eloquent silence; to vanish *inside* the Talmud is to slip into a silent eloquence, to slip into a *kol demamah dakah*, into the "thin voice of silence" that defines prayer as prayer. Slipping *inside* the Talmud, Rabbi Hanina becomes *part* of the Talmud, which is essential to any engagement with the Talmud: because he lived, the Talmud is alive.

"Yes" says Wiesel, "he prayed well. That was his principal virtue; his distinction. Some Masters were known for their wisdom or their social position, others were praised for their erudition or their piety; Rabbi

Hanina was praised for his prayers. And they disturb me. They reflect him, but not his times. The dramatic events that shook his generation are totally absent."[46] The history of humanity is about prayer and truth, the principles that were central to Rabbi Hanina, and yet, Wiesel asks, where is history in the prayers of Rabbi Hanina? Nowhere, for example, does the destruction of the Temple, which took place in his lifetime, appear in the tales of Rabbi Hanina.[47] How to explain this? No one wanted to serve God and thus draw the Divine Light of Torah into this realm more than Rabbi Hanina. He was, says Wiesel, "poorer than the poorest of the poor. He possessed nothing, literally nothing, except his burning desire to give God something—anything."[48] This longing for God lay behind his performance of miracles.

The evidence? "People who were in seemingly hopeless situations came to Rabbi Hanina ben Dosa. They expected him to do the impossible; and often he did. Because, to him, nothing was impossible; prayers made all things attainable. If only people knew how to pray. . . . But most never learned; others had forgotten."[49] To learn how to pray is to learn how to empty oneself of the ego and turn all concentration toward the well being of the other human being—*not to God*: the path to God leads through the other human being. In *Souls on Fire* Wiesel relates the fundamental Hasidic teaching that God "is not jealous of your happiness nor of the kindness you show to others. On the contrary: the road to God goes through man."[50] And it is for the sake of God Himself. Thus in the Book of Isaiah God refers to His own salvation (Isaiah 56:1). "The salvation of God," says the Midrash, "is identical with the salvation of Israel" (*Vayikra Rabbah* 9:3). Rabbi Hanina ben Dosa, it seems, had a profound sense of these truths.

"Consideration for others must precede scholarship," says Wiesel in his portrait of Hanina ben Dosa. "Abstract erudition may turn into a futile game of the intellect. Words are links not only between words but also between human beings. The emphasis on the *other* is paramount in Judaism: *Ahrayut*, responsibility, contains the word *Aher*, the Other. We are responsible for the other."[51] Thus, says Wiesel, when Hanina ben Dosa performed his miracles, "he did so almost unwittingly, unconsciously,"[52] aware only of the need to help. Wiesel elaborates on what is at stake in the loving kindness that we show toward the other human being:

> The Talmud extols modesty as much as justice. In its literature,
> the hero is above all endowed with qualities of the heart. Com-

passion for one's fellow man is one of the highest attributes in our tradition. We were born to help one another in our quest for perfection. Redemption is based on compassion for our people in exile, for the Redeemer himself, and for God, whose *Shekhina* dwells with us in exile. To hasten redemption is to perform the ultimate heroic act. But those who occasionally engage in this kind of mystical activity do so in secrecy. The ultimate hero remains invisible. The real hero is—unreal.[53]

Unreal, unseen, somehow elsewhere and yet closer to us than our own shadow. Our compassion for others must include compassion for the Invisible, for the God who longs for the redemption that is in our hands. As a master of prayer, Rabbi Hanina had mastered the ways of praying "on behalf of God's suffering," in the words of Levinas, "for the God who suffers both through man's transgression and through the suffering by which this transgression can be expiated."[54] Rabbi Hanina ben Dosa lived through a time of horrific suffering on the part of both God and humanity.

So where was Hanina ben Dosa in all this suffering? "He who could with words, with words alone, alter events and save lives, why didn't he use them to prevent the unspeakable disaster and spare Jerusalem the ultimate humiliation? Why didn't he do anything? Why didn't he say anything? Is that why the Hasidic world did not claim him as forebear?"[55] It is one thing, even if a hard thing, to note that he did not pray to lift his own family up from poverty. "He is satisfied with little—or even less than that. The result? His situation is so bad that his family has nothing to eat on Shabbat! Meanwhile, his wife, in order not to arouse pity, made believe that all meals were provided for [*Taanit* 24b–25a]."[56] But what about the destruction of the Temple? One explanation is that he died before the Romans destroyed it in the year 70 CE. Another possibility is that "he did not pray because he was unable to pray. In the presence of so many widows and so many orphans roaming through the ruins of Jerusalem, he lost his voice; his lips became sealed. The hero of prayer became a victim."[57] He did not pray because when widows and orphans are suffering, it is time to help, not pray.

Wiesel reminds us of the Midrash that relates another teaching from Rabbi Hanina ben Dosa. The ram, said Rabbi Hanina, that took the place of Isaac when his father Abraham raised the knife over him was created at twilight on the sixth day of the Creation. And nothing of that ram has been lost:

The ashes were dispersed in the sanctuary of the Temple. The sinews were used by David as string for his harp; the skin was claimed by the Prophet Elijah to clothe himself. As for the ram's two horns—the smaller one called the people together at the foot of Mount Sinai, and the larger one will resound one day, heralding the coming of the Messiah. From this poetic interpretation we learn of Rabbi Hanina's basic attitude toward life: all that exists contains a divine secret and a goal that transcends it. Reality and legend are intertwined: what is legend for *us* may have been reality for someone else. Memory and imagination are not necessarily incompatible; they may complement one another [*Pirke de Rabbi Eliezer* 31].[58]

There are, indeed, times when reality exceeds possibility. That is when legend comes to our aid and when memory is most needed.

Wiesel references a Midrash in which we are told that once Rabbi Hanina ben Dosa saw pilgrims bringing offerings to the Temple, and he grew sad because he had no offering to bring. Just then he spied a large stone, and he vowed that he would bring the stone up to the Temple. He chiseled and polished it and was ready to raise it up, but it was too heavy. Some workers offered to carry it for one hundred gold pieces, but, of course, he had very little money. Again Rabbi Hanina fell into despair. Suddenly five men appeared and offered to help but asked that the Rabbi also pitch in. The instant they picked up the stone, they somehow found themselves atop the Temple Mount. When Rabbi Hanina turned to pay them what money he had, they were nowhere to be found: God had sent His angels to assist Hanina ben Dosa with the offering (*Eykhah Rabbah* 1:1:1). Wiesel's closing comment: "Every word may evoke wonder, every man can hasten redemption, every human being is the center of creation. Like Rabbi Hanina, we wish we could go to Jerusalem with an offering, and like him, we are condemned to carry stones so heavy that they cannot be lifted—except that, unlike Rabbi Hanina, we carry them in our hearts."[59] This means the heart becomes our offering.

Portrait of Rabbi Ishmael

Wiesel relates a tale about the origins of one of Judaism's greatest sages, a man who lived between the destruction of the Second Temple in 70

CE and the Bar Kokhba Rebellion in 135. During a visit to Rome, the Talmud relates, Rabbi Yeoshua ben Hananya once found a Jewish child in a Roman prison. Upon seeing the child, Rabbi Yeoshua uttered the first portion of a verse from Isaiah 42:24: "Who gave up Jacob for a spoil and Israel to plunderers?" And the child uttered the second half of the verse: "Was it not HaShem? It is He against whom we have sinned and they would not walk in His ways or listen to His Torah." Amazed at the boy's learning, the Rabbi determined that he would save the child (*Gittin* 58a). The son of a priest, the child grew up to become the renowned Rabbi Ishmael.[60] Yes, Ishmael: the fact that the name Ishmael, unlike Esau, was used, writes Wiesel, "serves as proof, according to Talmudic commentators, that the first Ishmael, the son of Hagar, did repent [Rashi, commentary on Genesis 15:15]."[61] What did Ishmael have to repent for? No one really knows. That was between him and God.

In addition to studying with Rabbi Yeoshua ben Hananya, Rabbi Ishmael studied *Halakhah* with Rabbi Nehunya ben ha-Kana, the great Kabbalist and author of *The Bahir* (*Shevout* 26a).[62] Yes: he learned *Halakhah* from a great Kabbalist, for in the minds of the great Kabbalists, *Halakhah* is about the "Deeds of the Beginning" and the "Actions of the Chariot." Indeed, all of the great sages who authored codes of law—from Moses Maimonides to Moshe Isserles, from Joseph Caro to Rebbe Schneur Zalman of Lubavitch—were counted among the great mystics. For in Judaism, the realm of the mundane *is* the realm of the mystical, as Rabbi Ishmael understood. That is why he insisted that the study of Torah should be combined with a worldly occupation (*Berakhot* 35b). And that is why Rabbi Tarfon called him "a great scholar and an expert in *aggadot*," that is, the tales of the Written and Oral Torah (*Moed Katan* 28b). The proof? His *Mekilta de-Rabbi Ishmael*. Only a master of *aggadot* can sound the depths of the intimate bonds between the mystical and the mundane. So meticulous was Rabbi Ishmael about the systematic study of Torah, he drafted the Thirteen Principles for Torah analysis that we recite every morning in our prayers, something he learned from Rabbi Nehunya ben ha-Kana.[63]

Echoing a teaching from Rabbi Yohanan, the school of Rabbi Ishmael taught, "Every single word that went forth from the Holy One, blessed be He, split into the seventy languages [of the seventy nations]" (*Shabbat* 88b). The Midrash on Psalms contains a variation on this theme: "When the Holy One, blessed be He, gave forth the divine word, the voice divided itself into seven voices, and from the seven voices passed into the seventy languages of the seventy nations" (*Midrash Tehillim* 2.68.6). The Hasidic master Rabbi Yehudah Leib Alter of Ger elaborates further, saying, "All seventy languages flow forth from the holy tongue. It is the Torah that gives life to all those languages."[64] Proceeding from Rabbi Ishmael, then, we see that a portion of Elie Wiesel's Hasidic legacy concerns language and the bond between word and meaning. Torah itself is a revelation of that bond, and, inasmuch as the language of each nation issues from a spark of the divine utterance of Creation, each language harbors a trace of Torah.

"What else do we know about him?" Wiesel asks. "He was married— no one knows to whom. He had two sons who died before him[*Moed Katan* 28b]."[65] Knowing that he lost two sons tells us a lot about Rabbi Ishmael. It tells us that he had good reason to rebel against God—to cry out to God in anguish, despair, and anger—and perhaps he did: when a parent buries a child, God forbid, creation is turned on end. Nevertheless, this tragic horror did not turn him from his path, a path comprising not just erudition but also the joy that stems from true erudition: "Receive all men with cheerfulness," he taught (*Pirke Avot* 3:12). Rabbi Ishmael, more than any of the sages, erected a fence around speaking ill of our fellow human beings: the School of Ishmael, says the Talmud, taught that "whoever speaks slander increases his sins even up to [the degree of] the three [cardinal] sins: idolatry, incest, and the shedding of blood" (*Arakin* 15b). Thus, Rabbi Ishmael's devotion to Torah. And his reward?

Wiesel relates a tale from the tradition: Rabbi Ishmael was so handsome that just before his execution a Roman matron offered to save his life if he would lie with her. Just as Joseph had refused Potiphar's wife, so Rabbi Ishmael refused the Roman woman—whereupon she ordered him to be flayed.[66] The story continues:

And it came to pass that when the great and revered Rabbi Ishmael was tortured at the hands of the Roman soldiers for having studied Torah, his pain was so overwhelming that he cried out. And so powerful was that outcry that it shook heaven and earth. Nevertheless, the torturer continued to punish the saintly Jewish scholar who later shouted again, so terrible was the pain he was made to endure. His second outcry was more thunderous than the first: it shook the heavenly throne itself. "Why has he been made to suffer so much?" the angels asked. "Is this the reward for his devotion to learning?" "Once a decree has been issued it cannot be revoked," was God's answer. And he hastened to add: "If Rabbi Ishmael cries out once more, I shall restore the universe to its primary chaos." And so kind and considerate was Rabbi Ishmael that he remained silent, and thus the world was saved [*Otsar Midrashim, Esrei Harugi, Malakkot 6*].[67]

Even God could not bear to hear the screams of Rabbi Ishmael. So all of creation rested not only upon the martyrdom of a single witness but also upon the *silent* martyrdom of the most righteous of his generation!

In keeping with his Hasidic character, Wiesel asks: "Since when is God so sensitive to Jewish complaints?"[68] And under the circumstances, why would Rabbi Ishmael not want to restore the universe to its original, primeval chaos? Then we would have a condition of "never having been born" restored, the condition promoted by the House of Shammai that was deemed superior to the opposite view adopted by the House of Hillel. Are creation and the Torah of which it is made so dear to Rabbi Ishmael that he would choose to *silently* undergo such horrific torture? Indeed, he remained silent not only for the sake of creation and Torah but for the sake of God Himself, for there are times when being God's witness requires silence on our part, for the sake of Creation and the Creator.

The Hasidic legacy that comes to us through the example of Rabbi Ishmael? According to Wiesel it is this:

> What he told us—what he taught us—is as follows: Yes, I could destroy the world, and the world, ruled by cynicism and hatred, deserves to be destroyed; but to be a Jew is to have all the reasons in the world to destroy, and not to destroy. To be a Jew is to have all the reasons in the world to hate the executioners and not to hate them. To be a Jew is to have all the reasons in the world to mistrust prayer and faith and humanity and power and beauty and truth and language—and yet not to do so. To be a Jew is to continue using words when they heal, and silence when it redeems mankind.[69]

If God and the angels could not endure the screams of Rabbi Ishmael, his silence must have been even more unendurable. For his silence resembles the silence of the chaos and the void that haunts creation. But in the silence of Rabbi Ishmael the void is full of a silence that surpasses terror, a silence that swallows the scream before it can reach the lips. Stepping before the silence of Rabbi Ishmael, we collide with a place that is the opposite of *HaMakom*—"the Place," as God is called. If God insists upon silence, does He insist upon the radical indifference of the "It," the bystander? Is God merely a bystander? If not, how do we distinguish God's silence from the indifferent neutrality of Being, the blank and empty silence of the abyss, that is the legacy of the Greek philosophers?

Although he knew Greek—or *because* he knew Greek—Rabbi Ishmael forbade others to study the Greeks. Says Wiesel: "He was even harsher toward the miscreants, the heretics of his time—the Minim (the dissident sects), the Sadducees, the Christians."[70] Why? Because all of them, to varying degrees, came under the Hellenistic spell. The Talmud tells us that "Ben Damah the son of R. Ishmael's sister once asked R. Ishmael, May one such as I who have studied the whole of the Torah learn Greek wisdom? He thereupon read to him the following verse, 'This book of the law shall not depart out of the mouth, but thou shalt meditate therein day and night' [Joshua 1:8]. Go then and find a time that is neither day nor night and learn then Greek wisdom.' R. Samuel b. Nahmani said in the name of R. Jonathan, This verse is neither duty nor command but a blessing" (*Menahot* 99b). Yes, a *blessing*. The danger of the "Greek wisdom," as Rabbi Ishmael understood, is that it turns us over to the radical neutrality of being, to the chaos and the void overcome through the Creation, a void in which the scream held back is meaningless because *no one hears you scream*. Or worse, *you hear no one scream*.

No one hears, no one answers. The scream announces the demise of the soul of the mortal victim, as the torturer who would be as God takes absolute possession of it. The demolition of a man—the demolition of the *medaber* or the "speaking being," as Jewish tradition defines the human being—*is* the demolition of the word, the demolition of the scream held back, for which there is no word. And as Rabbi Ishmael understood, it begins with the demolition of the Jew. It is the demolition not only of the expressible but, more profoundly, of the inexpressible, the immemorial, the *hidden*. Rabbi Ishmael also understood that everything that sanctifies life is as unseen as it is unheard. For in the case of Rabbi Ishmael, the scream held back is deafening.

And so we realize the implications of this ancient sage for our own time: without the dimension of the hidden, there is no overcoming the chaos and the void that haunts us and no meaning attached to Creation. The chaos and void belong to a realm in which nothing is hidden. They lurk in the Greek wisdom. Where the Greek wisdom is concerned, nothing is hidden, as nothing can be hidden from the peering eye of the syllogism. Wiesel explains: Rabbi Ishmael declared that "there are seven things hidden from man: 'The day of our death, the day of our consolation, the depth and scope of the law, also, man does not comprehend what makes him worthy, what is going on in the heart of his friend, when David's kingdom will be restored, and when the sinful kingdom will be destroyed [*Pesahim* 54b].' "[71] We can see that this appeal to what Rabbi Ishmael identified as hidden and therefore essential to meaning and sanctity in human life came under assault not only in the time of the Romans but also in the time of those who would emulate the Romans. Rabbi Ishmael insisted that "God is loving,"[72] says Wiesel, and, his "love for his people was absolute."[73] Only by loving more, loving absolutely, will the messianic kingdom be established. This explains why in his portrait Wiesel relates that when the Romans took Rabbi Ishmael and Rabbi Shimon, they were ready to execute both of them, and each begged to be first so as not to witness the death of the other. They drew lots; Rabbi Shimon was murdered first.[74] That was the greatest torture that Rabbi Ishmael suffered: to see his friend tortured to death before his eyes.

According to Rabbi Ishmael, writes Wiesel, "Job belonged to Pharaoh's royal council. And when Moses came to the King to plead for the release of his people, Pharaoh asked his three learned advisors for their opinions. Jethro said, Let them go. Bileam said, Don't. As for Job, he remained neutral—and silent. *That* is why he was punished. In times of need and tragedy, neutrality helps the oppressor and not his victims [see *Haggadah Marbeh Lisaper, Maggid, First Fruits Declaration* 8]."[75] Rabbi Ishmael's "most sublime recommendation?" Wiesel asks. It is this: " 'Do not overburden the camel; do not place on its back a burden too heavy to carry!' [see *Sotah* 13b]."[76] This is a teaching that extends to humanity as well. The care for the animal begins with the care for the human being: if I do not care for the human being, I certainly will not care for the animal. Or is it the other way around?

Pairing and comparing Rabbi Ishmael and Rabbi Akiba, two giants of the Talmud—the *Yerushalmi* refers to them as "the fathers of the world" (*Rosh Hashanah* 1:1)—Wiesel notes that they engaged in many debates but always out of love for humanity and for one another. "Rabbi Akiba," he says, "emphasized imagination, Rabbi Ishmael realism. The first interpreted every word, every letter, every syllable in the Torah, whereas the second sought to clarify its greater meaning. For Rabbi Ishmael the spirit of the law was more important than the letter of the law."[77] But without the letter, there is no spirit. No one knew that better than Rabbi Akiba. Perhaps it was Rabbi Ishmael who led him to that realization. For Rabbi Akiba, the sage who was most meticulous with the *pshat*, the literal level of understanding—who attached the crowns to each letter, poring over every syllable—was the sage who ascended to the most dangerous realms of the upper worlds, where he alone "entered in peace and who departed in peace" (*Talmud Bavli, Hagigah* 14b).

Portrait of Rabbi Akiba

Rabbi Adin Steinsaltz writes: "The systematic organization of *halakhah* as a whole into clearly defined units was apparently carried out by Rabbi Akiva [sic]."[78] Which is to say, no other rabbi's influence on the generations of the last two thousand years is so profound and pervasive as that of Rabbi Akiba. Indeed, with Rabbi Akiba, Wiesel asserts, "the tale of the law became part of the law itself. For him, every word, every letter in Scripture carried special significance."[79] And special demand, special obligation, special responsibility—all that is necessary for meaning in life. That is why Rabbi Akiba's friend and interlocutor Rabbi Tarfon used to say, "Whoever separates from Akiba separates from life" (*Tosefta Mikvaot* 1). Akiba's "impact," says Wiesel, "was felt in the fields of *Aggada* and *Halakha*. 'If it were not for him,' says the Talmud, 'the Torah would have been forgotten.' Thus his life and work have inspired numerous legends and fables. He appeals to the imagination of the learned and the unlearned alike. He is loved by mystics and rationalists. . . . And yet, and yet—I have some difficulties with Rabbi Akiba. His attitude toward suffering troubles me."[80] Why? "I am troubled by his attraction to the suffering which precedes death—and therefore to death itself."[81] We shall return to Wiesel's concern. But first a little more background to prepare the canvas for this portrait.

Few of the great Talmudic sages had such modest origins as Rabbi Akiba. Born in Lydda around 50 CE, his father Yosef, the Talmud tells us, was a proselyte (*Sanhedrin* 96a). He grew up to become an illiterate shepherd in the service of a wealthy man named Kalba Savua, whose beautiful daughter Rachel fell in love with the young Akiba. When she decided to marry Akiba, however, her father cut her off from her inheritance so that the impoverished young couple slept only on straw. "If only I were able," Akiba told his bride, "I would present you with a Jerusalem of gold" (*Nedarim* 50a). One day the Prophet Elijah appeared at the door of the newlyweds disguised as a beggar in need of a bit of straw for his wife to lie upon, as she was about to give birth. Akiba gave him the straw and said to Rachel, "See? Some people are poorer than we are." Having witnessed her husband's compassion for the destitute, Rachel sent him to study with Rabbi Eliezer ben Hyrkanos and Rabbi Yeoshua. When he returned home twelve years later, she expressed her desire that he go back to study for another twelve years. When he returned home to his wife after the second twelve years, he had 24,000 disciples with him (*Nedarim* 50a). Another Talmudic source says that after 12 years he returned with 12,000 disciples, and after another 12 years he brought home 74,000 disciples (*Ketuvot* 62b–63a). His wife approached to greet him, only to meet with his disciples, who tried to keep her away. Rabbi Akiba chided them, saying, "Make way for her, for my learning and yours are from her" (*Ketuvot* 62b).

The only person wiser than Rabbi Akiba would probably have been his wife, Rachel. Poring over this Talmudic tale so central to his portrait, we understand a deeper meaning of Raba's teaching: "How precious is a good wife, with whom the Torah is compared" (*Yevamot* 63b). A good wife bears within her the wisdom of Torah. Bearing the most essential wisdom of Torah, the wisdom that *is* Torah, Rachel recognized the seeds of the same wisdom in her husband and sent him to study—not because of his erudition or his precocious mastery of the Tanakh but because of his love for other human beings, for the stranger, the beggar, and the one who has nowhere to turn. Without that love, without that *hesed*, there is no basis for the pursuit of wisdom and no soil from which the seeds of wisdom might grow: there is no Torah.

But wait a minute. He was *illiterate*, and yet the learned daughter of a wealthy man married him? Yes. And she sent him to study? Yes. At the age of forty he began by learning the *alef-beit*, saying, "When I was an *am ha-aretz* [an ignoramus], I would bite a scholar like a donkey" (*Pesahim* 49b). At the age of forty, the minimum age for studying the mysteries of the Kabbalah, the greatest of the mystics had only begun to learn the difference between an *alef* and a *beit*. The Talmud tells us that he and his son went to learn *alef-beit* together from a teacher of little children; he gathered straw and sold it so he could pay for lessons (*Avot d'Rabbi Natan* 6:2). There is Torah in this, too. We see in this portrait of Rabbi Akiba what leads a man out of the wilderness: the *alef-beit* of Torah. The number forty, of course, is associated with Torah, with the forty days it took to reveal the Torah to Moses, with the letter *mem* that begins the Oral Torah, whose gematria is forty. Moses, in fact, is part of this portrait of Rabbi Akiba.

Wiesel relates the account from the Talmud, where we are told that Moses overheard a rabbinic discussion concerning the Torah and *Halakhah*, and he understood none of it. When he asked God about it, God reassured him that this was indeed the Torah from Sinai, and Moses was satisfied. Suddenly, however, he saw a vision of Rabbi Akiba being tortured to death and asked God, "Is this the reward for devotion to Torah?" God rebuked him, saying that such things "are not to be questioned" (*Menahot* 29b). "And so Moses, in awe," says Wiesel, "like Rabbi Akiba after him, must have understood that there are moments when God wants His chosen to be silent."[82] What? The God who encourages questioning, who names His chosen *Yisrael*, meaning "he who strives with God," wants His chosen to be *silent*? It would seem that when the righteous suffer we should precisely *not* remain silent! What happened to God's declaration that His servant Job spoke rightly (Job 42:7)? Did not Moses confront God, when God was about to wipe out the Israelites, saying that if He should do such a thing, then He should erase the name of Moses from His book (Exodus 32:32)? *Is* such a horrific death the reward for Torah?

I am reminded of an insight from Emil Fackenheim: during the reign of the Third Reich Jews were murdered not because they abandoned Torah but because their grandparents adhered to it.[83] Wiesel is also reminded of something: "I remember the nocturnal processions of Jewish families walking toward death—it seems that they, too, like Rabbi Akiba, were offering themselves to the altar. It seems that they, too, had given up on life—as he had, many of them with the Shma Israel on their lips. Why didn't Rabbi Akiba opt for defiance? Why didn't he proclaim his love for life up to the very moment it was taken away from him?"[84] But what does "given up on life" mean? How, exactly, did they give up on life? By dying? I do not know what giving up on life means. Or how the clinging to life might manifest itself. There are times when clinging to life means dying with the Shma on your lips, as a chosen witness to the Holy One. But I do know, as I have learned from Professor Wiesel, that the affirmation of the sanctity of life in the midst of the desecration and destruction of life is the most essential, the most urgent aspect of wisdom.

And so with Rabbi Akiba we collide with the millennial task of retrieving meaning from the ashes of the obliteration of meaning, something that particularly belongs to the Hasidic legacy of Elie Wiesel. Rabbi Akiba dipped his hands into the ashes and felt around for the remnants of Israel, for the *atzmot*, the "bones" and "essence," of Israel that emerged from the ashes of the Temple that went up in flames. That is why he had such a fathomless and far-reaching impact on the generations of Jews who followed him: the ashes of the body and the shards of those bones of Israel would one day rain over the face of the earth. Says Wiesel of Rabbi Akiba: "A survivor of the destruction of Jerusalem, he had to find a way of conferring meaning upon it. . . . As one who walked amid the ruins of the Temple, he had to find a way to build—again—upon those very ruins."[85] Making our way through Wiesel's portraits, we tread through the ruins of the Third Temple. As we dig, with Rabbi Akiba and with Wiesel, among the ruins of the Second Temple, we sink into the quicksand of the ruins of the Third Temple. We sink into a sea of the mass graves of the Shoah, only to come across the body of a murdered Jew whose murderers will surely never be found.

And so it happened to Rabbi Akiba. Wiesel relates that he "sat in Rabbi Eliezer's presence for twelve years without ever uttering a single word. . . . One day Akiba stumbled upon an unknown corpse in the road—what we call a *met mitzvah*. Remembering that the High Priest, should this happen to him on Yom Kippur, must neglect all other duties and attend to the corpse, Akiba carried the man into town, arriving there exhausted, drenched in sweat—only to be reprimanded by his teacher: a '*met mitzvah*,' he was told, 'must be buried where he is found; with each step you took, you were guilty of shedding blood.'"[86] According to the *Kitzur Shulhan Arukh*, if we should happen upon the bloody body of someone who has been brutally killed, we are to bury the body as we found it, in all its bloody clothing (197:9). I once asked one of my teachers, a Lubavitcher rabbi, why we have such a custom. He said that we bury one who is found in such a condition, with no hope of finding the murderer, in order to put it in God's face and cry out, "See what has become of Your creation! What will You do about it?"

"Another episode in Rabbi Akiba's life troubles me," writes Wiesel. "Again, the adventure in the *Pardes*, the orchard of forbidden knowledge. Four friends entered it. One lost his mind, another lost his faith, a third lost his life—and only Rabbi Akiba entered in peace and emerged in peace [*Hagigah* 14b]. How is that possible? Had an event that destroyed his friends no effect on him?"[87] In the portrait of Ben Azzai and Ben Zoma that follows we shall delve into the details of this episode. Briefly, the four entered the uppermost reaches of the Hidden Wisdom known as the *Pardes* or the "Orchard" of mystical teaching, where the mysteries of the Chariot in Ezekiel's vision unfolded. They were Ben Azzai, Ben Zoma, Elisha ben Abouya, and Rabbi Akiba. Ben Azzai died upon entry, Ben Zoma went insane, and Elisha ben Abouya became an apostate. Only Rabbi Akiba entered in peace and departed in peace. So we see why this incident is so troubling to Wiesel. These were four of the greatest sages of their generation, four of the most righteous of Israel, four who were very close to one another; indeed, Rabbi Akiba loved them and warned them: "When you arrive at the stones of pure marble, do not shout, 'Water, water!'" (*Hagigah* 14b). So why no mention of outrage or pain on the part of Rabbi Akiba over the loss of his three friends?

Could it be that what befell his friends was part of the reason why Rabbi Akiba declared Bar Kokhba to be the Messiah at the time of the Jews' final rebellion against the Roman oppression, which lasted from 132 to 135 CE (*Talmud Yerushalmi, Taanit* 4:8)? As a mystic, Wiesel speculates, "he was mainly concerned with problems related to ultimate redemption. When his *Pardes* adventure failed, he may have decided upon a different strategy. Instead of waiting for a Messiah sent down from heaven, he would force heaven to accept a Messiah chosen by him. He may have thought, 'If I—and hundreds of thousands of children of Israel—proclaim this valiant young general the redeemer, God will have no choice but to anoint him as His redeemer.'"[88] The mystic's effort to hasten the coming of the Messiah may indeed entail forcing God's hand, even if it means endangering oneself. One must never, however, endanger others. Rabbi Akiba "was ready to endanger himself but not others," says Wiesel. "He was ready to advocate suffering for himself but not for others. That is why he taught clandestinely—unlike Rabbi Hananiah ben Teradyon, who persisted in teaching publicly."[89]

Still, Rabbi Akiba was not always so careful or so clandestine, as we see from this Talmudic tale:

> Once the wicked Government issued a decree forbidding the Jews to study and practice the Torah. Pappus b. Judah came and found R. Akiba publicly bringing gatherings together and occupying himself with the Torah. He said to him: Akiba, are you not afraid of the Government? He replied: I will explain to you with a parable. A fox was once walking alongside a river, and he saw fishes going in swarms from one place to another. He said to them: From what are you fleeing? They

replied: From the nets cast for us by men. He said to them: Would you like to come up on to the dry land so that you and I can live together in the way that my ancestors lived with your ancestors? They replied: Art thou the one that they call the cleverest of animals? Thou art not clever but foolish. If we are afraid in the element in which we live, how much more in the element in which we would die! So it is with us. If such is our condition when we sit and study the Torah, of which it is written, For that is thy life and the length of thy days [Deuteronomy 30:20], if we go and neglect it how much worse off we shall be! (*Berakhot* 61b)

Here, too, we catch a glimpse of the wisdom of one who began as a shepherd who knew only how to treat his fellow human beings with loving kindness—like the Prophet Micah's Seven Shepherds (Micah 5:4), whom we welcome into the Sukkah during the days of Sukkot: Abraham, Isaac, Jacob, Moses, Aaron, Joseph, and David. The shepherds are those who understand that the Torah is not just a text or a teaching—it breathes life into the soul. It is the *neshimah* of the *neshamah*. Understanding the profound meaning of the verse "Man lives not by bread alone but by every word from the mouth of God" (Deuteronomy 8:3), Rabbi Akiba was a kind of Eighth Shepherd, who understood that in the absence of Torah and its summons to love the soul suffocates.

"Chaos," writes Wiesel near the end of his portrait of Rabbi Akiba, "is the eschatological trauma in Judaism. Disorder on a universal scale, confusion and anarchy transcending time, space, and language. What is worse than evil? The triumph of evil—and that is chaos. For in chaos good and evil are intertwined and interchangeable. Evil triumphs where it poses as good."[90] Made of Torah, Creation is the overcoming of the *tohu vavohu*, the "chaos and the void" (Genesis 1:2), of the beginning. Creation is the Good, the *ki tov*, that overcomes the evil that is chaos. Evil triumphs not only where it poses as good but where it is indistinguishable from good, in a realm where there are no criminals or madmen, as Primo Levi describes the Lager.[91] "The world around us," he says of his emergence from Auschwitz, "seemed to have returned to primeval Chaos, and was swarming with scalene, defective, abnormal human specimens."[92] These are the creatures who mirror the image not of the Creator but of the chaos opposed by the Creator. "It was more than a sack," says Levi, "it was the genius of destruction, of anti-creation, here as at Auschwitz; it was the mystique of barrenness."[93] The anticreation is the creation of nothing out of something, a return to the void of what strives to overcome the void. It is the triumph of evil.

What does this have to do with Wiesel's portrait of Rabbi Akiba? He suggests one connection: "I remember, inside the kingdom of night, Hasidim singing not only *Ani Maamin* but also '*Amar Rabbi Akiba, amar Rabbi Akiba Ashrekhem Israel*—and Rabbi Akiba said, Blessed and happy are you, Israel—for you are purifying yourselves before Him who purifies you.' "[94] Like Rabbi Akiba, who sang his praise of God as he was tortured to death, these Hasidim cried out their praise to God—if only to defy or implicate God—from the depths of the anticreation, deep calling unto deep as never before. Perhaps it was the song of the Hasidim that kept Creation from slipping over the edge and back into chaos.

Portrait of Shimon ben Azzai and Shimon ben Zoma

Once again the portrait of the Talmudic sage is a portrait of a pair, each of whom tied to the other, complementing each other, with a tension between the two. As we have seen, Ben Azzai ascended to the uppermost realms only to succumb to death, while Ben Zoma succumbed to madness. Is there not a bond in this pairing of death and madness? In *The Town beyond the Wall* Wiesel writes, "The man who chooses death is following an impulse of liberation from the self; so is the man who chooses madness."[95] And yet Ben Azzai and Ben Zoma did not exactly choose death and madness. Indeed, in their ascent to the uppermost realms, they sought a certain liberation from the self, or at least from the ego, which is the greatest stumbling block in the relationship between the human being and the Holy One. In the transformation of the *ani* or "I" into *ain* or "nothing," which is necessary to the higher relationship, the ego must undergo a kind of death that from this side of the transformation looks like madness—not in order to ascend to the ecstatic heights but in order to elevate the earthly reality. As Wiesel says in a comment on the story of the four who entered the *Pardes*, "God does not expect man to join him in heaven. God wants man to remain human, to become more and more human—on earth."[96] Ben Azzai, the one whose soul left him, was especially attuned to this truth.

Ben Azzai was a disciple of Rabbi Yeoshua ben Hananya and of Rabbi Akiba. Like Ben Zoma, he never married nor had any children. Wiesel speculates that this was why he was never ordained rabbi.[97] The Talmud teaches, after all, that a man is not complete until he is married (*Yevamot* 63a). It is also written that a Jew who has no wife is among the seven kinds of men who "are burned by Heaven" (*Pesahim* 113b).[98] "What shall I do if my soul should yearn for Torah?" Ben Azzai explained his reason for not taking a wife. "The world can be perpetuated by others" (*Yevamot* 63b). It was because his love for Torah was so great that he was willing to run the risk of being burned by Heaven. "So great is his love for Torah," says Wiesel, "that it dominates his entire being. The Torah alone is life—it gives meaning to his life. One does not argue with the soul, the soul defies argument. It is reason which loves to argue, not the soul. The soul burns. One must nourish its flame; one must become its flame."[99] And Ben Azzai was, indeed, a soul on fire.

In the Midrash it is written: "Once, as Ben Azzai was expounding the Scriptures, flames blazed up around him, and being asked whether he was a student of the mysteries of the 'Chariot of God,' he replied: 'I string together, like pearls, the words of the Torah with those of the Prophets, and those of the Prophets with those of the Hagiographers; and therefore the words of the Torah rejoice as on the day when they were revealed in the flames of Sinai'" (*Shir HaShirim Rabbah* 1:10:2). To be sure, fire dominates the portrait of Ben Azzai. And Wiesel is taken by it. "Ah, how I would have liked to have been there, listening to Ben Azzai, watching his words dance in a circle of flames! Isn't this the dream of any writer, any teacher—to find words that will sing and dance, words that will burn?"[100] In the Talmud it is said of Yonatan ben Uzziel that when he studied Torah he became so intensely engaged with the Word that the birds flying over him went up in flames (*Bava Batra* 134a). The same might be said of Ben Azzai. He stressed the importance of observing even the most minor of commandments, and he taught that the reward for doing a *mitzvah* is that you will do another *mitzvah* (*Pirke Avot* 4:2). Like every little rivet in the wing of a jet airliner, every little commandment holds together Creation and our connection to the Creator. For the origin of the word *mitzvah*, "commandment," is the Aramaic word *tzavta*, which means "connection." Each time we perform a *mitzvah* we attain a deeper connection with the Creator and His Creation.

Wiesel tells us that "at the end of his life, Ben Azzai became melancholy. Listen to his sobering advice: 'Whoever remembers these four things will be saved from sin. Where does man come from? From darkness. Where is he going? To darkness. By whom shall he be judged? By the Creator of the universe, who knows everything and owns everything, and can be neither flattered nor cheated. Where does man go: To hell and nothingness [*Derekh Eretz Rabbah* 3].'"[101] Did Ben Azzai's melancholy have anything to do with his death upon the entry into the *Pardes*? Wiesel points out that the Midrash lists Ben Azzai as one of the Ten Martyrs who suffered horrific deaths under the Roman oppression (*Eykhah Rabbah* 2:2).[102] Tradition normally has it that all of the Ten Martyrs were rabbis. The Midrash places Ben Azzai in that category because, even though he was not a rabbi, his learning and love for Torah rivaled everyone in his generation—a love that led him to ascend to the uppermost realms to sound ever deeper the depths of Torah, even at the cost of his own life.

In the shadow of the death that befell Ben Azzai looms the madness that overwhelmed Ben Zoma, who "looked where he should not have looked. His reason was shaken, and it abandoned him."[103] In that shadow we discover the bond between Ben Azzai and Ben Zoma, the reason for Wiesel's pairing the two of them in this portrait. We also discover that in this portrait there is more than a trace of a portrait of Elie Wiesel himself. He once told me that in his novels there are only three characters: the old man, the child, and the madman. Is Ben Zoma, and not, say, Moishe the Beadle, the ultimate model for Wiesel's madman? One thing is certain: Elie Wiesel challenges Infinity and the Infinite One in his writing—including in this portrait—and that may be why Ben Zoma is so close to his soul. "Why do I write?" he asks. "Perhaps in order not to go mad. Or, on the contrary, to touch the bottom of madness."[104] And what lies at the bottom of madness? The heights of the *Pardes*.

Just a few examples will show how Ben Zoma found his way into Wiesel's world and why Ben Zoma is so central to his testimony. Wiesel's memories of his father are, understandably, pivotal to who he is and to his Hasidic legacy. In *Legends of Our Time* he writes, "In dying, my father looked at me, and in his eyes where night was gathering, there was nothing but animal terror, the demented terror of one who, because he wished to understand too much, no longer understands anything. His gaze fixed on me, empty of meaning."[105] In his eyes where night was gathering, madness was gathering. It is a madness that mirrors this madness, the madness of a mother systematically targeted for a most radical assault:

Yet the death of the child
Fails to save the others.
It is simply the first of many.
But I saw the mother.
The shudder went through her.
I offer you that shudder.
I saw her gaze fill with madness.
I offer you that madness.
As I offer you her gaze.[106]

The madness in the eyes of his father and the madness in the eyes of this mother flood the eyes of Elie Wiesel, flowing through this portrait of Ben Zoma.

In the words of Gregor's grandfather in *The Gates of the Forest*, "on your way through life you'll meet men who cling to reason, but reason gropes like a blind man with a white cane, stumbling over every pebble, and when it comes up against a wall it stops short and tries to tear it down brick by brick, quite in effectually, because an invisible hand builds it up again, higher and thicker than ever. We, on the other hand, believe in the power of faith and ecstasy, and no wall can stand against us."[107] Ben Zoma's mad desire to dismantle, brick by brick, the wall separating God from humanity, leads him ultimately to madness. Indeed, he had to go mad in order to approach the mysteries of the Hidden Wisdom, which concerns the mysteries of the *Maaseh Bereshit*, the "Deeds of the Beginning." Recall the assertion of Dr. Benedictus in Wiesel's *Twilight*: "In the beginning there was madness. . . . Christianity believes that in the beginning was the Word. But before the Word, what was there? Chaos? But what is chaos if not the loss of perception, sensitivity, language? A total pathological retrenchment. Before Creation, there was a vision of the future, and I tell you, that vision could originate only in great madness."[108] Note well: it is a vision not of the Deeds of the Beginning but the vision of *the future* that originates in great madness. Why might a vision of the future originate in madness? Because the future is the dimension of meaning, the dimension of the hidden, and only in a moment of "great madness" do we behold the hidden.

If Ben Zoma sought to fathom the depths of the meaning of Creation, he could not but plunge into madness—into "great madness," or what Wiesel calls "mystical madness." Says Wiesel:

There is something about him [Ben Zoma] that eludes me. A sage in torment—that much we understand. A sage in revolt, that, too, we understand. But a sage who has lost his mind? A sage who is mad? Right from the start, Ben Zoma aroused my interest—no; more than that: my excitement. Madness—and particularly mystical madness—is, after all, present in all my writings: Is it possible that Ben Zoma, without my noticing it, managed to slip into my stories under one alias or another? Ben Zoma has always belonged to my world, but it took me a long time to become aware of it.[109]

Mystical madness—that is the key to this portrait and to the Hasidic legacy of Elie Wiesel.

What distinguishes mystical madness from clinical madness? Most fundamentally, while clinical madness is damning, mystical madness is redeeming. The vision of the future that originates in mystical madness is a vision of the Messiah. Ben Zoma ascended into the uppermost realms to hasten the coming of the Messiah and to make evil disappear. He achieved neither. In his last novel, *Hostage*, Wiesel relates his main character's recollection of a mysterious figure, a mystic and a Messiah seeker named Paritus: "Shaltiel recalls that Paritus had given him a brief lecture on mystical madness. Is it a powerful and implacable rebellion against linear or discursive thought? What does it seek, except to push tradition and heritage to the bottom of the abyss? Is it the rejection of what seems stable, well-founded, precise, necessary and inevitable? Finally, it is the victory of words, Paritus had said, words that find meaning in the heart."[110] And what is the victory of words? It comes in the moment when we love with *all* the heart.

The victory of the word is the victory of meaning—that is what Ben Zoma sought in his ascent into madness. The sign of the victory of meaning? It is, above all, gratitude. "Throughout his days," says Wiesel, Ben Zoma "often spoke of life with gratitude. . . . A dreamer, reserved, secretive, he sought to lose himself in the mystical, in the blinding light of the obscure. His reward? Madness. The madness of a man who sought to understand that which escapes understanding; who aspired to knowledge that defies knowledge; who neglected the future because the past alone attracted him. Of the four companions, it is Ben Zoma who seems to me the most tragic."[111] Why the most tragic?

Reading further, we may have the answer, as Wiesel provides us with a glimpse of his own soul: "Did he know that he was losing his mind? Did he struggle to hold on to his sanity? Did he long for it, reach for it? These are dangerous questions. . . . Can we say with absolute certainty that Shimon ben Azzai and Shimon ben Zoma did not enter the *Pardes* looking, one for madness, the other for death? Or perhaps for shelter from the victories of the enemy?"[112] These dangerous questions are central to the portrait—indeed, the portrait is made of such questions. And surely Wiesel himself is looking for something in his portrait of Ben Azzai and Ben Zoma: the secret of the link between death and madness. If the connection is there, it lies in the death Ben Zoma died before his death. The death before death is the death that removes you from this world before you have been removed. It is the death that Wiesel portrays in three versions of a story about an encounter between Ben Zoma and his teacher Rabbi Yeoshua ben Hananya. In the first version, the Master asks him where he is coming from and where he is going. He says he is meditating on the mysteries of Creation, on the separation of the waters above from the waters below. Whereupon the Master said, "Ben Zoma is still outside," meaning outside of his senses (*Hagigah* 15a). The second version is the same, but this time the phrase "Ben Zoma is still outside" means he is beyond recovery. In the third version the Master asks him where his thoughts are right now. He answers: "My thoughts are on the mysteries of Creation," whereupon the Master says, "Ben Zoma is already gone." Ben Zoma died a few days later.[113]

Let us consider a Hasidic perspective on this episode, as it comes to us from Levi-Yitzhak of Berditchev:

It is related in *Hagigah* 15 that it happened once that Rabbi Yoshua ben Chananyah (one of the leading scholars in his time) was standing on one of the steps leading up to the Temple Mount, when he saw ben Zoma in front of him, and the latter did not rise in acknowledgment of the presence of his teacher. Rabbi Yoshua asked ben Zoma what subject he was so deeply immersed in that he had not noticed the presence of his teacher. The latter replied: "I was contemplating the significance of the difference between the 'upper waters,' and the 'lower waters' "[Genesis 1:7], and he had discovered that the distance between them was only three fingers' breadth. He

claimed that the proof was found in Genesis 1:2, where the
spirit of HaShem is described as hovering above the surface
of the waters. He considered the word *merahefet*, used by the
Torah there as describing the act of "hovering," as a reference
to a pigeon hovering above its young without touching them.
Upon hearing this, Rabbi Yoshua commented to his other
students: "ben Zoma is still on the outside." He meant that
ben Zoma had not yet become privy to hidden aspects of the
Torah. (*Kedushat Levi, Vayera* 33)

From the standpoint of tradition, Ben Zoma was "on the outside" because
he had taken leave of his senses and had not returned to sanity after ven-
turing into the inner sanctum of the Hidden Wisdom. From Levi-Yitzhak's
Hasidic standpoint, he remained outside the inner chambers of the Hidden
Wisdom and had not yet delved far enough into its innermost depths.

And yet Ben Zoma knew that the innermost depths of humanity lie
not in the ethereal flights of the pseudo-mystic but in the secret miracle of
mundane humanity. Says Wiesel: "Ben Zoma would say: Who is wise? One
who learns from every man. . . . Who is strong? One who overpowers his
inclinations. . . . Who is rich? One who is satisfied with his lot. . . . Who
is honorable? One who honors his fellows [*Pirke Avot* 4:1]."[114] Indeed, this
human orientation, Wiesel suggests, lay behind the four sages' longing
to ascend to the uppermost realms: the adventure was undertaken in an
effort to fathom what lay behind Jewish suffering, which in their time
was horrific. And yet, their concern was not uniformly for the sake of
their fellow Jews. Instead, the four of them represented four categories of
human reaction to the Jewish suffering: "The four friends of the *Pardes*
symbolize the various attitudes within the Jewish community toward the
Roman occupation. Ben Abouya represents active collaboration, Rabbi
Akiba active resistance, Ben Azzai passive death, and Ben Zoma flight
into meditation leading to madness."[115] Why madness? Because the flight
into meditation is a seeking after the *why* of Jewish suffering.

In yet another take, Wiesel writes: "Ben Abouya was concerned with
the present only, therefore he lost his faith; Rabbi Akiba was interested
in the distant future, therefore he was spared; Ben Zoma and Ben Azzai
were interested in the beginnings, and that is why they were punished."[116]
Still, are not the mysteries of the blinding present, the distant future, and
the remote beginnings interconnected? And notice the relation between
the *Who* and the *Why*. In the face of the martyrdom of the sages under

the Romans, "One sage [in the school of Rabbi Ishmael] went so far as to hurl a cry of despair at God: '*Mi kamokha baelim adoshem? Al Tikra elim ki imilemim*: Who is mute as you are, O God? You see your children humiliated, and you remain silent!' [*Gittin* 56b] Our four friends wanted to understand."[117] In the *Who* lies the outcry of *Why?! Lama*?! Rabbi Akiba sought a link between suffering and redemption. Elisha ben Abouya rejected any such link. Ben Azzai perished and Ben Zoma went mad because they beheld the mystery of the link between the *Who* and the *Why*.

Portrait of Rabbi Eleazar ben Azaryah

The portrait of Rabbi Eleazar ben Azaryah revolves around another renowned pair, neither of which, interestingly, is Rabbi Eleazar: Rabban Gamliel and Rabbi Yeoshua. They are the canvas, as it were, upon which Wiesel paints his portrait of Rabbi Eleazar. And yet we ask: is Rabbi Eleazar in the background or in the foreground of his own portrait?

Briefly, then, a few words about Rabban Gamliel. The Mishnah says that he often argued with Roman philosophers (*Mishnah Avodah Zarah* 3:4), who were the purveyors of the "Greek wisdom." He was also known to confront heretics, chief among whom were the early Christians (*Shemot Rabbah* 30:9). As the Nassi he worked for the unification of the Jewish people in the aftermath of the destruction of the Second Temple, and he led the academy at Yavneh to make it a center of learning and *halakhic* authority. It was the school that the Roman General Vespasian had granted to Yohanan ben Zakkai. The Talmud relates that when Jerusalem came under siege in the year 70 CE, the people of the city were starving. They approached Yohanan ben Zakkai and pleaded with him to do something to alleviate their horrific condition. But how to get out of the city? He determined that he would pretend to be dead. They put him in a coffin on top of some rotten meat and asked the Romans for permission to take the sage outside the city to bury him. Once outside the city walls, he approached the Roman General Vespasian and cried, "Peace to you, O Emperor!"

To which Vespasian replied: "Your life is forfeit on two counts: one, because I am not the Emperor and you call me Emperor, and two, if I am the Emperor, why did you not come to me before now?"

At that moment a messenger from Rome came running, saying, "The Emperor is dead, and the notables of Rome have made Vespasian Emperor!"

Realizing the prophetic wisdom of Yohanan ben Zakkai, Vespasian turned to him and said, "Make any request of me, and I shall grant it."

Said Yohanan ben Zakkai, "Give me a school in Yavneh and the family chain of Rabban Gamaliel."

And so Rabban Gamliel, the son of the famous Rabban Shimon ben Gamliel HaZaken and a descendant of Hillel, became the head of the academy in Yavneh (*Gittin* 56a–56b).

He was an extremely wealthy man and a profoundly compassionate man. The Talmud relates that Rabban Gamliel used to hear a bereaved mother weep every night for her dead son, whereupon he would break down into tears: he wept so much, in fact, that his eyelashes fell out (*Sanhedrin* 104b).

While Rabban Gamliel was quite wealthy, Rabbi Yeoshua was poor: he worked as a blacksmith (*Berakhot* 28a). This blacksmith, however, was a Levite who sang in the Temple before its destruction (*Arakin* 11b). He and Eliezer ben Hyrcanos carried Yohanan ben Zakkai out of Jerusalem in the coffin (*Gittin* 56a). He served as head of the Beit Din when Rabban Gamliel was Nassi of the Sanhedrin (*Bava Kama* 74b). He engaged in discussions with the murderous Emperor Hadrian and the philosophers of Athens (*Bekhorot* 8b; *Shabbat* 119a; *Hullin* 59b–60a). When asked what a man should cling to, he answered, "A good friend" (*Pirke Avot* 2:10). He taught that "more than the host does for the poor, the poor does for the host" (*Vayikra Rabbah* 34:8). Here we see the basis of the bond between Rabban Gamliel and Rabbi Yeoshua: it lay in their common understanding of the truth that the soul draws its breath of life from the midst of human relationship, whether it lies in hearing the weeping of a bereaved mother or in answering the call of a friend.

Now that we have the context, let us turn to the first strokes in Wiesel's portrait of Rabbi Eleazar ben Azaryah. A student once went to Rabbi Yeoshua and Rabban Gamliel with the question of whether the *Maariv* or evening prayer is obligatory. Rabbi Yeoshua said no, but Rabban Gamliel said yes. Rabban Gamliel won the argument. Afterward, however, quite contrary to tradition and custom, Rabban Gamliel did not invite the elderly sage Yeoshua to sit down. The members of the assembly were outraged and decided to unseat the Nassi Rabban Gamliel. Note: the decision to unseat Rabban Gamliel came not as a result of some *halakhic* technicality but due to a matter regarding the deference that one human being should show another. Also note that the wealthy man did not show the traditional respect toward the poor man, the blacksmith. And so Rabban Gamliel—the *great* Rabban Gamliel—had to be unseated as Nassi.

Rabban Gamliel commanded fear, Wiesel writes, but "he should never have shamed Rabbi Yeoshua."[118] This, however, was not the first time that Rabban Gamliel shamed Rabbi Yeoshua. It happened when the Sanhedrin had determined that Yom Kippur fell on a day other than what Rabbi Yeoshua thought it should be. Rabban Gamliel ordered Rabbi Yeoshua to come to him carrying a staff and money on the day that he, Rabbi Yeoshua, believed was Yom Kippur. Rabbi Yeoshua was deeply distressed. After he consulted with other sages, he took his staff and his money and went to Rabban Gamliel in Yavneh. Rabban Gamliel rose, kissed him on his forehead, and said to him, "Come in peace my master and my disciple, my master in wisdom and my disciple because you have accepted my words" (*Mishnah Rosh Hashanah* 2:9). Wiesel explains: "Rabbi Yeoshua, who walked, weeping, with Rabbi Akiba on the ruins of the Temple, understood that, having lost its sovereignty, the people of Judea needed another institution to symbolize royalty and authority: in effect, the president had succeeded the kings and princes of Judea and Israel. Thus for a scholar to disobey his leader would be tantamount to inciting general disobedience: the office would be adversely affected and so would the Jewish people. That is why he consistently chose to avoid open conflicts." To question the president's authority "ultimately meant to doubt that of Moses."[119] Therefore, despite his trepidation, Rabbi Yeoshua violated what he thought to be the holiest day of the year: the day when the fate of his soul would be determined.

When the Sanhedrin decided to oust the elderly Nassi, they replaced him not with Rabbi Akiba or another venerable sage but with the eighteen-year-old Rabbi Eleazar ben Azaryah, a young man known for his learning and a descendant of Ezra the Scribe. But really, a *kid*?! When approached, Rabbi Eleazar was very intimidated. He humbly said he must first consult his wife. She told him in no uncertain terms *not* to take the position because he was too young. When his wife told him he was too young, Rabbi Eleazar answered, "I look old, I look like a man of seventy" (*Mishnah Berakhot* 1:5). The "Talmudic legends," says Wiesel, "add that, indeed, at that moment, his hair turned, some say gray, some say white [*Berakhot* 28a]."[120] Because his hair miraculously turned white, he accepted the position, contrary to his wife's counsel, taking his sudden aging to be a sign from God.

"As for Rabbi Eleazar ben Azaryah," writes Wiesel, "he became president against his own will. He neither sought the position nor particularly wanted it. When it was offered to him, he did not grab it."[121] Wiesel points out some notable distinctions between the great Rabban Gamliel and the young new Nassi: "Rabban Gamliel cultivated the elite, Rabbi Eleazar broke down all social and intellectual barriers. Rabban Gamliel's principal interest was the law; Rabbi Eleazar loved poetry and legend: it was he who made the decision to incorporate the Song of Songs and the Book of Ecclesiastes into the canon [see *Tanhuma Tetzaveh* 5]. Whereas Rabban Gamliel chastised, Rabbi Eleazar comforted. Rabbi Eleazar's most ardent wish was to cleanse mankind from its sins, for, in his eyes, it had suffered enough."[122] And it was Rabbi Eleazar who said that a tribunal that imposes a death sentence once in seventy years is murderous (*Mishnah Makkot* 1:10). In the end, however, Rabbi Eleazar's wife proved to have given him sound advice, as Wiesel observes: several months later—some sources say one day later—they removed Eleazar ben Azaryah from the presidency. Rabban Gamliel reassumed the position; Rabbi Eleazar, however, was his deputy, so that Rabbi Eleazar retained a position of honor (*Berakhot* 28a). Says Wiesel, "The reason, then, for choosing young Rabbi Eleazar was that he could be easily demoted. Thus both Rabban Gamliel and Rabbi Yeoshua realized from the beginning that it was only an academic exercise, a game, so to speak. And he himself knew it."[123] A game? The purpose of the Sanhedrin is to enact God's will in this realm. Is that a place for game playing? Is this portrait a game?

Actually, Wiesel reminds us, Rabbi Yeoshua had a hand in the reinstatement of Rabban Gamliel. Rabban Gamliel and Rabbi Yeoshua disagreed on the question of whether an Ammonite or a Moabite can convert to Judaism; the former said no, the latter yes. Said Rabban Gamliel, "Since the law is according to Rabbi Yeoshua, it is time for me to go and ask for his forgiveness." At first Rabbi Yeoshua refused to forgive Rabban Gamliel. Only when he asked for forgiveness not for his own sake but for the sake of his father did Rabbi Yeoshua forgive him—whereupon Rabbi Yeoshua lobbied to have Rabban Gamliel reinstated as president (see *Berakhot* 28a).[124] The father of Rabban Gamliel, we recall, was Rabban Shimon ben Gamliel HaZaken; he was among the Ten Martyrs, the one slaughtered with Rabbi Ishmael as the first of the Ten Martyrs. Who he is can be found in his teachings. He was, for example, a teacher who understood the meaning and value of silence: "All my life I have been raised among the wise, and I have found nothing better for the body than silence. The essential thing is not study, but deed. And one who speaks excessively brings on sin" (*Pirke Avot* 1:17). Why better for the body? Because we perform the deeds of the commandments with the body—after we have fallen silent. Therefore too much talk, at the very least, brings on a delay in the observance of the commandments, which in turn increases human suffering in the world.

Wiesel directs us to a thread in *Pirke Avot* that traces a line from the father of Rabban Gamliel to Rabbi Eleazar.[125] Rabbi Eleazar taught:

> If there is no Torah, there is no common decency; if there is no common decency, there is no Torah. If there is no wisdom, there is no fear of God; if there is no fear of God, there is no wisdom. . . . He would also say: One whose wisdom is greater than his deeds, what is he comparable to? To a tree with many branches and few roots; comes a storm and uproots it, and turns it on its face. . . . But one whose deeds are greater than his wisdom, to what is he compared? To a tree with many roots and few branches, whom all the storms in the world cannot budge from its place. (*Pirke Avot* 3:17)

Noting the accent on the deed, we see that while Rabbi Eleazar may have briefly succeeded Rabban Gamliel as Nassi, he remained in debt to the great sage for the teaching and testimony transmitted over the ages, from Hillel, to Rabban Shimon ben Gamliel HaZaken, to Rabban Gamliel, to Rabbi Eleazar ben Azaryah. That is why, upon once again ascending to the office of Nassi, Rabban Gamliel retained Rabbi Eleazar as Av Beit Din, chief of the Sanhedrin's court of justice.

So Wiesel asks in the end: who was the disciple who initiated the dispute over the Maariv prayers and set this drama into motion? It was Shimon bar Yohai.[126] But we shall come to his portrait soon enough.

Portrait of Rabbi Tarfon and the Meaning of Humility

Wiesel's portrait of Rabbi Tarfon is not only the portrait of a sage—it is a portrait of humility. But what does being a sage have to do with humility? And what does humility have to do with being a sage? One place to begin is with Rashi's commentary on Genesis 1:26, where he explains that humility is an attribute of God Himself. Therefore if it is an attribute of the Holy One, then a sage who humbly strives to emulate the Holy One might aspire to the attribute of humility. The only problem is that one cannot *aspire* to be humble, since you cannot be humble and *know it*. Still, we may ask: how is it that humility—lowliness—can be an attribute of the Holy One, the Most High? The Kabbalists teach that HaShem undergoes a contraction or withdrawal in order to allow room for the existence of this finite world so as not to overwhelm our finitude with His infinity.[127] To be sure, the glory of the Infinite is manifest precisely in such a *tzimtzum*, to use the Hebrew term, manifest in what Levinas calls "an exasperated contracting" of the self for the sake of the other.[128] Creation is an act of entering into a relationship between God and humanity. As a movement into a covenant, creation is an act of divine humility.

Therefore if humility implies lowliness, it also implies the very height of the Most High. "Humility," Levinas explains, "is not to be confused with an equivocal negation of oneself, already proud of its virtue, which, in reflection, it immediately recognizes in itself. This humility is that of him who does not 'have time' to make a return upon himself and undertakes nothing to 'negate' the oneself, save the very abnegation of the rectilinear movement of a work which goes infinitely to the other."[129] Humility is not timidity, trepidation, or diffidence. On the contrary, humility requires vulnerability—which requires courage, confidence, fearlessness, and under-standing—the understanding of what there is to fear and what there is to fear *for*. Humility attests to the holiness of the other by affirming the height of the other. Thus, in order to understand what a sage has to do with humility, we must consider what humility has to do with height. "Let a single trace of pride be added to the quest," Wiesel elaborates on the wisdom of Rabbi Tarfon, "and it will lead to self-delusion and hypocrisy." When performing good deeds, he says, "one must think of what one does—and why." Not of one's own righteousness or salvation.[130] Humility seeks the Good, not the reward.

Rabbi Tarfon was among the sages of the third generation of the Tannaim, one of the sages of Yavneh during Rabban Gamliel's reign as Nassi. Interestingly, he was both a teacher and a colleague of Rabbi Akiba (*Ketuvot* 84b). Ironically, for one known for his humility, he was very tall, as it is written, the tallest in his generation (*Niddah* 24b): everyone literally looked up to him, even as he situated every other person in a position of height. Which tells us that the dimension of height is a meta-physical category and not a physical or spatial configuration. In fact, as we have seen, it is much more about time than it is about space. Because

Rabbi Tarfon had time for others, he had patience. Therefore, according to tradition, he would teach by asking questions (*Tosefta Berakhot* 4:16). Questions require more time, patience, and humility than do fixed formulas and ready answers.

In the words of Rabbi Yehuda HaNassi, humility means "knowing what is above you" (*Pirke Avot* 2:1). The dimension of height and humility lies in the You. Recall the teaching from the Zohar: instead of reading *Bereshit bara Elokim et ha-* as "In the beginning God created the—" we should read it as "In the beginning God created the *alef, tav, hey* of *atah*: You" (*Zohar* I, 15b). With this dimension of the You at the very foundation of Torah, as Wiesel points out, "another realm of humility exists in our relationship to the Torah. In its presence one can yield neither to pride nor to vanity. The commandment against idolatry, 'Thou shalt have no other gods,' refers to pride, according to Rabbi Shimon bar Yohai: you yourself must not be a god. . . . Whoever glorifies his or her own self will end in opposition to himself and to God."[131] Listen to Wiesel:

> It is through humility that Torah is preserved [*Tanhuma Ki Tavo* 3]. "Even if you are perfect in all things," says the Talmud, "if you lack humility, you have nothing [cf. *Sotah* 5a]" And the Midrash declares: "There are seven rewards given to the humble man or woman: they will have their share in the world to come, their teaching will be remembered, the Shekhina will rest on them, they will be spared all punishment, nothing evil will happen to them, the whole world will feel sorry for them, and, best of all, the humble man will not have to live with a wicked woman" That the Torah demands humility for those who study it is illustrated by the secret it harbors. This secret cannot be pierced, for it deepens as one comes closer to its gate. Let's call it the secret of the secret. Whoever pretends to know it still has a lot to learn.[132]

To say that the humble will be spared punishment is not to say that they will not suffer: suffering is not punishment, so that when they suffer, others will feel sorry for them. Further, the Talmud teaches that "he who humbles himself the Holy One, blessed be He, raises up, and him who exalts himself the Holy One, blessed be He, humbles . . . ; he who forces time is forced back by time but he who yields to time finds time standing at his side" (*Eruvin* 13b). And how do we yield to time? By beholding and heeding the dimension of height revealed in the face of the other human being, which is to say: to yield to time is to have time for the other human being—that is the key to humility.

The secret of secrets lies not in the uppermost celestial spheres but in the innermost recesses of the human heart—and in the compassionate, humble answering to the other, "Here I am for you!" Says Wiesel: "To be humble before God is easy; to be humble before another person is not. . . . True humility is judging oneself with severity and judging others with understanding. For a humble person, even the most obstinate sinner deserves respect, for we do not know the essential truth about someone else. Therefore I am unable to put myself in his or her place. Truth, in its totality, is known to God alone. And He desires to be humble in going down to the level of his creatures—and joining His people in exile."[133] Rabbi Tarfon shared with the Holy One this love for the people of Israel, for his "allegiance to Torah was absolute. In Talmudic literature he is called 'the father' and also 'the teacher of all the people of Israel'[*Talmud Yerushalmi, Yoma* 1:1]. Both titles point to his profound love for his people."[134] Indeed, a teacher or *moreh* is a kind of father or *horeh*, both of which are cognates of *Torah*.

Rabbi Tarfon was among those who have, God forbid, known the passing of someone *lo bekitzo*, "not in his time." Wiesel writes, "Fatherless, just as his children were motherless, Rabbi Tarfon showed great compassion to all orphans. To bring up an orphan, he would say, is to constantly fulfill the commandment of giving charity."[135] Giving charity, of course, includes giving Torah. Just so, in his portrait of Rabbi Tarfon, Wiesel tells the story of when Rabbi Akiba went to Rabbi Tarfon and told him he had some property that would be an excellent investment for him. When Tarfon later asked Akiba about the property, Akiba took him to a yeshiva where students, some of whom were orphans, were studying Scripture and said, "Here is your property." Rabbi Tarfon kissed Akiba on the forehead and gave him more money (*Pesikta Rabbati* 125:2; *Vayikra Rabbah* 34:16).[136] If to be an orphan is to be without a mother or a father, then, Rabbi Tarfon understood, to be without Torah is to be an orphan.

Rabbi Tarfon witnessed the destruction of the Second Temple, but "he rarely, if at all, spoke of it. One cannot help but be intrigued by his silence. Why didn't he refer to the ransacking of Jerusalem, the profanation of the Sanctuary, the children dying in the street? Was it simply a matter of discretion or shyness? Did he feel unable or unworthy to speak of a catastrophe of such magnitude? The same applies to his personal tragedies. He says nothing about the death of his wife and, later, of his children. Is it that he had *too much* to say?"[137] Or was he afraid that if he should speak of these things he might begin to weep so profoundly that he would never stop? With regard to Rabbi Tarfon's silence on the destruction of Jerusalem and the Second Temple, Wiesel raises another, more generous question: "Was he trying to tell us that silence too can be a response to extreme suffering? And that some secrets, protected by silence, must remain inviolate?"[138] The destruction of the Second Temple was the radical imposition of a silence upon the world that could be answered only with silence. "Before I write," says Wiesel, "I must endure the silence, then the silence breaks out. In the beginning there was silence—no words. The word itself is a breaking out. The word itself is an act of violence; it breaks the silence. We cannot avoid the silence, we must not. What we can do is somehow charge words with silence."[139] Here, as in all of these portraits, we discover the trace of a self-portrait in Wiesel's portrait of Rabbi Tarfon. Before Rabbi Tarfon speaks, he endures the silence that swept over the ruins of the Second Temple. He understands that the word itself now runs the risk of violence—hence his humility. And, in his humility, he sought to charge words with silence.

Amidst the rubble of the Temple Rabbi Tarfon cries out: "'No one is asking you to complete the task, but you must begin it' [*Pirke Avot* 2:16]. So we are beginning and beginning, again and again." Once more we are reminded of Wiesel's wisdom, steeped in humility: "It is not given to man to begin," he once wrote. "That privilege is God's alone. But it is given to man to begin again—and he does so every time he chooses to defy death and side with the living."[140] Wiesel's portrait of Rabbi Tarfon, his portrait of humility, is a portrait of a new beginning. It is a portrait of the infinity opened up in the again and again, couched in humility, each time a human being begins again.

Portrait of Rabbi Hananiah ben Teradyon

In the portrait of Rabbi Tarfon, we saw the dimension of height manifest in humility—in the water that assumes the lower level. In this portrait of Rabbi Hananiah ben Teradyon, we come to the dimension of height opened up through martyrdom—through the fire that ascends to the upper realms. The story of Hananiah ben Teradyon is among the most famous of the tales in the Talmud (*Avodah Zarah* 18a).

In the time of the Roman persecution, when the study of Torah was prohibited, there lived a sage named Rabbi Hananiah ben Teradyon. Fearing heaven more than he feared humanity, Rabbi Hananiah refused to bow to the injunction against learning and living by the Torah. Despite the threat of death, he continued to teach and to study, for he knew that without the Torah there is no life. One day the Romans found Rabbi Hananiah ben Teradyon in the midst of a public assembly. With his daughter Brurya at his side, he held the Torah scrolls to his heart and shared the Torah of Moses with the people gathered around him. The Romans decided to make an example of the rabbi. They arrested him and wrapped him in the scrolls of the Torah that he had been cradling in his arms. Once he was bound in the scrolls, they ordered bundles of dry wood to be piled around him. They soaked pieces of wool in water and applied them to the rabbi's chest so that his death would be slow and painful. And then they set fire to the wood.

When her father was taken to be executed, Brurya cried out and beat her head with her fists. Her father stopped her. "Now, at this supreme moment," says Wiesel, "she became his child again—she was reunited with her father, alone with him as never before."[141] Then she burst into tears and cried out, "Oh, father, I am cursed that I should have lived to see this!"

"Do not weep for me, my child," he comforted her. "The One who sees to the care of the Torah will see to my care."

She wept. "My tears are not only for you but also for the Torah that is to be burned with you!"

He answered: "You needn't shed tears for the Torah, little one. For the Torah is fire, and fire cannot burn fire."

As the flames began to rise, Rabbi Hananiah's disciples gathered around him and called out, "Rabbi, what do you see?"

"I see the parchment consumed in the fire," he replied. "But the letters . . . the letters are ascending into the heavens!"

"Rabbi!" they shouted to their beloved teacher. "Open your mouth and breathe in the flames, so that you may put an end to this terrible suffering!"

"Let the Holy One who gave me my soul take it from me," he said. "But let no man do injury to himself."

Beholding this scene and hearing these words, the executioner who set fire to the sage was overcome by the truth of the testimony he heard. "Rabbi!" he cried out. "If I should remove the tufts of wool from your chest, will you take me with you into the World to Come?"

"Yes," Rabbi Hananiah answered.

The executioner reached into the flames and removed the wet wool from the rabbi's chest. Within seconds the sage expired, and the executioner threw himself into the flames.

At that moment, all who were there heard a Voice from on high proclaim, "Rabbi Hananiah ben Teradyon and the executioner have found their place in the World to Come!" When, more than a century later, Rabbi Yehuda HaNassi heard the tale of Rabbi Hananiah's martyrdom, he wept and said, "Truly there are those who earn eternal life in a single hour, while others must labor a lifetime."

The Talmudic sages teach that there are six different kinds of fire: fire that eats but does not drink; fire that divides but does not eat; fire that eats and drinks; fire that consumes dry matter as well as moist matter; fire that pushes fire away; and fire that eats fire (*Yoma* 21b). Which fire shall we say is the fire that consumed Rabbi Hananiah ben Teradyon when he was wrapped in the scrolls of the Torah and burned alive? Recall the time when Rebbe Hersh, son of the Baal Shem, asked his father in his dreams, "How can I serve God?" Says Wiesel, "The Baal Shem climbed a high mountain and threw himself into the abyss. 'Like this,' he answered." Another time "the Baal Shem appeared to him as a mountain of fire, erupting into a thousand flaming fragments: 'And like this as well.'"[142] Rabbi Hananiah ben Teradyon became such a mountain of fire.

We realize how close Rabbi Hananiah ben Teradyon was to Wiesel when Wiesel tells us the following:

> I was especially moved by and proud of Rabbi Hananiah ben Teradyon. His poignant personal response to Rome's policy of violence appealed to me, to the Jew in me, to the Jewish child in me. The spirit is stronger than its enemy; the fire of Torah is stronger than fire; one can die for truth but truth never dies. This is what every Jew learned or should learn from Rabbi Hananiah ben Teradyon. His lesson is necessary, if not vital, to the understanding of our own existence and survival. . . . Whenever Jews were persecuted, we consoled ourselves with the martyr's statement: "*Gvilin nisrafin*"—only the scrolls are burning, only our homes, only our lives can be destroyed—our soul and our memory remain beyond our enemy's reach.[143]

The Torah remains beyond the enemy's reach. And as long as Jews cling to the Torah as Rabbi Hananiah did, their souls and their memory, their teaching and their testimony, remain beyond the enemy's reach.

Rabbi Hananiah ben Teradyon was a Tanna of the third generation. His teacher was Rabbi Eliezer ben Hyrcanos. Rabbi Halafta, father of the great Rabbi Yossi, was his friend. He was, however, haunted by tragedy. "His wife," says Wiesel, "was beheaded; one of his two daughters was placed in a house of ill repute; one of his two sons was executed by shady accomplices [*Avodah Zarah* 17b]."[144] Why was Brurya spared? Was it "because as a married woman," Wiesel wonders, "she no longer belonged to Rabbi Hananiah's household? Or because she and her husband were under the so-called protection of a Romanophile named Elisha ben Abouya [the apostate] who, everyone knew, was her husband's pupil?"[145] Here lies the greatness of Rabbi Hananiah, the dimension of height conveyed in this portrait: his response to his own horrific suffering was not malediction and bitterness but acts of loving kindness.

But there is more: "Rabbi Hananiah's entire life was filled with mourning. Many of his peers perished as martyrs. The people of Israel seemed to have been forsaken by the God of Israel. Judea was subjected to Hadrian's persecutions. Oppression, brutality, collective and individual cruelty were everywhere. The study and teaching of Torah meant mandatory capital punishment. As did the observance of Shabbat. And circumcision. And the reciting of Sh'ma. Challenged by the spirit of the Jewish people, Rome sought to distort and humiliate it."[146] According to the Hasidic master Levi-Yitzhak of Berditchev, "All the hatred of the Jews" comes "from our constant defense of You,"[147] which is a defense of the eternal You as well as the You of flesh and blood, both of whom announce an infinite responsibility that can be neither fulfilled nor abrogated. By their very presence in the world the Jewish people represent the presence of the Infinite One, of the You, who disturbs our sleep from beyond the world, from the inside, by proclaiming our infinite responsibility to and for the other human being. Subsequently the very presence of the Jews is unsettling to a world that longs to have matters—particularly matters of Redemption—settled.

Rabbi Yossi ben Kisma rationalized the Roman oppression of the Jews and justified God, and it troubled Rabbi Hananiah. "Because of the threat? No. Rabbi Hananiah was not easily frightened. More likely his sadness was caused by his colleague's rationalization of Jewish tragedy. If Jews are humiliated and slaughtered, it is because God wills it that way, Rabbi Yossi ben Kisma had said. God is on the side of Rome—on the side of Israel's enemy. If Rome is powerful, it is because God gave the Romans power."[148] Within a few days, the Talmud relates, Rabbi Yossi died, and many of the Roman dignitaries attended his funeral. It was on their way back from the funeral that they found Rabbi Hananiah publicly teaching Torah and ordered him to be wrapped in the scroll and burned alive (*Avodah Zarah* 18a). Hearing Yossi ben Kisma's rationalization of Jewish suffering may well have impelled Rabbi Hananiah to take up the Torah scroll and openly proclaim its teaching.

The Talmud teaches that God requires *Kiddush HaShem*, the "Sanctification of the Name" or martyrdom, on the part of one who might be forced to commit the sins of idolatry, adultery, or murder (*Pesahim* 25a–25b). If that is the case, it appears that Rabbi Hananiah and the other Ten Martyrs could have averted their cruel martyrdom. Says Wiesel,

> Upon closer scrutiny, the martyrs' deaths strike us as unwarranted even in the context of their times. Not one of them stood accused of adultery, idolatry, or bloodshed. Then why did they choose to die? Nowhere is it written that one must risk one's life for Torah. . . . I prefer to believe that, whatever they did, they did in conformity with the law. I believe that *Limud Torah*—teaching and studying—also implies *Kiddush-hashem*. I believe that it was not specified because it was self-evident: without *Limud Torah*, without learning, without knowledge, how would anyone even know about the other three laws never to be transgressed?[149]

Indeed, in the case of Rabbi Hananiah ben Teradyon, spreading the teaching and testimony of Torah was the capital crime. Under Jewish law, he could have ceased doing so and thus saved his life. But he knew that without teaching Torah, there is no life to save, neither for him nor for the Jewish people. So "Rabbi Hananiah was right," says Wiesel. "He knew that once Torah was forgotten everything would be forgotten."[150] The fire would be forgotten. The dimension of height would be forgotten. The commandment to choose life (Deuteronomy 30:19) would be forgotten. Rabbi Hananiah burned so that the Torah made of fire might not be forgotten. Wiesel's Hasidic legacy is the most ancient Jewish legacy: remember, so that the Torah made of fire might not be forgotten.

Wiesel ends his portrait with this: "It is said that when the news of Rabbi Akiba's tragic death reached Rabbi Hananiah ben Teradyon, he and his friends tore their clothes and began mourning their loss. And one sage exclaimed, 'The death of this sage and just man serves as a prediction of perilous times that are about to come upon us [*Mishnah Semahot* 8:9]." If the death of one man serves as an evil omen for humankind, what should one say about the death of six million men, women, and children, *children*?"[151] Yet again we come up against the children, the ones whose breath, says the Talmud, sustains all of creation (*Shabbat* 119b). The letters that Rabbi Hananiah saw ascending to heaven are reminiscent of the bodies and souls and ashes of the men, women, and children that were cast upon the winds in the time of the Shoah. Once again, as before, we enter into the collision: the ashen letters, like the ashen remains, rain down upon the earth and invade our souls.

Portrait of Rabbi Meir and Brurya

Wiesel opens his portrait of this most remarkable couple, the great Rabbi Meir and the brilliant Brurya, with a tale from the Midrash (*Midrash Mishlei* 31).[152] It is a tale that reveals the depths of each of these beautiful souls.

One Erev Shabbat, Rabbi Meir set out from the House of Study in Tiberius to spend the Sabbath with his wife Brurya and their two toddler sons. Often during the summer months the little ones would fall asleep before the arrival of the Sabbath. So when they did not greet him, the rabbi surmised that he would have to wait until morning to see his beloved children. His wife Brurya met him with a loving smile. She set the table with the loaves of challah and the cup of Kiddush wine. She lit the candles to usher in the Sabbath, and the rabbi recited the Kiddush. He sang to his wife the *Eshet Hayil*, "A Woman of Valor," said the blessing on the bread, and they sat down to enjoy the Sabbath meal.

"So our little ones are sleeping soundly?" Rabbi Meir asked his wife. But she did not answer. The rabbi wondered at his wife's unusual silence but he said nothing, supposing that she would speak when she was ready to speak.

Early the next morning, after her husband had finished his prayers, Brurya asked him, "May I have a word with you, my husband?"

"What is it, my love?"

"Not so long ago," said Brurya, "two very precious jewels were placed in our care. Yesterday, before you arrived home for the Sabbath, the one who entrusted to me those precious jewels came to reclaim them. I did not want to part with them, but I knew they belonged to him. I knew I had to return them."

"You have done the right thing," Rabbi Meir told her. "What is placed in our care must always be returned to its owner in good faith and in good cheer. But tell me, where are our little boys? Is it not time that they were up and about?"

Brurya said nothing but took her husband by the hand to their sons' room. As they approached the room the rabbi's bewilderment turned to dread: when they entered the room where their children lay still and cold, he realized the terrible truth behind his wife's question about the return of precious jewels. And he wept bitter tears.

"I did not know what to do," Brurya told him, her hand on his heaving shoulders. "I was afraid to disturb your joy in the Sabbath. But you just said that we must return what has been placed in our care, in good faith and in good cheer. God entrusted to our care these two precious jewels. But He has come to reclaim what belongs to Him."

"My own teaching now haunts me," Rabbi Meir sobbed. "We mustn't weep and mourn too much . . . lest it become a murmuring against the Holy One. . . . We must. . . . We must."

But his words could not break through his tears.

So crucial is this episode to the portrait of Rabbi Meir and Brurya, Wiesel offers an elaborate commentary on it:

> Believing in God and in His justice, he bows his head and accepts the judgment. What he feels is sadness, not rebellion. Disarmed in the face of misfortune, he lets himself go. . . . Rabbi Meir weeps; she does not. Rabbi Meir cannot control his emotions; she can. . . . Of the two, who touches and troubles us more? Rabbi Meir, because he is defenseless and innocent? Or Brurya, because of her willpower and composure? From Rabbi Meir's behavior, and his *repeated* inquiries, once senses his impatience, his anguish. The father has premonitions; he guesses that something is wrong, that something has happened to his children. . . . Yet, when facing a question of law, his mind is distracted. The father yields to the teacher until reality hits him head-on. Then he begins to weep and mourn. . . . As for Brurya . . . , why didn't she shout with pain—as any normal mother would have done? . . . She knows how to handle tragic situations because she has been through so much. . . . The verbal trap set for her husband? To be fair, it was a trap not against him but *for* him.[153]

Yes, a trap *for* him, *for his sake*. She was able to turn his attention, for a moment, to his learning and his wisdom as one of the great sages of his generation. He understood the truth that the Holy One, Blessed be He, the Creator and Sustainer of all life, is the One to whom all life belongs. Our lives are not our own, nor do our children belong to us. But his intellect was not enough to check his emotion and his anguish.

As for Brurya, her life was filled with tragedy, as we have seen: her father Rabbi Hananiah ben Teradyon was burned at the stake, her mother was beheaded, and her sister was made a prostitute. Then she lost her own children. In the end she was the sole survivor of her family. She lived in a time when many Jews endured horrific suffering—nothing unusual about her in that. What is unusual about her is her extraordinary intellect. Her learning ran so deep that she frequently engaged in *halakhic* disputes with the great sages of that generation, including her father Hananiah ben Teradyon. Says Wiesel, "No wonder she was feared in academic circles. Wherever she appeared, people took flight. Leaders of *yeshivot* avoided her. She literally paralyzed her opponents. She respected no official title, no social position; she recognized no authority. . . . Brurya: a woman of brains and heart whom one admires and loves because of her greatness— and *in spite of* her aggressive brilliance."[154] And yet she was so aggressive because her pain ran so deep.

One can see why Wiesel asserts, "For Rabbi Meir and Brurya the words are adventure and discovery. They live intensely, dangerously. There is never a boring moment. They stimulate, they wound, they search. In their presence everything moves, every string vibrates, sings, and breaks."[155] The Talmud relates that when Brurya's sister was taken away to be a prostitute, Rabbi Meir went to the brothel to ransom her. The man in charge of the brothel was afraid that he would be punished if he should release the girl. "When danger is about to befall you," Rabbi Meir told him, "repeat the acronym 'E.D.M.A.,'" which stands for the phrase *Elokei de Meir anani*, "God of Meir, answer me!" The man was arrested and sentenced to be hanged. When the noose was around his neck, the man cried out, "E.D.M.A.: God of Meir, answer me!" The noose broke, and the man was saved. When he told the story to the Romans, Rabbi Meir was forced to flee from the Holy Land (*Avodah Zarah* 18a). Wiesel reminds us that there was another reason why Rabbi Meir left the Land. After an argument concerning the susceptibility of women to temptation, Rabbi Meir had one of his students attempt to seduce his wife, Brurya. She succumbed: "Brurya, seized by remorse, hanged herself [Rashi on *Avodah*

Zarah 18b]."[156] And so Rabbi Meir and Brurya run the range of human experience, of Jewish experience, and of the response to that experience. It is troubling that the Talmud offers little elaboration on Rabbi Meir's reaction to her suicide, except to speculate that it was the reason why he left for Babylon, where he died (*Avodah Zarah* 18b; see also *Talmud Yerushalmi, Kilayim* 9:4).

Interestingly, the Talmud tells us that Rabbi Meir's real name was Rabbi Nehorai; he was called Rabbi Meir ("the Illuminator") because, says the Talmud, "he enlightened the eyes of the scholars in *halakhah*" (*Eruvin* 13b). And yet how darkened were his eyes when he gazed upon Brurya! He was also known as Rabbi Meir *Baal-haNes*, the Miracle Worker. Descended from converts—some say from the Roman Emperor Nero (*Gittin* 56a)—he studied with Rabbi Akiba and Rabbi Ishmael, as well as with Yehuda ben Baba and the apostate Elisha ben Abouya, whom he never shunned. Rabbi Meir traveled much of the world on urgent missions. He debated heretics and philosophers and, says the Talmud, even engaged Cleopatra in discussions (*Sanhedrin* 90b). That is why he was known as the Illuminator: he was a light unto the nations.

Rabbi Meir's light emanates not only throughout the nations but also across the generations, even unto the Messianic age, according to a Hasidic teaching, as Wiesel points out: "Although we know that *Stam Mishna kerebe Meir*, that whenever the Mishna is anonymous, it belongs to Rabbi Meir [*Sanhedrin* 86a], his views are rejected and his statements remain anonymous. Nothing can be more unfair to a scholar. Rabbi Pinhas of Koretz must have been disturbed by Rabbi Meir's fate for he tried to correct it. When the Messiah will come, said Rebbe Pinhas of Koretz, the *Halakha*—the law—will be according to Rabbi Meir [*Midrash Pinhas* 1:54–2:1]."[157] Thus, the unnamed source of a Mishnah is not exactly anonymous—the source, the teacher, rather, is hidden. And in the time of the Messiah all that is hidden will be revealed: the Messiah himself, it seems, will follow the rulings of Rabbi Meir.

Portrait of Rabbi Shimon bar Yohai and his Son Rabbi Eleazar

One thing that defines the Hasidism in Elie Wiesel's Hasidic legacy is the Jewish mystical tradition. The objection of the Mitnagdim, or the "Opponents," to the Hasidim was not the Hasidic accent on the mystical tradition; rather, they were concerned that the Hasidim were opening up the esoteric mysteries to too many people too fast. What makes the notion of *portrait* central to Wiesel's *Hasidic* legacy is a collection of Kabbalistic texts that come to us from Shimon bar Yohai, his son Rabbi Eleazar, and their disciples: the Zohar.

Here we must underscore once more Judaism's accent on the *Who*, which lies at the core of Wiesel's Hasidic legacy: his is the legacy of the *Who* transmitted precisely through the legacy of the *portrait*. That legacy stems from the Zohar that is so central to Hasidism and to Wiesel's testimonial tribute to Hasidism. As we have shown from the start, the legacy of the *Who* is what makes the portrait a portrait—the portrait of a soul. Each portrait reveals the *Who* that lies at the very core of the human being, and the *Who* defines the notion of portraiture. Thus these portraits, *as portraits*, convey a trace of the Holy One within the human one. Thanks to the teaching and testimony of Rabbi Shimon bar Yohai and his son, we have an opening into this mystery. "You see," writes Wiesel, "the child in me, the yeshiva student in me, the Hasid in me, feels close to Rabbi Shimon. Why? Because his imagination was boundless."[158] His imagination and his attunement to revelation. For the *Who* enters the world *only through revelation.*

The very presence of a *Who* in the midst of being is a transcendence of being. These portraits and their Hasidic legacy represent just such a transcendence. In the Talmud we are told that when his teacher Rabbi Akiba was martyred, Rabbi Shimon bar Yohai and his son Rabbi Eleazar were among the five who revived the Torah and saw to it that the Torah would not die. The other three were Rabbi Meir, Rabbi Yehudah, and Rabbi Yossi (*Yevamot* 62b). When the Romans discovered that Shimon bar Yohai was speaking out against them, they issued an order for his execution, whereupon the rabbi and his son went into hiding, first in a house of study and then in a cave. At the mouth of the cave a carob tree miraculously sprang up from the ground, and fresh spring water began to flow, so that they had food and drink. In order to keep their clothing from wearing out, they removed their garments, except during prayers and on the Sabbath. For thirteen years they studied the mysteries of the Torah with Elijah, until one day they heard a voice from heaven declaring that the Roman emperor had died and that the decree ordering their execution had been rescinded (*Shabbat* 33b). "Rabbi Shimon refused to die—even as a martyr," Wiesel comments. "Unlike his Master, Rabbi Akiba, who accepted martyrdom with exultation, Rabbi Shimon preferred hiding."[159] What happened when the father and son emerged from the cave? According to tradition, Wiesel relates, Rabbi Eleazar saw a man plowing and sowing in violation of the Torah, whereupon he cast a gaze upon the man, who immediately went up in flames. A voice from heaven cried out, "Did you come out to destroy My world? Return to your cave!" And so they went back to the cave for another year. The same happened when they came out again. But this time Rabbi Shimon healed whatever Rabbi Eleazar destroyed (*Shabbat* 33b).

The world that Rabbi Shimon and Rabbi Eleazar encountered when they left the cave was a world that had seen the mass murder and oppression of the Jews of Judea. Wiesel compares their experience to the experience of other survivors:

> When he left his prison-cave for the first time, he felt what our generation's survivors felt when they saw what happened— while they were away. Only then were they confronted with the real problem: what to do with their anger, their pain, and their despair. Like Rabbi Shimon, they could have destroyed Creation—and like him, they chose not to. . . . I think of him fondly because . . . I recall a time when I was with my father *there*, away from home. We were not alone, and yet we were. And because we were alone as never before, we grew close to one another as never before. Before—I rarely saw him. He was busy in the store or in the community. I saw him on Shabbat. Now I saw him all the time. We could finally talk and talk. He alone mattered to me, I alone mattered to him. I was as essential to his life as he was to mine. But unlike Rabbi Eleazar and his father, I left the cave alone.[160]

Recall the words of Moishe the Beadle to Eliezer, when Eliezer asked to study the esoteric teachings: "There are a thousand and one gates allowing entry into the orchard of mystical truth. Every human being has his own gate."[161] So, indeed, Wiesel passed through a gate embossed with the words *Arbeit Macht Frei* and entered another realm, a realm in which he attained a level of learning (if one may speak in such a way) unattainable anywhere else.

Just as one may speak of two Eliezers—the Hasidic child of Sighet and the one who rose from the mass grave of the Holocaust—so, says Wiesel, "it is customary to think that there are *two* Rabbi Shimons. . . . the one in Talmudic literature, the other in the Zohar. The first is human, the second quasi-divine. . . . Is it possible to combine or to reconcile the two portraits? Yes—for, in truth, there are two portraits of him in Talmudic literature, too. One precedes his entrance into the cave, and the other covers his return to society. The thirteen years spent in hiding underground had changed him greatly. The accumulation of so much solitude and silence had to have an effect."[162] Eliezer and his father were not alone, and yet they were, abandoned to the silence of the antiworld before which the world remained silent. Such solitude and silence had an impact upon him, an impact that at times shows up in these portraits.

With regard to the Shimon of the Talmud and the Shimon of the Zohar, Wiesel writes, "Yet it seems wrong, and would be misleading, to consider these two works [the Talmud and the Zohar]—of extraordinary importance and beauty—as belonging to two different domains. Instead I see them as two concentric circles: their center is one and the same."[163] Each, indeed, is a dimension of the other, related as word is related to meaning and the revealed is related to the hidden. There are many tales of the miracles that Rabbi Shimon bar Yohai performed after he emerged from the cave. Wiesel relates, for example, the story of how Rabbi Shimon was called to Tiberius, where human bones had been found, making it unfit for residency: people could not build homes on the site where others had been buried. Rabbi Shimon, however, "located the cemetery, thus opening up the rest of the city, which was destined to become a great center for Jewish learning [*Shabbat* 33b–34a]. (Why is it symbolic? Because Jewish renaissance has often sprung from the very ground where Jews have been killed. The Crusades, the Middle Ages, the pogrom periods provide a thousand and one examples. The latest one comes from Russia. Do you know where the first militant youths met to learn Hebrew and Hebrew songs? In cemeteries—at night.)"[164] Thus, says Wiesel, "all that occurred later had already begun to happen then."[165] Issues of exile and redemption go back to Moses, even back to Adam. Indeed, to be a child of Adam—a *ben adam* or "human being"—is to wrestle with matters of exile and redemption and of oblivion and memory.

Portraits of the Hasidic Masters

In the discussion of Wiesel's Hasidic legacy that opened this book, I presented a fairly thorough explanation of what Hasidism is, where it comes from, and its basic teachings as presented by Elie Wiesel, as well as several scholars of Hasidism. Therefore I shall not repeat what was said there. What can be added here and what must be kept in mind, as Wiesel says, is this:

> We must also remember that the Besht, the Maggid, and other early Masters were not interested in bringing forth a new religion but wished to create a new humanity, to humanize ancient words and offer them to those Jews who had forgotten their meaning. What was the new element? To teach man the secret power of love in relationship to God and His people. The Besht maintained that true love can envelop one's *entire* being; he who loves God loves His creation, loves His law, loves His people. And conversely; he who loves His people—meaning he who loves people—loves God; or, who loves, loves God.[1]

These words convey what Hasidism is about, what these selected portraits of the Hasidic Masters are about, and what Elie Wiesel's Hasidic legacy is about: whoever loves his or her fellow human being, loves God.

A major inspiration for Elie Wiesel's portraits of these Hasidic masters would be the tales his grandfather Reb Dodye Feig told him as a child: "He told stories too. . . . It is to him that I owe everything I have written on Hasidic literature."[2] As a Hasid who rose up from history's most radical assault on Judaism and Hasidism, his storytelling defines his Hasidic legacy as a response to the event. "In retelling these tales," he writes, "I realize once more that I owe them much. Consciously or not, I have incorporated a song, an echo, a word of theirs in my own legends and fables. I have remained, in a vanquished kingdom, a child who loves to listen."[3] Drawn from realms that transcend time and space, for the Hasid Elie Wiesel, these tales are manifestations of Torah, modes of prayer, and ways of connecting with the Holy One in the aftermath of the world's most radical assault on the Holy One.

If, as Wiesel suggests, Hasidic tales form the contexts for his story-telling, the Hasidic tales have their own Jewish contexts in the aggadic, midrashic, and Kabbalistic traditions. Those traditions, too, pervade Wiesel's portraits: Elie Wiesel's Hasidic legacy has its roots not only in Hasidism but in all of the written and oral Torah. "Prophets transmit the word of God," says Wiesel in his portrait of Rabbi Nahman of Bratzlav. "Just Men conceived it. Often in the form of tales. Every word is a tale, they said in Bratzlav. Example: Torah. Or Talmud. Or Zohar. The tale of the Law is as important as the Law. And it is more profound than the commentaries."[4] The Torah begins not with a catalogue of commandments but with the tale of creation. Why? Because the tale of creation is part of Torah, which means: *creation itself is made of the tale of creation.*

To receive a tale, as Wiesel has said, is "to become part of the tale,"[5] which happens when we transmit the tale in turn. Why is the Torah called "the Torah of Moses"? Because, says the Talmud, Moses offered it to others in the form of tales (*Shabbat* 89a). Created in the image and likeness of the Holy One, the human being not only *speaks*, as Maimonides says (*Moreh Nevuhim* 1:51)—he or she tells tales. And *listens*: a *medaber* or "speaking being" is a *listening* being. If the Nazi war against the Jews was a war against memory, as Wiesel maintains,[6] it was a war against the Jewish memory of Jewish tales. In the post-Holocaust era, more than ever, listening to the tale transmitted through these portraits is part of remembering who we are. "It is memory," says Wiesel, "that connects [a Jew] to Abraham, Moses, and Rabbi Akiba."[7] Just so, Wiesel himself struggles to remember, a portrait at a time. "When I write," Wiesel has said, "I feel my invisible teachers looking over my shoulders, reading my words and judging their veracity."[8] Just so, these Hasidic masters look over his shoulders—and into our eyes.

In the tales of the Baal Shem Tov, Wiesel points out, we have many of the "basic elements of Hasidism. The fervent waiting; the longing for redemption; the erratic wanderings over untraveled roads; the link between man and his Creator; between the individual act and its repercussions in the celestial spheres; the importance of ordinary words; the accent on fervor and on friendship, too."[9] Because "the force of the movement lay not in ideology but in life,"[10] the tales of the Hasidim, says Wiesel, are not about miracles but about friendship and hope—the greatest miracles of all."[11] To be sure, he points out, "friendship" is "a key word in Hasidic vocabulary. *Dibuk-haverim* for the disciple is as important as *Emunat-tzadikim*, faith in the Master. To follow a certain Rebbe means to relate to his pupils. A Hasid alone is not a true Hasid. Solitude and Hasidism are incompatible."[12] Thus the secret of the ascent into the upper realms lies in the oneness of a relationship—the very thing that came under a radical assault in the Nazi assault on the soul. Do we not see here Wiesel's Hasidic legacy in all of these portraits?

Relationship is central. The Holy One enters this realm through the between space of human-to-human relation. Only through that between space can understanding and insight open up. "Friendship or death, the Talmud says. Without friendship, existence is empty, sterile, pointless. Friendship is even more important in a man's life than love. Love may drive one to kill, friendship never. . . . The Hasidic movement owes its success to its emphasis on friendship among the faithful as well as fidelity to the master. Friendship is indispensable, essential."[13] To what? Not only to Hasidism but also to these portraits of the Hasidic masters, and there, too, lies the Hasidic legacy of Elie Wiesel: it lies in friendship, as well as in the summons to friendship underlying these portraits.

Menahem bar Rabbi Yose teaches that among the Ten Utterances that bring heaven and earth into being are the words from Genesis 2:18, "It is not good for the human being to be alone" (*Bereshit Rabbah* 17:1), and the Hasidim understand why: it is because all of creation rests upon human-to-human *relationship*. Even the company of God was not enough for Adam to overcome the solitude of being. Where meaning in life is concerned, we long for more than understanding—we long for the depth and dearness found only in the relation to another: *we long to love another*. Hence "this, too, is part of the Hasidic message: there is a solution to loneliness—and loneliness is no solution."[14] One thing overcome through the redemption that the Hasidim seek is loneliness. "Man's role is to mitigate solitude, whoever opts for solitude chooses the side of death," Wiesel's articulates the Baal Shem's core teaching. "Every encounter quickens the steps of the Redeemer, let two beings become one and the world is no longer the same; let two human creatures accept one another and creation will have meaning, the meaning they will have imposed upon it. That is the new idea introduced into Jewish life by Hasidism."[15] And that is the Hasidic legacy, the thoroughly *Jewish* legacy, of Elie Wiesel—but with a post-Holocaust difference.

Portrait of Israel ben Eliezer, the Baal Shem Tov

Each of the three verses relating the splitting of the Sea of Reeds contains seventy-two letters (Exodus 14:19–21). From this the sages determined that there are seventy-two names of God, one of which consists of seventy-two letters. A person who has mastered the secret of the various permutations of the seventy-two-letter name can influence creation itself (*Zohar* I, 7b). In the Jewish mystical tradition, one who has mastered the secret of the seventy-two letter name is known as a Baal Shem, or a "Master of the Name." Among the more noted ones are Eliyahu Baal Shem of Worms and Adam Baal Shem of Zamość, the teacher of Israel ben Eliezer, the Baal Shem Tov.

Unlike the other *baalei shem*, the Besht, as he is known by his acronym, is called not only Baal Shem but Baal Shem *Tov*, the "Master of the *Good* Name." What set the Besht apart from other *baalei shem*, Immanuel Etkes explains, were his spiritual powers: "By this we mean powers of a prophetic nature: remote vision, prognostication, ability to hear decrees from on high, and so forth."[16] In his *Shaar Emumah v'Yesod HaChassidut* (The gate of faith and the foundation of Hasidism) the nineteenth-century Radziner Rebbe, Rabbi Gershom Hanoch Leiner, provides us with a deeper clue: "The Baal Shem Tov opened up an inner gate that had been closed until his days. He opened it before the entire community of Yaakov, for the Torah is not in Heaven, but is the birthright and fiancée of every Jew. Everyone who seeks God with a full heart will find in the Baal Shem Tov's words the way of understanding and clear path for the upright in order to understand, discern, hear, learn, teach, guard, perform, and uphold all the words of the Torah."[17] The *Good* in the Good Name lies in bringing together what is most high and what is most human. No meditative flights into the empyrean realms here; rather, the "inner gate" is unlocked in the midst of flesh-and-blood human relationships, through acts of loving kindness—through *Hesed*.

As the bearer of this secret, Wiesel notes, the Besht "frequently had occasion to converse with the Messiah. In a letter to his brother-in-law, Reb Gershon Kitiver, the Baal Shem gives his account of one of these dialogues. To the question: 'But when, when will you come?' the Messiah answered: 'When your spring will run over, when your teaching will cover the land.' "[18] The Baal Shem was deeply troubled by this reply, says Etkes. It meant that "one need not expect the Redemption to take place in the near future, as it is inconceivable that such secrets as the Messiah revealed would soon be known to all an sundry!"[19] This may be the reason for why the *Ani Maamin* is so precious to the Hasid Wiesel, most especially the line "even though he may tarry, *yet* shall I wait."

Significantly, Wiesel's portrait of the Baal Shem Tov opens with a glimpse of his grandfather Reb Dodye Feig. His grandfather was the first to teach him about the foundations of Hasidism. "A Hasid must know how to listen," Dodye Feig taught him. "To listen is to receive."[20] Not only to listen but to heed—the most fundamental requirement of a Jew: *Shma, Yisrael*! "Israel, Jews, listen! Understand! Heed!" For if we do not know how to listen, we cannot entreat God to listen. Another memory of his grandfather that finds its way into his portrait of the Baal Shem Tov: "An objective Hasid," said Dodye Feig, "is not a Hasid." Wiesel's comment: "He was right. The Baal Shem's call was a call to subjectivity, to passionate involvement; the tales he told and those told about him appeal to the imagination rather than to reason. They try to prove that man is *more* than he appears to be and that he is capable of giving more than he appears to possess."[21] Here lies the *meod*: Hasidism summons the *bekol-meodekha* with which we are commanded to love God in the Shma (Deuteronomy 6:5).

And how do we love God with all our heart, all our soul, and all our "mores," loving more and even more, infinitely? By loving our fellow human being: there lies the infinite, the *bekol-meodekha*, with which we are summoned to love. When, for example, a man complained to the Besht that his son had forsaken God, the Baal Shem said, "Then love him more."[22] This good counsel from the Master of the Good Name illustrates one of the Baal Shem's most fundamental teachings, as Wiesel points out: "Not to judge others was one of the Baal Shem's principles; his function was to help, not to condemn."[23] Through the simple act of helping the *more* is revealed, the goodness that is more than all there is.

"This is one of the appealing characteristics of Hasidism," Wiesel writes, "everything is offered, yet everything remains to be done."[24] Because everything remains to be done, there is always *more* to do; doing *more*—*loving* more—we draw the Divine Presence into this realm. Here we discover what the Baal Shem Tov added to our understanding of the relationship between above and below and to our understanding of the ancient Kabbalistic teaching that the movement above is initiated by the movement below (see, for example, *Zohar* II, 31b; *Toledot Yaakov Yosef, Shelah* 7, 10). Indeed, the Baal Shem taught that the mystery of *teshuvah,* the movement of return, is that *God* does *teshuvah* (*Toledot Yaakov Yosef, Bo* 10). Says Wiesel: "'God is the shadow of man' was commented upon by the Baal Shem as follows: just as a shadow follows the gestures and motions of the body, God follows those of the soul. If man is charitable, God will be charitable, too. The name of man's secret is God, and the name of God's secret is none other than the one initiated by man: who loves, loves God."[25] The love of God requires the love of the other human being, and the love of the other human being requires the love of God.

This is one reason why the Baal Shem did not write any tractate or treatise of his own: the revelation of the Infinite One can happen only in the face to face of human relation. In the words of Emmanuel Levinas, "The face to face is a final and irreducible relation which no concept could cover."[26] If, therefore, "meaning is the face of the Other,"[27] it is because "the "exigency of the holy" emanates from the face,[28] which "*enters* into our world from an absolutely foreign sphere, that is, precisely from an absolute."[29] This entry of the face into our world is a *revelation*. Without such a revelation there can be no redemption. And so: "To the disciple who had transposed his verbal teachings to paper, the Master said, 'There is nothing of me in your pages. . . . I said one thing, you heard another, and you wrote a third.'"[30] Such a teaching implicates any writer who would presume to draw a portrait of the Besht through the use of words.

So where did this visionary come from? He revealed himself at the age of thirty-six, when he set out to spread not a new belief but a renewed elevation of creation through joy and gratitude. Says Wiesel, "More than any other Jewish historical figure, with the exception of the prophet Elijah, the Besht was present in joy as well as in despair; every *shtibl* reflected his light, his warmth."[31] Present in joy? What was there to rejoice about? "Traumatized by the nightmare of false Messiahs of the seventeenth century," Wiesel explains, "the rabbis looked askance at anything that seemed new, anything that was obscure."[32] And yet, "the Baal Shem was a moment of rapture and exaltation in times of mute lamentation. . . . He had been the spark without which thousands of families would have succumbed to gloom and hopelessness—and the spark had fanned itself into a huge flame that tore into the darkness."[33] Yes, *mute* lamentation. Because this muteness is the muteness of a human being, however, within it an outcry lies hidden.

The Baal Shem Tov did not bring hope to the Jews of Eastern Europe so much as he returned to them a sense of *purpose*, a sense of truth and meaning. And where do we find a sense of purpose? In joy and gratitude, precisely when we can see no reason for rejoicing or thanksgiving. Wiesel writes: "Song is more precious than works, intention more important than formulas. . . . One tear, one prayer can change the course of events; one fragment of melody can contain all the joy in the world. . . . And no elite has a monopoly on song or tears. . . . 'The man who looks only at himself cannot but sink into despair, yet as soon as he opens his eyes to the creation around him, he will know joy.' And this joy leads to the absolute, to redemption, to God; that was the new truth as defined by the Baal Shem."[34] Redemption lies in joy and gratitude? But what can that mean for someone who stands atop a mass grave?

If joy and gratitude, purpose and meaning, can be summoned in such an age, then it comes only with the realization that "God is not neutral. Nor is He an abstraction. He is at once ally and judge of man inside creation. The bond between them is irreplaceable, it is love. God Himself needs love. . . . It is in man that God must be loved, because the love of God goes through the love of man. Whoever loves God exclusively, namely, excluding man, reduces his love and his God to the level of abstraction. Beshtian Hasidism denies all abstraction."[35] Thus the Besht insisted that "study for the sake of scholarship is desecration; it is a transgression of the commandment against bowing before alien gods."[36] The Baal Shem Tov's devotion to flesh-and-blood humanity is at the core of his flesh-and-blood portrait. No one, he believed, is more out of touch with flesh-and-blood humanity than the purveyors of religious officialdom: "Only when it came to the official rabbis did the Besht show himself merciless. 'One day there will be no mercy, they will prevent the coming of the Messiah!' "[37] And yet he taught that "the Messiah is with us in every generation" (*Toledot Yaakov Yosef, Naso* 13), ever present, ready to help us draw upon a legacy from the past to open up a horizon for the future.

"What cannot help but astound us," writes Wiesel, "is that Hasidim remained Hasidim inside the ghetto walls, inside the death camps. In the shadow of the executioner, they celebrated life. Startled Germans whispered to each other of Jews dancing in the cattle cars rolling toward Birkenau: Hasidim ushering in Simhat Torah. And there were those who in Block 57 at Auschwitz tried to make me join in their fervent singing."[38] One recalls the chapter titled "The Dance of the Rabbis" in Sara Nomberg-Przytyk's memoir, where a transport of Hasidic rabbis broke into a dance upon being unloaded from the train.[39] Yes, they celebrated life amidst the ubiquity of death, in a realm where death itself came under a radical assault. Coming to that realization, one of Elie Wiesel's most prominent students, Alan Rosen, suggested to me, requires an adjustment, a *heshbon nefesh* or a reckoning, on the part of the reader who encounters these portraits.

Which brings us to one last tale and teaching from the Baal Shem Tov. There was once a deaf man passing through a village. He happened to walk by a house where there was a wedding celebration. He looked into the windows and saw the wedding guests dancing, but he could not see the musicians who were playing the music. "This must be an insane asylum," he concluded, "with all of these people leaping and whirling about." He thought they were mad because he could not hear the music (*Toledot Yaakov Yosef, Shelah* 3).[40] No doubt there are many who look upon those who embrace this Hasidic legacy as mad. But they do not hear the music.

Recall that in several of Wiesel's portraits of the Talmudic sages we saw a motif of pairs. Which tells us that the transmission of a legacy requires a pairing that is indicative of a community. Here, too, in the portraits of the Hasidic masters we shall see pairs: the Baal Shem Tov is paired with all of the masters in the pages that follow. "Every Hasid," write Wiesel, "had two Masters: his own and the Baal Shem."[41] This was part of the Hasidic endeavor to overcome solitude. In our own time, however, it comes in the aftermath of a time and place where solitude took on an unprecedented meaning.

Portrait of Dov Ber the Maggid of Mezeritch

Midrash is a characteristic mode of thought and of life for a *maggid*. Sharing a root with *aggadah*, a *maggid* is one who teaches through *aggadah*, through storytelling, as the Maggid Elie Wiesel teaches through storytelling. We have already noted the importance of storytelling in the Hasidic tradition. Like his master the Baal Shem Tov, Dov Ber wrote no commentaries or manifestos (he did, however, compile a collection of tales about the Besht known as the *Shivhei HaBesht* or *In Praise of the Baal Shem Tov*). His encounters were always eye to eye, ear to ear, face to face, soul to soul. Indeed, the face-to-face human relationship is the substance of the soul. And the Great Maggid's capacity for human relationship was inexhaustible: he had three hundred disciples, thirty-nine of whom became major Hasidic masters.[42]

Born in Volhynia in 1710, Dov Ber met the Baal Shem in 1752, eight years before the Baal Shem's death. Two other disciples who might have succeeded the Baal Shem were Yaakov Yosef of Polnoe and Pinhas of Koretz.[43] Yaakov Yosef is the author of *Toledot Yaakov Yosef*, the first attempt at gathering the teachings of the Baal Shem Tov, and Pinhas of Koretz, author of the *Midrash Pinhas*, was one of the major early Hasidic masters. With the Maggid of Mezeritch, says Wiesel, "Hasidism underwent its first structural, if not ideological mutation: from the realm of legend to that of history."[44] There was, in other words, a shift from the charismatic, hypnotizing figure to the teacher who transmitted a teaching and sent out disciples into all parts of Eastern Europe. The Baal Shem traveled the countryside to seek out disciples; the Maggid remained in Mezeritch, and the disciples came to him, only to be sent out once more into an often hostile world, thus "establishing and firmly implanting a Hasidic network spanning all of Eastern Europe."[45] Mezeritch became a kind of Third Temple for the Hasidim: like the light of the Holy One that emanated from the windows of the Temple into the world, the light of Hasidic teaching emanated from Mezeritch into the world of East European Jewry and, over the ages, into our own world, through the Hasidic legacy of Elie Wiesel. Yes, the Holocaust obliterated East European Jewry. And yet . . .

"Conceived by the Baal Shem," Wiesel elaborates, "the Hasidic idea owes the Maggid its adaptation, its practical application. Before him, it was impulsive, vague, fragmentary. Idealized in the extreme, it was vulnerable. Its core needed to be protected and strengthened, it needed a supporting framework and the external marks of an expanding movement. And most of all it needed to be anchored in reality."[46] To this end, the Maggid of Mezeritch established the category of Tzaddik or Rebbe. In a sense, the Rebbe is the opposite of what we might normally take to be a mystic: he is a materialistic mystic. The Rebbe is not some angelic or mysterious figure; rather, he is precisely the one who anchors the Hasidim in reality. Many times I have seen videos of the late Lubavitcher Rebbe Menahem Mendel Schneerson receiving hundreds of Jews lined up on a Sunday afternoon, as was his custom. Each time a Jew told him how much he or she had accomplished, he would always say, "And what *more* are you going to do?" He did not mean more study or meditation but what more are you going to *do*? That query from the Rebbe begins with the Maggid of Mezeritch.

The Baal Shem Tov once said of the Maggid of Mezeritch: "He does not just *know* the Torah; he *is* the Torah."[47] One of the Maggid's disciples, the great Rebbe Aharon of Karlin, was once asked, "What did you learn in Mezeritch?" He answered, "I have learned nothing in Mezeritch. Or to be more precise: I have learned the meaning of the word 'nothing'— the mystery which envelops all words. . . . I am nothing and yet I am *in* this world created by God, a man among men—isn't it strange to be nothing and at the same time to listen to you, talk to you, and—talk to God? . . . Well, that's what I learned in Mezeritch. As I told you: 'Nothing.' "[48] God creates "something" by becoming as "nothing"; in a mystical sense, God is "nothingness," the *ain* that precedes creation, otherwise than *all* there is. Commanded to be holy as God is holy (Numbers 15:40), we are commanded to do a kind of turnaround, shifting from *ani* to *ain*, from "I" or "ego" to "nothing." Just as God shifts from *ain* to *ani* as He undertakes the Creation, so must we shift from *ani* to *ain* in order to approach God. How does one go from *ani* to *ain*? By extending a helping hand to another human being, by loving *more*. Thus for Rebbe Aharon of Karlin, learning nothing is essential to learning how to *love more*.

Another instance of what was to be learned in Mezeritch comes to us from Rebbe Levi-Yitzhak of Berditchev. On one occasion when he returned home from Mezeritch for a holiday visit, his father asked him during the meal, "What did you discover at the Great Maggid's school?" He replied that he had "discovered that God exists, and He is in this world." His father called over the maid who was serving them their meal. He asked her: "Does God exist?" She answered, "Yes, of course." Said his father, "See, everybody knows that!" To which Levi-Yitzhak retorted, "She says, but *I know*."[49] To be sure, years later, when he had become the Berditchever Rebbe, once in a while he would send his servant to one synagogue or another, where the servant would march up to the *bimah*, pound his fist on the pulpit, and cry out, "Know ye, men and women, know that God exists and that He is in this world!"[50] That is, God is in this world as long as He is lived, and not merely studied between four walls.

How did Levi-Yitzhak know? He knew because he came to realize that to know God is to be known by God. He knew because every move in Mezeritch portended a cosmic move. He knew because he knew that in Mezeritch even a minor move had major implications: a single step in one direction or another would send other worlds into other orbits. "Know that everything above is due to you," the Maggid taught. "It is your life of holiness that creates holiness in Heaven."[51] That is why, when asked what he went to learn from the Great Maggid, Reb Leib, son of Sarah, replied, "I came to the Maggid not to listen to discourses, nor to learn from his wisdom; I came to watch him tie his shoelaces."[52] If everything comes into being through the Divine Word, nothing is trivial, not even tying your shoelaces.

Here we have the root and the reason for the Maggid's teaching that "whatever the event, *you* are its origin; it is through you, through *your* will, that God manifests Himself."[53] It is a teaching that extends into our own time, as we see in this reflection from Levinas: "To be an I means then not to be able to escape responsibility, as though the whole edifice of creation rested on my shoulders. But the responsibility that empties the I of its imperialism and its egoism, even the egoism of salvation, does not transform it into a moment of the universal order; it confirms the uniqueness of the I. The uniqueness of the I is the fact that no one can answer for me."[54] If, as Wiesel says, "they came to Mezeritch seeking human contact as much as knowledge,"[55] then they came to declare, "Here I am for you," in an affirmation of this infinite responsibility. For human contact is made of this responsibility of each for all, and I more than the others. Where knowledge alone is the aim, the knowing ego is imperial, as it appropriates the object of knowledge. To know Torah is the opposite of mastering Torah. It is, on the contrary, to know that Torah is my master. To know Torah, like knowing God, "is to know what must be done."[56] Therefore in Mezeritch there was no learning without doing; in Mezeritch Jews repeated what the Israelites declared at Mount Sinai: "*Naasei v'nishma!* We will do, and we will hear!" (Exodus 24:7). And doing meant doing for the sake of another.

Said the Maggid: "If you are content with black bread and water, you will come to the conclusion that the poor can subsist on stones and spring water. If you eat cake, you will give them bread."[57] Thus the Maggid sought ways to make what might appear to be an act of self-indulgence into an act oriented toward the other human being. This orientation toward the other person lies behind another saying from the Maggid: "A good speaker must become one, not with his audience, but with his words; the moment he hears himself speak, he must conclude."[58] When the speaker hears himself speak, he is no longer addressing others but rather has slipped into *self*-consciousness. When that happens meaning begins to slip away from the word. To be one with our words is to make our words human, words uttered for the sake of the *other* human. A scene from Wiesel's *Night* comes to mind. After Eliezer and the others had completed their initiation into the camp and were gathered in the block for the night, the young Pole in charge said to them, "We are all brothers and share the same fate. The same smoke hovers over all our heads. Help each other." And Wiesel comments: "Those were the first human words."[59] These are human words because they attest to the sanctity of human relation. They are words that retain their bond with meaning, for a word's tie to meaning lies in its capacity to draw one human being into a relationship with another.

This accent on human relationship is the hallmark of Jewish wisdom. "Who is wise?" Ben Zoma asks. And he answers: "He who can learn from every person" (*Pirke Avot* 4:1)—*every person*, from an infant to an Alzheimer's patient. There is Torah in all things and in all people. If "man is the language of God," as the Great Maggid's disciple Menahem-Mendl of Vitebsk teaches,[60] then man is the language of Torah. Therefore, as Rabbi Papa teaches in the Talmud, he who has only the Torah does not even have the Torah (*Yevamot* 109b). It is not so surprising that the Maggid would comment not only on what we can learn from the great sages of the tradition but also from a child and a thief. From a child, he explains, we learn (1) how to laugh, (2) how to cry, and (3) how to keep constantly busy. The thief teaches us the following: (1) whatever he does, he does secretly; (2) what he does not obtain today he will try to obtain tomorrow; (3) he is loyal to his accomplices; (4) he is ready to sacrifice himself for the object of his desire; (5) he is not afraid of hardship; and (6) he does not want to be anyone but himself—nothing can make him change trades.[61] Notice that, while each has wisdom to impart, each wisdom is different from the other. The wisdom of the child is the wisdom of emotion, of *ruah* or spirit, of fervor. The wisdom of the thief is oriented toward the accomplishment of a goal or a task, the wisdom of intellect and calculation, of *binah*. Both must come to bear in the pursuit of Torah, of *tikkun*, and of redemption.

"Let him who wants fervor not seek it on the mountain peaks," taught the Maggid of Mezeritch, "rather let him stoop and search among the ashes."[62] In the aftermath of the Holocaust, that is where we are, where we seek to dwell, where and how we pursue the mission of redemption: by rummaging through the ashes. Among the teachings of the Maggid most relevant to our post-Holocaust world is this one: "Zion is absolute in the world; it is the life of all countries."[63] The Nazis set out to obliterate the millennial Jewish teaching and testimony affirming the *absolute* sanctity of every human being and the *absolute* responsibility attached to that sanctity. In the post-Holocaust era—in the movement from Auschwitz to Jerusalem—the restoration of the Jewish state is precisely the restoration of that teaching. Every time Jews take the Torah scrolls from the ark they pray these lines from the prophet Isaiah: "The Torah goes forth from Zion and the Word of HaShem from Jerusalem" (Isaiah 2:3). As the Jews return to Zion, so does the Torah go forth from Zion. So does the Torah go forth from Mezeritch well before the rise of what we call "the modern Zionist movement."

In Wiesel's novel *The Sonderberg Case* the main character Yedidyah cries out: "How was I to reconcile Auschwitz and Jerusalem? Would the former merely be the antithesis, the antievent of the latter? If Auschwitz is forever the question, is Jerusalem forever the answer? On the one hand the darkness of the abyss, on the other the dazzling light of daybreak? At Birkenau and Treblinka, the burning bush was consumed, but here the flame continues to warm the hearts of messianic dreamers."[64] The flame warms the heart because we now "stoop and search among the ashes" for a redemptive spark. Elie Wiesel's portrait of the Great Maggid of Mezeritch is just such a spark.

Portrait of Rebbe Pinhas of Koretz

Born in 1728 in Shklov into a poor rabbinic family, Rebbe Pinhas of Koretz was one of the Baal Shem's closest disciples. As already noted, he was one of three candidates who might have succeeded the Besht as the leader of the Hasidic movement. He was a serious candidate for such an honor because, as Wiesel points out, "in his own gentle way, Pinhas distrusted all leaders. That is why he refused to become one himself."[65] Anyone who pursued the office would for that reason be disqualified. The role of Rebbe or Tzaddik is not something a man lays claim to; rather the role lays claim to the man. "If someone finds it necessary to honor me," said Rebbe Pinhas, "that means he is more humble than I. Which means he is better and saintlier than I. Which means that I should honor him. But then, why is he honoring me?"[66] The Rebbe's question was no doubt sincere, for humility was one of his defining qualities. Even when he prayed, Wiesel relates, "he prayed quietly, meditatively, shunning all visible demonstrations of ecstasy."[67] There was no "show" about Rebbe Pinhas. To be sure, he knew that the more show, the less truth, and truth was paramount to him: it was his "all-consuming passion," as Wiesel describes it. "If all men would speak the truth," said Rebbe Pinhas, "there would be no further need to bring the Messiah; he would be here already. Just as the Messiah brings truth, truth brings the Messiah."[68] As humility is required for truth, so is it required for the coming of the Messiah.

"Everything I know," he once said, "I learned before, sitting in the last row, out of sight. Now I am here, occupying a place of honor, and I don't understand."[69] This statement illustrates not only the Koretzer's characteristic humility but also his profound wisdom. He had the wisdom to realize that learning requires humility. It requires the courage to say, "I do not know, I do not understand." Wiesel, in fact, notes that "the legendary Reb Leib, son of Sarah, called him 'the brain of the world.' Hasidic tradition has it that the Besht left his knowledge to the Maggid of Mezeritch, his saintliness to Reb Mikhel of Zlotchov and his wisdom to Rebbe Pinhas of Koretz. In Hasidic literature, Rebbe Pinhas is called 'the Sage' "[70]—not because he knew the answers but because he knew the questions. "In Hebrew the word for 'question,'" Wiesel observes, "is she'elah, and the alef lamed of God's name [el] are part of the fabric of that word. Therefore God is in the question."[71] For Pinhas of Koretz, if God is in the question, He is also in the tale.

"When a Jew can provide no answer," Wiesel opens his portrait of Rebbe Pinhas, "he at least has a tale to tell." And so Wiesel proceeds to tell the tale of a tale. One day a young man came to Koretz for the Rebbe's help. He was in a state of despair over the meaninglessness of life. The wise Rebbe, however, had no answer for him: there is no fixed formula that can unlock meaning in life. Only a capacity for hearing can do that. Indeed, the Hebrew word for "meaning" is mashmaut, a word that has the same root as shma or "hear." To have a sense of meaning is to have a sense of having heard something—a calling, a summons, or . . . a tale. So, not knowing what to answer, Pinhas told him the tale of his own doubts and despair. He explained to the young man that he tried everything—prayer, study, repentance—but nothing worked. Then one day, the Rebbe related, he heard that the Baal Shem Tov would be passing through his town. He went to the shtibl for the prayer service and saw the Besht. When he walked up to the Baal Shem, the Besht said nothing but just gazed into his eyes. "The intensity of his gaze overwhelmed me," said the Koretzer, "and I felt less alone. And strangely, I was able to go open the Talmud, and plunge into my studies once more. You see," he explained, "the questions remained questions. But I was able to go on."[72]

For Rebbe Pinhas, the problem is not meaninglessness. No, the problem is loneliness and isolation. Curled up in the solipsistic solitude of his own being, the human being collides with his own emptiness, with a murmur of silence that is the murmur of no one; it says nothing, and we hear nothing but a rumbling. The rumbling of the "there is" washes over us, and we are filled with horror before the radical indifference of what is merely "there." "Man is not alone," the Besht told him when they first met. "God makes us remember the past so as to break up our solitude."[73] How does remembering the past break up our solitude? It does so because, as tradition or *mesorah*, which is a cognate of *meser* or "message," the past is not behind us: it is before us. How so? Because it places something infinitely precious into our care. It summons us to a task and to a future, which is the dimension of meaning: the future is the dimension of the *yet to be* that imparts to life a sense of mission and therefore of meaning.

Because this sense of meaning is opposed to the horror of indifferent emptiness, Wiesel writes, "God is not indifferent and man is not His enemy—this was the substance of the Hasidic message. It was a message against despair; against resignation. . . . God is everywhere, said the Besht. In pain too? Yes, in pain too—especially in pain. God *is*, and that means He dwells in every human being. In the unlearned too? Yes, in the unlearned too. In the sinner too. In the humble, in the humble most of all, He can be found. And He can be perceived by everyone."[74] Immediately one wants to ask: "In Auschwitz, too?"

Rebbe Pinhas taught that "God and Torah are One. God, Israel and Torah are One."[75] If this is so, then were God, Israel, and Torah present in Auschwitz? Israel was certainly there. Israel was gassed and burned there. But God? If, as the Koretzer taught, "no man can raise his voice in prayer except when the Shekhinah prays through it,"[76] then in the prayers of the Jews, and in the dance of the Hasidim that arose in Auschwitz, God was there, too. So God and Israel were there. The Torah was there, too: in Auschwitz, Wiesel studied the Oral Torah with a rabbi who knew it from memory. If there is something to transmit through testimony, it is because God was somehow present *even there*. And if He was present even there, then He must be present in the aftermath.

"He who assists another person," Rebbe Pinhas taught, "creates the Angel Azriel (Divine Helper)."[77] This teaching is, of course, based on the teaching of the Besht: "Of every good deed we do, a good angel is born. Of every bad deed, a bad angel is born" (*Toledot Yaakov Yosef, Haye Sarah*

3). How does one human being assist another to create the Angel Azriel? By setting out not to save the other's soul but to heal the other's body, as when even in the antiworld it happened that one man offered another a morsel of bread. "Take care of your own soul," said Rebbe Pinhas, "and of another man's body, but not of your own body, and of another man's soul."[78] On the Hasidic view and in keeping with Wiesel's Hasidic legacy, redemption does not lie in bringing people around to a particular belief or creed; in fact, such a view of redemption has led (and continues to lead) to the slaughter of millions of human beings. No, redemption lies in feeding the hungry, clothing the naked, and healing the sick, especially after the time when hunger, nakedness, and sickness plagued half of world Jewry. For God Himself is hungry, naked, and sick.

Gazing upon Wiesel's portrait of Rebbe Pinhas of Koretz, I am convinced that the Rebbe understood as much. On one occasion the countess who owned Koretz was passing by the Rebbe's window and heard him erupt in an anguished cry of pain. "I have never heard a cry filled with such truth," she told her escorts.[79] Truth requires anguish. Anguish over what? Over the physical plight of our fellow human being. "If only I knew how to sing," Rebbe Pinhas once whispered, "I would force Him to come down and be with His children, witness their suffering, and save them"[80]—save them as we are summoned to save them, not from "wrong belief" but from flesh-and-blood suffering, perhaps from a radical suffering and slaughter of which Rebbe Pinhas, like other Tzaddikim, may have had some premonition. Wiesel reminds us that the Jewish community of Koretz was obliterated on Sukkot 1941, just weeks after the *Einsatzgruppen* killing units moved to the East, with the prime directive of killing every Jew in their path. And he raises the question as to whether Rebbe Pinhas had had an intuition of their end. Was that why he slipped into a heavy melancholy?[81]

Indeed, more than melancholy, at the end of his life Rebbe Pinhas fell into a state of horror and despair. He who had told the young man a story to lift him up from despair had no one from whom to hear such a tale. What Wiesel refers to as his desperate fear of death is perhaps a fear of the meaninglessness and the isolation that the Rebbe opposed throughout his life.[82] Wiesel ends his portrait, saying, "His mystery remains intact. We don't know what happened to him at the end of his life—we never will. He who was always composed, calm and serene—why was he possessed by such fear at the end? What had he glimpsed? What visions did he have—and about whom? What were the questions? Were there any answers? Did he suddenly fully understand that the Jews had no friends—anywhere? Did it become clear to him that the Messiah would be late in coming—much later than he had anticipated, much later than he had feared?"[83] Yes, the Messiah. . . . We have not spoken of the Messiah or of Rebbe Pinhas's declaration that "to be Jewish is to link one's fate to that of the Messiah—to that of all who are waiting for the Messiah."[84] Is it the fate of the Messiah to be always late? If so, then it is because we are always late.

Portrait of Rebbe Aharon of Karlin

Rebbe Aharon of Karlin was born in 1736, the year the Besht revealed himself; he died at the age of thirty-six. He was famous for his ability to draw Jews into the fold of Hasidism. The Maggid of Mezeritch sent him to establish a Hasidic center in Lithuania, in the midst of the Mitnagdim. He was so successful that "for a time the Mitnagdim called all Hasidim 'Karliner.' "[85] Says Wiesel, "The Maggid of Mezeritch loved him—and so do I. The Maggid called him 'our best offensive weapon.' And rightly so. Rebbe Aharon had the special talent of being able to recognize the best young students, the most sensitive ones, and draw them closer to Hasidism. But he did not keep the newcomers with him; he immediately sent them to Mezeritch, to the great Maggid."[86] Rebbe Aharon could ignite a soul with just a simple word or two, as when he once delivered a one-sentence sermon: "He who does not improve, gets worse." When Reb Chaim-Heykel heard these words, he rushed to Rebbe Aharon and cried out for the Rebbe's help. He said, " 'Your words are now inside me, they tear me apart.' And the two men left together. 'I would like to follow you,' said Reb Chaim-Heykel of Amdur. 'So be it,' said Rebbe Aharon. 'Go to Mezeritch.' " Reb Chaim-Heykel became one of the Maggid's most illustrious followers and a close friend of Rebbe Aharon.[87] It was the next best thing to sending them to the Besht himself. Rebbe Aharon understood that the new movement was not about him, despite the fact that the Mitnagdim for a time referred to the Hasidim as "Karliner."

Rebbe Aharon used to say that when Hasidim meet, they should study the Zohar together. If they are unable to study Zohar, then they should learn Talmud. If they cannot learn Talmud, then they should open up the Bible. If that is too difficult, then they should exchange stories of the Hasidic Masters. If they do not know any stories, he said, let them sing a *niggun*, a wordless Hasidic melody that ignites the fire within the soul. "But what if, woe to us, they don't know a *niggun*?" Wiesel asks. "Well, in that case," he answers, "let them . . . love one another." And he adds: "This advice—more than any saying uttered by any Master—summarizes the attitude of the Hasidic movement: Ask the utmost of man, but accept him as he is"[88]—love him as he is. For the human being is already a child of the Holy One and is therefore infinitely precious. That is the message that Rebbe Aharon of Karlin was sent to deliver to the Jews of Eastern Europe. "What is the difference between the Mitnagged and the Hasid?" Wiesel reminds us. "The Mitnagged loves the Torah, whereas the Hasid loves the person who loves the Torah. The Hasid puts the accent on man, who is bound to change, while the Mitnagged places it on the Torah, which is above change. The Mitnagged finds his happiness in books, the Hasid in people; the Mitnagged seeks knowledge, the Hasid experience."[89] Recall Rabbi Papa's Talmudic teaching cited above: he who has only the Torah does not even have the Torah (*Yevamot* 109b). Rebbe Aharon of Karlin came to return the scholars of the Talmud to this Talmudic teaching.

Wiesel's portrait of Aharon of Karlin is a portrait of love: love is the key to the Hasidic movement, conceived not as one feeling among many but as a living presence between two. "Feelings one 'has,'" explains Martin Buber. "Love occurs. Feelings dwell in man, but man dwells in his love."[90] Just so, the soul on fire is a soul that rises up between two, and not just within. "What is a true Hasid?" writes Wiesel. "Beneath a torn overcoat, inside a hovel, a heart broken but yearning for perfection. And that yearning in itself is enough. Man's goal is to be worthy of God—but God accepts him even when he is not, provided he truly wants to be; provided, too, that he love his friend and neighbor. . . . Not everybody is capable of *Ahavat-Hashem*, love of God; or of *Ahavat-Torah*, love of Torah; but everyone must be capable of *Ahavat-Israel*, love of one's fellow man."[91] Said Rebbe Shlomo, a disciple of Rebbe Aharon, "I wish I could love the best of the just as deeply as God loves the worst of the wicked."[92] To seek that divine love for every human being is what it means to be holy as God is holy. To be sure, there is no *Ahavat-Torah*, no *Ahavat-Hashem*, without love of one's fellow human being, for in that love we realize our own humanity as one created in the image and likeness of the Holy One. And without love of the stranger, we might add, there is no *Ahavat-Israel*. In the end, love of the stranger is most crucial. Therefore the commandment to love, care for, and show kindness toward the stranger appears thirty-six times in the Torah, more than any other commandment.

The Torah commands us to love the neighbor (Leviticus 19:18) and to love the stranger (Leviticus 19:34) *k'mokha*, "as yourself." According to the Baal Shem, the commandment to love *k'mokha* is the basis of the entire Torah (*Toledot Yaakov Yosef, Korah* 2). If we examine the Hebrew word *k'mokha*, "as yourself," as well as the *le-* in *lereakha* or *leger*, "your neighbor" or "the stranger," a better translation would be: "You shall act in a loving manner *toward* your neighbor, *toward* the stranger, for that loving relation *is* who you are," as it is written (*Toledot Yaakov Yosef, Veethanan* 5). The commandment with regard both to the neighbor and to the stranger is followed by the phrase "I am HaShem," indicating that the human relation and the higher relation are of a piece. Where the human relation collapses, so does the higher relation. And the humanity of the human being resides in both relationships. This truth taught by Rebbe Aharon lay at the core of the ecstasy, of the literal dance for joy, that was so central to Hasidic wisdom.

What is the Hasidic ecstasy made of? It is made of awe and love. There are four levels of awe and love in the approach to the Divine Presence. First is the lower awe, which is nothing but fear, where we follow Torah out of fear of punishment. Then comes the lower love, which is the counterfeit of self-love, where we observe the commandments in hope of reward. Next is the higher love, where we embrace the commandments out of love for God. Finally, there is the higher awe, where we have an inkling of the greatness of God's holiness and love for His humanity. Beyond the higher awe is the realm in which the awe and love of God are of a piece. That is where the Tzaddik dwells. That is where Rebbe Aharon dwells. That is where his portrait is to be found. Says Wiesel, commenting on Rebbe Aharon's fear and love, "This terrible fear, this total awe he experienced did not stifle or diminish his love of God. He was a Hasid after all, and Hasidism was meant to combat fear—and solitude. Hasidism defined itself, and its relation to its members, in terms of love—exclusively."[93] What was the ecstatic fervor of the Karliner Hasidim made of? It was made of awe and love, which together transcend fear and solitude. With this merging of awe and love, in Karlin the fear of God was "the fear *for* God—the fear not to offend, not to hurt Him. And the one did not exclude or deny the other: on the contrary, the one completed and enriched the other."[94] Yes: a fear *not to hurt Him.* Perhaps God is not quite as invulnerable as we might suppose. Perhaps we must take care of Him and watch over Him as we would a newborn infant—or else He will die. There lies the fervor.

"That is what characterized Karlin: *hitlahavut*—fervor, enthusiasm," Wiesel sketches his portrait. "In Karlin one lived on summits of mountains all the time. In Karlin the Hasid was constantly singed by sacred fire."[95] The *k'mokha* is what takes the Hasidim to such heights. The fire is made of the *k'mokha*, as it opens up the infinite—the one infinitely dear, before us and beyond us, for whom we are infinitely responsible. Any other such responsibility would crush us. Which may be why, at least in some cases, this passion was so inimical to the isolation in the yeshiva found among the Mitnagdim, for whom the yeshiva was a kind of fortress: they "did not particularly appreciate the fervor, the exhibitionism of the Hasidim at services. The Hasidim shouted, sang, jumped up and down, danced and often even rolled on the ground to attain ecstasy."[96] Such behavior threatened the security of control sought in knowledge, where the one in control is the knowing self. And yet, the greater the reasoning self's control over the world, the more bankrupt its spiritual life. No, the soul, the *neshamah*, draws its breath, its *neshimah*, from the infinite responsibility to and for the one created in the image and likeness of the Infinite One—which requires coming out of the fortress of the House of Learning. It requires the *bitul hayesh* that is the utter abrogation of the ego, of the counterfeit "I," which seeks only security.

And so in this portrait we have the story of the stranger who came from Mezeritch and knocked on Rebbe Aharon's door. The Rebbe said, "Who is it?" The stranger answered, "It's *me*. Don't you recognize me?" Rebbe Aharon answered, "Only God and God alone may say 'I' or 'Me.' And if you have not as yet learned that, then you were wrong in leaving our Master. Better that you return to Mezeritch."[97] Therefore "in Karlin," Wiesel expounds, "one tried to attain inner fulfillment by negation of self. One hoped to create silence through words and a melody, a *niggun*, inside silence. And prayer inside the *niggun*."[98] A prayer inside the silence: that is where the *niggun* is created, inside the wordless melody, inside the *niggun* that surpasses utterance.

If in Karlin you lived on the summits of mountains, you need not go any farther than your living room to ascend those heights. "When a shepherd is overwhelmed by a feeling of wonder at the sight of a sunset," writes Wiesel in this portrait, "when a child wants to say something but cannot, and so repeats one word over and over again until he is understood—well, that is a sign that God's gaze is upon them. And that is the secret of all secrets: the Master of the Universe, who created three hundred and ten worlds [see Baal HaTurim on Genesis 1:1] and reigns over the infinite, has chosen to dwell in man's heart."[99] Thus, the Master of the Universe follows us from within us in every move we make. For "every man is a sanctuary and it is up to man to invite God inside. As Rebbe Mendel of Kotzk formulated it: God is where He is allowed to come in. God's favorite dwelling is neither a palace of gold nor an edifice of marble but man's heart."[100] How do we invite God inside? Through joy and thanksgiving, even—or especially—when we can see no reason for rejoicing or giving thanks.

Rebbe Aharon once returned home from one of his journeys into the world of the Mitnagdim, only to find Jews praying without fervor and studying without concentration. He said to them: "My children, my children, I want you to know that joy will lift you up to dizzying heights; I also want you to know that sadness will pull you down into the abyss."[101] Study? Yes. Understanding? Yes, absolutely. But without fervor, joy, and gratitude, these other qualities lead only to sadness. Indeed, who can gaze upon the world only through the eyes of reason and intellect and not succumb to despair? There are times when reason and intellect prove to be bankrupt. There are times when, in order to go on as the witnesses of God, we must seek the passion that is to be found only in the ashes. Those ashes are the medium for this portrait of Rebbe Aharon of Karlin.

"What did Rebbe Aharon die of and why so young?" Wiesel asks. "It happened in the month of Nissan 1772. The disciples of the Maggid chose not to go home to their families for Pesah, except for Rebbe Aharon, who decided to spend Pesah with his family, friends, and disciples. Even though the Maggid gave Rebbe Aharon his blessing that he should go, several times he sent representatives to plead with Rebbe Aharon not to go. Rebbe Aharon returned home and died two days later."[102] So what did Rebbe Aharon die of? Can a man—a Tzaddik—die of a vision? Did he, he Karliner Rebbe, have a vision of what would become of the Karliner Hasidim? Wiesel writes:

> Most Karliner and Stoliner Rebbes [descendants of Rebbe Aharon] and their followers were swallowed up in the kingdom of night and fire, as were other Hasidim and other Rebbes. Most of the victims who ascended the burning altar were Hasidim: the killers and they could not coexist under the same sky. And yet, and yet. There are still Karliner in Jerusalem and in

New York. . . . On Shabbat you will hear them sing the song composed by the great Rebbe Aharon in praise of Shabbat—a song of longing and tenderness. What was he longing for? Shabbat. God . . . love . . . redemption. . . . Is it possible that he died of love? Of longing? I wish I knew.[103]

None of us can ever know. And if we should presume to know, it would betray a profound disregard, a profound disrespect, and a profound incapacity to approach this portrait of Rebbe Aharon of Karlin. For to approach the portrait is to approach the prophetic vision of the Hasidic master that comes to us through the Hasidic legacy of Elie Wiesel.

Elimelekh of Lizensk and His Brother Zusia of Onipol

In Elimelekh of Lizensk and his brother Zusia we have a pair truly in the tradition not only of *Hasidut* but also of the *Zugot*. It is a tradition that picks up where we left off with Rebbe Aharon of Karlin, as Wiesel relates. One day the traveling Masters Rebbe Elimelekh and his brother Reb Zusia stopped at an inn in a little town as dusk was falling. "Soon the place fell silent. And dark. All of a sudden, they woke in a panic, overcome by an inexplicable fear. So violent was their fear that they left that inn and the village in the middle of the night. The name of the place: Oushpitsin—better known to our generation as Oświęcim, or Auschwitz."[104] What does it mean? It means that there may have been among the Hasidic masters a prescient insight not only into the destruction of their world but also what might be retrieved from the ashes of destruction, to see to the restoration of its legacy—without which there can be no redemption either for the Jewish people or for humanity.

And so we come to Elimelekh and his brother Zusia. "Without either, Hasidism would have been different," Wiesel asserts. "Together they gave its future a countenance. In years to come, for a Rebbe to be whole, he had to be both Rebbe Zusia—innocence and humility personified—and Rebbe Elimelekh, supreme incarnation of authority and power. Their two portraits—so distinct and intertwined—have remained singularly alive in Hasidic memory."[105] Yes, a future—if it *is* a future—must have a countenance, a face, a trace of holiness transmitted through a portrait. In Elimelekh and Zusia we realize that just as the soul lives in the midst of a relationship, so too does the face emerge only in the midst of a relationship, from the space *between* two. What emerges from this portrait of Elimelekh of Lizensk and Zusia of Onipol is the *face*.

Wiesel goes on to sketch the contrast between the two brothers by saying, "All his life Elimelekh aspired to fulfill himself through suffering, which taunted him by eluding him. Whereas Zusia, constantly beaten by life and tormented by Him who gives life, considered himself to be the happiest of men."[106] Did Elimelekh really think he had to go looking for suffering? Was he not patient enough to let it find him? Zusia is even more perplexing. When asked how he could be happy when he experienced so much suffering, Zusia did not understand the question: all he felt was gratitude. And gratitude engenders compassion. "Zusia, like Levi-Yitzhak of Berditchev," says Wiesel, "was incapable of finding fault with others; his brother wanted all men to be perfect. Elimelekh preached severity. Zusia advocated compassion. . . . Elimelekh was feared, Zusia was loved. Fear and love: the two feelings a Tzaddik must inspire."[107] As with the House of Shammai and the House of Hillel, we see the need for both to comprise the portrait—which is a portrait of neither the one nor the other; rather it is the portrait of a relationship out of which a legacy—a teaching and testimony—may emerge.

Zusia's insistence upon compassion was an insistence upon compassion not for himself but for others. The story is told that an innkeeper once mistreated a beggar, without knowing that the beggar was actually Rebbe Zusia. When he realized to whom he had been so cruel, he went to Rebbe Zusia and begged forgiveness. Rebbe Zusia told him to seek out the beggars in the street, invite them into his inn, and beg their forgiveness.[108] Beneath Zusia's admonition toward the innkeeper, one senses an admonition of Zusia toward himself. "In his own eyes," Wiesel explains, Zusia "was the worst of sinners. . . . Menahem-Mendl of Kotzk said of him: 'Just as there are scientific geniuses, there is one in matters of humility, and I mean Rebbe Zusia.' "[109] Said Rebbe Zusia, "When I shall face the celestial tribunal, I shall not be asked why I was not Abraham, Jacob or Moses. I shall be asked why I was not Zusia."[110] I shall be asked, in other words, why I did not take better care of the great treasure entrusted to me and why I was not more responsive when I was summoned by name. Thus we see the severity toward oneself that is necessary for compassion toward another.

As for Elimelekh, if he followed the path of judgment and severity, he judged himself most severely. " 'So many people come to me with their pleas,' he once asserted. 'One cries for health, another for bread, a third for a better life. Why do they come to *me*? Because in truth I am responsible for their sickness, their hunger and their misery!' Does that mean the Hasid's own responsibilities are diminished? Surely not. Only shifted. He is responsible for what happens to the Tzaddik—for *his* cries, for *his* spiritual anguish."[111] Responsibility is like an AC electrical current: it goes both ways. And yet, the insistence upon the stringency and authority of *Halakhah* is an insistence upon an infinite responsibility that devolves *not* upon the other person but precisely upon *me*. Hence, says Wiesel, "Lizensk meant total concern on the part of every Hasid for his fellow man."[112] And because the responsibility is infinite, it is a responsibility for redemption itself. At some point, Rebbe Elimelekh taught, "a Tzaddik *must* assume responsibility for the Messiah's *not* coming."[113] What heavier guilt can there be?

Said Elimelekh: The Celestial Tribunal "will ask me if I was just; I shall say no. Then they will ask me if I was charitable; I shall say no. Did I devote my life to study? No. To prayer perhaps? No again. And the Supreme Judge will smile and say: 'Elimelekh, Elimelekh, you speak the truth—and for this alone you may enter paradise.' "[114] If Elimelekh speaks the truth, it is a truth that lives in the midst of the face-to-face of a relationship—sometimes of a relationship that requires more difference than similarity. "Elimelekh's passion was the Talmud," says Wiesel, "whereas Zusia was a dreamer and leaned toward pure contemplation."[115] The implication? Elimelekh was more inclined toward *Halakhah*, or toward the *sefirah* of *Gevurah*, of severity and judgment; Zusia, on the other hand, leaned more toward *Aggadah*, or toward the *sefirah* of *Hesed*, of mercy, compassion, and loving kindness.

Recognizing the ability of the brothers to unleash the sparks of holiness from the stuff of creation, the Great Maggid sent Elimelekh and Zusia to traverse the Polish countryside, so as to spread Hasidut throughout the land, much as he had sent Rebbe Aharon of Karlin to Lithuania. "One tradition has it," Wiesel writes, "that every place they stayed—even for a night—became annexed to the Hasidic kingdom."[116] Just as the brothers brought a transformation to the Jews of Poland, so, says Wiesel, "nobody passed through Lizensk unchanged."[117] Rebbe Elimelekh settled in Lizensk in 1777 and died there in 1788. Among his disciples was the renowned Holy Seer of Lublin. The Hasidim used to declare that "after the founder—the Baal Shem—and the architect—the Great Maggid—came Elimelekh—the teacher"[118]—who through this portrait becomes our teacher.

Portrait of Moshe-Leib of Sassov

The great Yiddish writer Isaac Leib Peretz wrote a famous story called "If Not Higher" based on a Hasidic tale about Moshe-Leib of Sassov.[119] The hero of the Peretz story is the unnamed Rabbi of Nemirov. It takes place during the time of the Penitential Prayers leading up to Rosh Hashanah, the Days of Awe, and Yom Kippur. Each year during that time the Rabbi would disappear in the early hours of the morning. Some of the Hasidim would wonder: Where could he be? Why, where else? He had ascended to the uppermost realms of the uppermost worlds to plead the case of the Jewish people before the Most High, the Holy One Himself.

A Litvak Mitnagged, who happened to be passing through Nemirov one year, was of course skeptical. Determined to expose the Rabbi of Nemirov as a fraud and the Hasidim as fools, he sneaked into the Rabbi's room one night, hid under his bed, and waited. He was determined to find out just where the Rabbi had disappeared to. When the Rabbi rose, the Litvak watched him dress in peasant's clothes, with a heavy rope dangling from his coat pocket. He went out from his room, picked up an ax from the kitchen, and set out into the predawn darkness with the Litvak following behind.

The Rabbi made his way to the outskirts of Nemirov and into the woods. There the Litvak watched him fell a tree and chop it into sticks. The Rabbi then made a bundle of sticks, wrapped the rope around the bundle, and returned to town. The Litvak then saw the Rabbi stop at a broken-down shack where a sick old Jewish woman lived. The disguised Rabbi knocked on the door. She asked who was there, and he told her it was Vasily, a Russian peasant selling wood. She replied that she had no money, but he said, "No matter," and entered the shack. The Russian peasant Rabbi proceeded to make a fire and, while doing so, uttered the first of the Penitential Prayers. As the wood burned, he recited the second portion, and then the third—whereupon the Litvak became a disciple of the Rabbi of Nemirov. From that moment onward, whenever the Litvak heard one of the Hasidim of Nemirov declare that the Rabbi had disappeared into the uppermost realms to plead the case of the Jews, he simply nodded, smiled, and declared, "Yes, if not higher."[120]

In the Peretz version, Wiesel points out, the Rabbi of Nemirov is anonymous; according to the tale told by Reb Zvi-Hersh of Zhidachov, however, it is none other than Moshe-Leib of Sassov. The sick old woman is not Jewish but Christian, the episode takes place not during the Penitential Prayers but on a winter night, and the one who follows the Rebbe is not a Litvak but Reb Zvi-Hersh himself.[121] "This is the very substance of Hasidism," Wiesel comments. "The holy man must not necessarily look holy; he may appear as a peasant, a wanderer, a worker, a merchant. He must not necessarily stay within the covers of the Talmud, the Zohar, or the prayers—he may—and indeed should—leave his house, leave his shelter, leave his study and his work, and go into the forest, and perhaps chop wood in order to come closer to God."[122] If the holy man may not necessarily look holy, the same applies to the holy act.

One Erev Yom Kippur, Wiesel relates another tale of Moshe-Leib, the Hasidim of Sassov were gathered in the synagogue to hear the rabbi chant the Kol Nidre, the prayer that ushers in Yom Kippur and the holiest prayer of the year, chanted as only Moshe-Leib could chant it. Among the congregants was a young widow who had a small infant at home. She lived very close to the synagogue. She placed her baby in his crib and thought she might go to the synagogue just long enough to hear the Rabbi chant the Kol Nidre; it should have taken no more than about fifteen minutes. After waiting five, ten, then fifteen minutes—a voice cried out from within her: "Where could the Rabbi be, he who knew better than anyone the importance of being in the right place at the right time when coming before the Holy One?" So she left the synagogue and hurried home to her baby. "To her surprise she found that her infant was not alone. A man was cradling her child, singing to him softly. Said the Rebbe, 'What could I do? As I walked past your house I heard a child crying—I had to stay with him.'"[123] How do we ascend higher than the Kol Nidre takes us? By holding in our arms an infant in need of comforting.

Born in Brody in 1744, Moshe-Leib never met the Besht or the Great Maggid; he was a disciple of the great Talmudic scholar Reb Shmelke of Nikolsburg. Moshe-Leib's profound Hasidic love for the human being was a love that only seemed to eclipse his love for God; in fact, he knew there was no higher expression of his love for God than the love expressed by rocking an infant in his arms. I think this is true of anyone who has held in his or her arms a new soul entering this realm, no more than five seconds old, gazing into those eyes taking their first gaze upon this world. In that moment we attain the wisdom of the sages, a wisdom steeped in a love unlike any other, steeped in *a love for God*. Says Wiesel, "Moshe-Leib loved to walk and shout, and to be in love . . . with God."[124] His love for God led him to take the infant into his arms rather than pray the *holiest prayer of the year*! For the love of the infant *is not a means to loving God*—it *is* the love for God.

What, according to Moshe-Leib of Sassov, binds us most profoundly to our fellow human being? It is hunger—a teaching that must, in our post-Holocaust age, be pronounced with a certain fear and trembling and within a certain context. "You see, Moshe-Leib, he said to himself, hunger is more important than food. Think of all the overfed, over nourished prices and leaders who can eat and eat and eat until the end of their lives—are they happy? No, they are not. They are not happy because they are not hungry. But you are, Moshe-Leib. As hungry as a lion—so what are you complaining about? Thank God for your hunger! Louder Moshe-Leib! You have a strong voice, shout! Tell God how *grateful* you are—and not only how hungry you are."[125] And yet, in keeping with the Hasidic tradition and teaching, we who live in the post-Holocaust world must raise our own outcry against these words that now appear to undermine meaning. "The Lager *is* hunger," declares Primo Levi. "We ourselves are hunger, living hunger."[126] And yet even in that realm, if a shred of meaning was to be found, it was in the movement of ascent that characterizes snatching the bread from one's own mouth and offering it to another, a movement that in the concentrationary universe might indeed amount to dying for another. Where lies the key to unlock the highest gate leading into the uppermost realm of the Holy One? *In a piece of bread.*

"Do you wish to know, asked Reb Moshe-Leib of Sassov, whether whatever you are doing is right? Ask yourself whether it brings you closer to man. If it does not, then you are heading in the wrong direction—you are moving away from God. For even the love of God must be measured in human terms. One must love God *and* man and never act against man or without man—such was Hasidism as practiced in Sassov."[127] Rabbi Moshe-Leib could often be seen in the marketplaces of Sassov. "He felt he was more needed there," Wiesel explains, "he could accomplish more. . . . But how can you absorb so much pain? he was asked. How can you take in so much suffering from so many people? And he answered, If their pain is only *theirs*, then my work and my life is [*sic*] wasted. Their pain is also mine—so why shouldn't I try to alleviate it?"[128] If the holiness of the image of the Holy One binds us together as *benai adam*, as children of Adam, then *so does suffering*, for suffering is not only human, but it is part of the Likeness. Moshe-Leib's son once heard him on Rosh Hashanah praying in Yiddish, "Master of the Universe—we have been praying and praying, waiting and waiting, and redemption has not come. Why not? We can bear it no more, Master of the Universe. Do you hear me? We have reached the end."[129] And if God would not heed the prayers of Moshe-Leib of Sassov, then . . . *what?*

"Learn to listen," was one of Sassover's most urgent teachings. "Learn to care. Learn to be concerned, to be involved. The opposite of love is not hate but indifference; the opposite of life is not death but insensitivity."[130] This attitude of listening—this insistence on *Shma!*—is essential to our identity as human beings. If the face is the origin of speech and the revelation of difference as nonindifference, as Levinas has explained,[131] then *listening* to our fellow human being unlocks that speech and that revelation. Here the portrait of Moshe-Leib becomes, once again, a portrait of the face as such. The face enjoins us: "When it comes to helping someone in need, do not rely on prayer alone. Let the person in need pray, not you, your task is to help."[132] As another source states it, Moshe-Leib taught that there are times when we should behave as atheists: "If someone comes to you, entreating aid, do not say in refusal: 'Trust in God; He will help,' but act as if there were no God, and none to help but you."[133] Yes. None to help *but me*: no one either above or below can bring the help that I am summoned to bring.

One night, Wiesel relates, Moshe-Leib came home from the House of Study without stopping by the market, and his children asked him, "Papa, Papa, what did you bring?" Whereupon "he fainted. Later he explained: 'Suddenly I told myself that one day, upon arrival in the other world, I would be asked the same question: "Moshe-Leib, Moshe-Leib, what did you bring us?'"[134] But what could a mere human have to bring to God? His laughter? His tears? His prayers and good deeds? Or is it something else? Perhaps his anger and outrage, his questions and admonitions, as Wiesel implies when he writes, "My problem with Reb Moshe-Leib was that most tales about him—or by him—stress his joy, his warmth, his ecstasy; he seemed threatened by nothing, hurt by no one. Forever serene, at peace with himself and the world, forever singing and dancing and consoling and rejoicing—how could one not be disturbed by him? Then I found a clue which made me revise my perception of the man." The clue is this: in the Psalms it says, "Happy is the man who is chastised by God" (Psalms 94:12). "Reb Moshe-Leib translated it differently: Happy is the man who is chastising God, questioning Him, and taking Him to task for not fulfilling His obligations toward His people."[135] As we have seen, there are times when the challenge we put to God pleases God and hastens the redemption.

When we mutely accept everything that befalls our community—not ourselves but others—then not only does God refrain from smiling, but He retires to His hiding place to weep. There were times when Moshe-Leib would follow Him there. "Yes," writes Wiesel, "he too needed to be alone when he addressed God as defender of his people, and when he had to reveal his anguish to God, to God alone."[136] How did Moshe-Leib ascend to such heights? By dancing. Known for the power of his dance, he once said, "When somebody asks something impossible of me, I know what I must do: I must dance."[137] For the Hasid, the dance can transport the soul to heights unattainable through prayer alone. Recall what Wiesel says about the famous Shpoler Zeide: "He is the greatest dancer in Hasidic history. As Rabbi Barukh watched him dance, he said, 'What you achieve by dancing, others do not attain by praying.' The Zeide answered: 'That's because I had an excellent teacher: the prophet Elijah himself.'"[138] What does he achieve? Not just an ascent into the heights but an elevation of the depths. Here the soul *is* the dancing body that uses gravity to transcend gravity.

Could Moshe-Leib's capacity to ascend through his dancing take him to new levels of foresight? As he has done in other portraits of Hasidic masters, Wiesel hints that Moshe-Leib caught a glimpse of what would befall the Jews of Sassov: all fifteen hundred of them—*all*—Wiesel points out, perished in Belzec and Zlotchov.[139] "Toward the end of his life," Wiesel relates, "he had two friends who never left his side; they were jesters. And when his sadness became unbearable, they would tell him funny stories to make him laugh—and then his laughter became unbearable."[140] A dialogue from Wiesel's *One Generation After* that takes place in another, transcendent realm comes to mind:

> But . . . why are you laughing?

> So that you may remember my laughter as well as the look in my eyes.

> You lie. You laugh because you are going mad.

> Perfect. Remember my madness.[141]

This is the unbearable laughter that erupts from the Rebbe, the shriek of laughter that reverberates in a haunting silence. "How did Reb Moshe-Leib of Sassov, the symbol of compassion and love in Hasidism, put it? 'You who wish to find the fire, look for it in the ashes.'"[142] Echoing the words of the Maggid of Mezeritch, Moshe-Leib appears to have had a presentiment of a strange fire that lay in the future of the Jewish people. You wish to seek out the legacy? Look for it in these portraits made of ashes.

Portrait of Rebbe Levi-Yitzhak of Berditchev

Also known as Levi-Yitzhak Derbarmdiger (the Merciful), Rebbe Levi-Yitzhak of Berditchev was born in Galicia in 1740. He is the author of the mystical text *Kedushat Levi*. He and Moshe-Leib of Sassov had the same teacher: Shmelke of Nikolsburg. It was Shmelke of Nikolsburg who took Levi-Yitzhak to Mezeritch, where he became a disciple of the Maggid. Ever present, like a shadow, at the Great Maggid's side, "Levi-Yitzhak was to discover that the Jewish condition must be lived rather than studied,"[143] much in keeping with the words of the beggar in Wiesel's novel *The Oath*: "God too must be lived. . . . You must live Him, not study Him in books, between four walls!"[144] To be sure, only through the Hasidic impetus to take Judaism beyond four walls and into the world can there be a movement from our lower realm into the upper realms—in order to bring the upper realms into this realm. An example: Levi-Yitzhak once saw a coachman saying his morning prayers while greasing the axles of his coach. He did not scold him. Instead, he raised his eyes to heaven and cried out, "Look at Your people, God of Israel, and be proud. What does this man do while working on his cart? He prays. Tell me, do You know of any other nation that has You so completely in its thoughts?"[145] Thus we have a hint of what it might mean to live God.

Here lies Levi-Yitzhak's signature, the thread that twists and turns to weave his portrait. It is made not only of uproar and rebellion, as it may seem at first glance—but just the opposite: it is made of outcry and praise, of praise *in* outcry, of devotion through rebellion. "The most beautiful accounts and stories of his adventures," declares Wiesel, "are those that show him in his role of attorney for the defense, challenging and remonstrating the Judge. As a child, I loved them and saw in them nothing but love and friendship. Today I feel their weight of despair and revolt—and love them even more. I often look at them; I owe them much. Sometimes I dip my pen into their wealth before I write."[146] As a Hasid, Wiesel dipped his pen into the wellspring of Hesed, of love and loving kindness. That is what draws him to Levi-Yitzhak, who, for the sake of love for humanity, turns the tables: suddenly the Judge on High comes before—not a judgment but an outcry—a plea for the sake of the Judge Himself.

"Others," says Wiesel, "had carried on dialogues with God. But none had ever dared take a stand against God."[147] This is an important part of Wiesel's Hasidic legacy. This is how a devotion to God, after the Shoah, might be possible: look to Levi-Yitzhak. "If other mystics maintained I-and-Thou relations with God," declares Wiesel, "he, Levi-Yitzhak, threatened Him with breaking off these same relations. In this way, he wished to demonstrate that one may be Jewish with God, in God and even against God; but not without God. He was not content merely to ask God questions, like Abraham and Job before him. He demanded answers, and in their absence, drew his conclusions."[148] We must add this: if one cannot be Jewish without God, God cannot be God without the Jews, as it is written: "When you are My witnesses, I am God, but when you are not My witnesses, I am not God" (*Pesikta de-Rab Kaḥana* 12:6; see also *Sifre* on Deuteronomy 33:5). In the post-Shoah context of Wiesel's portraits these lines are especially implicating for God and humanity, as are these words from Levi-Yitzhak: "When a Jew sees tefillin on the ground, he runs to pick them up and kisses them. Isn't it written that we are Your tefillin? Are You never going to lift us up toward You?"[149] Yes, according to Jewish teaching, God, too, wears tefillin.

In the Talmud a question that provides the context for Levi-Yitzhak's question is raised: what did Moses see when God refused to show him His face but showed him His back (Exodus 33:22–23)? The answer: Moses saw the knot tied in the back of the tefillin around God's head, and that is how we know how to tie that knot (*Menaḥot* 35b). Elsewhere in the Talmud another question is posed: "Rabbi Nahman ben Isaac said to Rabbi Hiyya ben Abin: What is written in the tefillin of the Lord of the Universe?—He replied to him: And who is like Thy people Israel, a nation one in the earth [1 Chronicles 17:21]? Does, then, the Holy One, blessed be He, sing the praises of Israel?—Yes, for it is written: Thou hast avouched the Lord this day . . . and the Lord hath avouched thee this day [Deuteronomy 26:17–18]" (*Berakhot* 6a). This brings to bear certain other problems with regard to laying tefillin. Wiesel relates the story of the inmates having acquired a pair of tefillin in the camp and how Jews lined up to lay tefillin at the risk of their lives, each one, says Wiesel, praying with defiance and even anger.[150] At what hour in the morning, the rabbis ask, shall a Jew put on his tefillin, when the darkness succumbs to the light? The answer: when it is light enough for him to recognize the face of his neighbor (*Kitzur Shulchan Arukh* 10:2). When is it light enough for God to put in His tefillin? And whose face must He be able to behold? Surely it is the face of the human being, most especially when the darkness of the Kingdom of Night has effaced the human being.

Similarly, Levi-Yitzhak turns to the Torah of the Holy One to put to Him a question. "You order man to the aid of orphans [for example, Deuteronomy 10:18]," Levi-Yitzhak cries out. "We too are orphans. Why do you refuse to help us?"[151] Indeed, "We are Your tefillin" has come to mean "We are Your orphans." The God who sings the praises of Israel is known as the "Father of Orphans" (see, for example, Psalms 68:6). The vast majority of the survivors of the Shoah *were orphans*. As I have been told by numerous survivors from the DP camps, "Yes we had many weddings, and we celebrated, as people do in all weddings. The only difference was: there were no parents."

As powerful as the image of tefillin is, Yom Kippur, the Day of Atonement, is even more so. Who, other than Levi-Yitzhak of Berditchev, would presume to challenge the One who sits in judgment upon the Throne of Glory on Yom Kippur? "On the Day of Atonement," the tale is told,

> he once urged the town's humble tailor to speak up in front of the whole congregation; the man publicly made his confession: 'I, Yankel, am a poor tailor who, to tell the truth, has not been too honest with his work. I have occasionally kept remnants of cloth that were left over, and I have occasionally missed the afternoon service. But You, O Lord, have taken away infants from their mothers, and mothers from their infants. Let us on this Day of Days, be quits. If You forgive me, then I will forgive You.' At this the rabbi sighed: 'Oh, Yankel, Yankel, why did you let God off so lightly?'[152]

Yankel, however, was not the Rebbe. Levi-Yitzhak was. It was not a casual question. No, it was a question that was central to the Rebbe's own prayers. "He often fainted in the middle of services," Wiesel tells us. "The slightest prayer exhausted him; it involved more than his faith, it involved his life."[153] Yes, that is the point, and that is the legacy: there is a life-and-death stake in the confrontation with God, not only for humanity but also for God Himself. Yes, God Himself can, as it were, "die." Recall these lines from Nikos Kazantzakis: "Within the province of our ephemeral flesh all of God is imperiled. He cannot be saved unless we save him with our own struggle; nor can we be saved unless He is saved."[154] No, it is not only for the sake of Yankel that Levi-Yitzhak urges the tailor to confront the Creator: it is for the sake of the Creator and His Creation.

We have seen that the Jewish tradition of argument with God goes back to the first Jew, to Abraham himself, when he argued with God over the fate of Sodom and Gomorrah (Genesis 18:23–32). Why did God bother to consult Abraham in this matter? Because, says Wiesel, "God, knowing the fate of the Jews, wished to teach them the need of arguing, even against Himself."[155] Therefore, the Talmud teaches, "when the Holy One is conquered He rejoices" (*Pesahim* 119a). This tradition that arises in biblical times and unfolds throughout the Talmudic period continues into Hasidic tales and teachings; there, in the name of a love for humanity that is our only pathway to God, Rabbi Yaakov Yosef of Polnoe, a disciple of the Baal Shem Tov, maintains, "It is against the Creator of the universe and the Lord of history that accusation must be hurled. Ultimately, the exile—in body and spirit—is His doing. Ultimately, therefore, He must take mercy."[156] Thus Levi-Yitzhak is the inheritor rather than the originator of a Hasidic tradition of outcry, one that would carry over into the Hasidic legacy of Elie Wiesel.

As I have argued, the Hasidic tradition is not a departure from nor even a branch of Jewish tradition. It is an intensification of Jewish tradition: an intensification needed more than ever after the radical assault on that tradition and the decimation of the Hasidic world. "Jewish tradition," Wiesel writes, "allows man to say anything to God, provided it be on behalf of man. Man's inner liberation is God's justification. It all depends on where the rebel chooses to stand. From inside his community, he may say anything. Let him step outside it, and he will be denied this right. The revolt of the believer is not that of the renegade; the two do not speak in the name of the same anguish."[157] There is no believer whose passion and belief run deeper than that of Levi-Yitzhak of Berditchev; his outcry to the Holy One is rooted in *Ahavat Yisrael*, a love for the people of Israel, which is precisely the love for the Holy One.

That is why "the questions of the Berditchever Rebbe, and his challenges too, flung at the face of a sky in flames, have survived him. They follow us and give us the strength and courage to claim them and retell them as if they were our own."[158] The questions of the Berditchever Rebbe are part of Elie Wiesel's Hasidic legacy, as he makes those questions his own. Wiesel's first glimpse of the antiworld of the Shoah was a vision of a sky in flames, as he wrote in *Night*: "'The flames, do you see them?' (Yes, we saw the flames.) 'Over there, that's where they will take you. Over there will be your grave. You still don't understand? You sons of bitches. Don't you understand anything? You will be burned! Burned to a cinder! Turned into ashes!'"[159] Elsewhere in the Holocaust Kingdom, we know the Nazis were not content merely to desecrate the houses of prayer; they put them to the torch, with praying Jews inside, and thus consigned God Himself to the flames. In her Holocaust memoir, Judith Dribben relates the following: "One morning some Germans saw me on the stairs. Richard, a blond and fresh young man who spoke Ukrainian, stopped me. 'Last night we set your synagogue afire! Didn't it burn wonderfully? The Jewish God is burnt to ashes.'"[160] And yet, like the Torah, the questions and outcries inherited from the Berditchever Rebbe and transmitted through Wiesel's testimony are made of a fire that no fire can consume.

There is more wisdom—and certainly more holiness—in these questions and outcries than in all the erudition of the philosophers. A famous philosopher, Wiesel relates, once came to Berditchev to engage Levi-Yitzhak in an argument and prove that God did not exist. Before he could speak, however, "the Rebbe looked up straight into his eyes and gently said: 'And what if it were true after all? Tell me, and what if it were true?' The philosopher later confessed that this question had moved and troubled him more than all the affirmations and arguments he had ever heard before or since."[161] If it were true after all, then all of our questioning and outcry would be meaningless. If it were true, after all, there would be no legacy, no past, no future, no testimony, and no problem: without God there can be no atheism.

Because Levi-Yitzhak's outcry was steeped in a love for the children of Israel, writes Wiesel, "he always managed to invoke extenuating circumstances for others. He himself did not get off so easily; he was his own most severe judge. 'Why do all Talmudic tractates begin with page two? To remind us that even if we know them from one end to the other, we have not even begun.'"[162] Page one is not missing. Rather, like the silent *alef* that precedes the *beit* of Torah (the silent One that precedes the voicing of page two) page one silently signifies the infinite. Which is to say that no matter how often we have engaged the task, we have not even begun to attain the infinite level of righteousness and responsibility for our neighbor that we are summoned to attain. This, says Wiesel, was the Berditchever's motto: "man must criticize himself and praise his fellow man. He pushed this line of thought to the point of holding himself responsible if mankind was in bad straits. . . . By improving himself, the Rebbe affects others; that is a major principle of mystical thought. Let one human being attain perfection and the entire species shall be saved from falsehood."[163] Why? Because, as we have already seen, each human being is connected to every other, body and soul, physically and metaphysically. Each is responsible for all, and I more than the others.

The silence of the missing first page that precedes page two of the Talmud—the silence of the *alef* that precedes the *beit* of the Torah—may have found its way into another tale of Rebbe Levi-Yitzhak. Aharon of Karlin once visited Rebbe Levi-Yitzhak: "The two men sat down, one facing the other, without saying a word. Two hours went by; not a sound. Then, obeying the same impulse, they exchanged a smile—in silence. And that is how they parted—in silence. Neither one ever disclosed the meaning of that smile, the content of that silence. All we know is the result. The obscure visitor became a famous Tzaddik."[164] There were, in fact, Hasidic masters who taught through silence, as we may gather from a passage in Wiesel's novel *The Testament*, where his main character, the poet Paltiel Kossover, relates from a prison: "I spent hours with a disciple of the Hasidic school of Worke, whose rebbe had turned silence into a method. . . . Later, with Rebbe Mendel-the-Taciturn, we tried to transcend language. At midnight, our eyes closed, our faces turned toward Jerusalem and its fiery sanctuary, we listened to the song of its silence—a celestial silence and yet terrible silence in which both voices and moments attain immortality."[165] Of course, like Paltiel, the world would soon discover what he discovered: "No master had ever warned me that silence could be nefarious, evil."[166] One wonders whether Levi-Yitzhak himself could have anticipated the nefarious, evil silence that would cast its shroud over humanity. One wonders what sort of madness might there have been in the silence and in the smile exchanged by the two Rebbes.

"Levi-Yitzhak admired King Solomon, the wisest of our sovereigns," Wiesel writes. "Why? Because, according to the Midrash, he mastered all languages? Because he knew how to speak to birds? No. Because he understood the language of madmen."[167] What is the language of madmen? Perhaps it is the language of God. As in the case of other Tzaddikim, Levi-Yitzhak was drawn to the language of madmen because he foresaw a time when only madmen could fathom a reality in which more was real than was possible. "It would seem," writes Wiesel, "that he succumbed to a severe nervous depression, deeper than any he had experienced before.

We know, for example, that one night, having strayed into what was known as Tanner's Street, he was seized by infinite almost inhuman sadness and fainted. We know also that he was obsessed by the suicide of a poor little beadle who had hanged himself from the synagogue's main chandelier, thinking thus to 'honor' God. . . . He withdrew into himself, became a recluse. . . . He whose passion had kindled sparks in every heart was now burned out; a frightened, hunted man."[168] Hunted? Or haunted? Did he realize that despite all the disputes between the Tzaddik and the Holy One, nothing could alter the course of what awaited the Jews of Europe? "Had Levi-Yitzhak discovered that the soul can become the enemy of reason? Or that fervor, pushed to its limits, opens onto the abyss? That abrupt transitions may beget insanity? Could he have understood that his pleas were not bringing forth the expected results? That God could easily decide not to receive them, not to hear them? No one knows. And more surprisingly: no one even tried to find out."[169] Not that finding out would resolve anything. Indeed, it could lead to even darker questions.

Portrait of Rebbe Nahman of Bratzlav

The Hasidim count Rebbe Nahman of Bratzlav as the last in a series of five great *hakhamim*: Moses, Shimon bar Yohai, the Ari Isaac Luria, and his grandfather the Baal Shem Tov.[170] "Rebbe Nahman is close and precious to me on more than one level," says Wiesel. "He makes me dream. I love everything that touches him, everything that refers to his life, his work. I love everything that is impregnated by his universe. . . . 'Take my stories and turn them into prayers,' Rebbe Nahman used to say. Well, as far as I am concerned, I'll turn his prayers into stories."[171] If Wiesel's tales assume the character of prayer, as when he divides *Town beyond the Wall* into prayers and not chapters, it may well be due to the influence of Rebbe Nahman of Bratzlav.

According to David Biale and his coauthors, Rabbi Nahman's most important collection of tales is *Sippurei Ma'asiyot* (Stories and fairy tales (1815), published after his death. "Redemption could not come, he taught, until the human mind, prisoner of sinful imagination, was freed. His tales would provide an alternative imagination."[172] Wiesel opens his portrait of Rebbe Nahman with one of the Rebbe's many tales of madness. According to the story, there was once a king who had a vision of his subjects being stricken with madness after eating the coming harvest. He shared his vision with his counselor, who advised him that they should both avoid eating from the harvest. The king refused, saying that he could not bear to remain sane while his people were mad. The counselor saw the wisdom in the king's thinking, and he decided that he, too, would eat from the harvest. The king and his counselor, however, marked each other with the seal of madness so that when they looked upon each other, each would know that the other was mad.[173] In a land where everyone is mad, madness would be taken for normalcy. Imagine taking yourself to be "normal," like everyone else but suddenly realizing, upon seeing the seal of madness, that you and everyone else are mad. Such a realization would open the way to true sanity, a sanity that looks like madness in the land of the insane—like the apparent insanity of being a man in a land where there are no men, to borrow a phrase from Hillel (*Pirke Avot* 2:5). What does it mean to be a man, that is, to be a true human being? It means to be *good*, as Primo Levi has suggested.[174] And there are, indeed, times when goodness appears to be madness.

Then there is the Bratzlaver's tale of a mad prince who took himself to be a rooster. He stripped himself of his clothing, curled up in a coop, and ate food fit only for a rooster. People searched far and wide for a cure. Finally, there came along a man who, imitating the prince, stripped himself of his clothing, moved into the coop with the prince, and ate only chicken feed. The prince was suspicious of him and wondered whether he might be insane. By degrees, the man convinced him to adopt the ways of men and enter human society, even though both of them knew that the ones who were mad were in fact those who labeled the prince as mad.[175] The lesson? We cannot always tell who is mad or whether we ourselves are mad. If, however, we are mad, the cure for madness seems to lie in a movement into a loving human relationship with one another, a relationship steeped in *hesed*—a movement that, to some people, may itself appear to be madness. Continuing the legacy of Levi-Yitzhak of Berditchev and his accent on *hesed*, Nahman of Bratzlav said, "If we perform no kind deeds, we have no understanding."[176] Clinical madness lies in cruelty, while mystical madness is rooted in loving kindness.

According to Reb Nathan, the Bratzlaver's biographer, in 1806 Rebbe Nahman decided to become a storyteller, saying, "I can see that my ideas have no effect on you, therefore I shall tell you stories."[177] Could that be why Wiesel became a storyteller? Could it be that ideas cannot convey the infinite importance of a human touch or a kind word, both of which in a time of darkness seem to be madness? To be sure, the centrality of friendship in Wiesel's tales is tied to the centrality of mystical madness. The centrality of mystical madness for Wiesel, then, emerges not only from Ben Zoma but also from Nahman of Bratzlav. Mystical madness is about the restoration of the bond between word and meaning, between meaning and the soul—an article of wisdom that Wiesel gleans from Rebbe Nahman of Bratzlav. Listen to these lines from Wiesel's portrait: "'Words can silence rifles,' says Rebbe Nahman. And also: 'One may give life to words with words.' Words can tear down the most solid of walls. The word is the most exciting of all discoveries, the most terrifying too. 'It is written,' Rebbe Nahman says, 'that Just Men obey the word of God. This should be read differently: Just Men make the word of God.' A literal translation, which on the Master's lips means: Just Men compose the language with which God creates His universes."[178] Because "Just Men" compose the language of creation, they compose the language of revelation—the language of the commandments. Thus, the tale of the law is the tale of the commandment, which in turn is the tale of the act of loving kindness, an act that to many may seem to be an act of madness, which is why its meaning can be transmitted only through tales.

"'Time does not exist,' the Bratzlaver asserts, whether in his tales or in the world; he goes so far as to exclude it from primary creation. According to him, God gave man everything—except time."[179] As quoted in another source, the Rebbe adds: "It is through men who perform good deeds that days are born, and so time is born."[180] Time did not come into being until the sixth day of creation, the day from which we measure time on Rosh Hashannah because only on that day did one human being enter into a relationship with another. Only on that day did the bond between word and meaning emerge with the bond between human and human. This, according to Nahman of Bratzlav, means that human relation, grounded in the bond between word and meaning, is indispensable to the higher relation. Time unfolds in that relationship. "It is as though he wanted people to understand that it is more important for man to halt and consider the mystery of his own life than that of the world's origins."[181] To be sure, the world's origin is hidden within the origin of each and every life. That is why the actions of each affect all: so that each is responsible for all. "The duty rests upon *you*," the Bratzlaver insists. "This single person who is standing in *this* generation at *this* point in the whole of eternity. It has to be done by you. 'Not an angel! Not a seraph!' [Exodus 12:12]"[182] Where lies the mystery of our own life, a mystery that transcends even the origin of the world? It lies in the simple act of extending a helping hand to another human being, for whose sake the world was created: every soul that enters creation is *indispensable* to all of creation.

"As a Kabbalist he is accessible," says Wiesel of Nahman of Bratzlav, "as a Rebbe he is not. Ascetic, an enemy of doubt, he frequents the so-called emancipated intellectual circles whose vocation and pastime is to doubt and oppose asceticism. An intolerant believer, he plays chess with free-thinkers; their faith in nothingness intrigues him."[183] And his tales are the weapons he draws upon in this game of chess. "His tales?" Wiesel writes of this strategist. "Each contains many others. Imagine a series of concentric circles whose fixed centers are buried in a man's innermost being: the I inside the I, conscience becomes silence and peace, memory inside memory."[184] According to Jewish tradition, telling tales is the highest form of human-to-human relationship, the highest form of speech: to relate a tale is to enter into a relation. In the Zohar it is written that there are three kinds of speech: saying (*lemor*), speaking (*ledaber*), and relating [a tale] (*lehagid*) (*Zohar* I, 234a). Rebbe Menachem Mendel Schneerson explains: "Speaking and saying come from the surface, not from the depth of the soul. The mouth can sometimes speak what the heart does not feel. Even what the *heart* says can be at odds with what the man truly wills in his soul. . . . But 'relating' comes from the depths of a man's being."[185] How is Israel to endure its exile? By relating tales.

No matter how deep its fall into exile, writes Wiesel, "Israel must console itself by and in the Torah. It must retain a strong hold on the letter and the will of God."[186] The letter and will of God are to be found in the word—in the faculty of speech—that according to the mystical tradition stems from the Divine Presence, the Shekhinah. "The will of God" says the twelfth-century mystic Judah Halevi, "is His speech" (*Kitav al khazari* 4:25). Thus, the Bratzlaver Rebbe teaches, "However low you fall, you still have the faculty of speech. You should use it! Speak words of truth: words of Torah, words of prayer and the fear of Heaven. You should speak to God. Speak also to your friend, and especially to your teacher. The power of speech is such that at all times it enables you to remind yourself of the closeness to God, and so to bring strength to yourself, even in the places which seem furthest from holiness."[187] And yet speech derives its power from the faculty of hearing, as Rebbe Nahman suggests elsewhere: "The very foundation of the Jewish People's link with God is through *hearing*."[188] The link lies in hearing because the Jew not only hears the voice but also knows that he is heard; even though he may speak from the confines of his garret, he does not speak to a void.

Such a link lies at the heart of prayer. If, as Rebbe Nahman says, prayer "is a battle against evil,"[189] it is because the battle against evil is a battle against meaninglessness, emptiness, silence, and death. One of his disciples, Wiesel relates,

> left us this prayer: "Master of the Universe, You know the extent of my ignorance, since I don't even know if I shall die one day. Help me. Make me know, make me aware. Make me conscious of the death awaiting me without any chance of escape. And that I shall be alone to confront it. Alone. Without friends, without anyone. Alone and abandoned by memories, desires and passions. Make this image penetrate me. The yellowed image of a sullen corpse." No Rebbe before him had ever spoken of life and death in these terms. None had ever imposed such a nightmarish vision upon his disciples. . . . And so, Rebbe Nahman's peers had little use for him.[190]

Yes, the Bratzlaver taught that "the essence of everything is joy,"[191] and that "compassion is at the root of all Creation."[192] Still, he did not shy away from confrontation, even confrontation with himself. In fact, says Wiesel, the more he was attacked, the more he liked it, saying things like, "The Angel of Death enlisted the aid of physicians—who demolish the body—and of the 'celebrities'—who destroy the mind."[193] He was not, however, a misanthrope—far from it. His confrontations with humanity were rooted in a love for humanity.

As were his confrontations with God. "To blindly submit to God, without questioning the meaning of this submission," says Wiesel, "would be to diminish Him. To want to understand Him would be to reduce His intentions, His vision to the level of ours. . . . Revolt is not a solution, neither is submission. Remains laughter, metaphysical laughter."[194] To be sure, the laughter that permeates the Bratzlaver's stories has a metaphysical ring to it. As Wiesel points out, "Laughter occupies an astonishingly important place in his work. Here and there, one meets a man who laughs and does nothing else."[195] According to one of his tales, for example, there was once a country that contained all countries. In that country was a town that contained all towns. In the town stood a house that contained all houses. In the house lived a man who embodied all men—and that man was laughing. He laughed and laughed. "No one had ever laughed like that before," Wiesel proclaims. "Who is that man? The

Creator laughing at His creation? Man sending Him back His laughter as an echo, or perhaps as a challenge?"[196] These are questions that must remain questions, questions that themselves reverberate throughout the depths of metaphysical laughter.

Still, another tale told by Nahman of Bratzlav might shed a different light on how we understand metaphysical laughter. It is the story of a king who summoned a messenger to deliver a special message to one of his subjects, a man known for his philosophical brilliance. He was perhaps too brilliant, for due to his philosophical overanalyzing of everything, he could not believe that the king could possibly have any interest in him; in fact, he doubted the very existence of the king. When he asked the messenger for proof of the king's existence, all the messenger could do was point to the message: neither the philosopher nor the messenger could find anyone who could confirm the existence of the king. Their reaction? "They laugh. They laugh with such despair that in the end, they will understand that there must be a link between the voice and the call, between the man and his road; in the end they will understand that their feeling of despair is not absurd, for it may well be the link that binds them to the king."[197] How can a laughter steeped in despair bind anyone to the king, who, of course, is the King of the Universe? Can the laughter of the King of the Universe also be steeped in despair, if, indeed, He can laugh? Normally, one would think that despair separates us from the Holy One. But there may be a place where normality is no more and a time when reality exceeds possibility. Did Rebbe Nahman of Bratzlav, in the end, have a vision of such a time and a place? Is that why what Wiesel calls "metaphysical laughter" plays such a prominent role in the Rebbe's tales?

These, Wiesel tells us, are the Rebbe's dying words:

> Describing Rebbe Nahman on his deathbed, Reb Nathan speaks of "a kind of smile on his face" while he whispered: "And here there approaches an immense and terrible mountain. And I am not sure whether we are walking toward it or whether it is coming toward us." Taking notice of his sobbing faithful he threw them this sentence: "My flame will glow till the end of time. Don't cry, I shall not forsake you." His Hasidim took his words as a promise and gave them a literal interpretation. As a result, they decided that he would have no successor. For them, the Tzaddik of Bratzlav remains alive.[198]

Wiesel recalls the first time he met a Bratzlaver Hasid; it was in the midst of a terrible mountain of ashes in Auschwitz. The Bratzlaver Hasid, he says, repeated a teaching from the Rebbe: "Two men separated by space and time can nevertheless take part in an exchange. One asks a question and the other, elsewhere and later, asks another, unaware that his question is an answer to the first."[199] Can the questions we now ask, in an post-Shoah age, when we seek something like Elie Wiesel's Hasidic legacy, possibly be an answer to the questions and outcries that rose up to the silent sky aflame over Auschwitz? His legacy is, in any case, a legacy of questions.

Portrait of the Holy Seer of Lublin

The Holy Seer of Lublin was born Yaakov-Yitzhak Horowitz in 1745 in a Polish village near Tarnigrod. He studied under the renowned Talmudist Reb Moshe-Hersh Meisels and then under Reb Shmelke of Nikolsburg. Reb Shmelke sent him to Mezeritch, where, under the guidance of the Great Maggid, he "learned the vital importance of friendship in Hasidism. And of beauty. And sincerity. Mezeritch was a laboratory of the soul: those who came as disciples left as teachers. The Maggid loved Reb Itzikl. Of his disciple he said, 'A soul like this has not been sent to us since the times of the Prophets.' "[200] The Holy Seer was, indeed, something of a prophet: he saw things in his visions—at times terrifying things—that no one else could see. The Holy Seer could behold the destiny of the Jewish people and could also peer into the inner recesses of the soul as well. "In his presence," Wiesel relates, "one felt shaken, purified . . . transformed. What struck people most were his eyes—one larger than the other—which often took on a disquieting fixity when looking at someone. Hasidim were convinced that he was searching their inner depths."[201] Nothing was hidden from the Seer.

"Like other masters," says Wiesel, "the Seer advocated passion and compassion, and enthusiasm, fervor—*hitlahavut*—fervor, above all. 'I prefer a passionate Mitnagged to a lukewarm Hasid,' he said. For absence of fire, absence of passion, leads to indifference and resignation—in other words, to death. What is worse than suffering? Indifference. What is worse than despair? Resignation—the inability to be moved, to let oneself go, to let one's imagination catch fire."[202] Once again, fire is a dominant image in the portrait of this soul on fire. "People go to Riminov," said the Seer, "to get sustenance and to Kozhenitz to get cures. But they come to Lublin to get the Hasidic fire."[203] The Hasidic fire burns with a love for God and humanity; it burns in the realization that the love for humanity is the only way we can express our love for God.

"What he [the Seer] himself had to give," Wiesel explains, "was not learning, though he was learned, but the art of human relations, which, of course, goes beyond learning. He taught his followers not how to study but how to listen, how to share, how to feel, how to pray, how to laugh, how to hope—how to live. What the Besht had done for his followers, the Seer did for his: he gave them a sense of dignity."[204] Imparting to his followers a sense of dignity, Rebbe Yaakov-Yitzhak elevated them. How? By opening up to them a sense of height, which is a sense of mission and meaning. "Close to the Holy Seer, one found meaning in what seemed to have none. In Lublin one was again allowed to see Jewishness as a magnificent adventure."[205] Shaped by a covenantal relationship with God, Jewishness lies in the project of redemption. Such a mission is so daunting precisely because it stirs a profound sense of gratitude and joy—yes, joy—among those who take up the task: "In Lublin, Hasidim were urged to live not only in fear of God but also in fear for God and, above all, in joy with God."[206] The *hitlahavut*—the fervor and passion that would transport the Seer through the upper realms—was steeped in a dizzying joy. "Often he would remark: 'Strange—people come to me sad and leave happy; whereas I . . . I stay with my sadness, which is like a black fire.' In moments of doubt he would groan, 'Woe to the generation whose leader I am.' He sought joy with such intensity that he ignored other considerations. Said he: 'I prefer a simple Jew who prays with joy to a sage who studies with sadness.' "[207]

Paradoxically, it was the Rebbe's sadness, the black fire within him, that drove him to insist so fervently that the Hasidim of Lublin must rejoice, even—or especially—when they failed to see any reason to rejoice. "The Seer of Lublin said, 'A Hasid, like a child, should cry and laugh at the same time.' And he explained how he managed to combine the two when lamenting over the Shekhina's suffering every night at midnight: 'Imagine an exiled king who visits his friend; the friend is sad that the king is in exile, but still he is happy to be seeing him.' "[208] From Wiesel's portrait one gathers that as the Holy Seer grew older and the exile grew darker, the Rebbe's longing to rejoice in God and with God became ever more intense—as did the desperate sadness that fueled his longing.

This brings us to a tale told of the Holy Seer that is profoundly disturbing, even frightening, as Wiesel suggests: "This is one of the most mysterious and troubling episodes in Hasidic literature—an episode that chroniclers and storytellers are still reluctant to explain, or even explore."[209] But not Elie Wiesel. This strange tale, which is part of the Holy Seer's portrait, is central to the Hasidic legacy of Elie Wiesel.

The year is 1844. Many hundreds of Hasidim have gathered in Lublin for Simhat Torah, the most joyous of all the days on the holy calendar: this is when Jews gather to celebrate the renewal of yet another annual cycle of reading the Torah. "Surrounding their Master, people sing and dance with frenzy. Like him, with him, they lift the Holy scrolls higher and higher, as if to follow them—and follow *him*—and they do. He carries them away, far away. They trust him. No matter that they do not know the outcome or even the purpose of his secret plan. What matters is to be present. Hasn't he taught them that passion succeeds where reason fails? Tonight they are consumed by passion."[210] He has taught them about passion, about the ways in which worlds rest upon the human capacity to rejoice. And so the Holy Seer orders them to rejoice like they never have before, as if the Redemption of God and humanity depended on it. And they obey him.

The Hasidim, however, are so carried away in their flight of ecstasy that they do not notice when the Rebbe quietly slips away and goes up to his private study on the second floor of the house of prayer. "No one knows what he did there," says Wiesel, "no one knows what really happened to him then. All we know is that at one point the Rebbetzin heard strange noises coming from the Seer's study—sounds like those of a child weeping. She rushed into the room and shrieked with fear. The room was empty."[211] Some of the Hasidim hurried up the stairs in response to her scream and confirmed that, indeed, the Rebbe had suddenly and mysteriously disappeared. They ventured into the dark of night to search for him on the street below the window to his study. Not a trace of him was to be found. Suddenly, from about fifty feet away, they heard Reb Eliezer of Khmelnik calling out for help: he had found the Rebbe lying in the street in some sort of a trance. The Hasidim ran to him, picked him up, and carried him to his bed. One of the Hasidim who bore the Seer in his arms was Reb Shmuel of Karov, who heard the Seer repeating over and over, his eyes filled with terror: "And the abyss calls for another abyss."[212] What could the Holy Seer have seen? How might his insistence that the Hasidim dance with greater joy and fervor than ever before have been connected to the terrifying vision that had taken hold of him—a vision that somehow transported the Seer from his study and into the street, to the edge of the abyss?

"Hasidic literature," Wiesel comments, "has shrouded this disturbing episode in secrecy. It is considered taboo. A strange conspiracy of silence has shrouded it ever since it took place."[213] The scholar of Hasidism David Biale, for example, briefly mentions the fall from the window but says nothing more and makes no mention of a Great Fall.[214] Some sources refer to it cryptically as "the Great Fall—*Hanefila Hagdola*—without entering into details."[215] But why the *Great* Fall? A fall from where to where? It appears that the Holy Seer could not have fallen out the window in his study, as it was too narrow, and empty bottles were still standing on the sill. The general belief was that the Rebbe was punished, supernaturally, for attempting to use his powers during the Napoleonic Wars, when, taking the wars to be the birth pangs of the Messiah, he joined with Mendel of Riminov and the Maggid of Kozhenitz to use their powers to force the coming of the Messiah. In any case, he never recovered from the Great Fall: he was bedridden for forty-four weeks and then died.[216] We shall never know what exactly happened on that Simhat Torah, when the Great Fall occurred.

Shedding some light on some of the shadows in his portrait of the Holy Seer, however, Wiesel entertains a few questions:

> Was it a sudden attack of sadness, of depression? Was it his way of telling God, Either You save Your people or erase me from Your book? I no longer wish to go on living—unless You put an end to Jewish suffering? Could it be that, having failed to bring the Messiah through joy, he thought of trying . . . despair? . . . Perhaps he remembered the first time, in his youth, in Lizensk, when he had felt the irresistible urge to jump into the abyss and become an offering to God. To God—who had refused his gift of joy. Could it also be that in a sudden flash of fear the Seer had a glimpse of the distant future when night would descend upon the Jewish people, and particularly upon its most compassionate and generous children—those of the Hasidic community?[217]

As always, in the background of all of Wiesel's portrait, as though forming a kind of canvas for his brush strokes, lurks the specter of the Shoah. Here, however, it is more prominent, more ominous, than in most cases.

"Lublin," asserts Wiesel, "during the darkest hours, became a center for torment and death. Lublin, an ingathering place for condemned Jews, led to nearby concentration camps at Belzec and Majdanek. Lublin meant the great fall not of one man, nor of one people, but of mankind."[218] The Hasidic kingdom of Eastern Europe was utterly obliterated, and with it came a catastrophe of cosmic dimensions. Not just the Jewish people but all of humanity was turned over to the abyss that cries out to another abyss. Traces of that obliteration are bound to show up in these portraits of the Hasidic masters. But in the portrait of the Holy Seer of Lublin they are more pronounced than usual. And more ominous.

Portrait of Rebbe Menahem-Mendl of Kotzk

At least one other Hasidic master is associated with the vertiginous depths of the abyss: Rebbe Menahem-Mendl of Kotzk, who was known to declare, "I stand with one foot in the seventh heaven and with the other in the depths of the abyss."[219] Also similar to the Holy Seer, the Kotzker Rebbe's soul was aflame with a singular fire. Whereas on Simhat Torah the Seer stirred the Hasidim to rejoice as they never had before, Menahem-Mendl impatiently ordered them to dance as they never had before. "That's not the way to dance!" he shouted at them. Several times they attempted to dance differently, desperate to please the Master. "And," Wiesel relates, "the Rebbe exploded: 'Imagine yourselves on a mountain peak, on a razor's edge, and now: dance, dance I tell you!'"[220] The Kotzker understood that the only way to tread the razor's edge or to keep your feet on a shifting ground is to dance.

Born in Goray, Poland, in 1787, Menahem-Mendl broke away from his father and went to the Holy Seer of Lublin; it was the Holy Seer who ignited the fire within him. From Lublin he went to learn from the Hasidic Master known as the Holy Jew of Pshiskhe; his last Master was Rebbe Simha of Pshiskhe. Wiesel describes him as "The Master-against-his-will, the divine saint, the divine rebel," and "among the thousands of Hasidic leaders, great and small, from the Baal Shem's time to the Holocaust, he is undeniably the most disconcerting, mysterious figure of all. Also the most tragic."[221] The mystery and the tragedy surrounding the Kotzker Rebbe pose a certain challenge to anyone who would seek to render his portrait. For "he left no portrait," Wiesel says, "no personal possessions. It is as though he never existed."[222] He had *no personal possessions*: nothing to indicate that he had ever walked the earth.

To be sure, he appears to have wanted to obliterate every trace of his sojourn in this world: "It is said that he set his meditations to paper but that he destroyed the pages as quickly as he covered them; he burned at night what he wrote during the day. . . . On his deathbed he was still obsessed by the fear that his writings might survive him. . . . There remains only his oral teaching. And his legend. A legend of fear and trembling, lacking the joy that is a characteristic of Hasidism. One listens to it and feels bitten, scorched by a black and living fire shielded by a night without dawn."[223] Wiesel's Hasidic legacy bears the scar of that black fire. "The tales and sayings of the Kotzker Rebbe are easy to identify," he comments, "impossible to mistake them for another's. They bear his mark, his scar."[224] It is the scar left by drawing too close to the searing fire of a passion for truth. A scar, we are reminded, is a remnant of a wound—can a tale or a truth, the tale of the truth or the truth of a tale, *wound*?

Wiesel points out that "Mendl of Kotzk wants man to be thirsty for truth, for the absolute, and never mind if he never reaches his goal and never mind if truth blinds and kills whoever discovers it. . . . As far as Mendl of Kotzk is concerned, all the sins of the world weigh less than the conceit of self-deception. Man does not lower himself by his failures but by the alibis he invokes. Rather perish than mutilate the truth; that is Kotzk."[225] *Never mind if truth blinds and kills*? Is the truth worth such a price? If the truth kills, it is because there are times when the truth requires being killed, especially when it demands that we abandon self-deception. Self-deception inheres in a preoccupation with *my* person, *my* space, *my* status, *my* material being, and even *my* spiritual being. Languishing in its egocentric illusion, the self lives in the dative case, forever trembling over the questions of what will happen "to me" and what is in it "for me." Understood in such terms, then, *the self is just the opposite of the soul.* As Yitzchak Ginsburgh states it, *bitul*, or the "obliteration of self," is the doorway to truth, and "*bitul* produces a 'cavity' in the self, an opening and 'vessel' for truth to enter."[226] Truth enters when the soul enters into a responsive relation with another. It enters where the other human being enters to put to me the question put to the first human being: "Where are you?" (Genesis 3:9). The truth that wounds is the truth that shakes me from the deadly delusion that passes itself off as my "self." It is the truth that demands the full measure of my devotion: the truth of my infinite responsibility to and for the other human being.

And so we may understand the Kotzker Rebbe's reply to a disciple who went to him in tears for help so that he might be able to pray and study. The Rebbe said to him, "And whoever told you that God is interested in your studies and your prayers? And what if He preferred your tears and your suffering?"[227] In other words, what if he preferred your pursuit of truth to your studies and prayers? And so we see why, in his portrait of the Kotzker Rebbe, Wiesel writes, "In Kotzk, truth becomes obsession. It takes precedence over everything, shifts everything around. Even prayer, even study. And certainly joy, ecstasy and peace of mind. Man was created not to know happiness but truth."[228] This denigration of joy is a radical move in Hasidism. Wiesel has noted, for example, that "in his memoirs, the historian Emmanuel Ringelblum refers to a Bratzlav *shtibel* inside the Warsaw Ghetto. Over its entrance was the same inscription: JEWS, DO NOT DESPAIR. For a Jew, who bears a four-thousand-year-old memory, despair is equivalent to blasphemy."[229] Joy is not the same as happiness. Nor is despair the same as outrage or mourning or suffering. One can find joy in the search for truth, even if it entails outrage and suffering.

Indeed, if truth is tied to love, then it is tied to suffering: one cannot love another without suffering for the sake of another, suffering *because of* the suffering of another. "Everything can be imitated but the truth," said the Kotzker, "because an imitated truth is a lie."[230] Recall, for example, the midrashic account of the death of Haran, brother of Abram. When Abram's father Terah found that Abram rejected idol worship, he took the lad to King Nimrod. When Abram again affirmed the one true God and rejected the idols, Nimrod had him cast into a furnace of flames. Abram, however, emerged unscathed. His brother Haran was watching all the while. When Nimrod asked Haran whether he, too, refused to embrace the idols and worshipped instead the God of Abram, Haran decided he would imitate his brother and affirmed the one true God. He, too, was cast into the furnace, only to be consumed in the flames (*Bereshit Rabbah* 38:13). No, the truth cannot be imitated—it can only be lived. Because the truth unfolds in the movement into a relationship that only *I* can undertake, it is revealed in a responsibility that only *I* can assume. It summons me and thereby singles me out. And it is unrelenting.

Just as there is no relationship without contradiction, there is no truth without paradox. What is the paradox of Kotzk? It is this: "Kotzk, within the Hasidic movement, is an experience transmitted from being to being, lips closed and eyes meeting eyes. A question that continues, unreconciled with either time or life, Kotzk is neither philosophy nor social system; Kotzk is a narrow and solitary road whose beginning touches its end; a road where silence enters the word and tears it apart the way the eye tears apart what it sees. Kotzk means throwing off despair through despair. Kotzk means prison become sanctuary."[231] Thus "the song of the

Baal Shem was stifled in Kotzk, transformed into a call of warning and despair."[232] How could such a thing have happened? In these lines we have a hint: Jacob "fought the angel all night," writes Wiesel. "Victorious, he sent him away at dawn. That was a mistake. He should have guessed the angel would come back more than once, in more than one disguise, perhaps even disguised as Jacob. . . . All his life Mendl of Kotzk continued this struggle with the angel at night. Alone. Alone against man, alone against heaven, against generations of dead ancestors and ancestral traditions that weigh on every memory."[233] The stifling of the song of the Besht came with a retreat into solitude, isolation, and anguish. "The Rebbe's groping search, filled with existential anguish," as Wiesel states it, "progresses in a solitude culminating in delirium. For him, anxiety and solitude recover their rights in Hasidism."[234] In Kotzk this delirium eclipsed the ecstatic *hitlahavut* of Lublin. And yet in Kotzk one continued to cry out—silently. Wiesel elaborates: "In Kotzk one does not speak; one roars or one keeps quiet. . . . The Rebbe says: 'When one feels like shouting and doesn't, that is when one truly shouts.' "[235] For the cry one holds back transcends all words and every silence: it opens up a gate to the upper realms that otherwise remains closed.

"Certain experiences," Rebbe Menahem-Mendl added, "may be transmitted by language, others—more profound—by silence; and then there are those that cannot be transmitted, not even by silence."[236] This truth seems to have had a tremendous impact on Elie Wiesel and therefore on his portrait of the Kotzker, as we surmise when he says, "Writing becomes more difficult, more exhausting, more pressing. I need solitude. Silence. I become acutely aware of the ambiguity of words. Always the same questions, the same doubts. How to express that which eludes language?"[237] He needs solitude? The one who belonged to a Hasidic world that was all about the mitigation of solitude needs solitude? The one who, like his character Paltiel Kossover in *The Testament*, came to realize that "silence could be nefarious, evil"[238] needs silence? No. Wiesel is more like the Kotzker than like his character Kossover. Fortunately, however, unlike the Rebbe for whom he had immense admiration, Wiesel neither destroyed his writings nor receded into a dark and debilitating isolation. But he did, as he once told me, cut most of what he wrote. "You have to write it," he said, "in order to take it out. And yet, it remains . . . it remains."

"Silence in Kotzk," Wiesel tells us, "is so heavy, so dense that it tears the nights. One doesn't dream, one is delirious. One doesn't walk, one runs. One walks a tightrope, and it is he, the Rebbe, who holds both ends.

He is present in all eyes, all thoughts; he paralyzes. . . . It is enough for him to look into someone's eyes for the other to faint."[239] If his look could cause a disciple to faint, how was the disciple to follow his insistence that if we want God to be our Father, we must force Him? And how do we force the Holy One, blessed be He, Creator of heaven and earth, to do anything? The Kotzker himself shows us by his own example: it is said that he once cried out to God, "*Avinu malkainu*, our Father, our King, I shall continue to call You Father until You become our Father."[240] And yet he once told another disciple that God enters where He is allowed to enter, as if we were the ones who kept God from becoming our Father. If, as the Rebbe once said, "it is easier to extract Israel from exile than exile from Israel,"[241] then it is true. For the return from exile—the Redemption of God Himself—turns on our capacity to return meaning to the word *Father* in our outcry to the Holy One on high. For the word *Father* contains the dimension of height itself.

A turn in this portrait of Menahem-Mendl of Kotzk comes one Shabbat in the year 1839. As usual, the Hasidim are gathered in the House of Study awaiting the appearance of the Kotzker Rebbe. Suddenly Menahem-Mendl makes his entrance: "He is struggling with his breath like a sick man; his eyes, staring at the candles before him, reflect an ancient though nameless anguish. The assembled guests are silent, oppressed; something about him makes them uneasy, frightens them. . . . They wait for time to be torn open, for thoughts to be unveiled. And then the Rebbe—in his fifties but older-looking—his face fierce and terrifying, throws back his head and. . . . This is where the tale ends. . . . Something out of the ordinary happened in Kotzk that night; something incomprehensible, unspeakable."[242] He had to be carried out of the House of Study to his quarters, where he remained in complete seclusion until the end of his life twenty years later. What was the cause of the Rebbe's turn for the worse? Why had he come to reject all contact with his Hasidim, through whom, he surely knew, lay his only contact with God? How, in utter isolation, was he to maintain his remarkable ability to *listen*? After all, Wiesel reminds us that "in Hasidism, everything is possible, everything becomes possible by the mere presence of someone who knows how to listen, to love and give of himself."[243] Why would the Rebbe who knew *this* truth more profoundly than anyone else have undertaken such a radical retreat?

Wiesel offers one possible explanation: "Earlier he had been afraid never to discover truth; now he was afraid that he had already discovered it. Therefore, there was no solution; whether man turns to one side or to the other, he still encounters fear. The link between man and God, between man and his fellow man? Fear. God wants to be feared rather than loved. And Mendl of Kotzk protests: 'If that is life, I don't want it; I'll go through it as a stranger. If that is man, what is the good of saving him?' "[244] Even in this last desperate protest the Kotzker was bent upon forcing God to be *Father*, not only for the sake of Israel but for the sake of God Himself. Or, could there be something else? A vision akin to the vision of his teacher the Holy Seer of Lublin on the night of the Seer's Great Fall? Wiesel poses the question: "Could he have foreseen that one hundred years after his retreat another fire would set the continent ablaze, and its first victims would be Jewish men and women abandoned by God and by all mankind?"[245] The vast majority of the Hasidim were consumed in the black fire of that impenetrable night.

The Rebbe's last words were, "At last I shall see Him face to face."[246] But what might that mean? Did he utter these words with consolation or terror? After all, had he caught a glimpse of the future of the Jewish people, as Wiesel intimates, he might have caught a glimpse of the face of God before coming before Him face to face: "What man did to man at Auschwitz could not have been outside of God; in some way He too was at work—was He questioning man? Was He showing His face? What a face! In a sense, at Auschwitz God was afraid—afraid of Himself."[247] And if God is afraid of Himself, how can we help but be afraid? As for what the nature of that fear might be—whether it is awash in dread and horror, or steeped in joy and gratitude, or any combination of these passions—these portraits of the Hasidic Masters serve as a response to that question. Even if it is in the form of another question.

The Messiah

Portrait of an Anticipation

"The smoke of the crematoria," writes Gershon Greenberg, paraphrasing Wiesel, "clouded the path for entry into history, and the Messiah lost his way. With so many Jews murdered, none left to save, were the Messiah ever to come, he could not come as a savior. Further, as with God Himself, the disappearance of the Messiah into the endless distance meant his death. The Messiah's heartbeat was drowned out by the cries of the victims."[1] Yes, the ashes of Israel blind the Messiah, but the *silence* of the victims render us deaf to his heartbeat. And yet his heart continues to beat when it should have stopped. We are not saved, moreover, by his coming—we are saved, if ever we might merit salvation, by our waiting and working for his coming, even though he may tarry now and forever. If he should disappear—if he should die—it will not be because he faded into the distance: it will be because we have left off with the anticipation.

For these reasons, when attached to the Messiah, the very notion of a portrait is in a category of its own. Each of the patriarchs and prophets, the sages and Hasidic masters, has his or her own time and place, with each belonging to his or her own generation. The Messiah, however, lives in every generation. Other portraits in this volume are of individuals who have already walked the earth. The Messiah, however—though he abides in our midst—has forever *yet* to arrive and is forever on his way: he is the one whose appearance we anticipate at every moment, *despite* and *because of* his having faded into the distance. In the case of the others, we turn to them for their teachings, which form the substance of Jewish teaching and tradition—including Jewish teaching and tradition on the Messiah. Therefore, unlike other portraits, in the case of the Messiah we have a portrait of Jewish testimony itself. It is not, however, a portrait of ideas or concepts: a portrait can be drawn only of a *Who*, only of living flesh and blood. From the standpoint of Judaism—certainly from the standpoint of the Vizhnitzer Hasid—the Messiah is neither an idea nor the "spirit" of an age. No, the Messiah is living flesh and blood who comes for the sake of flesh-and-blood humanity.

Also unlike his other portraits, Wiesel's portrait of the Messiah has not appeared in print. While the published portraits that we have explored are based on oral presentations, as of now, "A Portrait of the Messiah" can be found only on the website featuring the video recording of a lecture that Professor Wiesel delivered at Boston University on October 16, 2006.[2] It is held in the Elie Wiesel Archives of the Howard Gottlieb Archival Research Centre at Boston University.

Just as the Baal Shem Tov often engaged in confrontations with the Messiah,[3] Rebbe Nahman of Bratzlav once declared, "The Messiah will be the one to comment on my work."[4] If, as Wiesel has said, the ultimate aim of mysticism is to bring the Messiah,[5] it is likewise the ultimate aim of Hasidism; indeed, to hasten the coming of the Messiah—to await, work for, and anticipate the coming of the Messiah—is the task to which the Jewish people and the seventy nations of the world are summoned. A legacy is, above all, just such a summons, and Wiesel's Hasidic legacy is a calling out not only to the Jewish people but to all of humanity. Further, answering the call of the legacy never ends: the more we respond, the more responsible we become. Responsible for what? Responsible for bringing the Messiah. And because that responsibility is infinite, the Messiah is the one who is forever *yet to come*: to engage in the task to which the legacy summons us is to engage an eternal *yet to be*. Meaning in life unfolds along the edge of the *yet to be*, even though it may be along the edge of annihilation. For Elie Wiesel, it rises up in the midst of the *and yet*. There the Messiah abides: in the *and yet*. "*And yet*," says Wiesel. "Those are my two favorite words."[6] After the Shoah those words are more powerful than ever. The Shoah forever altered the meaning of the Twelfth of Maimonides's Thirteen Principles of Faith, the *Ani Maamin*, the "I believe," that affirms a belief in the coming of the Messiah, even though he may tarry—an affirmation that would recur throughout the works and the life of Elie Wiesel.

Bearing witness to the truth and wisdom of Judaism's messianic tradition was, for Wiesel, the tie that most profoundly bound him to the Jewish tradition and therefore to his Hasidic legacy; to be sure, his bond

with Jewish tradition *is* his Hasidic legacy, and that legacy lies most profoundly in his link to the Messiah. In *Open Heart* he recalls the tale of a
survivor, a Hasidic rabbi, who after a lifetime of silence finally agreed to
say what happened to him "over there." But instead of telling his story,
the rabbi suddenly began to sing the *niggun* of "Ani Maamin," "the most
beautiful, most moving *nigun* [sic] I had ever heard. He added nothing:
For him, the song said it all. Shall I be able to sing up above? Shall I too
be able to intone this *nigun* that contains all that I have tried to express
in my writings?"[7] The words of the *niggun* are the words of the Twelfth
Principle of Faith previously mentioned, recited every day in our prayers:
*Ani Maamin beemunah shlemah beviat haMashiah; veaf al pi sheyiman-
meah, im kol zeh ahakeh lo bekol yom sheyavo* (I believe with complete
faith in the coming of the Messiah; even if he may tarry, *no matter what*,
I shall anticipate his coming every day). These words contain all that Elie
Wiesel struggled to express throughout his voluminous writings, the sum
of his legacy.

For a Jew, there is nothing passive about this wait, just as there is
nothing passive about the transmission of a legacy. To await the coming of
the Messiah is to work for his advent by laboring for the sake of humanity
and out of love for humanity, as Wiesel did, both in his writing and in his
life. A *living* human love is messianic to its core: like God, the Messiah
is not to be studied—he is to be *lived*. The legacy—and the responsibility—that Elie Wiesel transmits to humanity is steeped above all in such
waiting and working for the coming of the Messiah. Therefore, he says,
"one of the characters who has been present in all my writings is the
character of the Messiah, and who is the Messiah, what is the Messiah, if
not the embodiment of eternity in the present, the embodiment of eternity
in the future. He is waiting for us as long as we are waiting for him."[8]
In the words of Emmanuel Levinas: "To love one's neighbor is to go to
Eternity, to redeem the World or prepare the Kingdom of God. Human
love is the very work, the efficiency of Redemption."[9] Rarely have two
thinkers ever had a more intimate sense of the link between the Messiah
and time itself. Indeed, in a very profound sense, Wiesel's portrait of the
Messiah is a portrait of time.

"The awaiting of the Messiah," says Levinas, "is the duration of time
itself—waiting for God—but here the waiting no longer attests to the
absence of Godot, who will never come, but rather to a *relationship* with
that which is not able to enter the present, since the present is too small
to contain the Infinite."[10] That the Messiah tarries is what gives meaning to

life, for the dimension of meaning is the dimension of time. The Messiah, therefore, does not end history—the Messiah *is* history, inasmuch as the meaning of the Messiah lies in the wait for the Messiah. To link one's fate to that of the Messiah, Levinas asserts, is to affirm that salvation "remains *at every moment* possible,"[11] an affirmation that despite Levinas's Lithuanian background is thoroughly Hasidic. In fact, in the *Ani Maamin*, the word translated as "wait," *ahakeh*, means "expect" or "anticipate": I shall *anticipate* the coming of the Messiah and make ready for him because it can happen at any moment. Before we delve into Wiesel's portrait of the Messiah, however, we would do well to consider some of the Jewish teachings and traditions regarding the Messiah. After all, that is the palette from which Wiesel's portrait is drawn.

The Messiah in Jewish Teaching: A Brief Background

There are no teachings in Jewish tradition more confused and conflicting than the teachings on the Messiah. A few things, however, are clear. The one whom the Jews await is not the son of God any more than any other human being is a child of the Holy One. He is neither the incarnation of God nor part of a triune divinity; the Midrash, in fact, speaks of his mortal death, saying that when the Messiah dies, the World to Come will be ushered in (*Tanhuma Ekev* 7). Further, he is not born of a virgin, who in turn requires an immaculate conception. Indeed, from a Jewish perspective, the conception of any human being can be "immaculate," since in marriage the sexual union that produces a child is itself holy, as is the one born from that union. Because we do not inherit Adam's sin, we are born innocent and untainted, as we affirm each morning in our prayers: "The soul You have placed within me is pure."

According to Jewish teaching, children are not in need of redemption—they are the source of redemption, as the Vilna Gaon maintains.[12] In the Midrash Rabbi Assi teaches that children begin their study of Torah with the Book of Leviticus because "children are pure, and the sacrifices are pure; so let the pure come and engage in the study of the pure" (*Vayikra Rabbah* 7:3). Thus the Messiah whom the Jews await bears little resemblance to the one who the Christians believe has already come. The one we await is not the one whose blood will cleanse us of our *inherently* sinful being; rather, he will return us, body and soul, to the inherently holy *relation* to God and to one another. This may be one reason why the Midrash calls the Messiah the Son of Peretz (*Bereshit Rabbah* 12:6), the child born to Judah and Tamar (see Genesis 38:29): the name Peretz means "breach" or "opening," and the Messiah is he who creates the most complete opening for holiness to flow into this realm.

Recall what David Aboulesia, the Messiah Seeker, says to Paltiel in Wiesel's novel *The Testament*. The Messiah, he tells Paltiel, is "of this world, young man. The Talmudic sages place him at the gates of Rome, but in fact he lives among us, everywhere. According to the Zohar, he is waiting to be called. He is waiting to be recognized in order to be crowned. Remember, young man, the Messiah looks like anyone at all except a Messiah. His name, which preceded Creation, also preceded him. The story of the Messiah is the story of a quest, of a name in search of a being."[13] Jewishly speaking, the Messiah's kingdom is *in* this world and *of* this world. Therefore the Messiah comes not to deliver us *from* the world but to draw Torah *into* the world, so transparently that the word of the Holy One will be engraved upon every human heart, as it is written (Jeremiah 31:33), and justice and righteousness will reign throughout the nations (Isaiah 9:6). Swords will be beaten into plowshares, and "nation will not lift up sword against nation" (Micah 4:3). The Jewish anticipation of the coming of the Messiah is an effort to usher in such a world.

In the famous disputation at Barcelona held in 1263, Nahmanides pointed out that "you will never find in any book of Jewish tradition—neither the Talmud nor the Hagadoth—that the Messiah son of David will be killed, that he will be handed over into the hands of his enemies, or that he will be buried with the wicked."[14] Most prevalent of all the unfulfilled prophecies concerning the Messiah is that the Jews will be returned from exile. Various prophets invoke various signs of the coming of the Messiah, but almost all of them invoke this one: the ingathering of the Jews (e.g., Isaiah 11:11–12; Jeremiah 23:3, 29:14, 32:44, 33:7; Ezekiel 39:25; Joel 4:1; Zephaniah 3:20; Zechariah 10:8–10). The Midrash, in fact, teaches that in the time of the Messiah the nations of the world will assist in the return of the Jews to the Holy Land. And in the season of *Sukkot* or the Feast of the Tabernacles, they will come to Jerusalem to join the Jews in that celebration (*Shir HaShirim Rabbah* 4:8:2).

Beyond that, the teachings are less clear and often more mysterious. In the Talmud, for example, it is written, "Know that there exists on high a substance called 'body' [*guf*] in which are found all the souls destined for life. The son of David will not come before all the souls which are in the *guf* have completed their descent to the earth" (*Yevamot* 63b; *Avodah*

Zarah 5a; *Niddah* 13b; see also *Zohar* I, 119a). This mystical tradition underscores the connection between the upper worlds and this world. Such a view associates the completeness of creation with the coming of the Messiah; it also articulates a connection between each soul and all of creation—between each soul and the Messiah himself. On the day of his coming, says the prophecy, "HaShem will be One and His Name will be One" (Zechariah 14:9). Which is to say that in the Tetragrammaton the upper letters *yud-hey* and the lower letters *vav-hey* will be joined—God and humanity will be joined—so that the holiness of the Holy One will be manifest throughout the world, through the acts of loving kindness that each human being shows toward the other. Thinking and doing will be one. Teaching and practice will be one. Love of God and love of neighbor—love of stranger—will be one.

There are other teachings concerning the Messiah. The Talmud, for example, says that Gog and Magog will launch three wars against the Messiah in the winter month of Tevet. Messiah ben Joseph will fight those wars; in some accounts he will be killed and then followed by Messiah ben David, who will usher in the everlasting age of peace (*Sukkah* 52a; see also Rashi's commentary on *Sotah* 51; see also the *Or Hachayim* on Leviticus 14:9). In addition to Gog and Magog, the archenemy of the Messiah is sometimes called Armillus, who is spawned from Satan's mating with a stone statue in Rome. Forty days after the spawning of Armillus, Messiah ben David will rise up to build the Temple in Jerusalem and defeat the offspring of Satan.[15] That Armillus is born from a stone is indicative of the Messiah's defeat of the view that what is real is what can be weighed, measured, and counted and that power is the only reality. Further, it is said that the Messiah will reveal the meaning of the blanks between the words and in the margins of the Torah, the meaning of the white fire.[16] Perhaps he will also reveal the meaning of other flames.

Because we are prone to tarry, the Talmud teaches that two times are destined for the coming of the Messiah: now and the appointed time (*Sanhedrin* 98a). This teaching is based on the words from the prophet Isaiah: "I HaShem will hasten it in its time" (Isaiah 60:22); that is, I will either hasten it to make it now, or it will be in its appointed time. *Now*, if we perform the task for which we were created. *Now*, if we treat others with loving kindness. In short, now *is* the appointed time for *me* to act for the sake of another. Without the wait for the Messiah, there is nothing to hasten and no time appointed. Waiting for the Messiah, though he may tarry, is just the opposite of the languishing that characterizes so much of our intellectual game playing, which is no more than a means of marking time or killing time in a shameful waste of time. Thus Wiesel's portrait of the Messiah is the portrait of a wait like no other wait and a portrait like no other portrait.

How long must we labor for the coming of the Messiah? According to the *Pesikta Rabbati*, 365,000 years (1:7). Which is to say that the wait is infinite, as infinite as our responsibility. Thus, said Rabbi Samuel ben Nahman, in the name of Rabbi Yonatan, "Cursed be the bones of those who calculate the end. For they would say, since the predetermined time has come, and yet the Messiah has not come, he will never come. Nevertheless, wait for him" (*Sanhedrin* 97b). In this *nevertheless* we have the needful response to the despair that haunts the post-Holocaust world: do not calculate the time of redemption—hasten it. As we shall see, this refusal to calculate but rather to hasten is the substance of Wiesel's portrait of the Messiah. The time of the coming of the Messiah that is *now* is the time for which I am always too late because it is always *already*: the Messiah abides in the nexus of the *not yet* and the *already*—that is why the *and yet* is so central to Wiesel's portrait of the Messiah and, indeed to all of his work, the sum of which *is* his portrait of the Messiah. To be sure, in the Talmud it is written that there will be no Messiah because those days have already passed in the time of Hezekiah (*Sanhedrin* 99a); the point, however, is not to put an end to the task but to underscore its infinite duration. Even though—and precisely because—I am too late, *I must hasten to hasten* the coming of the Messiah.

As one might expect, there are many teachings on the Messiah found in the Kabbalistic tradition, one of the most notable of which is based on a passage in the Torah: "If a bird's nest chance to be before you in the way, in any tree or on the ground, with young ones or eggs, and the mother sitting on the young, or on the eggs, you shall not take the mother with the young: you shall surely let the mother go, but the young you may take to yourself" (Deuteronomy 22:6–7). The *Tikkunei HaZohar* says that the "bird's nest" refers to the exile of the *Shekhinah* (12b). The Zohar explains that the meaning of the bird's nest is revealed in the prophecy of Isaiah: "And they shall go into the holes of the rocks and into the caves of the earth, for fear of HaShem and for the glory of his majesty" (Isaiah 2:19). "The glory of his majesty" refers to the Messiah, who will reveal himself only to launch a war. After a time of tribulation, the Messiah will be crowned, and all the nations of the earth will behold him. And so Rabbi Shimon bar Yohai teaches his son:

> The Messiah is hidden in [Eden's] outskirts until a place is revealed to him which is called "the Bird's Nest." This is the place proclaimed by that Bird (the Shekinah) which flies about the Garden of Eden. . . . The Messiah enters that abode, lifts up his eyes and beholds the Fathers (Patriarchs) visiting the ruins of God's Sanctuary. He perceives mother Rachel, with tears upon her face. . . . Then the Messiah lifts up his voice and weeps, and the whole Garden of Eden quakes, and all the righteous and saints who are there break out in crying and lamentation . . . until it reaches the highest Throne. . . . Then from the holy Throne the Bird's Nest and the Messiah are summoned three times, and they both ascend into the heavenly places. . . . Then the Bird returns to her place. The Messiah, however, is hidden again in the same place as before. (*Zohar* II, 8a–8b)

Thus we see the depths from which Wiesel's portrait of the Messiah emerges. It is a portrait rooted not only in the passionate longing and working for the coming of the Messiah but also in the millennial Jewish tradition targeted for extermination in a time when the Messiah was more desperately needed than ever before.

This teaching from the mystical tradition may shed some light on a statement that Wiesel makes in his portrait of the Messiah. "For Christians," he says, "the Messiah is God's link to man; in Judaism man is God's link to the Messiah" ("A Portrait of the Messiah"). We find this insight unfolding in the teachings of the Jewish tradition: there is, throughout this tradition, a sense that somehow God's link to His own redemption as Creator is tied to humanity through the fate of the Messiah. If everything is in God's hands except the fear of God, as it is written in the Talmud (*Berakhot* 33b; *Niddah* 16b), then the advent of the Messiah is in the hands of humanity. The Talmud teaches that the name of the Messiah is among the seven things that preceded Creation (*Pesahim* 54a).[17] The Zohar teaches that "the 'spirit of God which hovered over the face of the deep' (Genesis 1:2) is the spirit of the Messiah" (*Zohar* I, 240a). The Messiah precedes the beginning to oppose the darkness that would undermine the beginning: bearing the name that preceded creation, the Messiah is essential to all of creation. Therefore the Messiah is present in every generation. It is a name in search of a man, as well as a man in search of a name, often disguised as a beggar, a leper, or an orphan—or as an old man, a child, or a madman—the three characters who, as Wiesel once told me, form the foundation of all his writing. Indeed, as Wiesel said to me, these three are the favorite disguises of the Messiah.

The Portrait

There have been numerous false Messiahs in Jewish history, ranging from Jesus of Nazareth to David Alroy (twelfth century), from Solomon Molcho (sixteenth century) to Shabbatai Zvi (seventeenth century). But how are we to understand the "false" in the false Messiah? The opposite of the true Messiah, says Wiesel in his portrait, is not the false Messiah but the unjust Messiah. To be unjust is to be false; to be false is to fall short of the commandment "Justice, justice, shall you seek" (Deuteronomy 16:20), and the task of the Messiah—of every Jew, every human being—is to seek justice. What is justice? It is not about being "fair" or balancing scales. Justice, above all, requires loving kindness, which, to turn to an insight from Levinas, "is established between unequals, and lives from inequality," without expectation of recompense.[18] Justice is *tzedek*, which is "righteousness," and is the root for the word *tzedakah* or "charity," or giving without expectation of return. The link between justice and truth tells us that truth is not a datum. Truth, rather, lies in this giving to another for the sake of another in an affirmation of the absolute sanctity of another; it lies in the "giving" that in Hebrew is *hav*, which is the root of *ahavah* or "love." The true Messiah is the giving Messiah, the one who, through his life more than through his teaching, ignites the love that defines the humanity of each of us through our own act of giving. Wiesel's portrait of the Messiah is a portrait of this love that is at the core of who we are as human beings created in the image and the likeness of the Holy One.

In his portrait of the Messiah, Wiesel states that a Jew can best be defined by his or her waiting and working for the coming of the Messiah, reiterating Rebbe Pinhas's declaration that "to be Jewish is to link one's fate to that of the Messiah—to that of all who are waiting for the Messiah."[19] His portrait of the Messiah is a portrait of that waiting, which is the measure of our days and the measure of time and wisdom. "The Messiah," Wiesel portrays him, "symbolizes our preoccupation with time instead of space" ("A Portrait of the Messiah"). The Jewish preoccupation with time is a preoccupation with the *already* and the *yet to be*. It is a preoccupation with the Holy One, and the preoccupation with the Holy

One is a preoccupation with the *other* one with the other human being: *the otherness in the other human being is the holiness in the other human being*. Like the Messiah, the other is the one whom I *have yet* to help, heal, feed, clothe, comfort, and shelter—the one whom I have *already* been commanded to help.

A tale from the Talmud drives home this point. One day the great third-century sage Yehoshua ben Levi was deep in meditation at the grave of Shimon bar Yohai, when suddenly the Prophet Elijah paid him a visit. Yehoshua ben Levi asked him, "When will the Messiah come?" And the Prophet replied, "Go ask him yourself. He is sitting outside the gates of Rome, a leper binding his wounds. But, unlike the other lepers, he binds just one wound at time, so that he may be ready to reveal himself at a moment's notice." Yehoshua ben Levi went to the gates of Rome, found the Messiah, and asked him, "Master and Teacher, when will you reveal yourself?" And the Messiah replied, "Today, if you will heed the voice of the Holy One" (*Sanhedrin* 98a). That is where the story ends. It is said, however, that if Yehoshua ben Levi had helped him with his wounds, the Messiah would have revealed himself.

As Wiesel states in his portrait, "It is the other that determines my humanity. What I do to the other shows who I am" ("A Portrait of the Messiah"). What I do to the other, I do to the Messiah. And what I *have yet* to do for the other, I *have yet* to do for the Messiah. Here lies the meaning of the Covenant of Torah. "The response to the love of God for Man," says Levinas, "is the love of my neighbour. Through this, the Revelation is already the Revelation of Redemption."[20] The Messiah is the highest expression of "the love of God for Man," and the commandment to love the neighbor—*and the stranger*—is the highest expression of the love of Man for God: it is the revelation of the Redemption wrought through the Messiah.

If, as André Neher says, "the human situation in history begins with the covenant,"[21] it is because the messianic mission of Redemption that imparts meaning to history is revealed in the covenant. If humanity is not summoned to such a mission, there is no meaning and no history. Through the summons to hasten the coming of the Messiah, humanity receives from the Most High a "memorial and a Name," a *yad vashem*, that we must weave into the fabric of time itself, which in turn receives its meaning from the merging of the ethical and the existential into a single injunction: "I have set before you this day life and good, death and evil . . . blessing and curse: therefore choose life, that you and your children may live" (Deuteronomy 30:15–19). A portrait of that summons, Wiesel's portrait of the Messiah is a portrait of the dimension of height that is the Most High. To be sure, in his portrait Wiesel reminds us of the Talmudic teaching that among the six questions the Celestial Tribunal will put to us when we stand before the Most High is: did you await—did you anticipate—the coming of the Messiah (*Shabbat* 31a)?[22] We now see what an affirmative answer might mean. We also see why we cannot measure up to an affirmative answer because the measure meted out to us is infinite.

In the Talmud Rabbi Yohanan teaches that "the son of David will come only in a generation that is either altogether righteous or altogether wicked" (*Sanhedrin* 98a). One immediately wonders, as Wiesel has wondered: was the generation of the Shoah not sufficiently wicked to bring the Messiah? While almost all of his other portraits are wrapped in emanations of light and beauty, of joy and gratitude, there is a dark, terrifying aspect to his portrait of the Messiah. If God was questioning humanity in the time of the Shoah, He may well have been asking us whether we are waiting and working for the coming of the Messiah. If He was afraid of Himself, He may well have been afraid of what will come about in order to bring about the Redemption of humanity—and of Himself. And if He was showing some hidden aspect of His face—the face no man can look upon and live—it may well have been the messianic aspect of His face.

With the dawning of the messianic era, Wiesel says in his portrait, good and evil, light and darkness, will become one, as in the time of the *Mabul*, the time of the Great Flood and the Great Confusion. All nations will hate the Jews. Hating the Jews, "they will hate themselves" ("A Portrait of the Messiah"). *Hate*. What a word! Can this word, indeed, be part of the advent of the Messiah? Wiesel's words: "Hate—racial, tribal, religious, ancestral, national, social, ethical, political, economic, ideological—in itself represents the inexorable defeat of mankind, its absolute defeat. . . . In all of creation, only man is both capable and guilty of hate."[23] And yet only a humanity that is both capable and guilty of hate can bring the Messiah. That guilt—that responsibility—is part of this portrait: only those who hate can bring about the messianic obliteration of hatred.

Here Wiesel turns to the Mishnah ("A Portrait of the Messiah"):

> In the period preceding the coming of *Mashiah*, insolence will increase and prices will soar. The vineyard will produce, yet wine will be expensive [since constant partying will cause excessive demand]. And government will turn to heresy and there will

be no admonishment. The [former] meeting place [of scholars] will be used for harlotry. . . . The wisdom of the Scribes will decay and those who fear sin will be utterly despised. Truth will be absent, the youth will blanch the faces of the elders, elders will rise in honor of the youth, the son will deride his father, the daughter will stand up against her mother and a daughter-in-law against her mother-in-law. (*Sotah* 9:15)

This is the mirror held up to us in Wiesel's portrait of the Messiah. The darkness of the messianic era is a darkness that lurks not only within human history but also within the human soul. And it is in our midst.

The Talmud identifies the signs of the coming of the messianic era that will be spread over seven years. In the first year it will rain on one city but not on another. The second year will be a time of unprecedented hunger, followed by a third year of widespread famine, both physically and spiritually, for in the third year "Torah will be forgotten." In the fourth year, however, some measure of plenty will return, followed by the overflowing of storehouses and the return of Torah in the fifth year. Year six will be a year of awe at "Heavenly sounds," and then the apocalyptic war will come in year seven. "In the generation when the son of David will come," Rabbi Yohanan taught, "scholars will be few in number, and as for the rest, their eyes will fail through sorrow and grief" (*Sanhedrin* 97a). The sage goes on to say: "If you see a generation whose wisdom and Torah study is steadily diminishing, await the coming of the Messiah, as it is stated: 'And the afflicted people You will redeem' [2 Samuel 22:28]." And he also says the following: "If you saw a generation whose troubles inundate it like a river, await the coming of the Messiah, as it is stated: 'When distress will come like a river that the breath of the Lord drives' [Isaiah 59:19]" (*Sanhedrin* 98a). Therefore even the absolute darkness is not altogether absolute. In his portrait of the Messiah, Weisel notes that it is only when night seems "irrevocably sealed" that the messianic light can break through ("A Portrait of the Messiah").

But it cannot break though without our help. Only we can bring the Messiah, says Wiesel. How? By being worthy of his coming. Just so, Wiesel's character Gregor in *The Gates of the Forest* realizes that "the Messiah isn't one man . . . he's all men. As long as there are men there will a Messiah."[24] For as long as there are men there abides the possibility of each man answering, "Here I am for you," to the other human being, which is the only way we can answer to the Holy One. If the Messiah is not one man but all men, his presence lies in the responsibility of every man to transmit the name that was before the beginning, so that the outcry of all humanity might be heard. We discover how deep this responsibility runs in the cry of a Hasidic master in *A Beggar in Jerusalem* as the Nazis are about to murder him and others: "We do not want to die, we want to live and build the kingdom of the Messiah in time and prayer. Someone opposes this wish and that someone is One and His name is One. We know that His eternal secrets transcend us. But does He know the pain they cause us? Even so, brothers: we shall make Him a gift of our lives and our deaths. We wish Him to use them as He pleases, and may He be worthy of them."[25] God opposes the wish of the Jews to live and build the kingdom of the Messiah? How can this be? And how can one wonder whether God Himself might be worthy of anything? This is where the Wieselian, the messianic "and yet" enters. It is a source of both terror and resolve.

Wiesel's portrait of the Messiah is a portrait of that terror and that resolve. The two combine to form a mystical madness, whose aim, Wiesel says, is to bring the Messiah: "Mystical madness is redeeming. The difference between a mystical madman and a clinical madman is that a clinical madman isolates himself and others, while a mystical one wants to bring the Messiah. What is the ultimate aim of mysticism? To bring the Messiah. To make evil disappear and bring people together."[26] Bringing the Messiah is the ultimate aim not only of mysticism but also of Judaism. According to the Hasidic masters Zadok ha-Kohen[27] and the Stretiner Rebbe,[28] within the soul of each of us there burns a spark of the soul of the Messiah, so that each of us bears an infinite responsibility to bring the Messiah. "In concrete terms," says Levinas, "this means that each person acts as though he were the Messiah. Messianism is therefore not the certainty of the coming of a man who stops history. It is in my power to bear the suffering of all. It is the moment when I recognize this power and my universal responsibility."[29] The Messiah summons humanity precisely to this infinite responsibility to and for the other human being, without which we are not human.

What makes a Jew a Jew? The Hebrew word for Jew, we are reminded, is *Yehudi*, which means "one who is grateful": gratitude, too, makes us human. Thus the Midrash tells us that with the coming of the Messiah, "all sacrifices will cease, but the thanksgiving offering will never cease; all songs will cease, but the songs of thanksgiving will never cease" (*Vayikra Rabbah* 9:7). In his portrait of the Messiah Wiesel asserts, "I truly believe that a community can be judged by its capacity to say thank you" ("A Portrait of the Messiah"), for the capacity to say thank you belongs to the messianic era itself. Gratitude is the key to meriting and thus bringing the Messiah who forever tarries. Gratitude for what? Gratitude for the wait, for the anticipation. Gratitude for the task. Gratitude not for the darkness of night that seems "irrevocably sealed" but for the opening in the darkness.

Each day brings its own trials, large and small. Therefore each morning when a Jew awakes, the first words on his or her lips are "Thank you." *Modeh ani*: I give thanks before you, the Living and Sustaining King, that You have returned my soul within me, great is Your faithfulness. The moment when we transition from night to day, from lying down to rising up, from dream to reality, from oblivion to vigilance is the moment when gratitude is most crucial, as Wiesel suggests ("A Portrait of the Messiah"). And so as soon as we can say anything, we say, "Thank you," and each "Thank you" hastens the coming of the Messiah. Thank you for what? Not for another day to enjoy the bounties of life. Rather, we rejoice in being blessed with the labor of hastening the coming of the Messiah—the labor that we cannot complete but must nevertheless engage (*Pirke Avot* 2:16)—and that is what makes each of our lives *matter*. That is why we follow the *Modeh ani* with the washing of our hands—with the *al nilat yadaim*, which is literally the "elevation of our hands": we elevate our hands in order to engage in the endless task of striving to merit the advent of the Messiah. This message is central to Wiesel's portrait of the Messiah.

But what if the Messiah should choose to tarry, despite our efforts? What if *he* is late for his appointment? Wiesel entertains this possibility, with the implications for how it complicates our task and our responsibility to merit the coming of the Messiah. In *A Beggar in Jerusalem* he relates that the three Patriarchs once came before the celestial court and reported to God that all is in keeping with His divine plan for the coming of the Messiah. And so the heavenly hosts gathered together to celebrate. Then God asked, "The Messiah, where is the Messiah? Why isn't he here taking part in the festivities?" The angel Michael reported that the Messiah has disappeared. God demanded that he be found and brought forward. His bidding was done: the Messiah was brought before the Holy One. God asked him, "Where have you been?" He answered that he had been in Jerusalem. He explained that he had decided to stay with God's people rather than join in the heavenly celebration, saying, "I had to join them, be one of them. Their will was stronger than mine, stronger than Yours, and so was their love. You see, they were six million."[30] And so we see how the Holocaust might forever complicate and even alter the messianic tradition.

Here it must be noted that a Jew is not only a *Yehudi*; another name that attaches to the Jew, both as an individual and as a people, is *Yisrael*—"one who strives and struggles with God"—the name conferred upon Jacob at Peniel, where he wrestled with a mysterious stranger until dawn (Genesis 32:22–30). The gratitude to God is a gratitude for the struggle with God that we must undertake in order to merit the coming of the Messiah, as Wiesel says in his portrait. This "prayer," this *tefillah*, is a "wrestling," a *naftolin*, with God for the sake of God and humanity to bring about the advent of the Messiah. This is Wiesel's prayer, the prayer of *Ani Maamin*:

> Pray, men.
> Pray to God,
> Against God,
> For God.
> *Ani Maamin*
> Whether the Messiah comes,
> *Ani Maamin*
> Or is late in coming,
> *Ani Maamin*
> Whether God is silent
> Or weeps,
> *Ani Maamin*
> *Ani Maamin* for him,
> In spite of him,
> I believe in you,
> Even against your will.
> Even if you punish me
> For believing in you.[31]

This opposition to God, this defiance of God—as though assuming the role of His bride, as the Jews did at Mount Sinai, and therefore of His *ezer k'negdo*, the "helper against Him"—is crucial to meriting the coming of the Messiah. Elie Wiesel's Hasidic legacy, which finds a definitive expression in his portrait of the Messiah, returns to us a capacity for prayers. It returns to us a capacity for the gratitude that might break through the darkness of night.

In the last pages of his last novel, *Hostage*, we have an episode that sums up Elie Wiesel's decades-long engagement with the Messiah, an engagement defines his Hasidic legacy. The main character, the hostage, is Shaltiel, whose name means "I have questioned God." Like Wiesel, he is a storyteller who fends off the terror of his captivity by telling stories to his captors and to himself. (Could Wiesel, in his storytelling, have been fending off another terror, a hostage to something else?) Shaltiel remembers a Hasidic tale that his grandfather related to him, the story of how the Baal Shem Tov once gathered together his closest disciples to teach them the mysteries of the final Redemption: "How and when to recite certain litanies; say the number for each of the heavenly angels; take the ritual bath and cite specific verses of the Psalms and the Zohar; practice an absolute asceticism of silence and chastity for a specific number of days and nights. All the things that had come down to him from his Masters—and to them from theirs, going back to Rabbi Hayim Vital and the Ari, and as far back as Moses, all the things concerning the advent of the Messiah—he passed on to them." They were to meet at an appointed time in a secret place in the forest, where they would confront the Messiah with the suffering of the Jewish people and, with the help of the Besht, force the Messiah to reveal himself.

But the Master was late. How was it possible? Understanding more profoundly than anyone what being in the right place at the right time meant for the Redemption, the Baal Shem Tov had never been for any appointment. What could have happened to him? Even the Messiah was kept waiting—until he could wait no longer.

Finally the Baal Shem arrived at the meeting place, but he was much too late. "On my way here, a few steps before reaching you," he explained, "I heard a child crying in a hut near the edge of the forest. His cries were heart-breaking. His mother had probably gone to fetch wood for the hearth, or milk. So, brothers and friends, I couldn't help opening the door to the hut, stepping inside, looking at the baby in his shabby cradle, singing a lullaby for him and consoling him. Do you understand? When a child cries like this, the Messiah can and must wait."[32] Do we understand?

With the help of Wiesel's portrait of the Messiah we may better understand why the wait for the Messiah is more important than being the Messiah, even more important than the coming of the Messiah: waiting for the Messiah—anticipating the advent of the Messiah—rests upon our ability to hear the outcry of a child. If the wait does not sharpen our sense of hearing and our capacity for answering, "Here I am for you," then it is truly in vain. Thus we hold the Messiah hostage—or is it the other way around? Perhaps we are his hostages, held as a ransom for the redemption of this world.

So what are we to conclude about these portraits and Elie Wiesel's Hasidic legacy? I think we have the trace of an answer in the trace of the Messiah that permeates all of these portraits. As Wiesel said, "Only when night seems irrevocably sealed can the messianic light break through" ("A Portrait of the Messiah"). Is the night upon us? If so, in Wiesel's Hasidic legacy we have a trace of the light, a particle or a wave, that penetrates the night. It is a legacy that leads us to realize that as long as a child cries out to us, we must first respond to that outcry with our own cry of "Here I am, for you!" Like firefighters—or lamplighters—we must be first responders to the child within each human being, each *ben adam* because there was a time when "with each hour, the most blessed and most stricken people of the world numbers twelve times twelve children less. And each one carries away still another fragment of the Temple in flames. Flames—never before have there been such flames. And in every one of them it is the vision of the Redeemer that is dying."[33] Through the Hasidic legacy that breathes in these living portraits, Wiesel breathes a breath of life into that dying vision.

It is a vision fraught with an overwhelming, unprecedented tension, a tension that Wiesel articulates in a passage from *Sages and Dreamers*: when the Rabbi of Kretchenev was deported to Auschwitz, "he began consoling his disciples: It is written, he said, that when the Messiah will come, God, blessed be He, will arrange a *makhol*, a dance, for the Just. *Makhol*, said the Rabbi, may also come from the verb *limkhol*—to forgive." And so, declared the Rabbi, "there will come a time, when the Just Men, the Tzaddikim, will forgive God, blessed be He."[34] Here we come to an ultimate realization: in the post-Holocaust era, God Himself needs the advent of the Messiah as much as His children do. And humanity is, indeed, God's link to the Messiah.

Notes

A Post-Holocaust Hasidic Legacy

1. Elie Wiesel, *A Jew Today*, trans. Marion Wiesel (New York: Random House, 1978), 172. I am indebted to John K. Roth for calling my attention to this passage. See John K. Roth, "Wiesel's Contribution to a Christian Understanding of Judaism," in Alan Rosen and Steven T. Katz, eds., *Elie Wiesel: Jewish, Literary, and Moral Perspectives*, ed. (Bloomington: Indiana University Press, 2013), 264.

2. Nikos Kazantzakis, *The Rock Garden*, trans. R. Howard and K. Friar (New York: Simon and Schuster, 1963), 105–6.

3. Kalonymos Kalmish Shapira, *Sacred Fire: Torah from the Years of Fury 1939–1942*, trans. J. Hershy Worch, ed. Deborah Miller (Northvale, NJ: Jason Aronson, 2000), 286–87.

4. Shapira, *Sacred Fire*, 286–87.

5. Elie Wiesel, *Souls on Fire: Portraits and Legends of Hasidic Masters*, trans. Marion Wiesel (New York: Vintage, 1973), 240.

6. Elie Wiesel, *Against Silence: The Voice and Vision of Elie Wiesel*, ed. Irving Abrahamson, vol. 2 (New York: Holocaust Library, 1985), 60; see also Elie Wiesel, *The Gates of the Forest*, trans. France Frenaye (New York: Holt, Rinehart and Winston, 1966), 63.

7. Wiesel, *A Jew Today*, 132.

8. Elie Wiesel, *The Trial of God*, trans Marion Wiesel (New York: Random House, 1979), 104.

9. Elie Wiesel, *Night*, trans. Marion Wiesel (New York: Hill and Wang, 2006), 3.

10. Elie Wiesel, *Somewhere a Master: Hasidic Portraits and Legends*, trans. Marion Wiesel (New York: Summit, 1982), 49–50.

11. David Biale et al., *Hasidism: A New History* (Princeton, NJ: Princeton University Press, 2017), 652.

12. Chaim A. Kaplan, *Scroll of Agony: The Warsaw Diary of Chaim A. Kaplan*, trans. and ed. Abraham I. Katsh (New York: Collier, 1973), 82.

13. Kaplan, *Scroll of Agony*, 179.

14. Victor Klemperer, *I Will Bear Witness: A Diary of the Nazi Years, 1942–1945*, trans. Martin Chalmers (New York: Random House, 1999), 277.

15. Elie Wiesel, *One Generation After*, trans. Lily Edelman and Elie Wiesel (New York: Pocket, 1970), 73.

16. Elie Wiesel, *Legends of Our Time* (New York: Avon, 1968), 25.

17. Elie Wiesel, *Open Heart*, trans. Marion Wiesel (New York: Alfred A. Knopf, 2012), 79.

18. Wiesel, *Souls on Fire*, 173.

19. See Ivan G. Marcus, *"Sefer Hasidim" and the Ashkenazic Book in Medieval Europe* (Philadelphia: University of Pennsylvania Press, 2018).

20. See the chapter on Jacob ben Hayyim Zemah and the *Shulchan Arukh Ha-Ari* in Marvin J. Heller, *The Seventeenth Century Hebrew Book: An Abridged Thesaurus*, vol. 2 (Leiden, The Netherlands: Brill, 2011), 827ff.

21. Moshe Idel, *Hasidism: Between Ecstasy and Magic* (Albany: State University of New York Press, 1956), 6.

22. Idel, *Hasidism*, 10.

23. Immanuel Etkes, *The Besht: Magician, Mystic, and Leader*, trans. Saadya Sternberg (Waltham, MA: Brandeis University Press, 2005), 50.

24. Idel, *Hasidism*, 13–14.

25. See Martin Buber's essay "Spinoza, Shabbatai Zvi, and the Baal-Shem" in his book *The Origin and Meaning of Hasidism*, trans. and ed. Maurice Friedman (New York: Harper & Row, 1960), 89–112; see also Gershom Scholem's essay "Hasidism: The Latest Phase" in his book *Major Trends in Jewish Mysticism* (New York: Schocken, 1974), 325–50.

26. Idel, *Hasidism*, 10.

27. Rachel Elior, *Mystical Origins of Hasidism* (Oxford: The Littman Library of Jewish Civilization, 2006), 180–81.

28. Elior, 182–83.

29. Elior, 186.

30. See, for example, Dov Ber, *In Praise of the Baal Shem Tov*, trans. and ed. Dan Ben-Amos and Jerome R. Mintz (New York: Schocken, 1970), 13–17.

31. Here it should be noted, as Immanuel Etkes points out, that "Yeshaya Tishbi, Gedaliah Nigal, Mendel Piekarz, Ada Rapoport-Albert, and others—all for their own reasons have rejected the notion that Hasidism transformed *dvekut* into a spiritual path that each and every Jews could access." See Etkes, *Besht*, 3.

32. Etkes, *Besht*, 53.

33. Biale et al., *Hasidism*, 17.

34. Moshe Rosman, *Founder of Hasidism: A Quest for the Historical Ba'al Shem Tov* (Berkeley: University of California Press, 1996), 69.

35. Rosman, *Founder*, 82.

36. Etkes, *Besht*, 79.

37. Biale et al., *Hasidism*, 86.

38. Biale, 93–99.

39. Biale, 168.

40. Biale, 169.

41. Idel, *Hasidism*, 199.

42. Idel, 202.

43. Wiesel, *Somewhere a Master*, 110.

44. Wiesel, *One Generation After*, 72–73.

45. Arthur Green, "Wiesel in the Context of Neo-Hasidism," in Rosen and Katz, eds., *Elie Wiesel: Jewish, Literary, and Moral Perspectives*, ed. (Bloomington: Indiana University Press, 2013), 51.

46. Elie Wiesel, *A Beggar in Jerusalem*, trans. Lily Edelman and Elie Wiesel (New York: Random House, 1970), 77.

47. Green, "Wiesel in the Context of Neo-Hasidism," 54.

48. Wiesel, *Somewhere a Master*, 152–53.

49. Wiesel, *Legends of Our Time*, 230.

50. Biale et al., *Hasidism*, 174.

51. Wiesel, *Souls on Fire*, 26.

52. Elie Wiesel and Mark Podwal, *A Passover Haggadah: As Commented Upon by Elie Wiesel and Illustrated by Mark Podwal* (New York: Simon & Schuster, 1993), 63.

53. Elie Wiesel, *Ani Maamin: A Song Lost and Found Again*, trans. Marion Wiesel (New York: Random House, 1973), 105, 107.

54. Wiesel, *Gates of the Forest*, 197.

55. Wiesel, *A Beggar in Jerusalem*, 12.

56. Wiesel, *Against Silence*, 3:1.

57. Wiesel, *Night*, 3.

58. Elie Wiesel, *The Sonderberg Case*, trans. Catherine Temerson (New York: Alfred A. Knopf, 2010), 46–47.

59. Wiesel, *Against Silence*, 1:206.

60. Elie Wiesel, *All Rivers Run to the Sea: Memoirs* (New York: Alfred A. Knopf, 1996), 16.

61. See Flavius Josephus, *The Complete Works of Flavius Josephus*, trans. William Whiston (Nashville, TN: Thomas Nelson, 2003).

62. See Yaakov ben Yitzchak Ashkenazi, ed., *Tz'enah Ur'enah: The Classic Anthology of Torah Lore and Midrashic Commentary* (Brooklyn, NY: Mesorah, 1989).

63. See Abraham Ibn Daud, *The Book of Tradition*, trans. Gershon D. Cohen (Philadelphia: Jewish Publicaitons Society, 2010).

64. See Hayim Vital, *Sefer HaHezyonot* (Jerusalem: Mekhon Ben-Tsevi, 2005).

65. See Dov Ber, *In Praise of the Baal Shem Tov*, trans. and ed. Dan Ben-Amos and Jerome R. Mintz (New York: Schocken, 1970).

66. Hillel Zeitlin, *R. Nahman Braslaver: der zeer fun Podloye* (New York: Matones 1952). It perhaps should be noted that some Christian commentators used the term *portraits* in their approach to biblical figures. See, for example, Arthur Penrhyn Stanley, *Scripture Portraits and Other Miscellanies* (London: Alexander Strahan, 1867); and John William George Ward, *Portraits of the Prophets: Character Studies of Men Who Blazed the Trail* (New York: Richard R. Smith, 1930).

The Portrait of the *Who*

1. Elie Wiesel and Josy Eisenberg, *Job ou Dieu dans la tempête* (Paris: Fayard-Verdier, 1986), 11; all translations for this text, throughout this book, are my own.

2. See Wiesel, *All Rivers Run to the Sea*, 11–13.

3. Wiesel, 60.

4. Elie Wiesel, *One Generation After*, trans. Lily Edelman and Elie Wiesel (New York: Pocket, 1970), 51.

5. Elie Wiesel, *Sages and Dreamers: Biblical, Talmudic, and Hasidic Portraits and Legends*, trans. Marion Wiesel (New York: Summit, 1991), 17.

6. Wiesel, *Against Silence*, 1:239.

7. Abraham Joshua Heschel, *The Prophets* (New York: Harper & Row, 1975), 2:267.

8. Elie Wiesel, *Evil and Exile*, trans. Jon Rothschild (Notre Dame, IN: University of Notre Dame Press, 1990), 159–60.

9. Emmanuel Levinas, "Dialogue with Emmanuel Levinas," in Richard A. Cohen, ed., *Face to Face with Levinas* (Albany: State University of New York Press, 1986), 23.

10. See Nahmanides, *Commentary on the Torah*, trans. Charles B. Chavel (New York: Shilo, 1971), 1:112.

11. See Milton Aron, *Ideas and Ideals of the Hassidim* (Secaucus, NJ: Citadel, 1969), 104.

12. Primo Levi, *Survival in Auschwitz*, trans. Stuart Woolf (New York: Simon & Schuster, 1996), 29.

13. André Neher, *The Exile of the Word: From the Silence of the Bible to the Silence of Auschwitz*, trans. David Maisel (Philadelphia: Jewish Publication Society, 1981), 141.

14. Neher, *Exile of the Word*, 63.

15. Ka-tzetnik 135633, *Shivitti: A Vision*, trans. Eliyah De-Nur and Lisa Herman (New York: Harper & Row, 1989), 158.

16. Wiesel, *Night*, 34; emphasis added.

17. Wiesel and Eisenberg, *Job ou Dieu dans la tempête*, 23.

18. Emmanuel Levinas, *Ethics and Infinity*, trans. Richard A. Cohen (Pittsburgh, PA: Duquesne University Press, 1985), 48–49.

19. Emmanuel Levinas, *Time and the Other*, trans. Richard A. Cohen (Pittsburgh, PA: Duquesne University Press, 1987), 77.

20. Wiesel, *One Generation After*, 72–73.

21. Gershom Scholem, *Major Trends in Jewish Mysticism* (New York: Schocken, 1974), 349–50.

22. Nehemia Polen, "Yearning for Sacred Place: Wiesel's Hasidic Tales and Postwar Hasidism," in *Elie Wiesel: Jewish, Literary, and Moral Perspectives*, ed. Alan Rosen and Steven T. Katz (Bloomington: Indiana University Press, 2013), 74–75.

23. Wiesel, *Night*, 110.

24. Levi, *Survival in Auschwitz*, 88.

25. Elie Wiesel, *From the Kingdom of Memory: Reminiscences* (New York: Summit, 1990), 62.

26. Elie Wiesel, *The Oath* (New York: Avon, 1973), 42.

27. Levinas, *Ethics and Infinity*, 87.

28. Levinas, 86.

29. Emil L. Fackenheim, *God's Presence in History* (New York: Harper & Row, 1970), 68–69.

30. Fackenheim, *God's Presence*, 67.

31. Wiesel, *Souls on Fire*, 46.

32. Wiesel and Eisenberg, *Job ou Dieu dans la tempête*, 69.

33. See Louis Finkelstein, *Akiba: Scholar, Saint and Martyr* (New York: Atheneum, 1981), 103.

34. Levinas, *Ethics and Infinity*, 86–87; emphasis added.

35. See Wiesel, *Evil and Exile*, 155; and Primo Levi, *The Drowned and the Saved*, trans. Raymond Rosenthal (New York: Vintage, 1988), 31.

36. Wiesel, *Legends of Our Time* (New York: Avon, 1968), 25.

37. Wiesel, *Against Silence*, 1:168.

38. Wiesel, *From the Kingdom of Memory*, 209.

39. Emmanuel Levinas, *Otherwise than Being or Beyond Essence*, trans. Alphonso Lingis (The Hague: Martinus Nijhoff, 1981), 193.

40. Levinas, *Ethics and Infinity*, 106.

41. Emmanuel Levinas, *Difficult Freedom: Essays on Judaism*, trans. Sean Hand (Baltimore: Johns Hopkins University Press, 1990), 17.

42. Wiesel, *Rashi: A Portrait*, trans. Catherine Temerson (New York: Schocken, 2009), 67.

Portraits from the Torah

1. Wiesel, *Sages and Dreamers*, 21.

2. Elie Wiesel, *Messengers of God: Biblical Portraits and Legends*, trans. Marion Wiesel (New York: Random House, 1976), x; emphasis in the original.

3. Wiesel, *Messengers of God*; emphasis in the original.

4. Wiesel, 3.

5. Joel Rosenberg, "Alone with God: Wiesel's Writings on the Bible," in *Elie Wiesel: Jewish, Literary, and Moral Perspectives*, ed. Alan Rosen and Steven T. Katz (Bloomington: Indiana University Press, 2013), 13.

6. Rosenberg, "Alone with God," 1.

7. Rosenberg, 1.

8. Elie Wiesel, *The Oath* (New York: Avon, 1973), 19.

9. Martin Buber, *I and Thou*, trans. Walter Kaufmann (New York: Scribner's, 1970), 54.

10. Wiesel, *Messengers of God*, 20.

11. Wiesel, 10.

12. Wiesel, 26.

13. Wiesel, 24.

14. Wiesel, 4.

15. Wiesel, 8.

16. See, for example, the teaching of the Chasidic master Zadok ha-Kohen in Norman Lamm, *The Religious Thought of Hasidism: Text and Commentary* (Hoboken, NJ: Ktav, 1999), 576–77; see also the teaching of the Stretiner Rebbe in Louis Newman, ed., *The Hasidic Anthology* (New York: Schocken, 1963), 248.

17. Wiesel, *Messengers of God*, 11.

18. Emmanuel Levinas, *Difficult Freedom: Essays on Judaism*, trans. Sean Hand (Baltimore: Johns Hopkins University Press, 1990), 33.

19. Wiesel, *Messengers of God*, 32.

20. Wiesel, 35–36.

21. Wiesel, 34.

22. Wiesel, 50.

23. Elie Wiesel, *Twilight*, trans. Marion Wiesel (New York: Summit Books, 1998), 58.

24. Quoted in Milton Aron, *Ideas and Ideals of the Hassidim* (Secaucus, NJ: Citadel, 1969), 243.

25. Wiesel, *Messengers of God*, 50.

26. Wiesel, 50.

27. Wiesel, *Legends of Our Time*, 177.

28. Wiesel, *Messengers of God*, 34.

29. Wiesel, 37–38.

30. Wiesel, 51.

31. Wiesel, 53–54.

32. Wiesel, *Oath*, 88.

33. Wiesel, *Messengers of God*, 53.

34. Wiesel, 40.

35. Wiesel, *Twilight*, 56.

36. Wiesel, *Messengers of God*, 52.

37. Wiesel, 51.

38. Wiesel, 60.

39. Wiesel, *Sages and Dreamers*, 24.

40. Wiesel, 25.

41. See Avraham Moshe Rabinowitz, *Hakhimah Birmizah* (Brooklyn, 1994), 282.

42. Emmanuel Levinas, *Proper Names*, trans. Michael B. Smith (Stanford, CA: Stanford University Press, 1996), 93.

43. Wiesel, *Sages and Dreamers*, 27.

44. Wiesel, 32.

45. Wiesel, 32.

46. Wiesel, 28.

47. Wiesel, 32.

48. Wiesel, 29.

49. Wiesel, *Twilight*, 172.

50. Yaakov Culi, *The Torah Anthology: MeAm Lo'ez*, Vol. 1, trans. Aryeh Kaplan (New York: Moznaim, 1977), 420.

51. Primo Levi, *Survival in Auschwitz: The Nazi Assault against Humanity*, trans. Stuart Woolf (New York: Simon & Schuster, 1996), 72–73.

52. Elie Wiesel, *Wise Men and Their Tales: Portraits of Biblical, Talmudic, and Hasidic Masters* (New York: Schocken, 2003), 27.

53. Wiesel, 27.

54. Wiesel, 28.

55. Wiesel, 31–32.

56. Wiesel, 24.

57. Wiesel, 34.

58. Wiesel, 35.

59. Isabel Wollaston, "The Absent, the Partial and the Iconic in Archival Photographs of the Holocaust," *Jewish Culture and History* 12, no. 3 (2010): 441.

60. Levi, *Survival in Auschwitz*, 39.

61. Levi, 82.

62. Wiesel, *Against Silence*, 239.

63. Rosenberg, "Alone with God: Wiesel's Writings on the Bible," 10.

64. Wiesel, *Messengers of God*, 73.

65. Wiesel, *A Beggar in Jerusalem*, 108.

66. Wiesel, 79.

67. Wiesel, *Messengers of God*, 64.

68. Martin Buber, *Between Man and Man*, trans. Ronald Gregor-Smith (New York: Routledge, 2002), 17.

69. Wiesel, *Messengers of God*, 78.

70. Wiesel, 79.

71. Wiesel, 69.

72. Wiesel, 66.

73. Wiesel, 74.

74. Søren Kierkegaard, *Fear and Trembling*, trans. Alastair Hannay (New York: Penguin, 1985), 46.

75. Wiesel, *Messengers of God*, 72.

76. Levinas, *Ethics and Infinity*, 106.

77. Wiesel, *Messengers of God*, 75–76.

78. Wiesel, 69.

79. Wiesel, 80–81.

80. Wiesel, 85–86.

81. Wiesel, 96.

82. Wiesel, 107.

83. Wiesel, 123; emphasis in the original.

84. Ka-tzetnik 135633, *Shivitti: A Vision*, trans. Eliyah De-Nur and Lisa Herman (New York: Harper & Row, 1989), 59.

85. Wiesel, *Messengers of God*, 94.

86. Nietzsche's most famous pronouncement on the death of G-d appears in Section 125 of *The Gay Science*. See Friedrich Nietzsche, *The Gay Science*, trans. Walter Kaufmann (New York: Vintage, 1974).

87. Wiesel, *Messengers of God*, 111.

88. Wiesel, 94.

89. Wiesel, *Night*, 34.

90. Wiesel, *Messengers of God*, 108.

91. Wiesel, *Night*, 37.

92. Wiesel, *Messengers of God*, 109.

93. Ka-tzetnik 135633, *Kaddish*, trans. Nina De-Nur (New York: Algemeiner Associates, 1998), 97–98.

94. Elie Wiesel, *Evil and Exile*, trans. Jon Rothschild (Notre Dame, IN: University of Notre Dame Press, 1990), 39.

95. Says Nahman of Breslov, "All a person's deeds are inscribed in his soul. That is why after death a person is asked if he remembers his name." See Nahman of Breslov, *Tikkun*, trans. Avraham Greenbaum (Jerusalem: Breslov Research Institute, 1984), 102.

96. See Levinas, *Difficult Freedom*, 17.

97. Wiesel, *Messengers of God*, 113.

98. Wiesel, 117.

99. Wiesel, 143.

100. Wiesel, 145.

101. Wiesel, 133.

102. Wiesel, 128.

103. Wiesel, 148.

104. Wiesel, 12.

105. Wiesel, 130–31; for the reference to Kierkegaard, see Søren Kierkegaard, *Stages on Life's Way*, ed. and trans. Howard V. Hong and Edna H. Hong (Princeton, NJ: Princeton University Press, 1988).

106. Wiesel, 142.

107. Wiesel, 143.

108. Kalonymos Kalmish Shapira, *Sacred Fire: Torah from the Years of Fury 1939–1942*, trans. J. Hershy Worch, ed. Deborah Miller (Northvale, NJ: Jason Aronson, 2000), 22.

109. Wiesel, *Messengers of God*, 144.

110. Wiesel, 151.

111. Wiesel, 168–69.

112. Wiesel, 142.

113. Adin Steinsaltz, *On Being Free* (Northvale, NJ: Jason Aronson, 1995), 22.

114. Wiesel, *Messengers of God*, 166–67.

115. Wiesel, 184.

116. Wiesel, 177–78.

117. Wiesel, 163.

118. The others were Enoch, who "walked with God, and he was not, for God took him" (Genesis 5:25); Abraham's servant Eliezer, who found a wife for Isaac (Genesis 24:14–15); Asher's daughter Serah, who brought Jacob the news that Joseph was still alive (*Sefer HaYashar, Vayigash* 9); the prophet Elijah, who ascended into the heavens in a chariot of fire (2 Kings 2:12); Hiram, King of Tyre, who sent help to Solomon for the building of the Temple (1 Kings 5:15); and Eved-melekh, the Ethiopian slave who rescued Jeremiah from the pit (Jeremiah 38:8–11). Some sources add Yehudah HaNassi's son Yaavetz, Rabbi Yehoshua ben Levi, and the Messiah (*Talmud Bavli, Derekh Eretz Zuta* 1); see Moshe Weissman, ed., *The Midrash Says*, vol. 1 (Brooklyn, NY: Bnay Yakov, 1980), 73.

119. Wiesel, *Messengers of God*, 164.

120. Wiesel, 172.

121. Wiesel, 178.

122. Wiesel, 174.

123. Arnošt Lustig, *A Prayer for Katerina Horovitzova*, trans. Jeanne Nemcova (New York: Harper & Row, 1973), 50–51.

124. Wiesel, *Messengers of God*, 180.

125. Wiesel, 180.

126. Wiesel, 181.

127. The other five are the remembrance of when God took the Jews out of Egypt, of one's own soul standing before God, of the affliction in the desert, of Amalek, and of the Sabbath.

128. Wiesel, *Wise Men and Their Tales*, 42.

129. Wiesel, 56.

130. Wiesel, 64.

131. Wiesel, 62.

132. Wiesel, 63.

133. Wiesel, 64–65.

134. Wiesel, 65.

135. The other nine are the manna that fell in the desert, and the rainbow, writing, and the writing instrument, the tablets of the Ten Commandments, the grave of Moses, the cave in which Moses and Elijah stood, the opening of the mouth of Balaam's donkey, and the opening of the earth's mouth to swallow the wicked in the incident involving Korah (*Pesahim* 54a).

136. Wiesel, *Wise Men and Their Tales*, 67.

137. Wiesel, 68.

138. Wiesel, 46.

139. Wiesel, 43.

140. Wiesel, 48.

141. Wiesel, 50.

142. Wiesel, 80.

143. Wiesel, 69; emphasis in original.

144. Wiesel, 69–70.

145. Wiesel, 77.

146. Wiesel, 71.

147. Wiesel, 72.

148. Wiesel, 73.

149. Wiesel, 72.

150. Wiesel, 73–74.

151. Wiesel, 75.

152. Wiesel, 75.

153. Abraham Joshua Heschel, *Man Is Not Alone* (New York: Farrar, Straus and Giroux, 1951), 47.

154. Wiesel, *Wise Men and Their Tales*, 78.

155. Wiesel, 79.

156. Wiesel, 81.

157. Wiesel, *One Generation After*, 13.

Portraits from the Prophets

1. Wiesel, *Wise Men and Their Tales*, 179.

2. Wiesel, *Wise Men and Their Tales*, 178.

3. Wiesel, *Somewhere a Master*, 191.

4. Wiesel, *Five Biblical Portraits*, 66.

5. Weisel, *Five Biblical Portraits*, 38–39.

6. Emmanuel Levinas, *Otherwise than Being or Beyond Essence*, trans. Alphonso Lingis (The Hague: Martinus Nijhoff, 1981), 83.

7. Levinas, *Otherwise than Being*, 143.

8. Wiesel, *Five Biblical Portraits*, 123.

9. Wiesel, 55.

10. Wiesel, *Night*, 20.

11. Abraham Joshua Heschel, *The Prophets*, vol. 1 (New York: Harper & Row, 1975), 7.

12. Wiesel, *Wise Men and Their Tales*, 167.

13. Wiesel, 161.

14. Wiesel, *Somewhere a Master*, 151.

15. Wiesel, *Wise Men and Their Tales*, 162.

16. Wiesel, 160.

17. Emmanuel Levinas, *Nine Talmudic Readings*, trans. Annette Aronowicz (Bloomington: Indiana University Press, 1990), 183.

18. Wiesel, *Wise Men and Their Tales*, 160.

19. Wiesel, 169.

20. Wiesel, 169–70.

21. Elaine Scarry, *The Body in Pain: The Making and Unmaking of the World* (Oxford: Oxford University Press, 1985), 27.

22. Levinas, *Ethics and Infinity*, 105.

23. See Levinas, *Difficult Freedom*, 8.

24. Wiesel, *Five Biblical Portraits*, 63.

25. Wiesel, 36.

26. Wiesel, 36.

27. Wiesel, 41.

28. Wiesel, *Against Silence*, 60.

29. Wiesel, *Gates of the Forest*, 63.

30. André Neher, *The Exile of the Word: From the Silence of the Bible to the Silence of Auschwitz*, trans. David Maisel (Philadelphia: Jewish Publication Society, 1981), 37.

31. Wiesel, *Five Biblical Portraits*, 38.

32. Wiesel, 41.

33. Wiesel, 45.

34. Wiesel, 52.

35. Wiesel, *A Beggar in Jerusalem*, 81.

36. Wiesel, *Five Biblical Portraits*, 46.

37. Ka-tzetnik 135633, *Star of Ashes*, trans. Nina De-Nur (Tel Aviv: Hamenora, 1971), 53.

38. Wiesel, *Five Biblical Portraits*, 53.

39. Wiesel, 35.

40. Wiesel, 35.

41. Wiesel, 55.

42. Wiesel, 63.

43. Wiesel, 56.

44. Wiesel, 58.

45. Wiesel, 56.

46. Wiesel, 58.

47. Wiesel, 60–61.

48. Wiesel, 60.

49. Wiesel, 62.

50. Shushani is the subject of the portrait "The Wandering Jews" in Wiesel, *Legends of Our Time*, 87–109.

51. Wiesel, *Wise Men and Their Tales*, 175.

52. Wiesel, 177.

53. Wiesel, 173–74.

54. Wiesel, 175.

55. Wiesel, 176.

56. See Markus Zusak, *The Book Thief* (New York: Alfred A. Knopf, 2007).

57. Wiesel, *Wise Men and Their Tales*, 174–75.

58. Wiesel, 178.

59. Wiesel, 178.

60. Wiesel, 187.

61. Wiesel, 173.

62. Wiesel, 185.

63. Wiesel, 182.

64. Wiesel, 183.

65. Wiesel, 183.

66. Wiesel, 185.

67. Wiesel, *Souls on Fire*, 227.

68. Wiesel, *Five Biblical Portraits*, 126.

69. Wiesel, *Wise Men and Their Tales*, 224.

70. Wiesel, *Five Biblical Portraits*, 104.

71. Heschel, *Prophets*, 1:9.

72. Wiesel, *Five Biblical Portraits*, 100.

73. Wiesel, 100–1.

74. Wiesel, *Against Silence*, 1:137.

75. Wiesel, *Five Biblical Portraits*, 123.

76. Wiesel, 105.

77. Wiesel, 112–13.

78. Wiesel, *Souls on Fire*, 227.

79. Wiesel, *Five Biblical Portraits*, 121.

80. Wiesel, 105–6.

81. Wiesel, 122.

82. Wiesel, 122.

83. Wiesel, 119.

84. Wiesel, 118.

85. Wiesel, 117.

86. Wiesel, 114.

87. Wiesel, 123.

88. Wiesel, 125–26.

89. Stephan Landsman, *Crimes of the Holocaust: The Law Confronts Hard Cases* (Philadelphia: University of Pennsylvania Press, 2005), 74.

90. Donna Rubinstein, *I Am the Only Survivor of Krasnostav* (New York: Shengold, 1982), 39.

91. Judith Dribben, *And Some Shall Live* (Jerusalem: Keter, 1969), 85.

92. Wiesel, *Sages and Dreamers*, 88.

93. Levinas, *Otherwise Than Being*, 57; emphasis added.

94. Wiesel, *Sages and Dreamers*, 83.

95. Wiesel, 83.

96. Wiesel, 89–90.

97. Wiesel, 97.

98. Wiesel, 80.

99. Heschel, *Prophets*, 1:12.

100. Wiesel, *Sages and Dreamers*, 89.

101. See Wiesel, *Against Silence*, 2:82.

102. Wiesel, *Sages and Dreamers*, 92.

103. Wiesel, 82.

104. Wiesel, 87.

105. Wiesel, 90.

106. Wiesel, 300–1.

107. Wiesel, 97.

108. Wiesel, 85.

109. Wiesel, *Against Silence*, 3:281.

110. Wiesel, *Five Biblical Portraits*, 150–51.

111. Wiesel, *Wise Men and Their Tales*, 70.

112. Wiesel, *Five Biblical Portraits*, 141.

113. Wiesel, 129.

114. Wiesel, 134.

115. Wiesel, 132–33.

116. Wiesel, 144.

117. Wiesel, 136.

118. Wiesel, 138.

119. Wiesel, 148.

120. Wiesel, 139.

121. Wiesel, 142.

122. Wiesel, 139–40.

123. Wiesel, 148–49.

124. Wiesel, 154–55.

Portraits from the Writings

1. Wiesel, *All Rivers Run to the Sea*, 321.

2. Levinas, *Nine Talmudic Readings*, 41.

3. Wiesel, *Sages and Dreamers*, 106.

4. Wiesel, 103.

5. Wiesel, 108.

6. Wiesel, 100.

7. Wiesel, *Gates of the Forest*, 201.

8. Wiesel, *Beggar in Jerusalem*, 115.

9. Wiesel, *Sages and Dreamers*, 105.

10. Wiesel, 113–14.

11. Wiesel, 109.

12. Abraham Joshua Heschel, *The Sabbath: Its Meaning for Modern Man* (New York: Farrar, Straus and Giroux, 1981), 100.

13. Adin Steinsaltz and Josy Eisenberg, *The Seven Lights: On the Major Jewish Festivals* (Northvale, NJ: Jason Aronson, 2000), 65.

14. Wiesel, *Sages and Dreamers*, 110.

15. Wiesel, 111.

16. Wiesel, *Oath*, 195.

17. Wiesel, *Sages and Dreamers*, 99.

18. Wiesel, 102–3.

19. Wiesel, 113.

20. Wiesel, 112.

21. Wiesel, *Five Biblical Portraits*, 63.

22. Wiesel, *Somewhere a Master*, 41.

23. Wiesel, *Sages and Dreamers*, 50.

24. Wiesel, 50.

25. Wiesel, 55.

26. Wiesel, 51.

27. Moshe Cordovero, *The Palm Tree of Devorah*, trans. Moshe Miller (Southfield, MI: Targum, 1993), 12.

28. Shalom Dovber Schneersohn, *Yom Tov Shel Rosh Hashanah 5659: Discourse One*, trans. Y. B. Marcus and M. Miller (Brooklyn, NY: Kehot, 2000), 26.

29. Wiesel, *Sages and Dreamers*, 54.

30. Wiesel, 55.

31. Wiesel, 58.

32. Wiesel, 59.

33. Wiesel, 59.

34. Wiesel, 61.

35. Wiesel, *Somewhere a Master*, 91–92.

36. Wiesel, *Sages and Dreamers*, 59.

37. Wiesel, 63.

38. Levinas, *Totality and Infinity*, 243.

39. Levinas, 34.

40. Wiesel, *Sages and Dreamers*, 134.

41. Wiesel, 140.

42. See Martin Buber, *The Legend of the Baal Shem*, trans. Maurice Friedman (New York: Schocken, 1969), 27.

43. The seven women prophets are Sarah, Miriam, Deborah, Hannah, Abigail, Hulda, and Esther.

44. Wiesel, *Sages and Dreamers*, 146.

45. Wiesel, 145.

46. Wiesel, 148.

47. Wiesel, 148.

48. Wiesel, 135.

49. Wiesel, 150.

50. Wiesel, *Messengers of God*, 198; my emphasis.

51. Elie Wiesel and Josy Eisenberg, *Job ou Dieu dans la tempête* (Paris: Fayard-Verdier, 1986), 163; all translations are mine.

52. Wiesel and Eisenberg, 127–28.

53. Wiesel and Eisenberg, 288.

54. Wiesel and Eisenberg, 288.

55. Emmanuel Levinas, *Existence and Existents*, trans. Alphonso Lingis (The Hague: Martinus Nijhoff, 1978), 60–61.

56. Wiesel, *Messengers of God*, 187.

57. Wiesel and Eisenberg, *Job ou Dieu dans la tempête*, 245.

58. Wiesel and Eisenberg, 188.

59. Wiesel and Eisenberg, 191.

60. Wiesel and Eisenberg, 27.

61. Wiesel, *Messengers of God*, 201.

62. Wiesel, 193–94.

63. Wiesel and Eisenberg, *Job ou Dieu dans la tempête*, 227.

64. Wiesel, *Messengers of God*, 200.

65. Wiesel and Eisenberg, *Job ou Dieu dans la tempête*, 398.

66. Wiesel, *Messengers of God*, 198–99.

67. Wiesel and Eisenberg, *Job ou Dieu dans la tempête*, 176.

68. Wiesel, *Messengers of God*, 206.

69. Wiesel and Eisenberg, *Job ou Dieu dans la tempête*, 364.
70. Wiesel and Eisenberg, 278.
71. Wiesel and Eisenberg, 155.
72. Wiesel, *Messengers of God*, 207.
73. Wiesel and Eisenberg, *Job ou Dieu dans la tempête*, 50.
74. Wiesel and Eisenberg, 279.
75. Wiesel and Eisenberg, 395.
76. Wiesel and Eisenberg, 373.
77. Wiesel and Eisenberg, 374.
78. Wiesel and Eisenberg, 392.
79. Levinas, *Ethics and Infinity*, 52.

Portraits from the Talmud

1. Reuven Kimelman, "Wiesel and the Stories of the Rabbis," in Alan Rosen and Steven T. Katz, eds., *Elie Wiesel: Jewish, Literary, and Moral Perspectives* (Bloomington: Indiana University Press, 2013), 38.
2. Adin Steinsaltz, *The Essential Talmud*, trans. Chaya Galai (New York: Basic Books, 1976), 47.
3. Steinsaltz, *Essential Talmud*, 246.
4. Steinsaltz, *Essential Talmud*, 100.
5. Steinsaltz, *Essential Talmud*, 163.
6. Wiesel, *Sages and Dreamers*, 184.
7. Steinsaltz, *Essential Talmud*, 262.
8. Steinsaltz, 268.
9. Wiesel, *Sages and Dreamers*, 178.
10. Wiesel, *Wise Men and Their Tales*, 216.
11. See Wiesel, *Oath*, 129.
12. Wiesel, *Sages and Dreamers*, 160.
13. Elie Wiesel, *Against Silence*, 318.
14. Wiesel, *Sages and Dreamers*, 346.
15. Wiesel, *Wise Men and Their Tales*, 258.
16. Wiesel, *Sages and Dreamers*, 331.
17. Steinsaltz, *The Essential Talmud*, 8–9.
18. Wiesel, *Sages and Dreamers*, 165.
19. Wiesel, 165.
20. Wiesel, 157.
21. Wiesel, 158.
22. Wiesel, 159.
23. Wiesel, 162.
24. Ibid., 162.

25. See Yehudah Leib Alter, *The Language of Truth: The Torah Commentary of the Sefat Emet*, trans. Arthur Green (Philadelphia: Jewish Publication Society, 1998).

26. Wiesel, *Sages and Dreamers*, 167.

27. Wiesel, 166.

28. Wiesel, 166.

29. Wiesel, 168.

30. Wiesel, 169.

31. Wiesel, 170.

32. Wiesel, 171.

33. Levinas, *Otherwise than Being or Beyond Essence*, 17.

34. Levinas, *Collected Philosophical Papers* 33.

35. Wiesel, *Sages and Dreamers*, 172.

36. Wiesel, *Town beyond the Wall*, 119.

37. Wiesel, *Against Silence*, 1:273.

38. Elie Wiesel, *Paroles d'étranger* (Paris: Éditions du Seuil, 1982), 171–72; my translation.

39. Martin Buber, *I and Thou*, trans. Walter Kaufmann (New York: Scribner's, 1970), 89.

40. Wiesel, *Sages and Dreamers*, 189.

41. Wiesel, 175.

42. Wiesel, *Legends of Our Time*, 151.

43. Wiesel, *Sages and Dreamers*, 176.

44. Wiesel, *Paroles d'étranger*, 169.

45. Wiesel, *Sages and Dreamers*, 177.

46. Wiesel, 180.

47. Wiesel, 189.

48. Wiesel, 175.

49. Wiesel, 181.

50. Wiesel, *Souls on Fire*, 208.

51. Wiesel, *Sages and Dreamers*, 184.

52. Wiesel, 176.

53. Wiesel, 183.

54. Emmanuel Levinas, "Prayer without Demand," trans. Sarah Richmond, in Sean Hand, ed., *The Levinas Reader* (Oxford: Basil Blackwell, 1989), 234.

55. Wiesel, *Sages and Dreamers*, 190.

56. Wiesel, 185.

57. Wiesel, 191.

58. Wiesel, 186.

59. Wiesel, 192.

60. Wiesel, 213–14.

61. Wiesel, 213–14.

62. Wiesel, 213–14.

63. Shulamis Freiman, *Who's Who in the Talmud* (Northvale, NJ: Jason Aronson, 1995), 370.

64. Alter, *Language of Truth*, 62.

65. Wiesel, *Sages and Dreamers*, 215.

66. Wiesel, 222–23.

67. Wiesel, 212.

68. Wiesel, 212.

69. Wiesel, 223.

70. Wiesel, 216.

71. Wiesel, 217.

72. Wiesel, 221.

73. Wiesel, 219.

74. Wiesel, 218.

75. Wiesel, 221.

76. Wiesel, 218.

77. Wiesel, 220.

78. Steinsaltz, *Essential Talmud*, 36.

79. Wiesel, *Sages and Dreamers*, 234.

80. Wiesel, 232.

81. Wiesel, 235.

82. Wiesel, 224–25.

83. See Emil L. Fackenheim, *God's Presence in History: Jewish Affirmations and Philosophical Reflections* (New York: Harper & Row, 1970), 6.

84. Wiesel, *Sages and Dreamers*, 226.

85. Wiesel, 226–27.

86. Wiesel, 230.

87. Wiesel, 235.

88. Wiesel, 237.

89. Wiesel, 238.

90. Wiesel, 239.

91. Levi, *Survival in Auschwitz*, 98.

92. Primo Levi, *The Reawakening*, trans. Stuart Wolf (Boston: Little, Brown, 1965), 33.

93. Levi, *Reawakening*, 128.

94. Wiesel, *Sages and Dreamers*, 240.

95. Wiesel, *Town beyond the Wall*, 100.

96. Wiesel, *Sages and Dreamers*, 242.

97. Wiesel, 244.

98. The others are "he who has a wife but no children; and he who has children but does not bring them up to the study of the Torah; and he who has no phylacteries on his head and on his arm, no finger on his garment and no *mezuzah* on his door, and he who denies his feet shoes. And some say: Also he who never sits in a company assembled for a religious purpose" (*Pesahim* 113b).

99. Wiesel, *Sages and Dreamers*, 245.

100. Wiesel, 251.

101. Wiesel, 253.

102. Wiesel, 246. According to tradition, the Ten Martyrs are Rabbi Akiba, Rabbi Hananiah ben Teradyon, Rabbi Yehuda ben Bava, Rabbi Shimon ben Gamliel HaNassi, Rabbi Ishmael Kohen Gadol, Rabbi Hutzpit the Interpreter, Rabbi Elazar ben Shamua, Rabbi Hanina ben Hakinai, Rabbi Yesheivav the Scribe, and Rabbi Yehuda ben Dama.

103. Wiesel, 247.

104. Elie Wiesel, *From the Kingdom of Memory: Reminiscences* (New York: Summit, 1990), 13.

105. Wiesel, *Legends of Our Time*, 18.

106. Wiesel, *Ani Maamin*, 39, 41.

107. Wiesel, *Gates of the Forest*, 11–12.

108. Elie Wiesel, *Twilight*, trans. Marion Wiesel (New York: Summit, 1998), 37.

109. Wiesel, *Sages and Dreamers*, 247.

110. Wiesel, *Hostage*, 191.

111. Wiesel, *Sages and Dreamers*, 254.

112. Wiesel, 254.

113. Wiesel, 247–48.

114. Wiesel, 246.

115. Wiesel, 249.

116. Wiesel, 255.

117. Wiesel, 250.

118. Wiesel, 199.

119. Wiesel, 205.

120. Wiesel, 205.

121. Wiesel, 204.

122. Wiesel, 206.

123. Wiesel, 204.

124. Wiesel, 208–9.

125. Wiesel, 207.

126. Wiesel, 210–11.

127. See, for example, Aryeh Kaplan, *Inner Space* (Jerusalem: Moznaim, 1990), 120–21.

128. Levinas, *Otherwise Than Being*, 114.

129. Levinas, *Collected Philosophical Papers*, 99.

130. Wiesel, *Wise Men and Their Tales*, 208.

131. Wiesel, 219.

132. Wiesel, 220–21; I do not find this reference in the Midrash.

133. Wiesel, 218–19.

134. Wiesel, 216.

135. Wiesel, 212.

136. Wiesel, 214.

137. Wiesel, 211.

138. Wiesel, 223.

139. Wiesel, *Against Silence*, 2:119.

140. Wiesel, *Messengers of God*, 26–27.

141. Wiesel, *Sages and Dreamers*, 281.

142. Wiesel, *Souls on Fire*, 52; this episode is also related in the anthology of sayings and teachings from the Baal Shem Tov, the *Tsavaat ha-Rivash* (Brooklyn: Kehot, 1999), 63–64.

143. Wiesel, *Sages and Dreamers*, 271.

144. Wiesel, 273.

145. Wiesel, 281.

146. Wiesel, 275.

147. Quoted in Victor Cohen, ed., *The Soul of the Torah: Insights of the Chasidic Masters on the Weekly Torah Portions* (Northvale, NJ: Jason Aronson, 2000), 98.

148. Wiesel, *Sages and Dreamers*, 277.

149. Wiesel, 280.

150. Wiesel, 280.

151. Wiesel, 285.

152. Wiesel, 286–87.

153. Wiesel, 287–88.

154. Wiesel, 289.

155. Wiesel, 296.

156. Wiesel, 297.

157. Wiesel, 298.

158. Wiesel, 302.

159. Wiesel, 308.

160. Wiesel, 310.

161. Wiesel, *Night*, 5.

162. Wiesel, *Sages and Dreamers*, 306–7.

163. Wiesel, 300.

164. Wiesel, 302.

165. Wiesel, 301–2.

Portraits of the Hasidic Masters

1. Wiesel, *Somewhere a Master*, 40.

2. Wiesel, *All Rivers Run to the Sea*, 42.

3. Wiesel, *Somewhere a Master*, 205.

4. Wiesel, *Souls on Fire*, 187. Elsewhere, he writes that with Rabbi Akiba "the tale of the law becomes part of the law itself"; see Elie Wiesel, *Sages and Dreamers*, trans. Marion Wiesel (New York: Summit, 1991), 234.

5. Wiesel, *Against Silence*, 187.

6. See Wiesel, *Evil and Exile*, 155.

7. Elie Wiesel, *The Forgotten*, trans. Marion Wiesel (New York: Summit, 1992), 71.

8. Wiesel, *From the Kingdom of Memory*, 173.

9. Wiesel, *Souls on Fire*, 5.

10. *Wiesel, Somewhere a Master*, 19.

11. Wiesel, 12.

12. Wiesel, 203.

13. Wiesel, *All Rivers Run to the Sea*, 45.

14. Wiesel, *Somewhere a Master*, 21.

15. Wiesel, *Souls on Fire*, 33.

16. Etkes, *Besht*, 43.

17. "Introduction to Beit Yaakov" in Gershom Hanoch Leiner, *Shaar Emumah v'Yesod HaChassidut: V'u HaKadamah v'Petach haShaar l'Beit Yaavov* (The gate of faith and the foundation of Hasidism: Entrance to the gate of Beit Yaakov), trans. Betzalel Edwards (Benei Brak: Machon Lehotzet, 1996), 24:2.

18. Wiesel, *Souls on Fire*, 24; see also Etkes, *Besht*, 81–82.

19. Etkes, *Besht*, 86.

20. Wiesel, *Souls on Fire*, 6.

21. Wiesel, 7; emphasis added.

22. Louis I. Newman, ed., *The Hasidic Anthology* (New York: Schocken, 1963), 116.

23. Wiesel, *Souls on Fire*, 20.

24. Wiesel, 25.

25. Wiesel, 31–32.

26. Levinas, *Totality and Infinity*, 291.

27. Levinas, 206.

28. Levinas, *Ethics and Infinity*, 105.

29. Levinas, *Collected Philosophical Papers*, 96.

30. Wiesel, *Souls on Fire*, 9.

31. Wiesel, 15.

32. Wiesel, 22–23.

33. Wiesel, 27.

34. Wiesel, 26.

35. Wiesel, 31.

36. Newman, *Hasidic Anthology*, 456.

37. Wiesel, *Souls on Fire*, 18.

38. Wiesel, 38.

39. Sara Nomberg-Przytyk, *Auschwitz: True Tales from a Grotesque Land*, trans. Roslyn Hirsch (Chapel Hill: University of North Carolina Press, 1985), 105–6.

40. This tale also appears in the Hasidic classic Dov Ber, *In Praise of the Baal Shem Tov*, trans. and ed. Dan Ben-Amos and Jerome R. Mintz (New York: Schocken, 1970), 80–81.

41. Wiesel, *Souls on Fire*, 15.

42. Wiesel, 56.

43. Wiesel, 63.

44. Wiesel, 57.

45. Wiesel, 65.

46. Wiesel, 66.

47. David Biale et al., *Hasidism: A New History* (Princeton, NJ: Princeton University Press, 2017), 76.

48. Wiesel, *Somewhere a Master*, 38–39.

49. Wiesel, *Souls on Fire*, 56; see also Milton Aron, *Ideas and Ideals of the Hassidim* (Secaucus, NJ: Citadel, 1969), 168.

50. Aron, *Ideas and Ideals*, 102.

51. Newman, *Hasidic Anthology*, 179.

52. Wiesel, *Souls on Fire*, 61.

53. Wiesel, 68.

54. Levinas, *Collected Philosophical Papers*, 97.

55. Wiesel, *Souls on Fire*, 76.

56. Levinas, *Difficult Freedom*, 17.

57. Wiesel, *Souls on Fire*, 73.

58. Wiesel, 71.

59. Wiesel, *Night*, 41.

60. Wiesel, *Souls on Fire*, 86.

61. Wiesel, 71.

62. Wiesel, 71.

63. Newman, *Hasidic Anthology*, 301.

64. Wiesel, *Sonderberg Case*, 46–47.

65. Wiesel, *Somewhere a Master*, 17.

66. Wiesel, 17.

67. Wiesel, 15.

68. Wiesel, 23.

69. Wiesel, 18.

70. Wiesel, 13.

71. Wiesel, *Against Silence*, 3:297.

72. Wiesel, *Somewhere a Master*, 11–12.

73. Wiesel, 15.

74. Wiesel, 20.

75. Newman, *Hasidic Anthology*, 147.

76. Newman, 335–36.

77. Newman, 36.

78. Newman, 451; Milton Aron attributes this teaching to Menahem-Mendl of Kotzk. See Aron, *Ideas and Ideals*, 256.

79. Wiesel, *Somewhere a Master*, 24.

80. Wiesel, 24.

81. Wiesel, 27.

82. Wiesel, 28.

83. Wiesel, 28.

84. Wiesel, 23.

85. Wiesel, 31.

86. Wiesel, 36.

87. Wiesel, 37.

88. Wiesel, 29–30.

89. Wiesel, 43.

90. Martin Buber, *I and Thou*, trans. Walter Kaufmann (New York: Scribner's, 1970), 66.

91. Wiesel, *Somewhere a Master*, 30–31.

92. Wiesel, 44.

93. Wiesel, 39–40.

94. Wiesel, 41.

95. Wiesel, 41.

96. Wiesel, 35.

97. Wiesel, 39.

98. Wiesel, 42.

99. Wiesel, 40.

100. Wiesel, 41.

101. Wiesel, 48.

102. Wiesel, 46–47.

103. Wiesel, 49–50.

104. Wiesel, 68.

105. Wiesel, *Souls on Fire*, 115.

106. Wiesel, 115.

107. Wiesel, 117.

108. Wiesel, 126.

109. Wiesel, 119.

110. Wiesel, 120.

111. Wiesel, 123.

112. Wiesel, 127.

113. Wiesel, 123.

114. Wiesel, 120.

115. Wiesel, 116.

116. Wiesel, 115.

117. Wiesel, 127.

118. Wiesel, 122.

119. See I. L. Peretz, *The I. L. Peretz Reader*, ed. Ruth R. Wisse, trans. Marie Syrkin (New Haven, CT: Yale University Press, 2002), 178–80.

120. Wiesel, *Somewhere a Master*, 95–98.

121. Wiesel, 98; for the version told by Reb Zvi-Hersh of Zhidachov, see Aron, *Ideas and Ideals*, 106–7.

122. Aron, 106–7.

123. Aron, 106.

124. Aron, 101.

125. Aron, 100.

126. Levi, *Survival in Auschwitz*, 74.

127. Wiesel, *Somewhere a Master*, 105.

128. Wiesel, 107.

129. Wiesel, 112.

130. Wiesel, 108.

131. See Levinas, *Ethics and Infinity*, 87.

132. Wiesel, *Somewhere a Master*, 110.

133. Newman, *Hasidic Anthology*, 494.

134. Wiesel, *Somewhere a Master*, 105.

135. Wiesel, 111.

136. Wiesel, 113.

137. Wiesel, 110.

138. Wiesel, *Sages and Dreamers*, 360.

139. Wiesel, *Somewhere a Master*, 99.

140. Wiesel, 113.

141. Wiesel, *One Generation After*, 48.

142. Wiesel, *Somewhere a Master*, 114.

143. Wiesel, *Souls on Fire*, 92.

144. Wiesel, *Oath*, 129.

145. Wiesel, *Souls on Fire*, 89.

146. Wiesel, 91.

147. Wiesel, 107.

148. Wiesel, 109.

149. See David R. Blumenthal, *Understanding Jewish Mysticism: A Source Reader*, vol. 2 (New York: Ktav, 1982), 95.

150. Wiesel and Eisenberg, *Job ou Dieu dans la tempête*, 82; see also Alan Rosen, "Capturing the Fire, Envisioning the Redemption: The Life and Work of Elie Wiesel," in Alan L. Berger, ed., *Elie Wiesel: Teacher, Mentor, and Friend* (Eugene, OR: Cascade, 2018), 46–57.

151. Wiesel, *Souls on Fire*, 110.

152. See Harry M. Rabinowicz, *Hasidism: The Movement and Its Masters* (Northvale, NJ: Aronson, 1988), 63.

153. Wiesel, *Souls on Fire*, 103.

154. Kazantzakis, *Rock Garden*, 105–6.

155. Wiesel, *Sages and Dreamers*, 378.

156. Samuel H. Dresner, *The Zaddik: The Doctrine of the Zaddik According to the Writings of Rabbi Yaakov Yosef of Polnoy* (New York: Abelard-Schuman, 1960), 239.

157. Wiesel, *Souls on Fire*, 111.

158. Wiesel, 112.

159. Wiesel, *Night*, 30–31.

160. Dribben, *And Some Shall Live*, 24.

161. Wiesel, *Souls on Fire*, 99.

162. Wiesel, 96–97.

163. Wiesel, 98.

164. Wiesel, 100.

165. Wiesel, *Testament*, 207.

166. Wiesel, 207.

167. Wiesel, *Souls on Fire*, 105.

168. Wiesel, 105.

169. Wiesel, 106.

170. Arthur Green, *Tormented Master: A Life of Nahman of Bratslov* (Tuscaloosa: University of Alabama Press, 1979), 10.

171. Elie Wiesel, *And the Sea Is Never Full: Memoirs: 1969– *, trans. Marion Wiesel (New York: Alfred A. Knopf, 1999), 291.

172. Biale et al., *Hasidism*, 116.

173. Wiesel, *Souls on Fire*, 169–70.

174. Levi, *Survival in Auschwitz*, 121–22.

175. Wiesel, *Souls on Fire*, 170–71.

176. Newman, *Hasidic Anthology*, 257.

177. Wiesel, *Souls on Fire*, 179.

178. Wiesel, 187.

179. Wiesel, 181.

180. Meyer Levin, *Hasidic Stories* (Tel-Aviv: Greenfield, 1975), 344.

181. Wiesel, *Souls on Fire*, 182.

182. Nahman of Breslov, *Restore My Soul (Meshivat Nefesh)*, trans. Avraham Greenbaum (Jerusalem: Chasidei Breslov, 1980), 47–48.

183. Wiesel, *Souls on Fire*, 175.

184. Wiesel, 180.

185. Menachem Mendel Schneerson, *Torah Studies*, adapted by Jonathan Sacks (London: Lubavitch Foundation, 1986), 74.

186. Wiesel, *Souls on Fire*, 188.

187. Nahman of Breslov, *Restore My Soul*, 24.

188. Nahman of Breslov, *Tikkun*, trans. Avraham Greenbaum (Jerusalem: Breslov Research Institute, 1984), 56.

189. Nahman of Breslov, *Advice*, trans. Avraham Greenbaum (Brooklyn, NY: Breslov Research Institute, 1983), 285.

190. Wiesel, *Souls on Fire*, 191–92.

191. Nahman of Breslov, *Restore My Soul*, 109.

192. Aron, *Ideas and Ideals of the Hassidim*, 160.

193. Wiesel, *Souls on Fire*, 193–94.

194. Wiesel, 198–99.

195. Wiesel, 198.

196. Wiesel, 199–200.

197. Wiesel, 174.

198. Wiesel, 200.

199. Wiesel, 201.

200. Wiesel, *Somewhere a Master*, 126.

201. Wiesel, 122.

202. Wiesel, 128.

203. Wiesel, 132.

204. Wiesel, 133.

205. Wiesel, 127.

206. Wiesel, 134.

207. Wiesel, 133.

208. Wiesel, 135.

209. Wiesel, 115; the story is also told in Shlomo Yosef Zevin, *A Treasury of Chassidic Tales on the Torah*, trans. Uri Kaploun (New York: Mesorah, 1980), 98.

210. Wiesel, 115–16.

211. Wiesel, 116.

212. Wiesel, 117.

213. Wiesel, 117.

214. Biale et al., *Hasidism*, 154.

215. Wiesel, *Somewhere a Master*, 117.

216. Wiesel, 118.

217. Wiesel, 137.

218. Wiesel, 138.

219. Wiesel, *Souls on Fire*, 235.

220. Wiesel, 235–36.

221. Wiesel, 231.

222. Wiesel, 231–32.

223. Wiesel, 232–33; some sources say that the Kotzker destroyed his writings each year on the eve of Passover; see Rabinowicz, *Hasidism*, 150.

224. Wiesel, 233.

225. Wiesel, 234.

226. Yitzchak Ginsburgh, *The Alef-Beit: Jewish Thought Revealed through the Hebrew Letters* (Northvale, NJ: Jason Aronson, 1991), 72.

227. Wiesel, *Souls on Fire*, 235.

228. Wiesel, 240–41.

229. Wiesel, *And the Sea Is Never Full*, 60.

230. Aron, *Ideas and Ideals*, 253.

231. Wiesel, *Souls on Fire*, 252–53.

232. Wiesel, 237.

233. Wiesel, 236.

234. Wiesel, 238.

235. Wiesel, 248.

236. Wiesel, 240.

237. Wiesel, *And the Sea Is Never Full*, 82.

238. Wiesel, *Testament*, 207.

239. Wiesel, *Souls on Fire*, 248.

240. Wiesel, *All Rivers Run to the Sea*, 85.

241. Wiesel, *Souls on Fire*, 245.

242. Wiesel, 228–29.

243. Wiesel, 257.

244. Wiesel, 254.

245. Wiesel, 254.

246. Wiesel, 254.

247. Wiesel, *Against Silence*, 3:309.

The Messiah

1. Gershon Greenberg, "The Hasidic Spark and the Holocaust," in *Elie Wiesel: Jewish, Literary, and Moral Perspectives*, ed. Alan Rosen and Steven T. Katz (Bloomington: Indiana University Press, 2013), 93.

2. A video of Elie Wiesel's lecture "A Portrait of the Messiah," delivered at Boston University on October 6, 2006, http://archives.bu.edu/web/elie-wiesel/videos/video?id=424836.

3. Wiesel, *Souls on Fire*, 24.

4. Wiesel, *Souls on Fire*, 194.

5. Wiesel, *Against Silence*, 232.

6. Wiesel, *All Rivers Run to the Sea*, 16.

7. Wiesel, *Open Heart*, 46.

8. Wiesel, *Against Silence*, 3:288.

9. Emmanuel Levinas, *Outside the Subject*, trans. Michael B. Smith (Stanford, CA: Stanford University Press, 1994), 58.

10. Emmanuel Levinas, "Revelation in the Jewish Tradition," in *The Levinas Reader*," trans. Sarah Richmond, ed. Sean Hand (Oxford: Basil Blackwell, 1989), 203; emphasis added.

11. Levinas, *Difficult Freedom*, 84.

12. Vilna Gaon, *Even Sheleimah*, trans. Yaakov Singer and Chaim Dovid Ackerman (Southfield, MI: Targum, 1992), 45.

13. Wiesel, *Testament*, 160.

14. Nahmanides, *Writings and Discourses*, trans. Charles B. Chavel, vol. 2 (New York: Shilo, 1978), 667.

15. Judah David Eisenstein, ed. *Otsar Midrashim* (New York: J. D. Eisenstein, 1915), 466.

16. Raphael Patai, *The Messiah Texts* (New York: Avon, 1979), 257.

17. The other six are Torah, Teshuvah, Gan Eden, Gehenna, the Throne of Glory, and the Temple.

18. Levinas, *Collected Philosophical Papers*, 44.

19. Wiesel, *Somewhere a Master*, 23.

20. Levinas, *Difficult Freedom*, 190.

21. André Neher, *The Prophetic Existence*, trans. William Wolf (New York: A. S. Barnes, 1969), 142.

22. The other five questions are: Did you try to make time to study Torah? Were you devoted to raising a family? Were you honest in your business affairs? Did you engage in the pursuit of wisdom? And did you cultivate a fear of heaven?

23. Wiesel, *And the Sea Is Never Full*, 369.

24. Wiesel, *Gates of the Forest*, 225.

25. Wiesel, *Beggar in Jerusalem*, 74.

26. Wiesel, *Against Silence*, 3:232.

27. Norman Lamm, *The Religious Thought of Hasidism: Text and Commentary* (Hoboken, NJ: Ktav, 1999), 576–77.

28. Louis Newman, ed., *The Hasidic Anthology* (New York: Schocken, 1963), 248.

29. Levinas, *Difficult Freedom*, 90.

30. Wiesel, *Beggar in Jerusalem*, 54–55.

31. Wiesel, *Ani Maamin*, 105, 107.

32. Wiesel, *Hostage*, 160-1.

33. Wiesel, *Ani Maamin*, 27, 29.

34. Wiesel, *Sages and Dreamers*, 131.

Bibliography

Abohav, Yitzchak. *Menoras Hamaor: The Light of Contentment.* Translated by Y. Y. Reinman. Lakewood, NJ: Torascript, 1982.

Abraham Ibn Daud. *The Book of Tradition.* Translated by Gershon D. Cohen. Philadelphia: Jewish Publicaitons Society, 2010.

Albo, Joseph. *Sefer HaIkkarim: Book of Principles.* 5 vols. Translated by Isaac Husik. Philadelphia: Jewish Publication Society, 1946.

Alter, Yehudah Leib. *The Language of Truth: The Torah Commentary of the Sefat Emet.* Translated by Arthur Green. Philadelphia: Jewish Publication Society, 1998.

Arama, Yitzchak. *Akeidat Yitzchak: Commentary of Rabbi Yitzchak Arama on the Torah.* 2 vols. Translated by Eliyahu Munk. Hoboken, NJ: Ktav, 2001.

Aron, Milton. *Ideas and Ideals of the Hassidim.* Secaucus, NJ: Citadel, 1969.

Ashkenazi, Yaakov ben Yitzchak, ed. *Tz'enah Ur'enah: The Classic Anthology of Torah Lore and Midrashic Commentary.* Brooklyn, NY: Mesorah, 1989.

Baal HaTurim. *Commentary on the Torah: Bereshis.* Translated by Avie Gold. Brooklyn, NY: Mesorah, 1999.

Bahya ben Asher. *Torah Commentary by Rabbi Bahya ben Asher.* Translated by Eliyahu Munk. 7 vols. Hoboken, NJ: Ktav, 1998.

The Bahir. Translated with commentary by Aryeh Kaplan. York Beach, ME: Samuel Weiser, 1979.

Berger, Alan L., ed. *Elie Wiesel: Teacher, Mentor, and Friend.* Eugene, OR: Cascade, 2018.

Biale, David, David Assaf, Benjamin Brown, Uriel Gellman, Samuel Heilman, Moshe Rosman, Gadi Sagiv, and Marcin Wodziński. *Hasidism: A New History.* Princeton, NJ: Princeton University Press, 2017.

Blumenthal, David R. *Understanding Jewish Mysticism: A Source Reader.* 2 vols. New York: Ktav, 1982.

Buber, Martin. *Between Man and Man.* Translated by Ronald Gregor-Smith. New York: Routledge, 2002.

———. *I and Thou*. Translated by Walter Kaufmann. New York: Scribner's, 1970.

———. *The Legend of the Baal Shem*. Translated by Maurice Friedman. New York: Schocken, 1969.

———. *The Origin and Meaning of Hasidism*. Translated and edited by Maurice Friedman. New York: Harper & Row, 1960.

Chayim ben Attar. *Or Hachayim*. 5 vols. Translated by Eliyahu Munk. Jerusalem: Munk, 1995.

Cohen, Victor, ed. *The Soul of the Torah: Insights of the Chasidic Masters on the Weekly Torah Portions*. Northvale, NJ: Jason Aronson, 2000.

Cohn-Sherbok, Dan. *God and the Holocaust*. Leominster, UK: Fowler Wright, 1996.

Cordovero, Moses. *Moses Cordovero's Introduction to Kabbalah: An Annotated Translation of His Or Neerav*. Translated by Ira Robinson. Hoboken, NJ: Ktav, 1994.

———. *The Palm Tree of Devorah*. Translated by Moshe Miller. Southfield, MI: Targum, 1993.

Culi, Yaakov. *The Torah Anthology: MeAm Lo'ez*. Translated by Aryeh Kaplan. Vol. 1. New York: Moznaim, 1977.

Dan, Joseph. *Sefer HaYashar*. Jerusalem: Bialik Institute, 1986.

Dov Ber. *In Praise of the Baal Shem Tov*. Translated and edited by Dan Ben-Amos and Jerome R. Mintz. New York: Schocken, 1970.

Dresner, Samuel H. *The Zaddik: The Doctrine of the Zaddik According to the Writings of Rabbi Yaakov Yosef of Polnoy*. New York: Abelard-Schuman, 1960.

Dribben, Judith. *And Some Shall Live*. Jerusalem: Keter, 1969.

Ein Yaakov. Translated by Avraham Yaakov Finkel. Northvale, NJ: Jason Aronson, 1999.

Eisenstein, Judah David, ed. *Otsar Midrashim*. New York: J. D. Eisenstein, 1915.

Elior, Rachel. *Mystical Origins of Hasidism*. Oxford: Littman Library of Jewish Civilization, 2006.

Etkes, Immanuel. *The Besht: Magician, Mystic, and Leader*. Translated by Saadya Sternberg. Waltham, MA: Brandeis University Press, 2005.

Fackenheim, Emil L. *God's Presence in History: Jewish Affirmations and Philosophical Reflections*. New York: Harper & Row, 1970.

Finkelstein, Louis, ed. *Sifra on Leviticus*. New York: Jewish Theological Seminary, 1983.

Finkelstein, Louis. *Akiba: Scholar, Saint and Martyr*. New York: Atheneum, 1981.

Flavius Josephus. *Josephus: The Complete Works*. Translated by William Whiston. Nashville: Thomas Nelson, 2003.

Freiman, Shulamis. *Who's Who in the Talmud*. Northvale, NJ: Jason Aronson, 1995.

Ginsburgh, Yitzchak. *The Alef-Beit: Jewish Thought Revealed through the Hebrew Letters*. Northvale, NJ: Jason Aronson, 1991.

Ginzberg, Louis, ed. *The Legends of the Jews*. 7 Vols. Philadelphia: Jewish Publication Society, 1969.

Green, Arthur. *Tormented Master: A Life of Nahman of Bratslov*. Tuscaloosa: University of Alabama Press, 1979.

———. "Wiesel in the Context of Neo-Hasidism." In *Elie Wiesel: Jewish, Literary, and Moral Perspectives*, edited by Alan Rosen and Steven T. Katz, 51–58. Bloomington: Indiana University Press, 2013.

Greenberg, Gershon. "The Hasidic Spark and the Holocaust." In *Elie Wiesel: Jewish, Literary, and Moral Perspectives*, edited by Alan Rosen and Steven T. Katz, 83–98. Bloomington: Indiana University Press, 2013.

Halevi, Judah. *The Kuzari (Kitav al khazari)*. Translated by Henry Slonimsky. New York: Schocken, 1963.

Hand, Sean, ed. *The Levinas Reader*. Oxford: Basil Blackwell, 1989.

Heller, Marvin J. *The Seventeenth Century Hebrew Book: An Abridged Thesaurus*. 2 vols. Leiden, The Netherlands: Brill, 2011.

Heschel, Abraham Joshua. *Man Is Not Alone*. New York: Farrar, Straus and Giroux, 1951.

———. *The Prophets*. 2 vols. New York: Harper & Row, 1975.

———. *The Sabbath: Its Meaning for Modern Man*. New York: Farrar, Straus and Giroux, 1981.

Horowitz, Isaiah. *Shnei Luhot HaBrit*. Translated by Eliyahu Munk. 3 vols. Hoboken, NJ: Ktav, 2000.

Idel, Moshe. *Hasidism: Between Ecstasy and Magic*. Albany: State University of New York Press, 1995.

Kaidanover, Tzvi Hirsch. *Kav HaYashar*. Edited by Avrohom Davis. Lakewood, NJ: Metsudah, 2007.

Kaplan, Aryeh. *Inner Space*. Jerusalem: Moznaim, 1990.

———. *Meditation and Kabbalah*. York Beach, ME: Weiser, 1982.

Kaplan, Chaim A. *Scroll of Agony: The Warsaw Diary of Chaim A. Kaplan*. Translated and edited by Abraham I. Katsh. New York: Collier, 1973.

Ka-tzetnik 135633. *Kaddish*. Translated by Nina De-Nur. New York: Algemeiner Associates, 1998.

———. *Shivitti: A Vision*. Translated by Eliyah De-Nur. New York: Harper, 1989.

———. *Star of Ashes*. Translated by Nina De-Nur. Tel Aviv: Hamenora, 1971.

Kazantzakis, Nikos. *The Rock Garden*. Translated by R. Howard and K. Friar. New York: Simon and Schuster, 1963.

Keter Shem Tov. Brooklyn: Kehot, 1972.

Kierkegaard, Søren. *Fear and Trembling*. Translated by Alastair Hannay. New York: Penguin Books, 1985.

———. *Stages on Life's Way*. Edited and translated by Howard V. Hong and Edna H. Hong. Princeton, NJ: Princeton University Press, 1988.

Kimelman, Reuven. "Wiesel and the Stories of the Rabbis." In *Elie Wiesel: Jewish, Literary, and Moral Perspectives*, edited by Alan Rosen and Steven T. Katz, 38–48. Bloomington: Indiana University Press, 2013.

Kitzur Shulchan Arukh [Code of Jewish law]. Compiled by R. Solomon Ganz-fried. Translated by Hyman E. Goldin. Rev. ed. 4 vols. New York: Hebrew Publishing, 1961.

Klemperer, Victor. *I Will Bear Witness: A Diary of the Nazi Years, 1942–1945.* Translated by Martin Chalmers. New York: Random House, 1999.

Lamm, Norman. *The Religious Thought of Hasidism: Text and Commentary.* Hoboken, NJ: Ktav, 1999.

Landsman, Stephan. *Crimes of the Holocaust: The Law Confronts Hard Cases.* Philadelphia: University of Pennsylvania Press, 2005.

Leiner, Gershom Hanoch. *Shaar Emumah v'Yesod HaChassidut: V'u haKadamah v'Petach HaShaar l'Beit Yaavov* (The Gate of Faith and the foundation of Hasidism: Entrance to the Gate of Beit Yaakov). Translated by Betzalel Edwards. Benei Brak: Machon Lehotzet, 1996.

Levi, Primo. *The Drowned and the Saved.* Translated by Raymond Rosenthal. New York: Vintage, 1988.

———. *The Reawakening.* Translated by Stuart Wolf. Boston: Little, Brown, 1965.

———. *Survival in Auschwitz: The Nazi Assault on Humanity.* Translated by Stuart Woolf. New York: Simon & Schuster, 1996.

Levi-Yitzhak of Berditchev. *Kedushat Levi.* Translated by Eliyahu Munk. Hoboken, NJ: Ktav, 2009.

Levin, Meyer. *Hasidic Stories.* Tel-Aviv: Greenfield, 1975.

Levinas, Emmanuel. *Collected Philosophical Papers.* Translated by Alphonso Lingis. Dordrecht: Martinus Nijhoff, 1987.

———. "Dialogue with Emmanuel Levinas." In *Face to Face with Levinas*, edited by Richard A. Cohen, 13–33. Albany: State University of New York Press, 1986.

———. *Difficult Freedom: Essays on Judaism.* Translated by Sean Hand. Baltimore: Johns Hopkins University Press, 1990.

———. *Ethics and Infinity.* Translated by Richard A. Cohen. Pittsburgh, PA: Duquesne University Press, 1985.

———. *Existence and Existents.* Translated by Alphonso Lingis. The Hague: Martinus Nijhoff, 1978.

———. *Nine Talmudic Readings.* Translated by Annette Aronowicz. Bloomington: Indiana University Press, 1990.

———. *Otherwise Than Being or Beyond Essence.* Translated by Alphonso Lingis. The Hague: Martinus Nijhoff, 1981.

———. *Outside the Subject.* Translated by Michael B. Smith. Stanford, CA: Stanford University Press, 1994.

———. "Prayer without Demand." Translated by Sarah Richmond. In *The Levinas Reader*, edited by Sean Hand, 227–34. Oxford: Basil Blackwell, 1989.

———. *Proper Names.* Translated by Michael B. Smith. Stanford, CA: Stanford University Press, 1996.

———. "Revelation in the Jewish Tradition." Translated by Sarah Richmond. In *The Levinas Reader* edited by Sean Hand, 190–210. Oxford: Basil Blackwell, 1989.

———. *Time and the Other*. Translated by Richard A. Cohen. Pittsburgh, PA: Duquesne University Press, 1987.

———. *Totality and Infinity*. Translated by Alphonso Lingis. Pittsburgh, PA: Duquesne University Press, 1969.

Lustig, Arnošt. *A Prayer for Katerina Horovitzova*. Translated by Jeanne Nemcova. New York: Harper & Row, 1973.

Maimonides. *The Guide for the Perplexed (Moreh Nevuhim)*. Translated by M. Friedlaender. New York: Dover, 1956.

Marcus, Ivan G. *"Sefer Hasidim" and the Ashkenazic Book in Medieval Europe*. Philadelphia: University of Pennsylvania Press, 2018.

Mekilta de-Rabbi Ishmael. Translated by Jacob Z. Lauterbach. 3 vols. Philadelphia: Jewish Publication Society, 1961.

Midrash Aggadah. Jerusalem: Mekhon Haketov, 1996.

Midrash Hagadol al Hamishah Humshe Torah: Sefer Bereshit. Jerusalem, 1947.

Midrash on Proverbs (Midrash Mishlei). Translated by Burton L. Visotzky. New Haven, CT: Yale University Press, 1992.

Midrash on Psalms (Midrash Tehillim). Translated by William G. Braude. 2 vols. New Haven, CT: Yale University Press, 1959.

Midrash Rabbah. Edited and Translated by H. Friedman, Maurice Simon, et al. 10 vols. London: Soncino, 1961.

Midrash Shmuel: A Collection of Commentaries on Pirke Avot. Translated by Moshe Shapiro and David Rottenberg. Jerusalem: Haktav Institute, 1994.

Midrash Tanhuma. 2 vols. Jerusalem: Eshkol, 1935.

Mikraot Gedolot: Multi-Commentary on the Torah. Translated by Eliyahu Munk. Hoboken, NJ: Ktav, 2003.

Nahman of Breslov. *Advice*. Translated by Avraham Greenbaum. Brooklyn, NY: Breslov Research Institute, 1983.

———. *Likutei Moharan*. 15 vols. Jerusalem: Breslov Research Institute, 2012.

———. *Restore My Soul (Meshivat Nefesh)*. Translated by Avraham Greenbaum. Jerusalem: Chasidei Breslov, 1980.

———. *Sefer HaMidot: The Book of Character [The Alef-Beit Book]*. Translated by Moshe Mykoff. Jerusalem: Breslov Research Institute, 1986.

———. *Tikkun*. Translated by Avraham Greenbaum. Jerusalem: Breslov Research Institute, 1984.

Nahmanides. *Commentary on the Torah*. Translated by Charles B. Chavel. 2 vols. New York: Shilo, 1971.

———. *Writings and Discourses*. Translated by Charles B. Chavel. 2 vols. New York: Shilo, 1978.

Neher, André. *The Exile of the Word: From the Silence of the Bible to the Silence of Auschwitz*. Translated by David Maisel. Philadelphia: Jewish Publication Society, 1981.

———. *The Prophetic Existence*. Translated by William Wolf. New York: A. S. Barnes, 1969.

Newman, Louis I., ed. *The Hasidic Anthology*. New York: Schocken, 1963.

Nietzsche, Friedrich. *The Gay Science*. Translated by Walter Kaufmann. New York: Vintage Books, 1974.

Nomberg-Przytyk, Sara. *Auschwitz: True Tales from a Grotesque Land*. Translated by Roslyn Hirsch. Chapel Hill: University of North Carolina Press, 1985.

Patai, Raphael. *The Messiah Texts*. New York: Avon, 1979.

Peretz, I. L. *The I. L. Peretz Reader*. Edited by Ruth R. Wisse. New Haven, CT: Yale University Press, 2002.

Pesikta de-Rab Kahana. Translated by William G. Braude and Israel J. Kapstein. Philadelphia: Jewish Publication Society, 1975.

Pesikta Rabbati. Translated by William G. Braude. 2 vols. New Haven, CT: Yale University Press, 1968.

Pinhas Spira of Koretz. *Midrash Pinhas*. Ashdod: Hotsa'at "Yashlim," 1990.

Pirke de Rabbi Eliezer. Translated by Gerald Friedlander. New York: Hermon, 1970.

Polen, Nehemia. *The Holy Fire: The Teachings of Rabbi Kalonymus Kalman Shapira*. Northvale, NJ: Jason Aronson, 1999.

———. "Yearning for Sacred Place: Wiesel's Hasidic Tales and Postwar Hasidism." In *Elie Wiesel: Jewish, Literary, and Moral Perspectives*, edited by Alan Rosen and Steven T. Katz, 69–82. Bloomington: Indiana University Press, 2013.

Rabinowicz, Harry M. *Hasidism: The Movement and Its Masters*. Northvale, NJ: Jason Aronson, 1988.

Rabinowitz, Avraham Moshe. *Hakhimah Birmizah*. Brooklyn, NY, 1994.

Rosen, Alan. "Capturing the Fire, Envisioning the Redemption: The Life and Work of Elie Wiesel." In *Elie Wiesel: Teacher, Mentor, and Friend*, edited by Alan L. Berger, 46–57. Eugene, OR: Cascade, 2018.

Rosen, Alan, and Steven T. Katz, eds. *Elie Wiesel: Jewish, Literary, and Moral Perspectives*. Bloomington: Indiana University Press, 2013.

Rosenberg, Joel. "Alone with God: Wiesel's Writings on the Bible." In *Elie Wiesel: Jewish, Literary, and Moral Perspectives*, edited by Alan Rosen and Steven T. Katz, 9–20. Bloomington: Indiana University Press, 2013.

Rosman, Moshe. *Founder of Hasidism: A Quest for the Historical Ba'al Shem Tov*. Berkeley: University of California Press, 1996.

Roth, John K. "Wiesel's Contribution to a Christian Understanding of Judaism." In *Elie Wiesel: Jewish, Literary, and Moral Perspectives*, edited by Alan Rosen and Steven T. Katz, 264–76. Bloomington: Indiana University Press, 2013.

Rubinstein, Donna. *I Am the Only Survivor of Krasnostav*. New York: Shengold, 1982.

Scarry, Elaine. *The Body in Pain: The Making and Unmaking of the World*. Oxford: Oxford University Press, 1985.

Schindler, Pesach. *Hasidic Responses to the Holocaust in the Light of Hasidic Thought*. Hoboken, NJ: Ktav, 1990.

Schneersohn, Shalom Dovber. *Yom Tov Shel Rosh Hashanah 5659: Discourse One*. Translated by Y. B. Marcus and M. Miller. Brooklyn, NY: Kehot, 2000.

Schneerson, Menachem M. *Torah Studies.* Adapted by Jonathan Sacks. 2nd ed. London: Lubavitch Foundation, 1986.

Scholem, Gershom. *Major Trends in Jewish Mysticism.* New York: Schocken, 1974.

Sforno, Ovadiah. *Commentary on the Torah.* Translated by Raphael Pelcovitz. 2 vols. Brooklyn, NY: Mesorah, 1987–1989.

Shapira, Kalonymos Kalmish. *Sacred Fire: Torah from the Years of Fury 1939–1942.* Translated by J. Hershy Worch. Edited by Deborah Miller. Northvale, NJ: Jason Aronson, 2000.

Shlomo Ephraim ben Aaron Luntschitz. *Kli Yakar, Shemos.* Translated by Elihu Levine. 2 vols. Jerusalem: Targum, 2002.

Sifre on Deuteronomy. New York: Jewish Theological Seminary, 1993.

Stanley, Arthur Penrhyn. *Scripture Portraits and Other Miscellanies.* London: Alexander Strahan, 1867.

Steinsaltz, Adin. *The Essential Talmud.* Translated by Chaya Galai. New York: Basic Books, 1976.

———. *On Being Free.* Northvale, NJ: Jason Aronson, 1995.

Steinsaltz, Adin, and Josy Eisenberg. *The Seven Lights: On the Major Jewish Festivals.* Northvale, NJ: Jason Aronson, 2000.

Tanna debe Eliyahu: The Lore of the School of Elijah. Translated by William G. Braude and Israel J. Kapstein. Philadelphia: Jewish Publication Society, 1981.

Tikkunei HaZohar. 3 vols. Jerusalem: A. Blum Sefarim Geshaft, 1993.

Tosefta. Jerusalem: Wahrmann, 1970.

Tsavaat ha-Rivash. Brooklyn, NY: Kehot, 1999.

Vilna Gaon. *Even Sheleimah.* Translated by Yaakov Singer and Chaim Dovid Ackerman. Southfield, MI: Targum, 1992.

Vital, Chayyim. *Sefer HaHezyonot.* Jerusalem: Mekhon Ben-Tsevi, 2005.

———. *The Tree of Life (Ets Chayyim).* Translated by Donald Wilder Menzi and Zwe Padeh. Northvale, NJ: Jason Aronson, 1999.

Ward, John William George. *Portraits of the Prophets: Character Studies of Men Who Blazed the Trail.* New York: Richard R. Smith, 1930.

Weil, Yedidiah Tiah. *Haggadah Marbeh Lisaper.* Edited and Translated by Mark B. Greenspan. Oceanside, NY, 2011.

Weissman, Moshe, ed. *The Midrash Says.* 5 vols. Brooklyn, NY: Bnay Yakov, 1980.

Wiesel, Elie. *Against Silence: The Voice and Vision of Elie Wiesel.* Edited by Irving Abrahamson. 3 vols. New York: Holocaust Library, 1985.

———. *All Rivers Run to the Sea: Memoirs.* New York: Alfred A. Knopf, 1996.

———. *And the Sea Is Never Full: Memoirs, 1969– .* Translated by Marion Wiesel. New York: Alfred A. Knopf, 1999.

———. *Ani Maamin: A Song Lost and Found Again.* Translated by Marion Wiesel. New York: Random House, 1973.

———. *A Beggar in Jerusalem.* Translated by Lily Edelman and Elie Wiesel. New York: Random House, 1970.

———. *Célébration biblique: portraits et légendes*. Paris: Éditions du Seuil, 1975.

———. *Célébration hassidique: portraits et légendes*. Paris: Éditions du Seuil, 1972.

———. *Evil and Exile*. Translated by Jon Rothschild. Notre Dame, IN: University of Notre Dame Press, 1990.

———. *Five Biblical Portraits*. Notre Dame, IN: University of Notre Dame Press, 1981.

———. *The Forgotten*. Translated by Marion Wiesel. New York: Summit, 1992.

———. *From the Kingdom of Memory: Reminiscences*. New York: Summit, 1990.

———. *The Gates of the Forest*. Translated by Frances Frenaye. New York: Holt, Rinehart and Winston, 1966.

———. *Hostage*. Translated by Catherine Temerson. New York: Alfred A. Knopf, 2012.

———. *A Jew Today*. Translated by Marion Wiesel. New York: Random House, 1978.

———. *Legends of Our Time*. New York: Schocken, 1982.

———. *Messengers of God: Biblical Portraits and Legends*. Translated by Marion Wiesel. New York: Random House, 1976.

———. *Night*. Translated by Marion Wiesel. New York: Hill & Wang, 2006.

———. *Night*. Translated by Stella Rodway. New York: Hill & Wang, 1960.

———. *La Nuit*. Paris: Les Éditions de Minuit, 1958.

———. *The Oath*. New York: Avon, 1973.

———. *One Generation After*. Translated by Lily Edelman and Elie Wiesel. New York: Pocket Books, 1970.

———. *Open Heart*. Translated by Marion Wiesel. New York: Alfred A. Knopf, 2012.

———. *Paroles d'étranger*. Paris: Éditions du Seuil, 1982.

———. *A Passover Haggadah*. Edited by Marion Wiesel. New York: Simon and Schuster, 1993.

———. *Sages and Dreamers: Biblical, Talmudic, and Hasidic Portraits and Legends*. Translated by Marion Wiesel. New York: Summit, 1991.

———. *Somewhere a Master: Hasidic Portraits and Legends*. Translated by Marion Wiesel. New York: Summit, 1982.

———. *The Sonderberg Case*. Translated by Catherine Temerson. New York: Alfred A. Knopf, 2010.

———. *Souls on Fire: Portraits and Legends of Hasidic Masters*. Translated by Marion Wiesel. New York: Vintage, 1973.

———. *The Testament*. Translated by Marion Wiesel. New York: Summit Books, 1981.

———. *The Town beyond the Wall*. Translated by Stephen Becker. New York: Avon, 1964.

———. *The Trial of God*. Translated by Marion Wiesel. New York: Random House, 1979.

————. *Twilight*. Translated by Marion Wiesel. New York: Summit, 1998.

————. *Un di velt hot geshvign*. Buenos Aires: Tsentral-farband fun Poulishe Yidn in Argentina, 1956.

————. *Wise Men and Their Tales: Portraits of Biblical, Talmudic, and Hasidic Masters*. New York: Schocken, 2003.

Wiesel, Elie, and Josy Eisenberg. *Job ou Dieu dans la tempête*. Paris: Fayard-Verdier, 1986.

Wiesel, Elie, and Mark Podwal. *A Passover Haggadah: As Commented Upon by Elie Wiesel and Illustrated by Mark Podwal*. New York: Simon & Schuster, 1993.

Wollaston, Isabel. "The Absent, the Partial and the Iconic in Archival Photographs of the Holocaust," *Jewish Culture and History* 12, no. 3 (2010): 439–462.

Yaavov ben Rabbeinu Asher. *Tur HaArokh: Tur on the Torah*. 4 vols. Translated by Eliyahu Munk. Hoboken, NJ: Ktav, 2005.

Yaakov Yosef of Polnoe. *Toledot Yaakov Yosef al HaTorah*. 2 vols. Jerusalem: Agudat Beit Vialipoli, 1944.

Yalkut Shimoni. 5 vols. Jerusalem: Chotzet Sefarim, 1993.

Zeitlin, Hillel. *R. Nahman Braslaver: Der zeer fun Podloye*. New York: Matones, 1952.

Zevin, Shlomo Yosef. *A Treasury of Chassidic Tales on the Torah*. Translated by Uri Kaploun. New York: Mesorah, 1980.

The Zohar. Translated by Harry Sperling and Maurice Simon. 5 vols. London: Soncino, 1984.

Zohar Hadash. 2 vols. Jerusalem: Yarid Hasfarim, 2005.

Zusak, Markus. *The Book Thief*. New York: Alfred A. Knopf, 2007.

Index